The left in disarray

Sean Matgamna

This book is dedicated to the new anti-capitalist generation – to those who will cleanse and regenerate an authentic socialism – because, despite everything, socialism remains the best hope of humankind.

The left in disarray

Sean Matgamna

Printed by Imprint Digital, Exeter EX5 5HY

ISBN: 978-1-909639-36-2

Published June 2017 by Workers' Liberty
20E Tower Workshops
Riley Road
London SE1 3DG
020 7394 8923
awl@workersliberty.org
www.workersliberty.org

Contents

The melding of left and right:
The Stalinist synthesis

Summary: aspirant socialism and "socialism" 71

The fate of the Bolshevik rearguard

The survivors of Atlantis

IMPERIALISM AND ANTI-IMPERIALISM IN THE MAKING OF THE CONTEMPORARY LEFT

Imperialisms and anti-imperialism 112

Bureaucratic Imperialism and the socialist revolution 133

Imperialism and the left: twenty case histories

Iraq and the "liberal interventionists" 194

The re-evaluation of values 214

The anti-imperialism of the fools: How Israel came to be the world's hyper-imperialism 231

THE LEFT IN DISARRAY: TEN POLEMICS 245

PEOPLE WHO SHAPED THE LEFT: FIVE ESSAYS 335

How not to fight the kitsch left: the Euston Manifesto 393

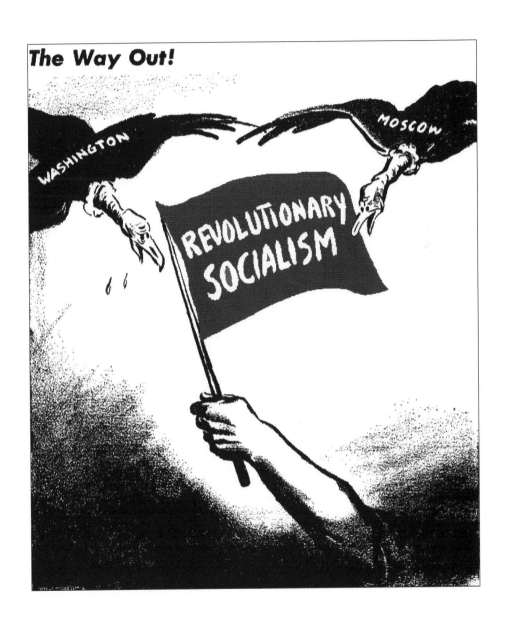

Introduction

"Tell the truth and shame the devil"

"To face reality squarely; not to seek the line of least resistance; to call things by their right names; to speak the truth, no matter how bitter it may be; not to fear obstacles; to be true in little things as in big ones; to base one's program on the logic of the class struggle; to be bold when the hour for action arrives – these are the rules" – Leon Trotsky †

The story in the Bible about the Tower of Babel is well known. Humankind starts to build a high tower so it can climb up to the heavens. Offended by this urge to independence in creatures he has created to be his supplicants and playthings, God punishes them. Where before there had been only one language, humankind wakes up one morning speaking many – all the languages of the earth. God has ensured that the divided humanity will not now be able to unite in such enterprises as building a tower up to heaven. Thus the old story-makers tried to account for the existence of many languages in the one human species.

The 20th century and after has done something very like that to the anti-capitalist left. Clear-seeming and once more or less precise terms – "democracy", "imperialism", "anti-imperialism", "socialism", "revolution" – that corresponded, more or less, to real things and relationships in the world in which the socialists existed, now convey nothing that is clear without additional explanation. All the key terms now have more than one, and sometimes many, meanings. Thus, most of the time they have no clear meaning; they express and convey emotion, not reason. They are tools of demagogy more than of reasoned discourse. Concepts and words have been stretched and reshaped, and then stretched, redefined, redesigned and reshaped again and again to cover many different and sometimes contradictory realities. They clog our minds and cloud our political eyes and judgement. Our language of politics is decayed, disablingly.

Where different languages have clearly defined meanings for words, translation and dialogue is possible. Where language has rotted and been corrupted by misuse or deliberate misrepresentation to such an extent that many or most of the key words have lost precise

---

† *The Death Agony of Capitalism and the Tasks of the Fourth International, 1938*

meaning, understanding is impeded and communication is often impossible. So too is useful polemic. Manipulative demagogy, the use of words to convey and evoke feelings, wishes, self-love, aggression, contempt, adoration, takes their place. That is one of the reasons why the left is divided into an archipelago of mutually uncomprehending segments, why it lives in self-isolated atolls. Incomprehension, in turn, deepens the intra-left divisions. Our capacity to think coherently about politics, history, society, ourselves and our history, and our capacity to communicate with each other, are enfeebled and often in some ways destroyed.

How did the left rooted in the tradition of Karl Marx, Frederick Engels, Vladimir Lenin, Leon Trotsky, Karl Liebknecht, James Connolly, Rosa Luxemburg, Clara Zetkin, Leo Jogiches, Keir Hardie, and all those whose lives made up the socialist movement of the past, get into the state it is in now? Why is the left in disarray?

Left-wing people are people who by political instinct and conviction side with the oppressed and the exploited, with the victims of exclusion, of malign power, of cruel indifference. We have fought against racism, for women's equality with men, and against all the social aristocracies – aristocracies of birth and genealogy, of gender, of the purse, of the skin. Defined broadly, the left in history has been a tremendous force for progress, enlightenment, liberty, tolerance, freedom, democracy, and the right to free criticism of religion and of other official political and social ideologies. It has fought tyrannies and tyrants, and the rule of mind-stifling priests and prelates. It has fought for civil rights and civil liberties, for free speech and free thought, and against censorship. It has been the locomotive for cranking history forward. It has organised and shaped labour movements that have established and broadened working-class rights against employers and their states; it has lurched the whole of society upwards. In the 20th century the authentic left fought fascism, the theocracies of different religions (Catholic, Islamic, Shinto), Stalinism, capitalism, and plutocracy.

The left, in a word, has fought for consistent democracy – for all-pervasive political, social, and intellectual democracy. The real left, in any situation, are the Consistent Democrats.

Not all of the left, all of the time, has embodied all of these virtues, of course. There is another side to the story. The left is produced, shaped, and reshaped, by different social environments, and, at any given moment, by its own prior history. It has had different strands, traditions, levels of awareness, degrees of consistency and coherence. It has had mutually antagonistic strands at war with each other. People thinking of themselves as of the left have sometimes done indefensible things and taken up terrible attitudes and positions, sometimes suicidally.

On antisemitism, for instance: in the Dreyfus affair, some socialists affected an above-the-battle incomprehension. Why, with their minds on the great structural elements in society, like the economy, should they bother with such a thing? Some socialists thought that agitation against "the Rothschilds" – wealthy Jews, portrayed as the epitome both of capitalism and of Jewishness – a permissible form of socialist agitation. Frederick Engels remonstrated: "antisemitism is merely the reaction of declining medieval social strata against a modern society consisting essentially of capitalists and wage-labourers, so that all it serves are reactionary ends under a purportedly socialist cloak... In addition, the antisemite presents the facts in an entirely false light... there are here in England and in America thousands upon thousands of Jewish *proletarians*..." (19 April 1890).

Some strands in the German Communist Party, in a brief attempt to create a "national Bolshevism" in the early 1920s (1920s, not 1930s), played with antisemitic agitation. The heroic Russian populist movement, Narodnaya Volya, welcomed the epoch-defining anti-Jewish pogrom movement that broke out in 1881 as a positive expression of the people's will to rebel against their conditions. In another vein, some socialist insurrectionists in early 1920s South Africa who had raised the slogan "Workers of the World, Unite for a White South Africa!" went the gallows singing The Red Flag. The very influential early 20th century US socialist novel, Upton Sinclair's *The Jungle*, has a chapter that is viciously racist against African Americans. Etc.

In such cases, left-wingers acted contrary to their own values of consistent democracy, judicious breadth of view, egalitarianism, and rationality in politics as in everything else. Other left-wingers knew that, and talked, wrote, and acted differently, criticising the socialists who fell short. To a great extent, socialism developed, made and remade itself, by criticism and self-criticism. Vladimir Lenin used, as the epigraph of his polemic *What Is To Be Done?*, Ferdinand Lassalle's comment: "Party struggles lend a party strength and vitality; the greatest proof of a party's weakness is its diffuseness and the blurring of clear demarcations".

The South African socialists, shouting "Workers of the World Unite", and nonsensically coupling it with "For a White South Africa", might have been the paradigm for the catastrophe that overwhelmed the left in the mid and late 1920s, when much of the revolutionary left was conquered by Stalinism in varying dilutions. The basic socialist critique of capitalism came to be fused with positive programs of Stalinist totalitarianism. That introduced a system of having one attitude to oppression in capitalist society, and a radically different attitude to the same or worse oppression in Russia and later in the other Stalinist states (China, for instance) – a pervasive system of double standards, and thus of no standards, in measuring social affairs. It established an all-pervading "doubleness" of outlook, attitude, feeling, judgement, language, which rendered much of the left radically incoherent. It merged genuine left-wing standards and attitudes into hybrids, encompassing their opposites. On imperialism, for the great instance which affects the left still. It amalgamated the proper socialist attitudes to the crimes of capitalism with an opposite attitude to similar, and very often worse, crimes of Stalinism. In its perennial peace campaigning, it fused appeals against the horrors of war with sly manipulation in favour of Russian foreign policy, whatever it was at that point. Those contradictions and tensions produced strong seams of hysteria in left-wing politics. We have still not purged the left of those catastrophic amalgams and hysterias †.

This book tries to account for the state of the left by analysing the historical and political evolution of the old 19th and 20th century left and its ideas, its defeats by the forces of Stalinism, of fascism, and of plutocracy, and their impact on its ideas. This discussion of what Stalinism did to the left is intended to make it easier to understand the character, causes, and faults of the contemporary left, and to help those who want to fight for a more consistent and more authentic left.

II

From the collapse of the USSR, until the onset of the 2008 credit crisis, international capitalism went through a vast expansion under the banners of free trade, neo-liberalism, and globalisation. That produced social and ideological conditions that were very unfriendly to the idea that capitalism needs to be replaced with socialism, that the working class can and should make a socialist revolution, that historically capitalism has outlived itself. After the fall of Russian and East European Stalinism, we went through a riot of bourgeois triumphalism, and an accelerated, disarray and decline, political, moral, intellectual, of the "actually existing left". The left was faced with the need to redefine itself. In so far as it has redefined itself, it has since

---

† *The great contemporary instance of this sort of double-faced and double-minded political hysteria concerns Israel. See the account in this book of the "warmongering anti-war demonstrations".*

2001 been in terms of an alliance with one of the most reactionary forces on the planet, "political Islam" – Islamic clerical fascism. And these conditions have helped many ex-Stalinists mutate into born-again advocates of bourgeois democracy and capitalism – something, all in all, better than their former Stalinist political mindset. Working-class socialist democracy was never even potentially real for those jaded power-worshippers, and naturally they do not regard it as a possibility now.

Since the collapse of the Stalinist Russian empire in 1991, world capitalist power has traded on the idea that there is no alternative to capitalism. There never was; there never will be: there cannot be. We should, as someone at a debate told us once, "marvel at the market's gifts to mankind". Be grateful for the things God gives you! Don't dream, don't scheme, don't rebel! For, warn the ideologues – the old Labour Party reform-socialists among them – if you rebel, then you will stumble into a nightmare of state terrorism, into the Gulag, into the Stalinist archipelago of slave labour camps and mass murder.

They build philosophies on the claim that Stalinism was Bolshevism; that Bolshevism was not overthrown in a Stalinist counter-revolution, as in fact it was, but continued and developed by the logic of its own inner nature into Stalinism. The Stalinist counter-revolution against the working class and against Bolshevism was really, they claim, Bolshevism itself in essentials. Bolshevism, which fought Stalinism to the death of the rearguard Bolsheviks – that was only immature, infant Stalinism. The anti-Stalinist Bolsheviks were only fighting against their other self.

In all this, the triumphant bourgeoisie has merely appropriated the core lies of Stalinism and put them to work. The story is nonsense in terms of the facts – nonsense as ridiculous as Stalin's indictment of the old Bolsheviks in the mid-thirties as having worked for British and other intelligence services when they were leading the 1917 Revolution. Yet aspects of the post-Stalinist left, for instance the accommodation of the ostensible left to Islamist terrorism, have been as if designed to prove the bourgeois ideologues' point.

III

But the story doesn't end there. The end of the story has not been written yet. In the socialist beginning is the class struggle. The world's working class is expanding; it has, maybe, doubled in size over the last 30 years. Capitalism is still rearing up fresh armies of its own gravediggers.

The movement that has gathered around Jeremy Corbyn and John

12

McDonnell to reclaim the Labour Party for the working class is a tremendous event, and for socialists and labour-movement activists and well-wishers, an inspiring and heartening one. It opens opportunities for socialists and socialism that had been blocked off for two decades since the Blair-Brown coup in the Labour Party in 1994-7. The socialist left, however, is in no state to do the positive work for socialism that is now possible. It is organised in an archipelago of sects. Each group's Marxism is in the main an in-house Marxism, some of it strange and bizarre, specific to the group. Like the overshadowing statues on Easter Island, grotesque personality cults loom in and above the left. Almost all the groupings are organised as factional tyrannies. They forbid or stifle internal discussion, and, for practical purposes, most of them, most of the time, outlaw dissent. Reason there is an abused and terror-stricken, half-starved, prisoner. Relations between the different groups are blindly hostile; intergroup discussion is usually shouts of abuse from the factional trenches. In some groups an aura of quasi-religious awe surrounds their special positions and doctrines and high priests. Demagogy reigns, and demagogy ruins. Yet the economic crisis that began in 2007-8 has exposed to many people the fundamental nature of capitalism – its instability, its needless cruelties, its domination by billionaire predators who run the system for their own benefit. The need for a vigorous, intellectually receptive and productive, anti-capitalist left is urgent and pressing.

IV

It can now be seen that the collapse and disarray in the left in the aftermath of 1991 was inevitable, after the way the left had been shaped and schooled in the preceding decades. Though the old European Stalinism, holding state power in many states, is dead, socialists, including the heirs of the old anti-Stalinists, live still, as is argued here, in the grip of the moral, political and intellectual chaos created by Stalinism. Cultural inertia is a gigantic and pervasive force in history. Stalinism was for many decades a world-wide entity, affecting not its own full or partial devotees alone, but many others. Stalinist ideology combined states of minds, feelings, reasonings or refusals to reason, doctrines, and beliefs, hybridised with concerns valid and important in themselves. The peace campaigns after about 1950 are the best examples here. There are many others. Much of the old culture is still alive on the left.

It is the contention of this book that the moral and political crisis of the present-day left is fundamentally a confusion of ideas, of identity and of historical perspective. Of an unexplored, and often startlingly unknown, history of the left itself, and of our language of politics. The crisis of the would-be left today consists in the continued influence within it, in its ways of seeing the world, of organising and thinking, of un-purged or often half-purged, essentially unrecognised, Stalinist politics, patterns, attitudes, and residues.

Stalinism is dead as state power in Europe. But Stalinism wasn't just state power. It was a vast interlocking political culture, containing a set of ideas, attitudes, states of mind, moralities, antagonisms, animosities. If that culture died with Stalinist state power in Europe, then this book is anachronistic, a case of refusal to move on, an unhealthy obsession with old, irrelevant events and issues. The point is that as a political culture, Stalinism is not dead. It survives even in much of that left which defines its historical anti-Stalinism with Trotsky's name. It survives in the ideological chaos that still engulfs the left. The concerns of this book are not, alas, only matters of history. One of its aims is to speed Stalinism on its way into the void of outlived, negated, and learned-from history.

This book offers an analysis and an indictment of the contemporary left, written from within the left and from a left-wing point of view. It is part of a drive to purge the debris of Stalinism which, it argues, pervades the contemporary left. It is a companion volume to *Can Socialism Make Sense? An Unfriendly Dialogue* (2016).

A note on terminology. It would be misleading to talk about "the left" without qualification, in part because this book is in many ways a self-criticism. We, the Alliance for Workers' Liberty, are ourselves of the left; and it is argued here that on many issues, on free speech for instance, and on Zionophobia and Judeophobia, the ostensible left today has taken over positions that were for a very long time the preserve of the right. Thus various terms are used – addled left, ostensible left, kitsch left, confused left. Kitsch left is the more precise: much of the left is in the grip of inorganic, pastiche, imitative, incoherent politics. †

Sean Matgamna, 12 June 2017

---

† *The book contains material written as self-contained pieces at different times. Some subjects are examined more than once, from different angles and under different headings. Some of the subjects covered in one of the lists of Stalinist traits are also covered in more detailed essays. Therefore there is some overlap between some chapters, and some repetition of arguments and summaries.*

Without many discussions and wranglings with Martin Thomas, this would be a poorer contribution to the discussion on imperialism. Mistakes and inadequacies, of course, are mine.

Preface

In the deep Middle Ages rumours began to circulate in Europe that the Islamic enemy of Christendom, God, and humankind had suffered tremendous blows and defeats at the hands of a new military power that had arisen in the far-away lands of the east. Who and what was this new power? Europe lacked information; it lacked the means of getting information.

Whoever they were, these warriors against Islam, the enemy of God and of humanity, were doing God's work. Nothing was known about them, and therefore much had to be surmised, inferred, imagined. Who could do God's work against Islam but Christians? If you doubt that, you put in question the place of Christians in God's scheme of things and the cosmic significance of the centuries of Christianity's struggle with Islam. You are saying that some force other than Christianity can be God's instrument in this great work. You downgrade the historical role of the one true, holy, and apostolic Catholic Church. No: it had to be Christians who were doing this work, with a great Christian leader at their head.

Thus the legend of Prester John was conjured up and refined and retold to fill the great gap in what was known, and to license Christian jubilation at Islam's difficulties. It came to be widely believed that the victorious enemies of Islam in the east were Christian, and led by a Christian prince, Prester John.

The reality, of course, was that the Mongols had inflicted those defeats on Islam. The armies doing God's work against Islam were a force of triumphant herdsmen so primitive that at one point there was a discussion among its leaders as to whether they should kill off all the farming peoples of northern China and so clear the land for herds and herdsmen and the better sort of society they embodied.

Stalinism has not been buried yet

Anarchist militia fighters in the Spanish workers' revolution of 1936-7, which was suppressed by the Stalinists and the Republican bourgeoisie before Franco's fascists then defeated the Republic. Facing page: graphic by Walter Crane.

17

The Stalinist roots of the present crisis on the left

1. Defining an age

In the summer of 1933, a few months after the Nazis had consolidated power in Germany, a conversation that defines a whole political age, and in so doing offers a key to understanding the political malaise of the left today, took place in a group of young members of the Communist Party, in Cambridge. Some of the participants in that conversation would serve the USSR as double agents within the British secret services for decades to come, and be exposed piecemeal in the 1950s, 60s and 70s. The story of that conversation is told in Andrew Boyle's *The Climate of Treason*.

Kim Philby, just back from Germany, reported to his friends. Hitler had been allowed to come to power peacefully. The strong German Communist Party (KPD) had had six million voters and hundreds of thousands of militants. It had had its own armed militia, which until the Nazis consolidated their power had had the strength to repress the fascists in the working-class districts of Berlin. And yet the KPD had allowed itself to be smashed. When the bourgeoisie called the Nazis to power, the Stalinist-controlled KPD had been paralysed. It had slunk into its grave. It did not put up even token resistance.

During the two and a half years from the September 1930 elections to the consolidation of Nazi power in January-March 1933, as the Nazis grew spectacularly, the KPD had refused to try to unite with the Social Democrats to oppose them. Instead they formed united fronts with the Nazis against the SPD, the "social fascists". In 1920, a general strike had defeated an attempt at a right-wing coup, the so-called Kapp Putsch. In 1933 the KPD did not even attempt to organise a general strike! The Social Democratic Party leaders in the Reichstag pledged to be a loyal, legal opposition to Hitler. Between them the KPD and SPD destroyed the possibility of a general strike. They ensured that the call for a general strike made by the small Trotskyist organisation met with no response.

It was one of the great pivotal events in the history of the labour movement, and in the history of the 20th century, leading into the final consolidation of Russian Stalinism, World War Two, Stalin's conquest of Eastern Europe, the decline and decay and ultimately the complete destruction of the revolutionary working-class movement that had rallied to the Russian October Revolution.

In fact, the KPD acted as it did on Stalin's direct orders. Stalin had decided that it was in the USSR's interests to let Hitler come to power because Hitler would try to revise the Treaty of Versailles imposed on defeated Germany by the victors of the First World War and "keep them busy in the West while we get on with building up socialism here", as he put it to the German Stalinist leader Heinz Neumann. Stalin would later have Neumann shot: his wife Marguerite would be one of a trainload of German Communist refugees from Hitler who were transferred – in an act that symbolised and summed up Moscow's relationship with the international "communist" movement – from Stalin's concentration camps to Hitler's, in 1940, as a gesture of goodwill to the German ally, after the Hitler-Stalin Pact in 1939. Most of them died, but she lived to tell the story.

In Cambridge in that summer of 1933 the young men listening to Philby's report tried to make sense of events – and of their own political world. The Communist International was still denying that any defeat at all, still less a catastrophe, had occurred in Germany: it denied that the KPD had been destroyed. It played with idiotic ideas such as: "The establishment of the open fascist dictatorship, which is destroying all democratic illusions among the masses and liberating them from social-democratic influence, is accelerating the rate of Germany's advance towards the proletarian revolution" (Comintern executive statement, 1 April 1933).

Those who wanted to stay in Stalin's "Communist International" had to accept that way of looking at it. This was the period of "High Stalinism": the Pope in Moscow decided such things and brooked neither disagreement nor sceptical reserve. Even so, the question forced its way through: were the leaders of the Communist International correct? Or had they made a gigantic "mistake" in Germany? Some of the young men suggested that, maybe – maybe – mistakes had been made. Maybe they should have fought the Nazis rather than let them consolidate fascist rule peacefully? Perhaps Stalin's critics were right? Maybe the Trotskyists had been right in calling for a general strike. Perhaps, after all, Stalin did not quite know, or always know, what he was doing.

"No!", said Philby, the future KGB general, very heated. The KPD had not made mistakes, and Stalin had not got anything wrong in Germany. To talk of even the possibility that Stalin was mistaken was to miss the point, Philby insisted: he denied that, where the affairs of the labour movement were concerned, Stalin *could* be mistaken and wrong. Like the infallible Pope, who cannot err where Catholic "matters of faith and morals" are concerned, Stalin could not err where the affairs of the left were concerned. Philby put it with unanswerable neatness and clarity. "W... why", he stuttered, "W... what-ever Stalin does – th... tha... *that is the left!*" There was no left other than the left defined by Stalin's words and deeds. Stalin was the left.

2. "Communism" and the left

It is a statement that sums up an entire epoch in the history of world and of the left. And, to call things by their proper names, what in many or most respects was becoming the ex-left: for the hitherto left and right were now melding in a new Stalinist synthesis. What Stalin did, what the Russian and later other Stalinists in power did, whatever they did, even the things that had previously been characteristic of the right, whatever they said in the name of socialism and communism – that was now socialism. That, deed and doctrine, was now the left. That was now Marxism. The left today is the child and grandchild of that "left", of a "left" that collapsed catastrophically when the USSR collapsed.

Defence of what that "socialist state" did, and generalisations from what it did, whatever it was – that now defined the "revolutionary" left. The official accounts of what they were and what they did; the rationalisations, fantasies and lies which disguised the real nature of what they were and what they did; the learned In-House-Marxist or Stalinist commentaries on the "reasons" for what they did; the deep "theoretical", "dialectical" arguments that were concocted to explain what they did and why "socialism" in the USSR was so very far from the old hopes and socialist goals of the old left; the codifications of Stalinist practice, written over and into the basic texts of socialist learning, memory, and aspiration, turning "communism" and "Marxism" into incoherent and ever-changing Stalinist palimpsests – that was now "the left".

With the Stalinist counter-revolution, what had for decades been socialism, a powerful progressive force in the world, the implacable enemy by instinct and belief of oppression, social inequality, sexual bigotry and repression, exploitation, superstition, unreason, censorship, and of its own opposite, the right in instinct and conviction, was transformed into a "socialism" that, amongst other things, incorporated the basic traits of the old right and was itself the negation of the old socialism. Everything socialistic was transformed, over time, and not without resistance, into its opposite. All that had been holy to socialism was profaned, and adulterated, and turned inside out.

3. The old left and the new

The Marxist left had developed its ideals and goals and norms out of the realities of the bourgeois society in which the working class and the Marxists lived, and from the wishes, hopes, and goals of the defeated plebeian left in the bourgeois revolutions, right back to the Renaissance, the English Revolution of the 1640s and the French Revolution at the end of the 18th century (the Levellers and Diggers, the sans-culottes, Noel Babeuf). It had carried forward their drives for democracy and equality against the shallower pluto-democratic, bourgeois, versions of these ideas. Thomas Rainsborough had expressed this goal and this spirit beautifully during the "Putney Debates" at the end of the English Civil War: "I think that the poorest he that is in England hath a life to live as the greatest he…"

Before the Russian Revolution, "socialism" was interchangeable with terms such as "the Cooperative Commonwealth", the "Workers' Republic", the "Republic of Labour". It meant the reorganisation of the means of production, of the means of life around which the citizens expend most of their time all over the world, under the collective control of the producers. It was synonymous with liberty and its expansion and cultivation throughout society. Because the Marseillaise had been the anthem of the liberating French revolution, before World War One it was sung at working-class meetings all over Europe.

Old socialism proposed to substitute for capitalism and wage slavery common ownership of the means of production, distribution, and communication, and, irreplaceably, democratic common administration for the common good. Collective ownership by all of society is necessarily democratic ownership: otherwise "collective ownership" by those who "own" the state which administers the "collective" economy is in fact minority ownership and control.

The democracy at every level of socialist society would, socialists believed, be profound and all-embracing. Where now, what Marxists call bourgeois democracy or pluto-democracy is at its best a shallow, money-warped, and one-dimensional political democracy, socialism would remake the whole of society in a democratic image. Democracy would finally become real – real and full self-administration by the working class. Under socialism, socialists believed, there would be equality for all, irrespective of gender, race, sexuality, or any other aristocratic principle which disadvantages some people now. The sis-

21

terhood and brotherhood of all people would be realised. Reason, and not the blind forces of market economics and old superstition, would govern society. The democratic Commonwealth of Labour would replace rule by aristocrats of the bank account, skin, inherited status and privileged education.

What, with their different methods, tempos, and perspectives, had all the different strands of socialism in common? All of them – the socialist reformists such as Keir Hardie or Nye Bevan or R H Tawney, no less than the revolutionaries – sought to abolish capitalism and the exploitation and wage-slavery on which it rested, and to replace it with a non-exploitative, rational, humane society. *In Place of Fear*, the title of Nye Bevan's 1952 book, was not a bad indication of what socialists tried to do: to put solidarity in the place of the fear that regulates capitalism, the fear of unemployment, poverty, jail, wars.

Their ideas of what would replace capitalism, and how to get to that point in history, differed greatly, for instance, as between anti-politics anarchists and Marxists (though Marxists and revolutionary anarchists – who are not by any means all anarchists – agree on the ultimate goal, a society emancipated from state power). But all the socialists sought to replace private ownership of the means of production and exchange and the exploitation of the producers that goes with it, by collective social ownership by the workers themselves.

All of them, in one way or another, with one qualification or another, looked to the working class, the slave-class of the capitalist era, to achieve this great social transformation. They saw themselves as educators and organisers of a working class striving for social betterment and for the socialist transformation of society.

Before the spread of the Stalinist plague, Marxist socialists were guided by adherence to the working class, to the working class side in the class struggle – always and everywhere and in all circumstances; and to the education of the labour movement in consistent democracy, in working-class political independence, and in unrelenting anti-capitalist militancy.

Plekhanov, the founding father of Russian Marxism, expounded the idea that governed what the Russian Marxist movement did and aimed to do. It was what all socialists, more or less, did and thought they existed to do. This rock-basic statement of what socialists do cannot be repeated too often †.

"What is the socialist movement?... To a contemporary socialist

---

† G V Plekhanov: *The Tasks of the Socialists in the Struggle Against the Famine in Russia, 1891.*

the socialist movement does not look anything like it did to a [utopian] socialist in the [18]30s [for whom] 'future history resolves itself into propaganda and the practical implementation of their social plans...' What did the [Marxists] see in it? Above all class struggle, the struggle of the exploited with the exploiters, the proletariat with the bourgeoisie. In addition they saw in it the inevitability of the impending triumph of the proletariat, the fall of the present bourgeois social order, the socialist organisation of production and the corresponding alteration in the relationships between people, i.e. even the destruction of classes, among other things.

"If, therefore, for the [Marxists] the whole future history of bourgeois society resolves itself in the struggle of the proletariat with the bourgeoisie, all their practical tasks are prompted by precisely this class struggle. Standing resolutely on the side of the proletariat, the new Socialists do everything in their power to facilitate and hasten its victory. But what exactly can they do? They 'agitate, educate and organise' the working class and raise it to the position of an aspirant ruling class. A necessary condition for the victory of the proletariat is its recognition of its own position, its relations with its exploiters, its historic role and its socio-political tasks.

"For this reason the [Marxists] consider it their principal, perhaps even their only, duty to promote the growth of this consciousness among the proletariat, which for short they call its class consciousness. The whole success of the socialist movement is measured for them in terms of the growth in the class consciousness of the proletariat. Everything that helps this growth they see as useful to their cause: everything that slows it down as harmful. Anything that has no effect one way or the other is of no consequence for them, it is politically uninteresting."

4. The basic beliefs of old socialism

Marx had argued that socialism would grow out of advanced capitalist society, which had developed the forces of production far enough that scarcity and want in the basic means of life could be abolished almost immediately; that socialism would be the creation of the mass of the people, led by the working class, which would rule, could only rule, collectively and, by definition, therefore, democratically. That socialism would immediately destroy the old state machine, replacing it with an accountable system of working-class self-administration.

In capitalist society the relationship between, on one hand, the

23

owners of the social means of production, and, on the other, the sellers of labour power, is exploitative. Marx uncovered the mechanics of it. The participants in the exchange are legally free and in law equal, and yet it is exploitative. Capitalism is a regime under which, in order to live, workers are compelled to sell their labour-power to employers who own the means of production, exchange, and communications, and who, by setting the workers to work, get those workers to produce far more value than is paid to them as a wage. As the peasant serf worked some days a week for the overlord, so the proletarian works part of the day for the capitalist. The system is regulated by fear – fear of poverty, deprivation, penurious old age, of the future of the young generation, and of course each capitalist's driving fear of being gobbled up by another capitalist who wrings more profit out of the workers. It operates in the workplaces as a pitiless tyranny designed to exact, wring out, use, the labour power purchased by the capitalist – what the old socialists defined as wage slavery.

Marx explains: "The value of the labouring power is determined by the quantity of labour necessary to maintain or reproduce it, but the use of that labouring power is only limited by the active energies and physical strength of the labourer. The daily or weekly value of the labouring power is quite distinct from the daily or weekly exercise of that power, the same as the food a horse wants and the time it can carry the horseman are quite distinct. The quantity of labour by which the value of the workman's labouring power is limited forms by no means a limit to the quantity of labour which his labouring power is apt to perform.

"[For example], to reproduce his labouring power, [a worker may need to produce new value equivalent to] working [three] hours daily… But… the capitalist has acquired the right of using that labouring power during the whole day or week. He will, therefore, make him work say, daily, [nine] hours. Over and above the [three] hours required to replace his wages, or the value of his labouring power, he will, therefore, have to work six other hours, which I shall call hours of surplus labour, which surplus labour will realise itself in a surplus value and a surplus produce [profit, interest, rent, etc.]"

"The worker cannot become rich in this exchange, since, in exchange for his labour capacity as a fixed, available magnitude, he surrenders its creative power… Rather, he necessarily impoverishes himself…because the creative power of his labour establishes itself as the power of capital, as an alien power confronting him. He divests himself of labour as the force productive of wealth; capital appropriates it, as such… The productivity of his labour, his labour in general in so far as it is not a capacity but a motion, real labour, comes to confront the worker as an alien power; capital, inversely, realises itself through the appropriation of alien labour." (*Wages, Price and Profit*; *Grundrisse* Notebook III).

The Marxian socialist program is no more than the solution to this radical contradiction in bourgeois society, and the lesser contradictions at all levels which arise from it, which have shaped and continue to shape capitalist society.

5. Bolshevism, Marxism and the Russian Revolution

The Bolsheviks, in power in Russia after 25 October (7 November) 1917, took the lead in establishing a new, Communist, International – the "Third International". They worked to reorganise the old socialist movement. Bolshevism and the Communist International saw their movement as continuing the best of the old movement – those who had held to their principles when European bourgeois civilisation broke down in 1914 – armed for the new time of open revolutionary battles.

The Bolshevik Communist International picked up many of the threads of earlier socialism, and wove them into a more or less coherent strategy of working-class struggle for power – the direct action of the French, British, Irish and American syndicalists, the political "syndicalism" of the De Leonites, James Connolly, and Jim Larkin, the revolutionary parliamentarianism of Liebknecht, the sometimes acute criticism by communist-anarchists of the parliamentarians of the pre-1914 Socialist International, the concern with national liberation of such as James Connolly and of the Bolsheviks themselves – all in previous socialist activity and theorising that was healthy, all that was above all indomitable in its commitment to the workers' cause and in its will to fight the class struggle to working-class, socialist victory.

This was at the start a living movement of self-respecting, politically-educated militants. It conducted its affairs according to reason; it took it for granted that honest differences of opinion inevitably arise even among very like-minded people honestly pursuing the same goals, and that they can be resolved only by reason, discussion, and democratic decision-making.

All present-day notions, from both ignorant or unscrupulous anti-Bolsheviks and quasi-Leninist socialist sects, of socialist and communist popes possessing infallibility – and various forms of coercion to compel compliance – came alive in the era of triumphant Stalinist and bourgeois reaction. Every member of Lenin's Bolshevik party Central Committee of October 1917 had opposed him at some turning point or another, some of them even on the October insurrection itself. For instance, after the October Revolution, when Lenin proposed that the Bolshevik central committee expel two prominent Bolsheviks, Gregory Zinoviev and Lev Kamenev, who had on the eve of the revolution denounced the Bolsheviks in print for planning an insurrection, he got only one vote, his own. Trotsky too found himself opposed by all his close comrades at one point or another.

This is how Lenin, writing in 1906, defined the relationship between party democracy and majority rule in action: "The principle of democratic centralism and autonomy for local Party organisations implies universal and full freedom to criticise, so long as this does not disturb the unity of a definite action... Criticism within the basis of the principles of the party program must be quite free... not only at party meetings but also at public meetings." (*Collected Works* 10 (442-443)).

The Bolsheviks denounced bourgeois democracy and parliamentarism in the name of the fuller democracy of workers' councils and only in the name of a better, more potent democracy. Stalinism would denounce it in the name of an authoritarianism misnamed "new democracy". The Russian working class, in its unprecedented creativity – for a great instance, in creating the soviets (workers' councils) – and the Bolsheviks who led them to victory had in life found solutions (or, to put it at its weakest, pro-tem solutions) to many of the problems that had perplexed earlier socialist thinkers. The Communist International was experimenting, exploring, drawing provisional balance sheets when it was cut down by the Stalinist counter-revolution against the 1917 working-class revolution. But by the time of Trotsky's death at the hand of Stalin's assassin on 20-21 August 1940, the great socialist tradition had dwindled down to a few tiny organisations in a couple of dozen countries. It would dwindle further. Stalin's counterfeit socialism, which cut it down, would for most of the 20th century replace, dwarf, and overshadow socialism. After the collapse of the USSR, socialism would be buried under the ruins of Stalinism.

6. Old socialism and Stalinism

Lenin, Trotsky and the Bolsheviks did not believe that socialism was possible in the ex-Tsarist empire, backward and historically retarded as it was. What they believed was that the workers could take power there, and make the first in a chain of revolutions that would encompass the advanced countries where socialism was possible. As Rosa Luxemburg, who was also the Bolsheviks' friendly critic, wrote in 1918: "The fate of the revolution in Russia depended fully upon international events. That the Bolsheviks have based their policy entirely upon the world proletarian revolution is the clearest proof of their political far-sightedness and firmness of principle and of the bold scope of their policies".

The working-class revolutions in Europe between 1918-1923 were defeated – Germany, Italy, Hungary. In isolation, the Stalinist mutation, a new form of class society, took form, with "collective" property and a privileged elite of exploiters who, in fact if not in name, collectively "owned" the state which owned the economy. It triumphed by way of a bloody one-sided civil war against the workers of the USSR, and against the resistance of those Bolsheviks who held to the ideas under which they had made the October Revolution, Trotsky and his comrades. After World War Two Stalinism spread, rolling into Eastern and central Europe on the caterpillar tracks of Russian tanks, and in Yugoslavia, China and other states by Stalinist organisations at the head of peasant armies winning civil wars.

"Socialism" after the victory and reconsolidation of the bourgeoisie in the west and of Stalinism in the USSR and in the Communist International, was no longer conceived of as the rule of the working people in a world created by advanced capitalism, as in Marx's and Lenin's conception of socialism it had to be, but as the de facto rule of an oligarchy over the producers in underdeveloped or even pre-capitalist societies, with the historical mission of developing those societies to what advanced capitalism had achieved. Values were turned inside out and upside down.

The place of "socialism" in history, the very shape and sequences of history as hitherto conceived by Marxists was radically revised. The idea of what socialist militants were and did, and of what they were not and would not do, was turned inside out. Socialism was no longer, as in Marxism it had to be, the offspring of advanced capitalist society, impossible without what advanced capitalism achieves in history, not least the creation and social education of a working class that would create socialist society.

The Bolsheviks had believed not in building "socialism in one country", but only that the Russian workers could take power, as part of a wider social revolution in advanced capitalist Europe. This was improved to the belief that the main task of socialism was to do what capitalism had done in the "advanced countries" – to develop backward countries and enable them to catch up with and outstrip the advanced countries of capitalism.

"Socialism" became a thing of savage self-contradiction. "Marxism" became a pidgin religion whose paradoxes, conundrums and mysteries-of-the-faith could properly be understood only by those who approached them with the right "method", frame of mind, and "dialectical" flexibility and adaptability – those able to understand the special new meanings that now inhered in old words.

7. Socialism as state slavery

A bureaucracy which collectively "owned" the state had expropriated the workers in the USSR, depriving them of all rights and using them far worse than the workers in capitalist countries were used, worse even than in pre-war Nazi Germany, as Trotsky wrote in the program adopted by the Fourth International in 1938. It turned them into state slaves or, as Trotsky wrote in 1939, "semi-slaves".

The new ruling class continued to call itself communist and Marxist; it defined and camouflaged its own brutal rule over the working people as the rule of the working class over itself; it represented its anti-socialist and anti-working-class counter-revolution as the living continuity and embodiment of the October revolution.

By repeated purges, ideological bamboozlements, double talk, demagogy, and bribery, they took control of the Communist International, the powerful international network of revolutionary working-class organisations made up of people who had rallied to the Russian revolution. Stalinism was totalitarian utopianism – and this is centrally important for what concerns us here, the state of socialism today. In its role in the history of political institutions and ideas it was above all a movement of social and political misrepresentation and parody, of falsification and fraudulent substitution. It was a fatal mixture of internal party demagogy and unbridled bureaucratic machine control.

The gap between what it was and what it claimed to be would, on the stage, have been a farce of the blackest humour; in life it was stark tragedy that engulfed enormous masses of people. As a survivor of Stalin's prison camps, Joseph Berger, put it, it was the shipwreck of a generation.

In the USSR, and later in other Stalinist states, they ran fake trade unions, fake parties, fake elections, fake rule by the working class, fake national autonomies, and fake, utterly and grotesquely fake, socialism. Stalinism, in its account of itself and what it was doing, was a gigantic historical masquerade, sustained for nearly six decades.

International "Communism" changed in the 1920s and 30s from being a genuine revolutionary working-class movement into a series of totalitarian organisations in the capitalist states, working to serve the USSR, that is, the USSR's rulers. The Communist Parties' own local leaders aspired to become what in the USSR the "communists", the bureaucratic ruling class, were. They created immense ideological confusion in the working-class movement. They cut off the Left Opposition, and later the Joint Opposition of Leon Trotsky, Gregory Zinoviev, Lev Kamenev, and Nadezhda Krupskaya, and the international opposition movement, led by Trotsky, from the mass army of would-be communists, who saw in the Stalinist parties the local battalions of the Russian Revolution, but whose idea of the Russian Revolution was changed from the historical truth of Bolshevism to the misrepresentations of Stalin.

At first they used subtle political misrepresentation, then violent demagogy, then force and repression. Stalinism became increasingly reckless and intense, until in the years from 1935 onwards, it culminated in mass murder in the USSR, in Spain, and, on a much smaller scale, in other countries. At the end of World War Two, Stalinists in Vietnam and Greece massacred Trotskyists on a large scale. The Stalinist secret police assassinated individual Trotskyists and other socialist opponents in France, Belgium, Italy and the USA.

Everywhere in fascist and then Stalinist-ruled Europe, the cadres of Bolshevism, of Leninism, of Trotskyism, were persecuted, stifled, jailed, and murdered. They did splendid deeds here and there in that Europe, for example in producing *Arbeiter und Soldat*, an underground paper for the German workers in uniform in the army of occupation in France, an enterprise which cost the lives of two dozen Trotskyists, most of them German soldiers. But those were mere episodes only, not part of a great socialist movement or its harbingers. At the end of the Second World War Stalinism loomed in the world as a great and expanding power, surpassed only by the USA.

The USSR in 1939 made up a sixth of the world. At the end of an expansion which reached its peak with the proclamation of the Stalinist People's Republic of China in October 1949, but would not end until the Russian defeat in Afghanistan (1979-89), Stalinism controlled one-third of the surface of the earth. It had mass parties, which were the main parties of the working class in a number of capitalist countries, France, Italy, Indonesia, etc.

8. In service to a bleak utopia

Stalinism was a regression to pre-Marx "utopian socialism" – a bleak and strange mirage. Utopianism on a gigantic scale, yes, but utopianism is what it was, totalitarian utopianism. Many of the features of Stalinism – like the collective-superman "party of a new type" – could be understood by analogy with the traits of old utopian socialism.

The Bolsheviks knew and proved in practice that the Russian workers could take power; they did not "know" or believe that socialism could be built in backward, and in addition civil-war-ruined Russia. They knew perfectly well that it couldn't. That isolated Russia, in which the Bolsheviks clung to power, should be built up and its economy developed was self-evident. The anti-Stalinist Bolsheviks were pioneer advocates that this should be done. That it could be done as far as the building of socialism, a socialism more advanced than the most advanced capitalism in its economy and its social relations, occurred to nobody before the end of 1924, when Stalin formulated the idea and the program of "Socialism in One Country".

Russia would be built up out of its deep backwardness and outstrip the capitalist world? It was the program, but on a gigantic scale, of the old utopian colony-builders who attempted in some wilderness to start society anew, in parallel to existing capitalist society. Socialism would come, so to speak, from outside capitalism, not from inside, not by the working class in advanced capitalism taking power and building on what had been achieved. The Marxist objections to it were as many as the lessons Marx and Engels had drawn from the experience of the old colony-builders, Owen, Cabet, Thompson. In practical revolutionary politics it was objected to by Trotsky and others because it implied that Russia would remain isolated for many decades, that there would be no socialist revolution anywhere in that time, that capitalist armies would not militarily "intervene" in the process. It implied that the communist parties would become "frontier guards" in their own areas for the "Socialism in One Country" a-building in the Russian state.

Totalitarian-utopian Stalinism unravelled all of the assumptions and concerns of the old Marxist movement. It redefined the role of parties – in Russia as the agent of development, outside Russia as a significant network for the "defence of the Soviet Union". It displaced the working class as the protagonist in the socialist movement and offered as its substitute, The Party, which might be tied to the working class but then again, might not, but in either case was the decisive, the irreplaceable agency. It implied redefining the relationship of the "party" to the working class: not to educate in order to develop consciousness and political independence but to manipulate and use.

9. The creative tension between science and utopianism: Vladimir Lenin and Marxism

Marxist socialism and "political socialism" in general was the socialism that proposed to revolutionise capitalist society from within, basing itself on one of the fundamental classes inside capitalism. No saviour from on high or from outside would change society, but an agency coming from out of advanced capitalism, the proletariat. That socialism rose necessarily on the grave of mid-19th century romantic "utopian socialism", the socialism that proposed to create socialist societies in colonies in some wilderness and compete from outside, by building a better society in parallel with capitalism, which one day it would supersede. Today the Marxist project itself is dismissed as utopian in the sense of unrealisable by people who themselves have nothing coherent to offer as the goal to pursue in advanced capitalist society. Stalinism was a form of utopian socialism; so to an enormous extent is the would-be left still.

One of the best accounts of the "anti-utopian" nature of authentic Marxism is Lenin's *State and Revolution*, written when he was forced to go into hiding in the middle of 1917. It is both demonstration and exposition of what living Marxism is.

The book is a sustained argument that the leaders of the pre-1914 socialist movement had ignored or falsified the ideas of Marx and Engels on the state. It is an attempt by the analysis of texts to re-establish what Marx and Engels really thought. An exercise in arid scholasticism, one might fear. Scholasticism, it is not. It is the opposite of that.

Lenin analyses the old texts to discern and establish what Marx and Engels really said. He traces the development of their opinions on the state towards the conclusions they drew from the experience of the Paris Commune, in 1871, namely, that the revolutionary working class could not simply take over the old bureaucratic state machine – the civil service, the army, the police – and make it serve them: the workers would, following the example of the Communards, have to break it up and replace it by a "Commune state", self-administering working-class democracy, without a permanent state bureaucracy; a self-armed people instead of a standing army. He relates the views of Marx and Engels, and the way their views evolved from point to point, to the experience that shaped and refined those views. He assesses and judges their views in the light of those experiences and uses their method to shed light on his own situation.

For instance, Marx had thought that there could be a peaceful revolution in Britain and America – and perhaps, Holland, about which he felt he knew too little to judge. To the view put forward by Karl Kautsky, who was a scholastic in Marxism, that that settled it – Marx thought there could and therefore there could be a peaceful revolution in those countries – Lenin counterposed Marx's method, his way of arriving at that conclusion. To establish whether the opinion formed by Marx and Engels half a century earlier might still be valid, he analyses the way the institutions of these countries have evolved. Why, he asks, did they think what they did think then and there?

He reconstructs their reasoning from their writings and from the historical context. Britain and the USA then had nothing like the typical state bureaucracy of the European countries, had small armies, and no great military-bureaucratic apparatus of state. He asks: is that still true? He establishes by concrete argument, from the facts, that it is not.

Repeatedly he argues – and this is what most concerns us here – that Marx and Engels were not utopian socialists, not panacea-mongers, advocates of ideal solutions plucked out of their imaginations; not only advocates of a better world, but empirical scientists of society, who extrapolated from the actual world, from its tendencies and possibilities, building on the experience of the working class (especially of the French workers who had made or lived through a number of revolutions). Lenin explains why he thinks it is permissible to take that necessarily limited experience as representative.

(Incidentally, nobody who takes Lenin's way of working seriously, applying Lenin's way of approaching the work of Marx and Engels to Lenin's own work, could be both a consistent "Leninist" and a "Leninolator", or any other sort of "olator". Consistent Lenin-olatry would carry its own antidote and thereby generate its own dissolution.)

Within Marxism there is forever a tension between the empirical, scientific, sociological basis and the extrapolations and pre-figurations spun from them, which, of course, when they seem desirable, come to encompass hopes and feelings and loyalties. At which point might an extrapolation or projection that is considered desirable, and in which, therefore, people have invested their emotions and their active lives, need to be revised in the light of subsequent experience? At which point, if at all, might the governing ideas about the nature of capitalist social reality have to be abandoned? At which point might some or all extrapolations need to be jettisoned? What role would jettisoning some or all of the basic ideas or the extrapolations play in the contemporary class struggle? Would the jettisoning – prematurely or entirely mistakenly – by the Marxists work to defeat a desirable development, work to help the bourgeoisie in the ideological class struggle against the workers? These of course are questions in the realm of judgment, opinion, argument, "character": there is no one answer at a given time.

For instance, the German socialist Eduard Bernstein concluded in the late 1890s that, though the labour movement was a force for the evolutionary transformation of capitalist society, by way of cumulative reforms, the whole notion of proletarian revolution, of a socialist negating of capitalism, had been invalidated by experience: "the movement", he summed up his conclusions, is everything, the goal nothing. Karl Kautsky, Rosa Luxemburg, George Plekhanov, rejected that conclusion. Bernstein worked with a vulgar notion of evolution: real evolution necessarily includes revolutionary breaks. He based himself on too limited an experience. He was making an invalid induction.

In the Europe of two decades later, and greatly more so three decades later, as Bernstein was reaching the end of his life (1932) and Hitler was on the eve of taking control of Germany, Bernstein's thesis was unsustainable. In the early 1960s it seemed valid again. On the eve of World War One, Karl Kautsky, the leading Marxist of that epoch, postulated from the development of imperialism, a future "ultra-imperialism" that would organise the world without wars between the big powers. That idea did not win many supporters in the Armageddon of the World War, the succeeding international turmoil and the Second World War that broke out a quarter of a century after the first. An approximation of it became truth as the US keystoned a new world order in the decades after 1945.

Ideas of smooth, endless capitalist progress and prosperity formed in the decades before 2008 have been shaken and in part toppled by the economic crisis that has engulfed us. The point is that, though advocacy of socialist ideals is an important part of what Marxists do, real Marxism is not utopia-mongering but rooted in the necessary evolution of capitalist society. What is "Marxist" at a given time can only be established by argument and, ultimately by the test of experience.

The Stalinist counter-revolution in socialism and in Marxism

1. The Stalin-refashioned left

The story of Stalinism is well-enough known amongst political people. But Stalinism and Stalinism's characteristic traits are seen as things of the past, attributes of a dreadful time and of a dreadful movement – of the past. It is not a matter of the past: the political mindset and the habits of thought – and hypnotic thoughtlessness – fostered and entrenched by Stalinism over the decades of its domination of "left-wing" politics, still shape much of the left long after the collapse of Russian Stalinism. The Stalinist nature and origin of the characteristics of the present day left, its mindset, its habits of thought and lack of thought, and its methods, are obscured by the fact that most of that "left" is made up of the seeming heirs of Trotsky, the great historical antagonist of Stalin and Stalinism.

The Stalinist "left" came to be the predominant "Marxism", and, with modifications and some criticism of it, the common conception of socialism, for the two-thirds of the 20th century that remained after Stalin's counter-revolution was accomplished. The anti-Stalinist Bolshevik left was extirpated or marginalised, diminished and discredited by defeat, for generations, or transformed by the pressure of Stalinism and by its example. It was restyled out of all recognition.

Living in a political world hegemonised by Stalinism the old distinctions between what was "left" and what "right" – always imprecise and conventional as such terms are, and by their nature must be – was more or less destroyed. Major aspects of what had been the old left and the old right were merged and cross-bred, producing often strange and unexpected hybrids. Hal Draper would note a layer of 1940s and 50s "Stalinist sympathisers who do not even consider themselves socialists of any kind", attracted by "a feeling of new possibilities inherent in a completely statified economy which is not burdened by concern for the masses nor slowed up by pandering to them". (*New International*, January 1948).

The left today, including most of those with Trotskyist movement roots to them, grew out of the Stalinist revolution in the politics of "socialist" revolution, which denuded it of class, of political integrity, of program, of standards, of its own real history, and of its old objectives.

That Stalinist counter-revolution in the politics of revolution took place on three fronts – social and economic in the USSR and political all over the world in the labour movement and on the left. The difference between the old socialism and the movement reshaped by the Stalinist counter-revolution was not only in day to day activities and in program, but in the mindset and personality of "socialism". The shift in mindset is the point here, because much of it still dominates the left. As the capitalist world went into its deep early 20th century economic, political, social and military crisis – a crisis that many, friend and enemy of capitalism alike, thought was terminal – fully a sixth of the world was already "socialist": a parallel world was being created in Russia.

In consequence, Stalinist influence came to be far wider than the labour movement and socialist and "Communist" circles. Much was made of the seeming contrast between the thriving economy of the "communist" world and the devastating slumps in the capitalist world. In the USSR there was planned progress, spectacular progress, not capitalist chaos and regression. There was no "mass unemployment", no great slump, no economic semi-paralysis. Many in the west who had scorned, rejected, or fought actively against the October Revolution of the Russian working class, rallied to the Stalinist counter-revolution and its statified economy – whose typical waste and destruction and inhumanity were not blazoned forth across the world, as those of capitalism were.

Those – Trotsky and others, surprisingly few others then – who pointed to the realities of Russia, to the semi-slave and state-chattel labour conditions, and the helplessness before the all-powerful state to which the workers were reduced, were shouted down and driven off the highways of public discourse. Stalinistic sympathies extended in the 1930s to the US liberal publications *The Nation* and *The New Republic*, the liberal daily in London, the *News Chronicle*, the *New Statesman* and the British Labour left publication *Tribune*. *Tribune* was politically a Stalinist paper up to the Hitler-Stalin pact and World War Two. The virtual indifference with which the liberal establishment as well as the broad Labour and socialist left responded to the Stalinist terror and totalitarianism in Russia in the 30s is one of the oddest things in modern history.

The anti-Stalinist left was stifled. George Orwell's account of his difficulty in getting his reports on the real situation in Republican Spain and the Stalinist police terror there published is nowadays well-known. When Trotsky pointed out the elements of Jew-baiting in the Moscow Trials, he was denounced by even right-wing Jewish leaders in America as a malevolent defamer of a Russia which had in fact destroyed antisemitism. An example of just how topsy-turvy the old left-right polarisation became is the fact that Victor Serge's report on the Stalinist counter-revolution was circulated in Britain by "The Right Book Club", a weak would-be counterpoint to the Stalinist-controlled and very influential Left Book Club. Meanwhile, many on the political right approved of Stalin because he was destroying the Bolshevik left. Mussolini at the time of the Moscow Trials claimed Stalin as one of his disciples, and said that Stalinist Russia was fascist. Some Russian émigré fascists made the discovery that Stalinism was Russian fascism and Stalin their rightful "Führer".

It was in Russia that the future of humanity was, somehow, being forged by Stalinism. Miraculously, courtesy of the ruling party, socialist Russia had leapfrogged ahead to show the more economically-developed countries the way to the future. By 1950 a third of the world was "socialist". Countries like China, which were among the least developed, now appeared to be marching at the head of history's column; the losers so far in the modernisation and industrialisation of the world, were turning into the winners, humankind's pioneers, leaders, and saviours. So tens and tens of millions of people all over the world believed. Stalinism's success reshaped the thinking of the left everywhere. Even those who in Trotsky's time had been the implacable critics and denouncers of Stalin's Russia. The Fourth International had by the mid 1950s come to believe that Russia and the other Stalinist states were irreversibly "in transition" to socialism.

We are concerned here with the changes Stalinism brought in the principles, attitudes, political morality, standards of behaviour, mores, mindset, norms of the left.

Why did the Stalinist counter-revolution maintain an international "revolutionary" "communist" movement at all? It was of enormous value to the Russian state to have subservient movements in most countries and sometimes mass movements, legions of adherents and militant propagandists across the world such as no other state could match, and which it could even lend out, for example to Hitler during the Hitler-Stalin pact in 1939-40.

In the place of what the old socialism had done and tried to do in educating and organising the working class into intellectual and political independence and anti-capitalist politics, those legions put expediency – the brute expediency of the Russian ruling class. There was nothing in old socialism that could not be sacrificed, turned inside out, stood on its head, or declared to be treason to socialism. The USSR and its external Communist Parties, controlled and, to a serious extent, financed by the Russian ruling class, came to be everything. The Stalinists concentrated and distilled all that was authoritarian, "nihilistic", Jesuitical, Machiavellian into a world outlook in which rifled remnants of a bowdlerised Marxism were recast as the philosophy of manipulation in the service of the "socialist fatherland", for use by the Communist "party of a new type". Anything thought useful was true and socialist. Anything.

Old bourgeois and pre-bourgeois agitational and propagandist techniques of manipulation were brought to new levels of concentration, intensity, and completeness by the Stalinist rulers and their agents and allies across the world. Politics, history and, they thought, "History", were freed from the primitive slavery to facts. Politics that were virtually fact-free and virtually truth-free became possible on a mass scale. Great political campaigns could now be lied into existence, and were.

To be sure, this was not something unknown before Stalinism; but the Stalinists, beginning with their lies about what the Soviet Union was, and what socialism and communism were, made it an all-embracing permanent way of intellectual, spiritual, and political life. Truth did not exist, only "class truth", which meant "party truth", which meant Russian truth, which meant whatever suited the bureaucratic autocracy – which meant anything they though would be useful. Consistency was a vice of lesser, unemancipated mortals. Now you could say and do anything and it was your political and moral duty to do whatever was most useful. Logic? Anything was logical so long as you got the "context" right and understood the "historical process". It was all a matter of perspective. Dialectics, comrade!

Truth? No such thing! There is no "objective" truth, only shifting, socially and historically relative truth. In fact that meant "feeling", intuition, subjective thinking. And therefore? Applying the rules of Stalinist dialectics, and putting things properly in "context" and "perspective", anything that is useful can be shown to be true. Morality? No such thing "in the abstract"! What serves the struggle is moral. The end justifies the means. But means condition ends; and therefore ends should condition means? No! That was "petty-bourgeois moralism". History? There is no "objective" history, only class history. Therefore? "History is only current organisational needs read backwards", as one Stalinist professor put it. Therefore, to get the most useful history, select, suppress, construe, spin, mythologise, lie and misrepresent as much as necessary. Wherever Stalinists had the preponderant influence, there was a giant intellectual step backwards to the standards and norms of the pietistic, authority-fixated scholastic ideologues of the Dark Ages who saw nothing wrong in interpolating into ancient texts, if that served the greater glory of God and of the Church.

Wherever the Stalinist influence ran, it worked to falsify history and current politics. If it is true that those who do not learn from history are apt to repeat it, then those who have had their own and other history falsified simply can not learn from it: they have had their retrospective, historical, eyes put out. At different times Trotsky described this condition as "syphilis" and "leprosy". In the summaries of the proper revolutionary communist approach which he wrote in the 1930s, the demand to be truthful and to "be true, in little things as in big ones" is always central. The fact that such a "demand" had to be made and that it was made only by a tiny pariah minority, as incapable of imposing the necessary norms of behaviour as they were incapable of doing what they knew had to be done to defend the working class – that was one measure of how far the "Marxist" movement had fallen, how deeply it had regressed, and how much had to be done to restore it.

Trotsky was a voice crying out of the grave of Bolshevism, of the early Third International, and of old socialism. He contended against the amoralism of Stalinism:

"Permissible and obligatory are those and only those means, we answer, which unite the revolutionary proletariat, fill their hearts with irreconcilable hostility to oppression, teach them contempt for official morality and its democratic echoers, imbue them with consciousness of their own historic mission, raise their courage and spirit of self-sacrifice in the struggle. Precisely from this it flows that not all means are permissible. When we say that the end justifies the means, then for us the conclusion follows that the great revolutionary end spurns those base means and ways which set one part of the working class against other parts, or attempt to make the masses happy without their participation; or lower the faith of the masses in themselves and their organisation, replacing it by worship of the 'leaders'." (*Their Morals and Ours*).

The Stalinists answered not with arguments but with lies, abuse, truncheon-blows and bullets, and in Trotsky's case, with an alpine ice-pick.

Much of the popularly accepted history of workers' and other struggles is still today shot through with Stalinist myths, lies, anathemas and demonology: for instance, the Spanish working-class revolution of 1936-7, which was bloodily suppressed by the Stalinists, is buried in the handed down concept from that time of "The Spanish Civil War" (in which the Stalinists and some other sensible people encountered a little local Trotskyist-Anarchist difficulty in Barcelona in May 1937, and dealt with it with the necessary civil-war severity.) There was, indeed, a Spanish Civil War, but within that there was also the most important working-class revolution since 1917.

There was never any honest self-criticism and analysis of acknowledged mistakes; there was no possibility of democratic discussion other than "discussion" authorised by the leaders from time to time to batter some alleged dissident or heretic and intimidate the others. Like intellectual and political honesty, integrity and fair dealing, the faculty for recognising and correcting mistakes atrophied, along with the old ideas of socialism. If everything is decided by what the rulers of the USSR think best serves them at a given moment, as it was, then starkly contradictory positions – the most notorious example: anti-Nazi, then pro-Nazi, then anti-Nazi again, in 1939-41 – may indeed have all been equally "correct" and all perfectly self-consistent from a Russo-centric point of view.

The standards of honesty and the criteria of truth that have the working class and its social and political development at their heart, and even civilisation and rationality in general, were pushed aside. Yet if they fall into disuse – or if the ascendancy of other criteria and standards makes their employment dangerous or impossible – then we cannot recognise our mistakes and where we went wrong. The historical memory of the working class is destroyed or falsified, and that adds to the tremendous difficulties which its existence as the basic wage-slave class in capitalism already places in the way of the working class developing an independent political identity.

Trotsky truly said that the revolutionary party – if it is a revolutionary party – is and has to be the memory of the working class. It has to be the memory of truths. The Stalinist parties were the parties of enforced amnesia, hysterical delusion, of the substitution of historical myths and lies for the memory of a working-class socialist movement which is truly itself, and knows what it is, and therefore has no need to lie about it, either to itself or anyone else; a movement which accumulates experience and learns and unlearns, from its experience, and from its own mistakes as it goes along.

If the revolutionary Marxists are the good and full memory of the working class, the Social Democrats were the bad limited, partial, and selective memory, of the working class. And the Stalinists? They were memory filtered through raging paranoia, obsessions and self-obsessions, murderous hatreds and the recollections and justifications of mass murder. That is one of the reasons for the tremendous regression in working-class consciousness in the late 20th century. When George Orwell wrote about the "memory hole" in his book *1984*, and about the systematic rewriting of history to get it into line with the eternally changing now, he invented nothing. He merely read off, and gave an imaginary physical expression – physically redoing and updating old newspapers – to what he saw happening in and around the Stalinism-infected labour movements and in the USSR.

2. Reactionary-romantic a-historical anti-capitalism

For Marxists advanced capitalism is the irreplaceable mother of our socialism. And not a good mother: a poisonous old harridan-spider who eats her own young. Or tries her best to. The working class has to fight its way out of her physical, ideological, and political webs.

There were of course communists before Marx and Engels. There were utopians and blueprint-makers; there were also activists such as Auguste Blanqui, for whom Marx and Engels had great and well-merited respect. But the typical Blanquist idea of the road to communist revolution was that, whenever the revolutionary communist secret society had enough guns, gunpowder and fighters to put up barricades and rise in rebellion, it would do that at the first politically favourable moment. They had no proper idea of the necessary evolution of capitalist society, of its forces of production, as the irreplaceable ground-preparer and seed-sower for socialism; no idea of the necessity of the social, intellectual, political, and moral preparation of the proletariat through both capitalist evolution and communist education and organisational work, to make it able to seize power and replace capitalist society with working-class socialist rule.

Marxism had seen the rise of bourgeois society and of the bourgeoisie on the ruins of feudalism as a great step forward for humankind, preparing the objective prerequisites of socialism. It created bourgeois freedom of the individual, freedom of speech, assembly, press, and religion. (It is true, of course, that those freedoms, those "Rights of Man and of the Citizen", were not won by the female half of humankind for many, many decades after they were won by men. For instance, in France women won the right to vote only in 1945; in Switzerland, only in 1971).

40

The "bourgeois revolutions" were most often won by the efforts of the plebeians, and the "bourgeois" freedoms were won, or their extension to the whole of the people was won, by the efforts of the working classes. Socialism became possible only when capitalism had created a mass proletariat and created means of production which, liberated of the drives and unreason of capitalism, can create abundance for all in the basics of life. The program of abolishing bourgeois society depended on whether or not that society was advanced enough and objectively capable of generating something better and more progressive than itself. On a world scale, in the 20th century, it was. In Russia, though the workers could and did take power, it was not.

The Bolsheviks' conception of the Russian revolution was that the spread of the revolution to advanced capitalist Europe would link Russia to advanced worker-ruled societies, of which Russia would then become a developing appendage. The implication embedded in Socialism in One Country was the opposite of that. Now Russia would advance and develop and grow towards socialism on its own strength and growth. Autarky became a fixed principle of other Stalinists – in China, for three decades over the "high Stalinist" period, for example. The Bolshevik Left Opposition criticised the cutting off by Stalinism of the world market from Russian development.

For the Stalinist movement the program of abolishing advanced bourgeois society, objectively ripe for socialism, was a commitment to create... a replica of a Russia where Stalinism had wiped out all the conquests of liberty and the human and democratic rights of the citizen – and of economic enterprise – and replaced it with Stalinist totalitarianism. In France this program was sometimes called the policy of "liberticide". That is what it was. Reactionary anti-capitalism: an "alternative" development to capitalism that was in a thousand ways, and not least in terms of liberty and democracy, a regression to pre-capitalist society

3. The consequences of Stalinist utopianism

Stalinism, cutting adrift from the dominant currents of history, flying in the face of the most fundamental Marxist idea of the "shape" of history and of advanced capitalism as the nurturer of socialism and creator of the social and economic pre-requisites of socialism – Stalinism was a reactionary utopianism. The Marxist project of subverting and overthrowing advanced capitalism from within gave place to the Stalinist project of building up backward Russia in a long-term

41

competition from outside with advanced capitalism.

In that work, the Communist Parties, which had been founded in and after the First World War to overthrow capitalism, now had only the role of supporting the USSR, in any and every way its rulers thought necessary. If socialism was to be built "in one country", then there would, by definition, be no other socialist revolutions for a whole epoch.

That meant supporting the Stalinist ruling class – of whose system the 1938 founding program of the Trotskyist Fourth International wrote that it differed from fascism only "in more unbridled savagery". This core utopianism shaped and reshaped everything else. It stood the historical perspective of Marxism on its head. I will list the main ways in which it transformed or negated Old Socialism.

4. The suppression of class politics

The axis on which everything now revolved was not the class struggle, not the education of the working class, not the development and organisation of working-class political independence, not the centrality of the working class, the protagonist of "old Socialism", but whatever would best serve the USSR, that is, the rulers of the USSR. Class criteria were obsolete except as demagogic recruiting-cries to the foreign legions of the USSR's frontier guards. What in old socialism had been attributed to the working class, was now attributed to the USSR, its rulers, and its international parties. For all practical purposes the "working class" was a cipher, a notional thing in whose name another class, the Russian bureaucratic autocracy, acted and pontificated.

In the early 1930s this approach led the German Communist Party to block with the Nazis against the Social Democrats. At various periods in the mid-1930s and after the creation of cross-class Popular Fronts in France, Spain, Britain and other countries became the goal of the Communist Parties. What were Popular Fronts? With or without the formal involvement of the Communist Party, they were the broadest possible bloc of middling or right-wing and labour or socialist parties, around the axis of a very limited program (and for their "communist" supporters mainly a negative one: anti-fascism). In Britain, the CP wanted to include the Labour Party, the Liberals, and the "progressive wing" of the Tory Party in the broad Popular Front alliance. As Trotsky pointed out, this put them to the right of the Labour right wing, who wanted a Labour government.

The truth is that even right wing bourgeois liberals were comparatively progressive compared to the Stalinist parties, whose victory would have led to the replications of the Russian Stalinist regime. But our concern here is with the influence of the Stalinists in pulping the idea of a class politics among a broader left – their influence on people like Nye Bevan, for instance, the late-40s Labour minister who founded the NHS, who was expelled from the Labour Party as a Popular Frontist in 1939.

The Stalinists perverted the idea that in history the bourgeoisie plays a progressive role and made it something entirely arbitrary: a given bourgeoisie was good or bad, historically progressive or reactionary, depending on its relations, for now, with the USSR. They even found good and bad, patriotic and traitorous (pro-German) fascists! In France, the CP appealed to "patriotic" French fascists – that is, those French fascists who were not hooked up with Nazi Germany – to join their popular front. The consequence of the Popular Front period was the abandonment and destruction of even nominal commitment to independent working-class politics.

The later Stalinists found "good" bourgeoisies primarily in the Third World countries emerging from colonialism, but also, for example, in the 26-County Irish state. The bourgeoisie there was wretchedly stunted, and in social and political terms very reactionary, relentlessly grinding down and driving out the proletariat of the countryside, the towns, and the cities. It preened itself in the heroic light of the Irish rebellions in which itself and its ancestors had played no part, or opposed and denounced. (For example, the *Irish Independent*, the paper of the Catholic-nationalist bourgeoisie, after the suppression of the 1916 Rising, had called on the British to shoot the wounded socialist and trade-union leader James Connolly). It allowed the Catholic hierarchy to run the nearest thing to a theocracy in Europe, not excluding clerical-fascist Franco Spain and Portugal. It lived by exporting meat – cattle and people, hundreds of thousands of people, wretchedly educated, cast adrift on the tide. But it was out of step with Britain because of the partition of the island. Decisively it took a neutralist line in foreign policy, standing out against great pressure to let NATO have bases in the 26 Counties. You couldn't be more "progressive" than that! So for decades the Stalinists – in Ireland and among the Irish in Britain through the CP's Irish front organisation, the Connolly Association – devoted themselves to promoting the idea that the Irish bourgeoisie ran "the most progressive state in Western Europe", as Desmond Greaves once expressed it.

5. Uncoupling Marxist anti-capitalism from the socialist program

In the beginning of modern socialism is the Marxist-communist critique of capital and capitalist society. It consists of a negative and a positive side – the negative criticism of what exists, and the positive alternative, the socialist program of working-class self-emancipation, the pursuit of which determines what the Marxists do in every situation, place, and condition. The positive proposals are, for Marxists, extrapolated from the criticism of capitalism. Marx refused to make any detailed picture of the future post-capitalist society. The future society would evolve out of the expropriation by the workers of the expropriators (the bourgeoisie), and out of the society in which that revolution was made. We have seen what Lenin wrote of that aspect of Marxism.

But the Marxist critique of capital, rooted in advanced bourgeois society and the needs of the working class in that society, and the Marxist working-class program, can be sundered and separated. The positive working-class Marxist program can be cut away from the negative criticism and condemnation of capitalism. Different "utopias" can be substituted. To the anti-capitalism can be attached the program of another class, indeed, of a number of other classes or fragments of classes. Fascism, for example, demagogically criticises capitalism, attributing what it denounces to "Jews", "Jewish finance", etc.

Among people still calling themselves and thinking themselves communists, valid criticism of capitalism and of capitalist democracy can be combined with something other than working-class socialism – with positive support and advocacy of a worse, Stalinist, social order. One consequence of the combination was the creation among communists of a comprehensive dualism that was in practice a political split personality. Things given heartfelt condemnation in capitalist society were defended, or their existence denied, in the Stalinist world. Genuinely indignant at wrongs and ruling-class crimes in Britain, would-be communists simultaneously defended similar and far worse things in the USSR, China, and Eastern Europe. The less worldly-wise simply denied what they didn't want to know; the knowing, more sophisticated ones might, in a lucid moment, have summed up their attitude like this: the concentration camps, jails and torture chambers of a socialist state are not the same thing as identical things that, under capitalism, are damnable.

Stalinism took over and demagogically exploited the Marxist and communist criticism of capitalism and bourgeois democracy, and put, in the place of the Marxist program of expanded democracy and working-class self-ruling socialism, a drive to replicate the Russian system.

When communists criticise bourgeois democracy, we criticise it for not being real democracy. We criticise not representative government, but the limitations, class bias, one-dimensionality and hypocrisies of the bourgeois version of representative government. The "dictatorship of the proletariat", for Lenin and Trotsky and the Bolshevik Party, meant only the dictatorship of the working class, a class dictatorship of the mass of the people, exercised democratically, by way of what Lenin called "a state of the Paris Commune type". It meant "dictatorship" only in the sense of political rule outside the existing laws that protect the bourgeoisie and bourgeois property, overruling those laws and old norms where necessary by working-class will and plebeian direct force.

Disparaging bourgeois democracy, Stalinism counterposed to it not working-class democracy but lawless perpetual bureaucratic dictatorship. Where the communist program stipulated, and socialism as a social system required, a collectivised economy run and owned democratically, the Stalinists put in its place a collectivised economy run by a totalitarian autocracy. The "communist" parties, building support as critics of capitalism, complemented that critique with a non-socialist, Stalinist alternative, much of it, as we will see, derived from what had been the social and political Right.

6. The protagonist: not the working class, but the "party of a new type"

For Marxists, though party and class are not the same thing, there is an unbreakable link between them. "The Communists… have no interests separate and apart from those of the proletariat as a whole," as the Communist Manifesto puts it. Not so the Stalinist parties. The Communist Parties were "Bolshevised" in the early mid 20s, and completely remoulded by the end of the decade. The idea of "the party" now became "the party of a new type", a Stalinist army – in some countries, a very large army – operating with mechanical discipline under the command of Moscow. As Trotsky wrote in 1940: "The present 'Communist' bureaucrats'… ideal is to attain in their own country the same position that the Kremlin oligarchy gained in the USSR. They are not the revolutionary leaders of the proletariat but aspirants to totalitarian rule". (*The Comintern and the GPU*, Writings 1939-40, p.348).

45

This term, "party of a new type", was attributed to Lenin (though he used it only once, in passing, and with different connotations) or to Gramsci (who used the term not at all, but wrote about "intellectuals of a new type", meaning critically-minded politically educated workers, nothing like the typical Stalinist intellectuals) †.

In fact it was a Stalinist term for a new protagonist, a bureaucratic machine which replaced the working class. The Jesuits demanded "Poverty, Chastity and Obedience" from their militant priests. With Stalinism, "discipline and obedience", and often poverty, and unlimited self-sacrifice, came to be the prime qualities of the militant in its parties. The old idea of the party member as a politically-educated, self-respecting, thinking militant, retaining the right and the duty to think and argue and dispute even while acting as a disciplined executor of the democratic will of the majority of the organisation or of the elected leadership acting within its proper competence – that was condemned as "petty bourgeois", or as "Trotskyite", or Luxemburgist, sabotage of the proletarian movement. Working-class "discipline" now meant adherence to the "party line", whatever it was, and the surrender of every old working-class and socialist position, integrity, loyalty, instinct, conscience, to "The Party" and its leaders. For the militants, political life came to be an endless succession of Jacob-like acts of obedience to a savage God – but where God in the Bible relented, sparing Jacob's son, Isaac, once Jacob had agreed to cut his throat as a sacrifice to him, the Stalinist Moloch demanded that the blood be drained and many millions of Isaacs eviscerated on its altar.

The propensity to reason and to think politically beyond the decision to submit to "discipline" and rationalise "the line", variously and repeatedly, was eradicated in the militants of such parties and in the parties as collectives. Militants were taught to put the USSR at the centre of their world outlook. Stalinist "democratic centralism" meant military-style discipline and hierarchy in any and all conditions, with politics essentially the province of the leadership only – and, ultimately, in all essentials, of Moscow only. There was no provision for what members would do if the leaders were mistaken. Only Moscow could anoint and remove a CP leadership.

7. The return of the superman-saviours

The Internationale, insisting on the basic truth of Marxist socialism – "the emancipation of the proletariat must be the work of the proletariat itself" – declares: "No saviour from on high deliver us/ No faith

46

have we in prince or peer/ Our own right hand the chains must shiver/ Chains of hatred, greed, and fear". Stalinism counterposed to that a "leader" principle. The cult of individuals, in the first place of Stalin, followed by many other Stalins, including Mao and "Fidel", became in the Stalinist system as intense and all-pervasive as it is in fascism. It is often now forgotten that even Stalinist leaders in countries like Italy, the USA, Britain, and France had their own miniature cults, around leaders like Togliatti, Browder, Pollitt, and Thorez.

8. Revival of the old "force theory"

"Force", wrote Karl Marx, "is the midwife of every old society pregnant with a new one". Force could smash away obstacles to the new society, including entrenched old forces tied to the past and obstructing the future. Force is not itself a creative power. In a society that is not ripe with an evolved new system, it cannot work the miracle of creating socially what does not exist. And vice versa: force cannot suppress economic development for long. For example, the defeat of Germany in World War 2 did not for long hold back Germany from developing as a dynamic capitalist society. But force can, and for a long time, appear to work miracles. The Stalinist monopoly of violence, concentrated in the totalitarian state, and its status as a great military power, seemed to make real and potential force a great independent power in the world as well as within the USSR.

Isaac Deutscher, in volume one of his acclaimed biography of Trotsky, *The Prophet Armed*, asked himself about Trotsky's expectation that a worker-ruled Russia would collapse or be defeated if it remained isolated. "Trotsky himself, indirectly and unknowingly, provided in advance the clue to his own error – it is to be found in his appraisal of the Russian peasantry. Its political helplessness and lack of independence best account for the survival of a collectivist regime... and also for the forcible and relatively successful imposition of collectivism upon [the peasantry]... Trotsky... did not imagine... that the revolution would seek to escape from its isolation and weakness into totalitarianism". Trotsky had not reckoned with the emergence of totalitarianism, and the Russian autocracy's willingness to use its power with inhuman recklessness to "engineer" society.

This sort of thinking led even the Orthodox Trotskyists to see Maoism, in a phenomenally underdeveloped and impoverished China,

---

† *Gramsci, "Some preliminary reference points", in the Prison Notebooks; Lenin, letter to Alexandra Kollontai, 17 March 1917, Collected Works 35 (297-299).*

as a giant step in the empowerment of humankind over nature and society. It led many Orthodox Trotskyists to believe the official claims for the Great Leap Forward (1958-62), which in reality led to starvation for millions of people.

Trotsky had no illusions about the self-sufficiency of force as a creative power in society. He expected that the Russian state would be overthrown, despite Stalin's entrenched totalitarian force, by either a new workers' revolution or bourgeois restoration. But for decades the prestige of the USSR led much of the left to defer to the apparent ability of Stalinist force and of the Stalinist-type party to work social miracles.

9. Substitution of Apparatus-Marxism for Marxism, and of authority for reason

Restating the basic idea of the old socialism and communism, in the program the Trotskyist movement adopted in 1938 Leon Trotsky insisted that it was a cardinal rule for Marxists to "be guided", not by the interests of "the party", but "by the logic of the class struggle". There is at any given moment an objective truth, and for Marxists it cannot be dismissed just because it is inconvenient to "the party". But in Stalinist politics, everything inconvenient to the USSR and its parties was buried under lies, under an enormous accumulation of lies.

Millions revolted against capitalism and wanted to fight for socialism. Their political spirit and energy, mesmerised by the utopian delusion about socialism a-building in "Workers' Russia", was annexed, with their willing and fervent agreement, by the Stalinist movement, at the core of which was the Stalinist ruling class of the "USSR". The revolt was transmuted into something else, into something other than itself, into its opposite. They tied themselves to the Russian equivalent of their own ruling classes. Marxism, as a guide to analysis, and reason itself, were replaced by Authority; sacrosanct, unchallengeable, doctrinal authority; party authority; the authority of party leaders and ultimately of Moscow. They laid down the line, sanctified selected texts, interpreted those they blessed, and told the comrades what, "dialectically", they meant "here" and "now". This was Stalinist "Party Marxism". Mystification and mumbo-jumbo became a central part of the "Marxism" of the Communist Parties. "Marxism" came to be the esoteric knowledge of a secular priesthood who alone, under Moscow, could decide what it meant and what adherence to it implied in politics for any given situation.

The Catholic Church calls some of its doctrines "mysteries of religion". Those are the doctrines that defy the rules of logic, things that, by everyday standards and to the untutored human mind, are outright gibberish. The "Trinity", the dogma that God is both one divine person and, simultaneously, "three divine persons in one God"; or the belief that though the bread remains bread by every test of human senses and scientific analysis, still each little piece of bread really is (is "host" to) the real body and real blood of Jesus Christ, which is there in "real presence". They belong to a higher order of things. The bishops know better; the cardinals understand; the Pope is guided by God himself in these matters. These things are beyond you and your puny reason, little man, and all you little men!

That is what the Stalinists said too, in their own way – creating an ever-shifting swamp of moral, political, social, historical and intellectual relativism. It all depends, comrade! Stalin's 1939 alliance with Hitler is an outright betrayal of what the Stalinists had previously made central, "the anti-fascist struggle"? Not at all! As the Great Stalin said: "Germany did not attack France and Britain; France and Britain attacked Germany, and it is they who are responsible for the present war". Put it in context and you will see that objectively Hitler has capitulated to the Soviet Union: that is the inner dialectical meaning of the Hitler-Stalin pact, comrade! (See for example R Palme Dutt's editorials in the Communist Party journal *Labour Monthly* in the months immediately after the Pact. And the report of the February 1940 "anti-war" conference of nearly 900 labour movement people: *Labour Monthly*, March 1940). What was fascism, now that Hitler had allied with the USSR? It was "a matter of taste", said Molotov in 1940.

Strike breaking is outright treason to the working class? Not at all! In this context, comrade, strike-breaking is the highest form of class consciousness! As Harry Pollitt, the Secretary of the Communist Party of Great Britain, once put it: Today it is the class-conscious worker who will cross the picket line. †

At least we can be certain of one thing: the big capitalists and the financiers are in all circumstances the enemy? It depends, comrade! It depends. In the period of the US-USSR alliance, Earl Browder, secretary of the Communist Party of the USA proclaimed that he would gladly shake the hand of the notorious and much hated financier J Pierrepoint Morgan. Class treason? Not at all, comrade! It flows from the Russian-US alliance. And there is nothing more central to the

---

† *Kevin Morgan, Harry Pollitt, p.136*

cause of socialism, and therefore to the cause of the working class, which is exactly the same as the cause of the USSR, than that. Is there? Browder's proclamation is the highest form of class consciousness! Things are not always what they may seem to you, comrade little man!

And so on. And so on. It was an eternal metaphysical dance of rationalisations around whatever the Russian autocracy did and said and wanted. Only an autocratic, Great Russian chauvinist state, deeply contemptuous of the workers outside Russia as of those inside, could have demanded from the Communist Parties in the capitalist states such a self-gutting mode of existing and operating. It pulverised and destroyed the norms and standards of socialism and of working-class democracy. It did the same with the standards of reasons and intellect on which Marxism stood and which it needed if it was to sustain and renew itself at each historical turning point.

Take, for example, the Moscow Trials. In 1936, 1937 and 1938 Stalin put the surviving leaders of the Russian October Revolution on trail as traitors. Most of them were shot. Now CP members had to accept as an all-defining article of their socialist faith, of Marxism, an absurdity as mind-bending as the doctrine of the Trinity – that all the leaders of the Russian revolution in 1917 and after, except Lenin and Sverdlov, both safely dead, and one or two others, and Stalin, "Lenin's faithful disciple", had been agents of hostile foreign government. Accept it or break with "The Party", The Revolution", and "Communism".

Russia and its rulers, whoever they were, whatever they were, whatever they did, whatever they said, could not be wrong. That conviction was the lodestar. Philby in 1933 saw very clearly how things were – and faced the implications. So, if less lucidly, did vast numbers of other would-be communists.

The "cadres" of the "parties of a new type", the "Communists", good decent well-meaning people most of them, initially honest but insufficiently self-examining militants, surrendered themselves body, mind, soul, and integrity, to "The Party". They became in politics depoliticised sleep walkers. The true portrait of a mainstream 20th century "revolutionary" is that of a rigidly controlled, and rigidly self-controlled, "communist", involved in varying struggles, whose functional politics was a blind loyalty to the government of a foreign country and to a political apparatus, the CP, its franchised local representative.

Both of them were thought to embody socialism and could be trusted to lead the workers on to socialism. "The Party of a New

Type", comrade! The USSR and "The Party", the USSR's party, these were the fixed reference points in a world in which politics and policies were mere artefacts to be used, or jettisoned, as Stalin thought fit…

At each turn there was of course a shake out. But a hard core remained, most of it, and new hard-core elements were formed on the basis of Stalinist, not Bolshevik, politics. They learned to think according to Stalinist "dialectics". Everything was relative, forever in flux, adjustable in line with the Russia rulers' foreign policy needs. These once-critically-thinking, rebellious, individually and collectively aspiring people surrendered everything to those they took for the pre-ordained leaders of the world socialist revolution – and by doing that, they became the very opposite of what they started out to be, working-class revolutionary socialist militants.

A whole new, reshaped mutant political species numbering many millions was made and bred all across the world. Details would be different from person to person, from country to country, from CP to CP, from time to time, but the twisted utopianism and corrupted personal idealism embodied in the "utopian socialist" fetish of the USSR, accepting it as the measure of all things, now and in the future, and its local CP, its vicar in a given country, its franchised sub-group, was common to them all. It was what made them Stalinists, whatever detailed politics they were for now promoting. The quotient of un-reason was kept at delusional level by the necessary self-defence of labelling as "bourgeois propaganda" all news and facts about the USSR, etc., that were uncongenial and in contradiction to the teachings of the Stalinist church.

The typical Stalinist-movement militant was depoliticised, irresponsible except to "the party", crassly ignorant of the socialism she or he sought to serve and of how to serve it, and therefore, an obedient tool in the hands of the Russian Stalinist ruling class and its franchised "Communist Parties". These were "communists" who – never mind what they thought they were – fought not for a cause and for principles consciously understood and used to measure societies, organisations, people, political events and themselves, but for a fetish. The fetish of the USSR and its "communist" parties throughout the world had in their minds and feelings replaced the great socialist cause and come to substitute for it. They might have adopted an inside-out version of the catch cry of Eduard Bernstein, the right wing "revisionist" of old socialism, who said: the movement is everything, the goal (socialism) nothing.

Now the USSR and "the Party" was everything, the working-class movement nothing. W B Yeats' play "Caitlin Ni Houlihan" tells of a Queen who sacrificed her soul to the cause of her people. Generations of CP members did that too, without fully knowing that they did it, and without getting, without ever having had even a remote chance of getting, what they thought their self-submission and self-sacrifice would bring – working-class socialism. It is impossible not to sympathise and empathise with such people on a human level, and with their tragedy, which was also the tragedy of humankind in the mid-Twentieth Century. Impossible not to find something heroic in the doggedness of the best and – necessarily – least critical-minded and most self-hypnotised of them. That is what makes the story tragic – the terrible, murdering, effect on the cause which they sought to serve, whatever the cost to themselves, of the depoliticised, soul and mind-surrendering, mindless way they worked for it.

But, even so, they were thinking, reasoning beings. They have equivalents now. They made political choices. Even if their thinking never got beyond the "Kim Philby position", that "the USSR is the measure of all things socialistic", and that "Stalin" – like the Catholic Pope when speaking from St Peter's Chair on "matters of faith and morals" – "could not be wrong", thinking people is what they were. They made choices which meant their own destruction as socialists and led to the degradation and rot of socialism, so far for generations. Two lines from a fine song by an unteachable Stalinist, Ewan McColl, about miners entombed in a pit disaster, sum up their tragedy too: "Through all their lives they dug a grave/ Two miles of earth for a marking stone." The present state of the labour movement – and much of the contemporary kitsch left – is the marking stone over the grave which they inadvertently dug for 20th century socialism.

10. One-sided, arbitrary pacifism

Socialists and communists are natural "pacifists", in the sense that we want relations between states to be governed by reason and agreement and compromise rather than by war. But to make a cardinal all-defining principle of pacifistic methods is to mislead and disarm peoples who can only win liberation or emancipation, or avoid conquest, by war. It is to preach support for the status quo until those in power can peacefully be persuaded to agree to change. And in history most pacifists have rallied to "their own" side in wars once they have started. Socialists therefore came to see pacifism as a treacherous snare.

True, the British pacifist opponents of the First World War did rather better than the old guard Marxists around Henry Hyndman, who self-blinkeredly supported the war as an international "police action" against German militarism. Even so, pacifism erected into the central pillar of a world outlook is for socialists a nonsense or a hypocrisy. So the Bolshevik Communist International taught, and it was right.

For the Stalinists, pacifism, one-sided, arbitrary, temporary pacifism, was a force to be manipulated and appealed to against bourgeois governments, in any case when the USSR was the antagonist of their own country's government. In Britain the CP used pacifism very successfully – advocating peace on Hitler's terms – for the first nine months of World War Two, and less successfully for the rest of the 22 months from September 1939 to the invasion of Russia in June 1941. Thus pacifism with all its ambiguities and contradictions was rehabilitated in the would-be revolutionary movement. It survives Stalinism.

Precarious workers: the Picturehouse cinemas dispute, 2016-7

The melding of left and right:

The Stalinist synthesis

1. Stalinism and religion

Stalinism was in serious degree religious, without God or traditional ideas of the supernatural, but with "the future" as its "other" world, for other generations. Stalinism itself was the opium of most of the 20th century socialists.

In 1920 the liberal-socialist Bertram Russell branded Communism as a religious movement akin to early Islam. That was unfair. The leaders of the Comintern, Lenin, Trotsky and others, dealt in fact, reason, logic, albeit leavened by daring extrapolation, and the will to attempt things of such enormous scale and scope that less daring people were intimidated at the very thought of what the Bolsheviks dared to do and were trying to do. What was wrongly said of Bolshevism, falsely, unjustly, malevolently said, came to be true of Bolshevism's grave-digger, Stalinism. From now on, blind, fanatical, incorrigible, with the religious fervour of a death-and-Paradise-obsessed Islamist devoutly fighting a holy war, in which he thinks death can only bring him advantages in a wonderful afterlife, "Communists" championed a tyrannical state ruled by a narrow, intolerant, ignorant elite. For the religious fanatic, a personal afterlife, for the "Communist" a socialist future life for humanity. For both of them delusion.

2. Contempt for reason; an "other-worldly" focus

Stalinism taught contempt for reason outside of the lines of pseudo-reason laid down by the Stalinist church. It taught the elevation of feeling, of faith, of leader-trust and leader-worship, above reason, sometimes as all-encompassing as in the attitudes of the traditional mystical nationalists and the fascists. For instance, it was made an article of faith that the biological charlatanry of Trofim Lysenko was unchallengeable truth. Outside Russia and the satellites, Stalinism

54

necessarily operated under the criticism of non-Stalinists, and so in an atmosphere full of inner contradictions, hysterical denials, faith-driven assertions, and mental blocking-off – a parallel mental world. Demagogy was its tool of choice, misrepresentation of reality its core necessity.

When the de facto goal and central concern of communism and socialism became not socialism and the development and education of the working class towards being able to make a socialist society, then socialism was reduced to something parallel to the right's worship of God, tradition, "order", or, now, "the market" – with the promise that it comes right in the future. In both cases there was deception – indifference to life in the here and now.

The bourgeoisie tells the people that liberty is inseparable from its own limited "bourgeois democracy", thus trying to "sell" its gutted and severely curtailed democracy as the only way to preserve liberty. The Stalinist-influenced "left", idealising the methods of the bureaucratic counter-revolution in Russia, broke with the very idea of liberty – vis-a-vis the state, "the party", and, for minorities, society – except in demagogy against the capitalist ruling class. This was an anti-democratic negativism, combined positively with its opposite – worship of force and of Stalinist state-slavery, in which they accepted the same ground as the Old Right.

Free speech was a left-wing value. Under Stalinist influence, swathes of the left became opponents of free speech, people whose default response to ideas they dislike was to seek to ban and silence them. Opposition to monarchy was basic to the left. But Stalin was a monarch, a pope-emperor. Loyalty to Stalin became the paramount virtue of a good communist. The same with Mao, Tito, Ho, Castro... "No faith have we in prince or peer", the line from the Internationale, rang hollow and mocking in the mouths of the Stalinist-influenced left. Antisemitism, passed down through the ages in Christian society, mutated in the 19th century into zoological racism, given tone and verve by pseudo-science. It became the most potent social and political poison of the twentieth century. The presently dominant "absolute anti-Zionism" on the "Trotskyist" kitsch left, defined and fuelled not by just and necessary criticism of Israel's treatment of the Palestinians and advocacy of a Palestinian state, but by demonisation of Israel and commitment to destroying it – that comes straight from Stalinism. It is anti-Israel more than it is pro-Palestinian. In this too the political spirit of the (anti-Jewish) Old Right prevails in the ostensible left.

3. Imperialist "anti-imperialism"

Marxists are consistent democrats. We are against the coercion, domination, and exploitation of one people by another; and therefore we are for the self-determination of nations, and, where they want it and it is practically feasible, for fragments of nations. Where full self-determination is impracticable (because of the geographical interlacing of peoples), we are for autonomy for minority areas which want it. The Bolsheviks put it very well in 1913, in a resolution written by Vladimir Lenin:

"In so far as national peace is in any way possible in a capitalist society based on exploitation, profit-making, and strife, it is attainable only under a consistent and thoroughly democratic republican system of government... the constitution of which contains a fundamental law that prohibits any privileges whatsoever to any one nation and any encroachment whatsoever upon the rights of a national minority. This particularly calls for wide regional autonomy and fully democratic local government, with the boundaries of the self-governing and autonomous regions determined by the local inhabitants themselves on the basis of their economic and social conditions, national make-up of the population, etc." (*Collected Works* 19 (417-431))

The USSR itself, which did not export capital, was an empire in the same sense that Austro-Hungary had been up to 1917-8. A vast number of the people, a majority in the USSR, belonged to subject nationalities oppressed by the dominant minority. Where the Bolsheviks had hammered down the walls of the Tsarist "prison house of nations", the Stalinist counter-revolution erected them again, lined them with spikes and gun-turrets.

In international politics the Stalinists emptied the terms "imperialism" and "anti-imperialism" of all "objective" content. They presented predatory Russian imperialism, ruled over by a savage and sometimes crazily chauvinistic autocracy, as the expansion of the socialist revolution, and therefore, by definition, right on everything over which its rulers – not the imaginary working-class rulers, the real ones – clashed with the capitalist-ruled world or were criticised in it.

As vicarious Russian nationalists, the Stalinist parties were vicarious racists at the bidding of the Russian rulers. Toward Germans, for example in World War Two and afterwards, when many hundreds of thousands of German women were raped by Russian soldiers and 12 to 14 million Germans were driven west from Stalinist controlled Eastern Europe. The Yugoslav Stalinists massacred tens of thousands of Albanians when they occupied Kosova in 1945. There are many other examples.

The Stalinists identified imperialism as only capitalist imperialism; and they identified advanced capitalism, ipso facto, as imperialism, and therefore historically reactionary (except when in alliance with the USSR; thus, the great imperial powers were not meaningfully imperialist so long as they helped or might help the USSR). They educated the left to see the seizure, "ethnic cleansing", plunder and exploitation of countries as good or bad, imperialist or socialist, progressive or reactionary, according to who was doing it. It wasn't put like that – but there could be such things as "socialist", "working-class" ethnic cleansing, slaughter or exploitation.

This was an aspect of the comprehensive dualism and political split personality that still exists in the post-Stalinist would-be left, a malign legacy of Stalinism, even to some of the "anti-Stalinists". The Stalinists expunged from the left the very propensity to judge such matters according to observation, facts, reason, and principles of consistent democracy. It was the prerogative of the Russian (and for some, later, the Chinese or the Yugoslav or the Albanian or the Cuban) Caesar-Pope to decide such things.

4. Stalinism: "hydra-headed" nationalism and chauvinism

Vicarious Russian nationalism was the core of the Stalinist movement. Lesser nationalisms were adopted and sanctified as progressive, too, in so far as they could be aligned with, or made useful to, the custodians of the greatest nationalism, the Russian ruling class. In the early 1930s, in chorus with the Nazis, the Stalinists campaigned for German "liberation" from the victors in World War One. From the mid-1930s onwards, they operated with categories of good and bad, or worse and better, imperialisms, and, in effect, of good and bad peoples. The bad of one period could turn out good, and the good turn again bad. What was good and what bad at any moment depended on the USSR's alliances or desired alliances, and its antagonisms.

In the second half of the 1930s, Britain, France, Belgium, Holland, "the democracies" which had colonial and semi-colonial control of much of the globe, were the good imperialists. For 22 months before Germany attacked Russia in June 1941, the German Nazis who had overrun most of Europe in May-June 1940, were not imperialists but victims of the old imperialist powers, Britain, France, Belgium and Holland, who had forced war on them.

When Hitler invaded Russia, the Stalinists switched back to glo-

rifying and helping the "democratic imperialists", now Russia's allies. They opposed anti-imperialist movements in India. In their zig-
zags from right to pseudo-left and back again, the Stalinists built up
a repertoire, like a music hall artist of old, from which they could dust
off old routines and costumes and bits of political patter for new situations, combining them sometimes in strange mixes. After 1945,
they supported the restoration of the old empires in "their" old territories, the French in Indochina, for example (where the local Stalinists opposed restoration of French rule), and Algeria. Russia tried to
take a UN mandate for some of Italy's old territory in Libya. It tried
to stay in Iran, which Britain and Russia had jointly occupied in 1941,
after Britain had withdrawn.

In the 1950s and long after, the CPs of France, Italy, Britain, etc.,
campaigned against "Yankee imperialism" and for British, French,
etc., "liberation" from the American "occupiers". They did not succeed in pitting Britain or France against the USA, but they did, with
slogans like "Yankee bastards go home!", poison sections of the European working class with root and branch anti-Americanism. The
Stalinists treated nations and parts of nations as they treated the
working-class and labour movements – as tools and instruments,
pawns and diplomatic make weights for USSR foreign policy.

In place of the general principles of what Lenin called consistent
democracy in such questions, they placed another general principle:
support whichever nationalism and chauvinism best serves USSR
foreign policy, and change sides when that will serve Russian interests. "Anti-imperialism" came to be riddled with double-standards,
arbitrariness and frequent absurdity. Trotsky observed at the outbreak of World War Two that both imperialist camps were telling the
truth – about each other. The Stalinists told a lot of the truth about
their enemies, and lies and justifications about their allies and looked-
for allies. At any given moment only part of the truth was told about
world imperialism. "Anti-imperialism" as a conception, as a principle, and as a program, became detached from its rational democratic
core meaning and progressive political content, and came to be only
an emotion-charged mystification in the service of one of the great
empires after the fall of Hitler.

There was widespread support from the left, and from all Orthodox Trotskyists (except AWL), for Russia's own old-colonial style war
in Afghanistan after December 1979. The syndrome can still be seen
today when the rise of clerical-fascist terrorism in the forging-ground
that Afghanistan came to be in the decade after Russia's invasion is
blamed on the USA, for backing the resistance, but not on Russia for

invading and trying to annex Afghanistan and make it a colony.

5. The uses of the national question: Yugoslavia and Ireland

The project of "socialism in one country", implicitly and then more or less explicitly, meant socialism in no other country for the epoch in which "socialism in one country" would be built in the USSR. The road to world socialism was to build up the USSR so that its example would inspire the rest of the world. Communist Parties outside would serve the USSR in any and every way necessary. Instead of relating to the world from the point of view of preparing and carrying through working-class revolution, the Communist International, under Russian control, related to it manipulatively, as Russian chauvinists.

One of the earliest consequences of this was the substitution of Croatian nationalism for the program (from 1910) of the old Balkan Socialist Federation and the early Yugoslav communists. At the beginning it seemed to the Yugoslav communists that, in line with the old idea of a democratic federation of the Balkans to link together the peoples and fragments of peoples in the region, peaceful agitation for democratic reform of the Yugoslav state founded in 1918 and for full Croatian autonomy was the way forward.

Serbian-dominated Yugoslavia was militarily the most important power in the region, the chief ally of France there, and thus a threat to the USSR. The Comintern imposed on the Yugoslav communists a policy of backing Croatian nationalism in order to weaken and disrupt the Yugoslav state and its military capacities. Until 1935, when Stalin signed a pact with France, they allied even with the extreme Croatian nationalists, the Ustashe, the organisation that under Nazi German patronage would set up a fascistic state during World War Two, pursuing ethnic and religious (Catholic) sectarian goals and massacring Serbian Orthodox Christians.

Something similar happened in Ireland. The early Communist International backed the Irish in the Anglo-Irish war of 1919-21, but it never made a full analysis of Ireland. In the Irish civil war it backed the Republicans against the Free State government. It made no accounting of the intra-Irish divisions that received distorted and untenable expression, and additional complexity, in Partition. The early Comintern legacy on Ireland was soon overtaken by the Stalinist degeneration of the Communist International. In Ireland, too, manipulation in Russia's interest became the axis of everything. Like Croatian, Irish nationalism was, or might be, or could be made into, a force for disrupting the enemies of the USSR. Therefore the Communist Party became a source of nourishment for Irish nationalism.

After the years of World War 2, when the Communist Party of Ireland partitioned itself (from December 1941) at the Border and in Northern Ireland was vehemently Unionist, in the 1950s and 60s the CP resumed a pro-nationalist role. When the IRA's Border Campaign of 1956-62 failed, disastrously for the IRA, the British and Irish Communist Parties and their Connolly Association helped keep alive the Carbonari-Republican tradition. †

In the 1930s the Communist Party of Ireland and its Republican friends and fellow travellers such as Frank Ryan, Paedar O'Donnell, and George Gilmore had gained great influence in the Republican Movement. They split it into left and right segments and controlled the left-wing segment, the Republican Congress. The Stalinists sterilised it politically by insisting that it should not advocate an Irish workers' republic, but a populist nationalism focused against Russia's enemy Britain.

Then, as Russia orchestrated a campaign for a "democratic alliance" against Germany and played down anti-colonialism in the "democratic" empires of France, Britain, Belgium, and Holland, the Stalinists tried to turn the movement into one supporting British imperialism.

In the Hitler-Stalin Pact era (August 1939 to June 1941) the Stalinists turned into a pro-German movement. When Germany invaded Russia in June 1941, they partitioned the Communist Party (December 1941) to free the Northern segment for British patriotism and Unionism. In the early and mid 1960s the Stalinists again succeeded in gaining control of the rump IRA, and turned it towards agitation for civil rights in Northern Ireland. Out of that came the Six Counties Catholic civil rights movement, and from that erupted the Provisional IRA, from December 1969.

No-one needed to exaggerate the misdeeds and crimes on every level of the Orange-sectarian government that ruled the Six Counties from Belfast. But the just agitation on civil rights was used to tell and sell a fundamental lie: that democracy would be achieved by abolishing the Six Counties state and replacing it by Dublin rule in a united Ireland, or direct rule from Westminster. The Communist Party used agitation, justified as far as it went, to obscure the funda-

---

† *The Carbonari were a network of underground revolutionary groups in Italy and France in the early 19th century, characterised by a focus on military conspiracies and a disregard for social program. As revolutionaries they were sterile.*

mental fact of the political, social, and national situation in Ireland: two peoples, who can only be reconciled by an agreed democratic solution of the "constitutional question".

6. Defamation of socialist equality, defence of inequality

Stalin himself branded the egalitarianism at the centre of socialism as "petty-bourgeois". In his "Report to the 17th Congress" (1934) he repeatedly denounced "wage equalisation", "petty-bourgeois equalisation". "Equalisation in the sphere of requirements and personal, everyday life is a reactionary petty-bourgeois absurdity... It is time it was understood that Marxism is an enemy of equalisation". He declared that "cadres" – bureaucrats, hierarchs, managers – "decide everything", and the privileges of the "cadres" were blatant.

7. Denigration of democracy and liberty

The Stalinist and Stalinist-influenced "left" abandoned the core working-class fight to extend democracy. They took the Stalinist state tyrannies as models for their "democracy". They abandoned what the Communist Manifesto summed up as the historic task of the working class – "to win the battle of democracy", that is to win democratic control of society on the political level as the means to democratic self-rule in society and economy. The communists had been consistent democrats; the Stalinists were consistent and comprehensive authoritarians. The communists disparaged bourgeois democracy, and the Social Democrats' fetish of it, in the name of a higher, more comprehensive, more substantive democracy; the Stalinists denounced and misrepresented bourgeois democracy in the name of no democracy and of previously unheard-of autocratic rule over the people.

The Stalinists redefined democracy away from any concern with working-class or any other self-rule. Where the extension of democracy was seen by the older socialists as essential for the education of the working class to become a self-ruling class, the Stalinists gutted "democracy" of all meaning. They substituted double-talk redefinition. "Democracy" in Eastern Europe was full employment, low-rent housing, etc. Even if the claims about social benefits had been true about the Stalinist societies – and largely they weren't – the argument would have been a negation of democracy as self-rule, its obliteration as a social and political concept. As the bourgeoisie identified democracy with liberty and with their own cropped and docked one-dimensional democracy, the Stalinists, concurring, condemned democracy and liberty as bourgeois and necessarily bourgeois.

The working class and the plebeians in history are usually the creators of the advanced democracy in bourgeois-democratic societies and the fighters for it. In an important sense, that democracy is a prefiguring element of socialist society within capitalism. The Stalinist pseudo-left saw liberty as only a token, something of interest only when counterposed to the claims of their bourgeois enemies, only when used as a criticism of them, not as something which socialists must defend and expand. They did not see it as an irreplaceable part of any socialist program in which working-class action is central and working-class power is the goal.

After 1917, social democracy differentiated from Bolshevism, in favour of a specific limited form of democracy: parliamentary plutodemocracy. Trotskyism differentiated from Stalinism in favour of working-class (soviet) democracy. In reaction to what the Social Democratic right did with "democracy" in the service of counter-revolution, for example in Germany in 1918-19, the early Communist Parties tended to glorify and erect into a norm the emergency civil war measures forced on the Bolsheviks in the course of the Civil War, in which Soviet democracy shrank and almost disappeared. They tended to disparage democracy. That was part of an ultra-left infection, and a mistake, an understandable one, of the whole Communist International leadership. Stalinism was different. All through its existence, the Stalinist movement oscillated between opportunistic and demagogic appeals to a classless democracy on one side, and utter contempt for any democracy on the other. Contempt, though differently expressed at different times, was continuous.

Democracy? Comrade, a society where there is no unemployment, no hunger, where rents are cheap and there aren't any capitalists – that is more democratic than the bourgeoisie's parliamentary-demo-

---

† *"If we take the American imperialist regime as a whole, with all the Shahs that comprise it, any workers' state, whether it be bureaucratic or totalitarian, evidences a colossal extension and not limitation of the democratic rights of the proletariat compared to those which it enjoys under bourgeois (imperialist) democracy. The vast majority of the workers and peasants in the imperialist democratic regimes, the hundreds of millions of Iranian, Brazilian, Chilean, and Philippine workers have practically no democratic freedom compared to the Russian or Chinese proletariat."* – Nahuel Moreno, The Revolutionary Dictatorship of the Proletariat, English translation p.38. Chris Harman of the SWP wrote in a not-very-different vein: see section in this book on "Sterile anti-imperialism".

†† R. M. Douglas: Orderly and Humane: The Expulsion of the Germans after the Second World War.

cratic system: it is a higher form of democracy, a higher form of society. Even neo-Trotskyists could be found subscribing to this gobbledygook and repeating it (the late Nahuel Moreno wrote a book to prove it as late in Stalinism's political day as 1979). †

At the least, that could not but spread confusion. In practice it created utter chaos on the question of democracy in large swathes of the left. In substance the Stalinists taught people that the freedoms dismissed as bourgeois democracy meant nothing to the working class.

8. Identification of "bad peoples", distinct from "us" and our allies

The idea that people of all origins and nations are brothers and sisters was central to left-wing thinking. Stalinism shaped a terrible case of the opposite: the demonisation of the German people during and after World War 2. That demonisation helped generate one of the great crimes of the 20th century: the driving-out from central and eastern Europe of almost all the ethnic German population settled there over many centuries. Inside the USSR it led to the transplantation far to the east of over half a million "Volga Germans". Stalinism also infected the thinking of the left with a demonisation of the traditional demons of the right – the Jews, designated as "Zionists".

At the end of World War Two, twelve to fourteen million Germans were forcibly uprooted and driven west into a ruined Germany. This had been decided in advance by the Great Powers meeting at Potsdam. Probably half a million, and perhaps as many as a million, died in the expulsions and deportations. East Prussia, German since the early Middle Ages, was "ethnically cleansed" of two million Germans to make it fit for incorporation into Russia, and part of it into Poland.

As many as a quarter of the present population of Germany, according to one estimate, are immediate descendants of those 12 to 14 million expellees ††. A German Trotskyist "action program" of 1950 said this about the expulsions:

"We condemn the Oder-Neisse frontier [between Germany and Poland] established by the victors and the practice of mass expulsions as inhuman measures which can never be approved by socialists. But we warn the refugees against the illusion that their problems can be solved through conquest by force of their former homeland through World War III. A new war would destroy their homeland along with the rest of Europe. At present, it is important to absorb these refugees into economic life with equal rights and in accordance with their occupations. Reactionary elements among the 'displaced persons' attempt in collaboration with their West German friends to distract the refugees from defending their real interests by illusory promises of a return to their former homes. But we tell them that they can get a life worth living only by joining in the common struggle with the socialist labour movement" – *The Militant*, New York, 29 January 1951.

Only what the Stalinist press called "West German revanchists" talked of reversing the 1945 "settlement". Any attempt to run that horror film backwards would have entailed war with Russia.

9. Antisemitic "anti-Zionism"

The Stalinist poison in the way the Jewish-Arab conflict is seen in the labour movement is with us still. A petrol bomb is petrol and soapy water in a bottle which shatters. It works by the soapy water carrying and spreading the burning petrol. Just indignation against Israel's mistreatment of the Palestinians has worked to spread the poison of the root-and-branch "anti-Zionism" which is the kitsch-left dialect of antisemitism.

The Stalinists backed Israel in 1947-8 in the UN, and the Stalinist state in Czechoslovakia, acting as proxy for the USSR, broke the international embargo on guns for the Palestinian Jews, because that disrupted the British plans in the Middle East. Then they did an about-turn, in 1949 and thereafter, for similar motives of power politics. They filled the left with an absolute "anti-Zionism" that identified Zionism with Nazism and grossly falsified the history that had led to the creation of Israel. From 1949 to the death of Stalin in 1953, only a few years after Hitler and the Holocaust, the Stalinists made Arab or Islamic chauvinism, and antisemitism, everywhere "respectable" and good "anti-imperialism" by demonising the Jewish nationalists, the "Zionists"; by treating Israel as a historical aberration, an illegitimate spawn of history; and by equating the Zionists with the Nazis and attributed to them part at least of the responsibility for the Holocaust. They revived this agitation in the 1970s. They operated, if not completely then in effect and inescapably, with the idea that there are good and bad peoples – peoples deserving democratic rights, and peoples so vile, so imperialistic, so much puppets and tools of imperialism, that they and their rights do not come within the proper concerns of socialists. Demagogically, exploitatively, and one-sidedly advocating the rights of one side in various other conflicts, they had no concern with the idea that to reverse the roles between oppressed and oppressor is not part of a socialist, nor of any democratic solution to such conflicts. On the contrary, it is to adopt the chauvinism of one side.

Confused anti-imperialism is a central root of the absolute anti-Zionism dominant on the addled left today. "The Arab Revolution" was seen as a sub-section of the world revolution unfolding in the 1960s. The Arab Revolution would inexorably find its way to being a socialist revolution. And Israel? Israel was the ally of imperialism against the Arab Revolution.

The Arab Revolution had to be supported and helped to turn leftwards. The Arab nationalists, as distinct from the old feudalists, who were collaborators with imperialism, were progressive, at least in the first stage, and some of them could go all the way to socialism – for example, the leadership of the FLN, which defeated French imperialism in an eight-year war and assumed control of Algeria in 1962. The defeat and destruction of Israel was a detail in the unfolding revolution. It was to be recommended by all the logic and feeling of the Orthodox Trotskyists. They qualified their stance by putting forward a formula for a Socialist United States of the Middle East with "national autonomy for the Jews, Kurds, and other minorities". Now the formula, and the hopes for an Arab Revolution "growing over" to socialism, are long gone. The wish to defeat Israel remains.

10. All-pervading doubleness: a split-world, two-worlds view of reality

To Marxists the world was one entity. The Marxist program of socialism was a single world program. Socialism could be built on what the world market had made in capitalism, and only on that. Marxism had one set of values, one program, one historical protagonist, one agency for the program – the working class. All those derived from the most advanced civilisation, capitalism. Marxism understood that different levels and types of civilisation produced ideological differences and different ideas of morality; it based itself on the most advanced. The working class was the protagonist in the account of history which Marxists spun from the past, in their extrapolations of the future, and in the perspective which they chose to fight for.

It was that, also, in less developed countries, even countries where Marxists thought other classes – such as the agencies of capitalist development, the bourgeoisies – might play or were playing a progressive "civilising" role. There too Marxism was concerned with the working class. There too the working class was, for the Marxists, the protagonists of the story which they saw taking shape and being won in contemporary history. There too the Marxists looked to, champi-

oned, and defended the working class; there too, to expanded democracy. For the Marxists, it was one world, one protagonist (the working
class), one central concern, one standard of judgement, one fundamental program, with variations according to the level of social development. In all conditions the focus was on the education,
organisation, and social advancement of the working class. Marxists
were everywhere in favour of raising the productivity of labour –
thus augmenting the prerequisites of socialism – and they were also
and simultaneously in favour of the working class fighting for the
best wages and conditions. In any clash or seeming clash, they were
for the workers.

Stalinism broke that unitary view, program, concern, and outlook,
that socialist and communist self-identification with the working
class. It replaced it with a dualism that was little less than politically
schizoid. Routinely severe critics of capitalist society and champions
of the working class became, in relation to the "socialist" world, radically different. They sided with the ruling elites and with their "comrades" of the ruling parties.

Their central concern became the development of the economy
and of the country as a whole (and whatever else the rulers of the
"socialist" world decided was important). They became developmentalists, champions of industrial development in countries still working their way towards the productive levels of advanced capitalism
– the advanced capitalism that, in Marxist theory, had to be the starting point of socialism – and no longer champions of the working class
and other working people.

They looked at the two parts of the world with different eyes, different filters for what they would let themselves see and care about,
different standpoints, different heroes in the stories they saw unfolding, different programs, and, for practical purposes, different minds.
Everything was relative. There was nothing that couldn't be abandoned or reshaped out of all recognition.

Essentially, they looked at the "workers' states" with minds blank
for whatever the ruling Stalinist parties would choose to write on
them. They were different people in the way they related to the capitalist world, and in the way they related to the other, the "socialist"
world. They were Manichean: the advanced capitalist world was hell,
the developing countries trying to catch up were the realm of the
gods, a heaven where what wasn't good was a stage of the ultimate
good. In terms of Marxism, it was an upside-down view. Doubleness, double-mindedness, double-program-ism became central in
left-wing politics.

The facts of the Stalinist world, and our lack of consistent positive definitions, pushed us towards a comprehensive and sometimes arbitrary negativism in relation to advanced capitalism. The other side of that has been that descriptions such as "fascist" are disbarred for less-advanced states in conflict with the USA, for example for Iran. This attitude is rooted in Orthodox Trotskyist stances on Stalinist Russia, which required that all perception of its "fascistic" aspects be subordinated to higher considerations of the economic structure and the USSR's ascribed place in history.

10. Built-in hysteria and guilt

To a big extent the pro-Russian CP members and the large number of non-member sympathisers in the British Labour Party and elsewhere lived in a storm of horror stories about their "socialist fatherlands". In response, they themselves lived in a make-believe view of reality, a mix of rationalisation, denial or half-denial, and delusion about "socialism" in the USSR. They fed trustingly on a diet of "good news only" about it, most of it untrue and therefore open to challenge. They held to a picture of recent history that was repeatedly refuted in the bourgeois, social-democratic, and Trotskyist media, and to a version of their own history that was often at stark odds with the true history. On faith, they had to accept whatever they were told to accept. They lived in a mentality that paralleled that of the religious devotees who accept as dogma whatever they are told to believe by the authorities of their religion. They lived in a "double" world outlook in which they had one set of standards for assessing their own world and another, often its opposite, for assessing the other world of the socialist fatherlands.

From 1950 onwards Catholics had to believe that Mary the Mother of Jesus had not died but had been beamed up to Heaven alive by her loving son. Stalinists had to believe in Trofim Lysenko's ideas about bypassing evolution. Sometimes they would "break". Professor J B S Haldane was a very prominent British Stalinist who took the Moscow Trials in his stride but "broke" on the biological theories of Lysenko from his previously robust and impervious faith in Stalin's church-empire.

In other words, the Stalinists steered by emotion, feeling, make-believe, wish-fuelled delusional commitment, and denial on several levels at once. That was true also, to an extent, of the Orthodox Trotskyists after 1948-50. Unlike the "Communists" the Orthodox Trotskyists registered a lot of the truth about Russia and the other Stalinist states. But they also held as dogma to ideas about the Stalinist world flatly contradicted by facts and by common sense. You needed a special sort of reasoning to sustain their system of ideas. They lived in a state of painful ambivalence, constrained by feeling and commitment to a special construing, unique to themselves, of known facts.

Out of those difficulties emerged a politics necessarily streaked with the hysteria of people permanently under strain over their ideas, and relying heavily on faith, denial, and special meanings of words. Collective hysteria was central to the culture. And of course some individuals would carry a load of purely personal hysteria too.

The most malignant hysteria on the left concerns Israel and the Palestinians. All sorts of other things are expressed in intense hostility to Israel. That hostility is out of all proportion to the facts. And selective: no demonstrations and not much comment on, for instance Sri Lanka, where Tamils have been butchered by the Sinhalese majority on the island. Today a sense of guilt is commonplace in the culture of "anti-imperialism". It disarms, inhibits, urges tolerance of what elsewhere would be intolerable.

In cultural relativism it theorises and recommends ideological and political self-distrust, self-disavowal, and even cultural and political self-loathing, to the citizens of the advanced capitalist world. It induces masochistic moral submission in relation to the "Third World". It produces double and triple standards in appraising and judging cultures outside the advanced capitalist world. The idea that some are backward, reactionary, is seen guiltily and uneasily as "racist". Among people who revolt against injustice and inhumanity in their own advanced capitalist societies it produces a numbing, craven tolerance for the same things, and worse, sometimes far, far worse, in societies outside the metropolitan capitalist world and among migrants to the advanced capitalist countries. It produces a selective cultural and political regression below and behind the best produced by history and by decades and centuries of working-class and popular struggles for progress in the advanced capitalist societies.

It produces something akin to racist double standards in the idea that one would or should not expect from "them" – many "thems" – what you expect for and from people in advanced capitalist society. It generates political trollism, a culture which cries "racism" against rational critics of aspects of the culture of the peoples of ex-colonies. It "outlaws" the natural scorn and sometimes justified loathing of non-religious people for mind-shaping, culture-shaping and society-shaping religions rooted in the dark ages of human history. It disarms when judging the internal affairs of ex-colonies, where states have often inherited from the old colonialists the work of repressing and, sometimes, murdering national, religious, or cultural minorities.

There are many counts on which to feel anger and hatred against the behaviour of the richer, more advanced countries towards, say, Africa, left to rot with AIDS and other avoidable and terrible things. The paradox here is that, by definition, guilt is mainly generated in people who are critical of the rulers of the advanced countries and hostile to them, who think of themselves as the mortal enemies of the rulers of the capitalist world, and sometimes and in some regards really are; and who, themselves and their political ancestors, were enemies of old colonial imperialism – people who opposed, in words and sometimes in deeds, the crimes committed by the capitalist ruling classes against the peoples of the less developed parts of the world when those crimes were being committed.

Retrospectively, imperialist crimes inspire guilt in people whose political ancestors felt angry, not guilty, about them. Left-wing activists fought those crimes, in almost all cases, and knew themselves for certain not to be responsible for them in any degree, except in being too weak to stop their own ruling classes committing those crimes. What has the wage-slave class in the old colonial-imperial countries got to be guilty about? What have the political and cultural heirs of those in the advanced countries who fought and opposed imperialist crimes as they happened to be guilty about? Why should those who fought the old ruling classes in retrospect shoulder the guilt for the crimes of those ruling classes and of their system, which we fought and opposed, which our political ancestors fought and we fight now?

All this is a residue of the old "revolutionary" Maoist culture of the 1960s and 70s, in which the whole population of the metropolitan countries was seen as guilty towards the Third World. Measured against conditions in the Third World, metropolitan workers were seen as sub-exploiters and de facto aristocrats. One of the roots here is the culture of international Stalinism, with its two-minded tolerance of things in Stalinist societies that were considered intolerable at home – its mystified, muddled hostility to advanced capitalist society in the "name" of far worse, historically, culturally, politically, intellectually, in the Stalinist states. The widespread doubleness in respect to Stalinism made positive programs impossible for partisans of states and systems that outraged the old fundamental and irreplaceable positions of socialism. In Orthodox Trotskyists the unstable attitude to Stalinism bred a culture of self-distrust, of fear of "sectarianism", of once again (as in 1945-9) failing to "recognise" a revolution, because of a too-strong attachment to positive criteria. Above all, the experience for many decades of defending and excusing the Stalinist world, which outraged everything positive aimed for by socialists and was the opposite of the program applied in advanced capitalist societies, produced deep political, ideological, and cultural lacunae.

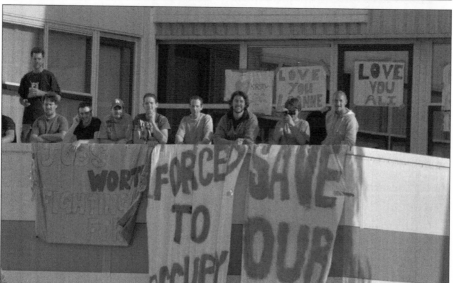

Above: the Grunwick dispute, 1977. Below: Vestas wind turbine factory occupation, 2009

Summary: aspirant socialism and "socialism"

The old aspirant socialism promised freedom; the new "socialism" brought slavery.

Socialism was "the free association of producers"; "socialism" brought a murderous intensification of labour exploitation under a ruling class which concentrated in itself all the worst traits of all the ruling classes of history (as Trotsky put it, at the end of the 1930s).

Aspirant socialism was the victory of the working class in the class struggle against the bourgeoisie, what the Communist Manifesto defined as "winning the battle of democracy". "Socialism" was the victory of a bureaucratic ruling class over the workers and peasants; the bureaucrats winning the battle of totalitarianism.

Aspirant socialism's protagonist was the proletariat acting as a "class for itself". The protagonist of "socialism" was a bureaucratic and militarised party machine, called "the party of a new type".

The core of aspirant socialism was working-class activity for self-liberation: "the emancipation of the working class must be the act of the working class itself". "Socialism" was a view of the world in which totalitarian states, peasant armies, machine-parties without internal democracy, that is, without a socialist intellectual or spiritual life, became the protagonists, the "saviours from on high" or from outside.

Aspirant socialism saw the working class, its education, development of political independence, trade-union-level well-being, as central to all it did and aspired to do. "Socialism" put the interests of anti-working-class states, that is of their rulers, at the centre of its concerns.

Aspirant socialism was republican liberty and equality; "socialism" was an absolute monarchy whose King-Pope-Caesar-Caliph-Sultan could truly say of society what Louis XIV had said of the French state: "society, c'est moi". Society – it is I.

Aspirant socialism was democracy, consistent democracy, all through society and in the economy, a world with neither slave nor ruling brigand. "Socialism" was political and social tyranny of an unparalleled intensity.

Aspirant socialism sought to build on the achievements of bourgeois civilisation and political democracy. "Socialism" excised and denounced the gains of centuries in culture, everyday rationality and human rights – most relentlessly, it repressed working-class rationality, working-class political and social rights, working-class aspiration to emancipation from class society.

Aspirant socialism was the victory of reason over the murderous unreason of class society; "socialism", floating on a cloud of reason-conquering hysteria, raised irrationality to the pitch of nightmare, and sometimes of outright madness.

Aspirant socialism was reason in revolt; "socialism" was reason in captivity to a church-state, ruled over by a Pope-Caesar, with cardinals, bishops and local clergy, preaching and enforcing his pronouncements all across the world.

Aspirant socialism meant to cut down the state's repressive functions and its power, to begin the withering-away of the state; "socialism" was the rising up of a totalitarian state to the exercise of absolute power over society, and a state-worship identical with that of fascism and sometimes transcending it.

Aspirant socialism was the triumph of the moral principles of comprehensive human solidarity over class society's morality of the capitalist jungle and petrified superstition. "Socialism" knew only the morality of the slave market, of the venal courtier, of canting priests; of the self-abasing suppliant to a tyrannical God, of an insecure, hypocritical ruling elite, of the conscienceless bureaucrat luxuriating in office, of the unfeeling, greedy, privileged consumer in a world of scarcity, general want, and sometimes widespread famine.

Aspirant socialism was the ruthlessly truthful and critical appraisal and reappraisal of reality. "Socialism" was consoling cant and a cosmology of degrading lies, armed against truth.

Aspirant socialism was a coherent, developing view of history, of social evolution, of the working class, and of socialism itself as the child and heir of advanced capitalism in society and in history. "Socialism" disarranged all the ideas, meanings and perspectives of socialism, shuffling and reshuffling them into arbitrary meanings, interpreted by a caste of state-licensed priests.

Aspirant socialism proposed to reorganise and reconstruct advanced capitalist society and on the basis of capitalism's own prior achievements to liberate first the workers and then all of humankind from class society; "socialism" took as its goal the development of backward societies towards what capitalism in the advanced countries had already achieved.

Aspirant socialism saw one world, with different stages and combinations of development in it, and approached it, all of it, with working-class interests as its norm and principle; "socialism" developed a political split personality, a comprehensive dualism in which what was condemned, resisted, and fought in one part of the world, could be simply ignored, or proclaimed good and praiseworthy, in the other.

Aspirant socialism expressed its revolutionary spirit, plebeian independence, and working-class self-assertion in the words of the Internationale: "no saviour from on high deliver ". "Socialism" worshipped supermen-saviours, philosopher-kings, and God-like deliverers of the proletariat from capitalist bondage.

Aspirant socialism organised revolutionary political parties in which discipline in action was prepared and made real by freedom of thought, of initiative, of criticism and of dissent. "Socialism" created monolithic sect-parties without freedom of thought or criticism or dissent: parties organised not according to reason and the needs of the working-class struggle but by the Jesuit rules of hierarchy, mechanical obedience, self-hypnosis, and self-suppression.

Aspirant socialism had a clear and adequate conception of its ends and means – of how and how not, of why and why not; of what would serve its goals and what would pervert and defeat them. It knew that its means had to be consonant with its end, commensurate with its goals. It had a clear notion not only of what it was against, but also, and self-definingly, of what it was for. "Socialism" used, to its ends, any and every means to hand, even the most foul, even those that most contradicted its notional goals.

For socialists the "dictatorship of the proletariat" meant the workers and working farmers organising democratically in soviets to rule themselves, riding roughshod over existing bourgeois and bureaucratic laws where they needed to. In "socialism", the "dictatorship of the proletariat" was the totalitarian rule of a privileged, self-serving autocracy, riding in tanks over the backs of peoples reduced to semi-slavery or (millions of them) outright forced-labour slavery.

Socialism was the great clean, un-won truth of the 20th century; "socialism" was the foulest lie of the 20th century.

Socialism is, remains, socialism; "socialism" was, of course, Stalinism. For over half a century, socialism, in common discourse, was the "socialism" that existed in the USSR; for many, friends and opponents of socialism alike, that's what it still is. The ideas conveyed by the words socialism and communism before Stalin established his system faded into the mists of pre-history, often denounced as "utopian socialism" or "petty-bourgeois socialism" or "moralising" socialism. "Socialism" came to be the prattle and practice of Stalinism – what became known in the 70s and 80s, to its ex-Stalinist critics and others, as "actually existing socialism".

Slave Labor --- Before Yalta and After

From The Militant (USA). Above: Laura Gray's cartoon of 17 March 1945. Facing page: top, a Trotskyist response (19 March 1938) during the Moscow Trials. They didn't know the fate of some of the people pictured. Lomov and Berzin would be shot later in 1938; Kollontai had survived and was Stalin's ambassador to Sweden. Bottom, 17 April 1950.

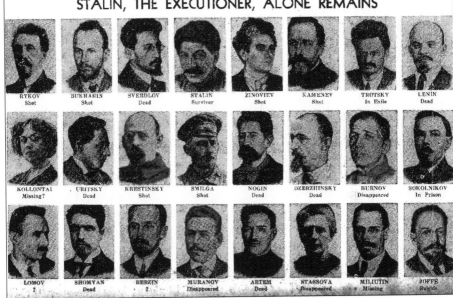

Lenin's General Staff of 1917

STALIN, THE EXECUTIONER, ALONE REMAINS

RYKOV Shot	BUKHARIN Shot	SVERDLOV Dead	STALIN Survivor	ZINOVIEV Shot	KAMENEV Shot	TROTSKY In Exile	LENIN Dead
KOLLONTAI Missing?	URITSKY Dead	KRESTINSKY Shot	SMILGA Shot	NOGIN Dead	DZERZHINSKY Dead	BUBNOV Disappeared	SOKOLNIKOV In Prison
LOMOV ?	SHOMYAN Dead	BERZIN ?	MURANOV Disappeared	ARTEM Dead	STASSOVA Disappeared	MILIUTIN Missing	JOFFE Suicide

The fate of the Bolshevik rearguard

1. The terror and tragedy of the twentieth century

The twentieth century was full of terror and tragedy, and mass murder on a scale that beggars imagination and almost defies comprehension. It was also in terms of things attempted, perhaps the most heroic in the history of humankind.

It was terrible in its murderous and enormously destructive wars of mechanised, automated, and finally automatic machines of mass murder – wars in which many millions died, by no means only combatants, and whole cities in considerable parts of Europe were levelled to rubble.

Terrible in its peacetime social devastation and the destruction of countless lives wreaked by economic dislocation and slump. Terrible in the recreation of the medieval Jewish ghettos in many cities, in the middle of the twentieth century, as preparation for the slaughter of six million European Jews in industrial factories designed for mass murder.

Terrible in the spawning of totalitarian Leviathan states able to use the technology of industrial society to exercise an unprecedented level of control, and without interruption for decades, over hundreds of millions of people. The East German workers who fell under the wheels of the fascist juggernaut in 1933 did not emerge from totalitarian rule for 56 years!

Terrible, in the decline of Marxism and socialism. And tragic above and beyond the many millions of individual human tragedies which these events entailed, because none of it was necessary in the sense of unavoidable. Better, immeasurably better, was possible by humankind and to humankind in the twentieth century.

The technology used to produce horror and slaughter was itself an aspect of an overall situation where not only better was possible, but where it was necessary and overdue, and where its retardation was the precondition for the horrors that engulfed humankind in the middle of the twentieth century.

At the core of the tragedy of the twentieth century was the fate of a socialist labour movement that had been built over decades to ensure what might be called an orderly historical succession – of work-ing-class socialism to capitalism – but proved unable to do that. It proved unable, despite tremendous efforts, to resolve its problems and difficulties. Was it, as it began to look to Trotsky at the end, and as the threat of it looked to Max Shachtman a decade, and three decades, later, a case of looming mutual ruination of the contending classes of capitalist society? The Communist Manifesto had listed such a thing as one of the possible outcomes of the class struggle.

In the 1920s Trotsky had used as a metaphor for the effect of dog-matic reformism in the British labour movement, the image of chick-ens bred so fine that they could not peck their way out of the eggshell and stifled in it. It seemed to many by the late mid-1940s to be the very image of the working class in recent history. The man who had spent most of the 30s living with Trotsky as his secretary, Jean van Heijenoort, who had also been one of the secretaries of the wartime Fourth International centred in New York, abandoned politics in 1948. He declared that the working class had definitively failed as a revolutionary class able to take humankind beyond capitalism and class society. He took refuge in mathematics. Large numbers of hith-erto revolutionaries came to the same conclusion, without like van Heijenoort writing about it lucidly to explain themselves.

To the dilemma before humankind, posed by socialists as the al-ternatives of "socialism or barbarism", History's answer seemed to be capitalist stasis, Stalinist barbarism spreading over much of the world, and a weak and faltering bourgeois democracy in a histori-cally privileged part of it, western Europe and the USA.

2. The heroism of the working class in the Twentieth Century

"Revolution is the only form of 'war' – and this is another peculiar law of history – in which the ultimate victory can be prepared only by a series of 'defeats.' What does the entire history of socialism and of all modern revolu-tions show us? The first spark of class struggle in Europe, the revolt of the silk weavers in Lyon in 1831, ended with a heavy defeat; the Chartist move-ment in Britain ended in defeat; the uprising of the Parisian proletariat in the June days of 1848 ended with a crushing defeat; and the Paris commune ended with a terrible defeat. The whole road of socialism – so far as revolu-tionary struggles are concerned – is paved with nothing but thunderous de-feats. Yet, at the same time, history marches inexorably, step by step, toward final victory! Where would we be today without those 'defeats,' from which we draw historical experience, understanding, power and idealism? Today, as we advance into the final battle of the proletarian class war, we stand on

77

the foundation of those very defeats; and we can do without any of them, be-cause each one contributes to our strength and understanding" – Rosa Luxemburg, Order Reigns in Berlin, 14 January 1919.

With the tragedy of mid-twentieth century humanity, within it, an essential part of it, went the heroism of the working class – not all of it, not everywhere, not always, but enough of it, in enough places, enough times, to indicate what had been possible. In country after country, decade after decade, heroically the workers had risen.

The class war is a serious affair and a dangerous undertaking. Those who lose pay a heavy price for having presumed to question the rulers. The image of that history is the 6,000 defeated slaves crucified along both sides of 120 miles of the Appian Way after the defeat of the great slave revolt in 73 BC. There are other forms of crucifixion and retaliation. The anarchist Errico Malatesta commented, after the defeat of the Italian workers who had seized the factories in September 1920 and failed to take state power: "The bourgeoisie sooner or later will make us pay with tears of blood for the fear that we have instilled in them today". The fascist regime, in power after 1922, did that. Under Thatcher, the British workers paid a terrible price for frightening the bourgeoisie in the 1970s.

Within that working-class heroism, within the best of it, there was another heroism – that of the revolutionary left, in many countries, many times. The list of working-class movements, strikes, political campaigns, armed revolts, against capitalism and Stalinism, is a tremendous one. A long series of movements, aspirations and revolts against usually great, sometimes very great, and often insuperable, odds. The list is vast. A near-arbitrary selection – things I know a little about – is very long. The Russian workers moved in great waves of strikes, from the 1890s. In the Russian Revolution of 1905, which was ultimately defeated, the workers created in the soviets – elected workers' councils – the beginnings of their own democratic system. In the same year, in the most advanced and most historically privileged of advanced capitalist countries, the USA, the Industrial Workers of the World was founded to organise the "unskilled", migrant and other workers, irrespective of race or creed, initially as a socialist and industrial-unionist-led movement. Its strikes were often small, and sometimes not so small, civil wars in which the working-class side would suffer numerous casualties.

After 1908 and the founding of the Irish Transport and General Workers' Union, and especially in the great "Labour War" of 1913-14, the workers of Dublin, then the second city at the heart of the leading capitalist and imperialist power, rose off their knees to "seize the fierce beast of capital by the throat". James Connolly's summary description of the workers of Dublin and their movement can not be bettered: "The Irish Transport and General Workers Union found the labourers of Ireland on their knees, and has striven to raise them to the erect position of manhood. It found them with no other weapons of defence than the arts of the liar, the lickspittle and the toady, and it combined them and taught them to abhor those arts and rely proudly on the defensive power of combination..."

In Russia, in 1917, the workers covered the country with a network of workers' councils. In February/March they overthrew the empty-headed butcher they knew as "Tsar Nicholas the Bloody" (now a saint, no less, of the Russian Orthodox Church!) and in October/November they set up a soviet state. At the end of 1918 soviets covered Germany and Austria, but instead of consolidating the power of the working class, their leaders set up the bourgeois Weimar Republic.

Communists took power for a few weeks in 1919 in both Hungary and Bavaria. Even in backward rural Ireland striking workers in small dairy-produce factories, creameries, ran up the red flag and proclaimed their strike committees to be soviets, in perhaps three dozen separate cases. Limerick City was controlled for a while in 1919 by the Workers' Council (in British terms, Trades Council), which declared itself a soviet and contested control of the city with the British administration and its army.

In the 1920s the workers of China acted as a powerful independent force, fought great strikes and other battles. In 1936 the workers of France organised a general strike, and won large reforms to wages and conditions. In the USA the workers organised great sit-in strikes and organised a powerful industrial federation, the CIO. In Catalonia, the workers took power in 1936/7, to be smashed by the unwitting combination of their anarchist leaders, who did not believe in taking state power, on one side, and on the other, the Stalinists, who physically crushed them, opening the way for four decades of fascist rule.

In Britain in the mid 1940s the working class, which had its own deep-rooted parliamentary tradition, voted for the socialist transformation of Britain, and got instead very big reforms, the modern welfare state, achieved by the Labour Government. In France, in 1944, working-class revolt challenged the Nazi occupiers. The magnificent Warsaw Ghetto uprising in 1943 was led by socialists – some of them socialist Zionists – and workers did most of the fighting.

In the 1950s, workers in the Siberian slave-labour camps, in East

German, in Poland and in Hungary rose against Stalinism. In Poland they won serious concessions, making Poland at that time the least totalitarian of the Stalinist states. In Poland, the workers moved again in 1970 – hundreds were shot down at the Gdansk Shipyards. In 1968, nine million workers seized France in a tremendous General Strike. In 1969 the Italian workers mounted great strikes. In Britain between July 1971 and December 1975, nearly 150,000 workers took part in over 200 workplace occupations. In 1974, in waves of militant industrial action, the high point of which was a miners' strike, the working class drove the Tory government out of office – an ill-judged appeal to the electorate against the miners led to the dismissal of the government – and put in the Wilson Labour Government. In August 1980, the workers seized effective control of Poland and started on a struggle that eventually led to the overthrow of Stalinism, to be replaced, alas, by bourgeois democracy and capitalism. In Britain in 1984/5 the miners fought a bitter 13 month long strike in which they faced the mounted police of the Thatcher government – a strike in which a victory that would have smashed the ruling class offensive was possible, and much that has followed its defeat was avoidable.

There are many, many, many other examples of working-class industrial battles, rebellions, seizure of factories, general strikes, armed risings, electoral victories – back to the Paris Commune of 1871, where the workers held power for nine weeks in the first workers' state in history; back to the Chartist General Strike of 1842 in the north of England – in bourgeois history "the Plug Riots"; and beyond that, a dozen years earlier, the seizure of Lyons by the silk workers; and back beyond that...

3. The paradoxical "anti-socialist" revolutions in Russia and Eastern Europe

But, it may be argued, the greatest manifestations of the revolutionary power of the working class for the last third of a century were working-class revolts in eastern Europe and Russia, not for but against socialism, not against but for market capitalism. Those great deeds of the working class did not point in the direction of post-capitalist socialism but straight ahead to capitalist restoration in the Stalinist states.

Socialism died of shame, failure and self disgust in Eastern Europe. Socialism was tried and is now deservedly rejected as an all-round social and historical shame and failure. The workers wanted capitalism, and socialism, "history's great dream" – so bourgeois and ex-socialist propagandists alike say – goes the way of other ignorant yearnings and strivings, taking its place in the museum of ignorance and quackery alongside such relics of intellectual barbarism as alchemy.

Yes, at the end of the 1980s, which had opened with a self-confident Russian Stalinist invasion of Afghanistan at Xmas 1979 (the last in a series of expansions during the 1970s, which even saw a Russian-financed Cuban army fighting in Africa), "socialism" seemed to die of shame and self-disgust, first in Eastern Europe and then in its USSR heartland.

Not since the Italian Fascist Grand Council met in 1943 and declared the Fascist system at an end, had anything like it been seen. "Socialism", so the bourgeoisie's ideologists brayed, had been tried and was being rejected as a failure and a curse on those who had lived with it. And, yes if the Stalinist systems were any sort of socialism, then socialism at that point died, and it deserved to be dead. It was rotten and stinking for decades before its outright collapse. It was a historical blind alley.

Yes, that "socialism" was rejected most explicitly by the working class in Eastern Europe and the "USSR". In Poland it was a working-class movement, Solidarnosc, that made the anti-Stalinist revolution the anti-Stalinist bourgeois revolution. "Actually existing socialism" melted like islands of ice in the thawing and surging seas of international capitalism. Its most implacable enemies included the very working class in whose name the "socialist" states claimed their social and historic legitimacy.

Yes, but what was it that the workers and working farmers, the office workers and the intelligentsia, revolted against, when they revolted against "socialism"? They revolted against:

• National oppression by the USSR and within the USSR (and by Czechs in Czechoslovakia, Serbs in Yugoslavia, etc.)

• The subordination of individuals, social groups, and nations to an all-powerful state, through which a bureaucratic ruling class exercised its economic exploitation and political tyranny.

• The denial of free speech, free press, free assembly, free organisation.

• Exploitation and poverty, combined with outrageous privilege. They wanted instead:

• National and individual freedom.

• Democracy.

• Prosperity and equality – or an end, at least, to the arbitrary and peculiarly glaring sort of inequality imposed on the Eastern Bloc by bureaucratic privilege. Like the Parisians seeking equality in the French Revolution, they would find that equality and capitalism are incompatible.

That the workers thought they could get what they wanted, or at least get more of it, under a market system – that it was Western Europe and the USA that gave them their positive idea of the desirable alternative to Stalinism – is very important: that determined what happened in 1989-91. But it is not the whole story, nor the end of the story.

4. What did the failure of Stalinist "socialism" prove?

That rigidly bureaucratic systems, where all power, decision, initiative and resources are concentrated in the hands of the state, cannot plan economies effectively.

That the workers become alienated from a supposed "workers' state" when in fact it means tyrannical rule over them by privileged bureaucrats.

That socialism is impossible without freedom and democracy, without free initiative and comprehensive self-rule.

That socialism is a dead end when it is posed as a way, under a totalitarian state, driving the people, to develop backward national economies, rather than as the working class seizing power in an advanced capitalism-prepared society.

The collapse of European Stalinism proved all these things. But then paradoxically the experience vindicates, rather than disproves, Karl Marx's idea of what socialism is, what it is not, and its place in the succession of class societies. No pre-Stalinism Marxist ever believed that such bureaucratic tyrannies could, or should, succeed as "socialism". As we have seen, Lenin, Trotsky, and the Bolsheviks, who are cited as the fountainheads of Stalinism by people who either know no better, or refuse to "know" what they know, did not think they could.

For the socialism of Marx, Engels, Luxemburg, Mehring, Lenin, Trotsky, Connolly, Gramsci, it is good that millions of people in Eastern Europe and in the Soviet Union rose in revolt against "socialism" and "communism".

Stalinism was never socialism. But (like the revolts in Europe in 1848) the revolt against it was socialism in embryo. The mass self-assertion and revolt of millions of people is the raw material of socialism – socialism as liberation and self-liberation, here self-liberation from state tyranny and grotesque state-organised inequality.

Such revolt does not, of course, necessarily develop into conscious mass socialism; yet, it is its necessary starting point and one of its essential components. There can never be a viable socialism without it. Socialists had hoped for socialism to replace Stalinism. In retrospect we can see that it would have been a true miracle if the workers in the Stalinist countries had attained political clarity after many years in darkness. It would be remarkable if the workers had not been confused and bewildered by the official "socialism" which meant tyranny and poverty, and by the capitalism of Western Europe which meant comparative prosperity and liberty. Men and women such as Lech Walesa, the hero of Solidarnosc who looked for his ideal society to the capitalist world, the opposite of the society he had grown up in, and Arthur Scargill, who led the miners' strike in 1984-5 and in his own confused way was an honest militant working-class leader but who looked east, to Stalinism, the opposite of the society he lived in, were tragic mirror images of each other's limitations.

What East European and Russian workers gained in 1989-91 was the freedom to think and to organise, the freedom to struggle and to learn from their struggles. Out of this, the first steps towards socialism – independent workers' organisations, trade unions, and even parties – have emerged again in countries in which history seemed to have ended in Hell with the imposition of Stalinism half a century earlier. In the east, working-class history began again.

The East European and Russian revolts of the working class against Stalinism vindicated the anti-Stalinist Bolsheviks, those who made the Russian workers' revolution and died, most of them. fighting to defend it against Stalinism.

5. Stalinism and Bolshevism

Lenin and Trotsky led the workers organised in a democratic political party – the Bolsheviks – and in democratic workers' councils, soviets, to power. They fought with adequate ruthlessness against the bourgeoisie and the opponents of socialism. They smashed the walls of the Tsarist prison-house of nations and gave liberty to the oppressed nations – a majority of the population – in the Tsarist Russian Empire. Far from substituting themselves for the working class, the Bolshevik party, by its leadership and farsightedness, allowed the working class to reach and sustain a level of purposeful mass action hitherto unparalleled in history.

The Bolsheviks were fallible human beings, acting in conditions of great difficulty, trying to achieve and hold something which had never before been achieved and held. Mistakes they may have made in the maelstrom of civil war and economic collapse are proper subjects for historians and for socialist discussion and debate. As their critic and comrade Rosa Luxemburg wrote in 1918, the Bolsheviks would have been the last to imagine that everything they did in their conditions was a perfect model of socialist action for everywhere at all times.

When things began to go wrong the Bolsheviks stood their ground. The workers' risings were defeated in the West. Invasions, civil war, and economic destruction wrecked the soviets. The Bolshevik party itself divided. One section took a path on which it ended up leading the bureaucratic counter-revolution. The surviving central leaders, in the first place Trotsky, fought the counter-revolution on a program of working-class self-defence and of renewing the soviets. Those Bolsheviks went down to bloody defeat. Stalinism rose above the grave of Bolshevism, just as it rose hideously above the murdered socialist hopes of the Russian and international working class. That working-class hope turned into nightmare, and we are still gripped by its legacy. By the late 1930s Stalin had slaughtered the leading activists not only from the Trotskyist, but also from the Right (Bukharinist) Communist and even the original Stalinist faction of the Bolshevik party of the 1920s.

Stalinism was not Bolshevism, any more than it was any kind of socialism. Trotsky, who was to die at the hands of Stalin's assassins, put it well and truly when he said that a river of working class and communist blood separated Stalinism, from Bolshevism.

The dying Lenin, in the first place, and then the Left Opposition founded in Moscow in October 1923, whose leaders were Trotsky and Rakovsky, fought the Stalinist counter-revolution that overthrew the workers' state. Fought it to the death of large numbers, almost all of them, in Stalin's concentration camps, jails, and homicide chambers.

6. The Trotskyists

Trotskyism was no arbitrary, episodic, or merely personal creation. The Trotskyists took over, developed and fought for the ideas of the early Communist International – the International which itself inherited the progressive work and root ideas of the previously existing socialist movement. The ideas of what came to be called Trotskyism were the continuation and summation of the whole history of the socialist working-class movement.

The Trotskyists held to the goal of winning working-class power in the advanced capitalist countries. But that program could only be fought for effectively by a mass movement; those perspectives depended for their realisation on the living activity of millions of revolutionary workers. And the millions-strong world-wide army of "communism" was in the grip of the delusion that Stalinism was communism. Organisationally, it was in the grip of totalitarian "communist" "parties" controlled by the Moscow Stalinist bureaucracy, which used lies, corruption, and gangsterism to keep its hold.

In the 1920s and with decreasing conviction up to the Moscow Trials of 1936-8, Trotsky and his comrades saw USSR Stalinism as, to an extent, a progressive alternative to capitalism and to capitalist imperialism. But they registered also that it was neither an adequate, nor a viable, nor a desirable alternative. And from 1937, when after six months' internment in Norway he arrived in Mexico and resumed regular comment, Trotsky became increasingly hostile and negative about the "USSR" which at the end of his life he defined as only potentially progressive. (See the present writer's introduction to *The Fate of the Russian Revolution*).

Max Shachtman, adapting an old joke about the Holy Roman Empire, pointed out that in the name "Union of Soviet Socialist Republics" there were at least four lies: it wasn't a free union, there were no soviets, it was in no way socialist, and it was more a Stalinist absolute monarchy than any kind of Republic.

Trotsky did not properly name Stalinist imperialism "imperialism", but he described it in fact, and counterposed to it a working-class programmatic alternative. Thus, for example, Trotsky championed independence for the Ukrainian nation, oppressed by Great Russian Stalinist chauvinism.

What if "the separation of the Ukraine threatens to break down the economic plan and lower the productive forces", asked Trotsky. "This argument, too, is not decisive. An economic plan is not the holy of holies. It is impermissible to forget that the plunder and arbitrary rule of the bureaucracy constitute an important integral part of the current economic plan... The question of first order is the revolutionary guarantee of the unity and independence of a workers' and peasants' Ukraine in the struggle against imperialism on the one hand, and against Moscow Bonapartism on the other". (*Writings* 1939-40 p.44ff). Trotsky understood perfectly that the USSR was a Great-Russian Empire.

The Trotskyist rearguard of Bolsheviks were comprehensively defeated, inside Russia and everywhere else. They could not rise politically when the working class had been defeated and beaten down.

Let one of those Stalinists who crushed Bolshevism and lived to finally understand what had happened, Leopold Trepper, describe them for us.

Leopold Trepper was the head of the USSR's spy network in Nazi-occupied Europe. After the war Trepper was imprisoned by the KGB and only released during the post-Stalin thaw in the mid 1950s. In his autobiography *The Great Game*, Trepper honours the Trotskyists for their unyielding opposition to Stalin thus:

"The glow of October was being extinguished in the shadows of underground chambers. The revolution had degenerated into a system of terror and horror; the ideals of socialism were ridiculed in the name of a fossilised dogma which the executioners still had the effrontery to call Marxism. And yet we went along, sick at heart, but passive, caught up in machinery we had set in motion with our own hands. Mere cogs in the apparatus, terrorised to the point of madness, we became the instruments of our own subjugation. All those who did not rise up against the Stalinist machine are responsible, collectively responsible. I am no exception to this verdict. But who did protest at that time? Who rose up to voice his outrage? The Trotskyists can lay claim to this honour. Following the example of their leader, who was rewarded for his obstinacy with the end of an ice-axe, they fought Stalinism to the death, and they were the only ones who did. By the time of the great purges, they could only shout their rebellion in the freezing wastelands where they had been dragged in order to be exterminated. In the camps, their conduct was admirable. But their voices were lost in the tundra. Today, the Trotskyists have a right to accuse those who once howled along with the wolves. Let them not forget, however, that they had the enormous advantage over us of having a coherent political system capable of replacing Stalinism. They had something to cling to in the midst of their profound distress at seeing the revolution betrayed."

7. Ambassador Coulondre, Hitler, Trotsky; and Trotskyism after Trotsky

On the very eve of the Second World War, the German fascist dictator Hitler had a last meeting with the French ambassador Coulondre. Soon, for the second time in a quarter-century, France and Germany would be tearing each other to pieces in war. Coulondre remonstrated with Hitler about the Nazi deal with Stalin, the Stalin-Hitler pact. It would mean war, he told Hitler.

He conjured up for Hitler the memory of what had happened at the end of the last world war. Working-class revolt had swept across Europe. Revolutionary workers brought down the German Emperor; they took and held power in Russia; they took power but were overthrown in Hungary and in Bavaria. Europe was swept by strikes, factory seizures, and great mass movements of workers determined not to go on in the old way and desperately looking for a way out of war and capitalism, a way to a socialist society.

That, said Coulondre, is what you risk unleashing once again. To dramatise his point, and to evoke as vividly as he could for Hitler the horrors he was conjuring up, Coulondre pronounced the name under which he, and the European bourgeoisie, thought of the socialist revolution.

"The real victor (in case of war) will be Trotsky. Have you thought of that?"

Trotsky! Together with Lenin, Trotsky had led the Russian workers' revolution in 1917. He, with Lenin dead, had opposed the tyrannical Stalin regime in the USSR. Now a hunted exile, he preached the need for socialist revolution as the only alternative to the barbarism into which capitalism and Stalinism were plunging the world. For the bourgeoisie of the world and for the Stalinists who ruled the USSR he still personified the threat of working-class revolution.

Almost exactly a year after the conversation between Coulondre and Hitler, on 20 August 1940, in Coyocoan, a suburb of Mexico City, the Spanish Stalinist Ramon Mercader, posing as a co-thinker in order to get close to him, smashed Trotsky's skull with an ice-pick and he died the following day. When, at the end of World War Two, a wave of working-class revolt did sweep Europe, it was controlled or repressed by the Stalinist organisations.

Trotsky left behind him a weak and tiny movement – a small splinter from the gigantic world communist movement of those who had rallied to the Russian Revolution. Most of the would-be communists stayed with Stalin, who controlled the "Soviet" state, because they did not understand that a political and social counter-revolution. had taken place within the collectivist property forms that continued to exist in the Soviet Union.

By the second half of the 1940s, the USSR had survived and had conquered a new Stalinist empire covering half of Europe. Its European borders were carved out in the middle of Germany, a hundred miles west of Berlin. Russia had become one of the two great world powers. In Eastern Europe, systems like that of the USSR were created; in China and other countries, Stalinists made revolutions which were against the big capitalist powers, and against the bourgeoisie, but also against the working class. In the West, in France and Italy for example, the Stalinist movements, on Russia's orders, helped the bourgeoisies to rebuild their states.

Stalinism expanded into new areas, covering one third of the world. Capitalism, which had seemed almost on its last legs in 1940, entered a post-war boom. The mass labour movements of the advanced countries settled in to live with and under capitalism. Capitalism experienced such lightning-flash revolts as the general strike in France by nine million workers in May 1968, but easily survived them.

The majority of the forces making up post-Trotsky Trotskyism continued to see the Stalinist states as degenerated or (the new ones outside Russia) deformed "workers' states", socially in advance of and superior to capitalism. Russia, Eastern Europe, and China were, they believed, "post-capitalist", in transition between capitalism and socialism.

Trotskyism thus seemed to be the embodiment of an idea whose time had come – and somehow passed it by; a movement whose program, or the economic fundamentals of it, had been made reality by its Stalinist enemies, and grotesquely twisted into horrible shapes in the process.

8. Stalinism and the inertia of political cultures

The precondition for the direct and indirect effect which Stalinism still has on the current left is the fact that a culture, once established, has a tremendous power of inertia. Inertia itself becomes a force in events, affecting decisions which may be turning points in history, shaping events for a long time ahead. A culture can be extirpated, wiped out, adulterated, or turned inside out, as the previous socialist and Marxist political culture was by Stalinism; but it can also, left to "itself", go on for a very long time, especially if it still seems to "work" and nothing better replaces it. The degenerated social-democratic culture in the working class is a case in point. It survived long after the political and moral collapse of social democracy in 1914, even where it had to compete with the vigorous early Communist International.

Antonio Gramsci: "Mass ideological factors always lag behind mass economic phenomena... at certain moments, the automatic thrust due to the economic factor is slowed down, obstructed or even momentarily broken by traditional ideological elements... Hence ... there must be a conscious, planned struggle to ensure that the exigencies of the economic position of the masses, which may conflict with the traditional leadership's policies, are understood. An appropriate political initiative is always necessary to liberate the economic thrust from the dead weight of traditional policies".

9. The revolutionary Marxist tradition

Today we live in conditions where the tradition of revolutionary Marxism passed on by Trotsky and the Trotskyism of his time is highly fragmented. Its elements are disassembled and sometimes needlessly counterposed to each other, that is, dogmatically overemphasised aspects of what should be one integrated whole, or even made into substitutes for larger concepts ("the party" for socialism). This situation has much in common with the state of revolutionary socialism before the Communist International, after the October Revolution, began to reintegrate the contributions of the Social-Democratic left, the revolutionary syndicalists, and the best of the anarchists, into a coherent whole.

Yet the revolutionary socialist tradition is immensely important. Again: the revolutionary movement is, in Trotsky's words, "the memory of the working class". The bourgeoisie has a vast retinue of intellectuals to record, construe, explain, slant, spin current and past events from the point of view of the ruling bourgeoisies. It has a many-faceted educational apparatus which teaches its history, its values, its outlook, which glorifies its system. It tells the young that capitalism and bourgeois democracy are the culmination of history. It fights the bourgeois class war on the "ideological front", waging a never-ending ideological war on the bourgeoisie's behalf. (For instance, the way the oil and other "interests" have systematically worked to discredit the evidence about global warming.) The bourgeoisie also has social and political institutions which "socialise" people in general and the working class in particular, into the values, the outlook, and the tradition which expresses its interests.

The working class has none of that. It exists in a bourgeois world, dominated by commerce, which inculcates active or passive acceptance of bourgeois thinking and bourgeois values. We are constantly under bombardment by the bourgeois media, which do the same. Against all that we have our under-resourced educational and propaganda work; and a large part of that depends on the written residues of the socialist past – what we have of them – and is enriched by them. The working class, the basic exploited class in capitalist society, faces great difficulties in remaking society. It cannot develop control of a portion of the means of production within the old system, as in its time the bourgeoisie did within and under feudalism and absolutism. The working class, unlike the bourgeoisie in its historical journey, does not develop its own culture within this system. Its class-consciousness and historical awareness and aspirations fluctuate. Habitually its leaders – its trade union as well as its political leaders – help the capitalist rich and powerful against their own people in return for personal advancement.

Though the working class has known its age of reform under capitalism, we accumulate many defeats, and the working class or its organisations are not able to learn from all of them. We sometimes have to live through again and learn things earlier workers knew. What the things listed, and all the other similar things not listed, indicate is that though the working class has not failed to fight, again and again, and again, there are special difficulties to be overcome if the working class is to emancipate itself. The question for socialists is: what can be done to overcome those difficulties?

The historical record refutes the idea that the working class has no inbuilt antagonism to the capitalist class, their system, and their society. It refutes any suggestion that workers lack the tendency and

---

† *This is how, in 1981, the predecessors of the AWL saw the problem of the Trotskyist organisations:*

"Given that our real opinion is that we should in honesty defend the article in court, to make an insincere apology would be to allow ourselves to be forced to tell lies under the compulsion of Ms Redgrave's wealth.

"We are not prepared to tell lies to the labour movement or to the youth. That is in general a rock-basic rule. It is urgent to preach it and to live by it because for fifty years deliberate and systematic lying and other falsifications of truth have been a major part of the labour movement.

"Spreading outward from the totalitarian Stalinist state via the Stalinist parties, the politics of lies and doubletalk, of the double standard or none, of 'anything goes' for my organisation or for my faction, the politics of the numbed or dead conscience and of the supple spine – these have wreaked havoc with the political consciousness and the political morality of the labour movement, They are not the sort of politics we exist to promote. Not for nothing did Leon Trotsky preach and insist again and again that one of the first principles of revolutionary politics was 'to tell the truth to the labour movement and to the masses'. We subscribe to Trotsky's principle. And we will fight for it".

We have learned much from the Heterodox Trotskyists and from attempting to reintegrate the positive contributions of others – the De Leonites and revolutionary syndicalists, for example – into our work. Much of what we had been doing had been done earlier by the Shachtmanites, and done better because the Workers' Party and ISL emerged as part of a general Bolshevik-Trotskyist culture much richer and deeper than was the culture of the politically impoverished Orthodox Trotskyist dialects of the movement out of which the AWL tendency evolved.

capacity to rebel against capitalism. The long absence of open big-scale class battles in Britain does not point to a death of class struggle, but to the fact that the bourgeois won great victories over the working class in that struggle in the 70s and 80s. The virtual destruction of the old Labour Party by the New Labour disciples of Thatcher was part of that series of defeats.

The Russian workers, led by the Bolsheviks, proved in 1917 that the working class can take and consolidate power, when certain objective and subjective preconditions are met. That is one of the reasons why the bourgeoisie sustains an ideological offensive against the memory of the October Revolution, identifying it with the Stalinist counter-revolution against Bolshevism, the Stalinism that destroyed the working-class power, though not in the same way that the bourgeoisie tried to destroy it at the time of the revolution. They conflate and identify the rule of the workers with the rule of those who overthrew the workers' power, and massacred the Bolsheviks!

Our traditions embody our history, our collective, codified experience, spanning generations and the work of generations of socialists. They exemplify our Marxist methodology, our models of how to analyse and think. We cannot at will take the working class through the enlightening experience of a general strike. We can teach workers about the general strikes of history, like Britain in 1926 and France in 1936 and 1968, about such half-buried events as the British general strike of 1842, and about the Russian Revolution. In times of adversity, one-sided "sects" can sometimes play a positive role, by preserving valuable ideas, even in a decayed, desiccated, or petrified form.

The Orthodox Trotskyists did that, and so in their different ways did the others. AWL, over decades, evolved its own political tradition out of the Orthodox Trotskyism of James P Cannon. We separated from that decisively in 1979-80, when all the Orthodox Trotskyists backed the Russian army in Afghanistan, and we refused to do that. We then "discovered" the literary work in the 1940s and 50s of Max Shachtman, Hal Draper, Al Glotzer, Irving Howe, and others. †

We exist in a situation where the living aspects of our tradition are dislocated, and embedded in partly, or sometimes greatly, alien traditions, for instance, that of the Orthodox Trotskyists, from which AWL has evolved. Therefore, in striving to integrate the sundered elements of the Trotskyism of the Trotskyists we face the danger of vapid eclecticism. To a shaping extent, such political and theoretical eclecticism is central to the SWP-UK.

Avoiding that is a question of striving for consistency, critical understanding of what we take as our "tradition", and above all in living by the cardinal rule of Marxist politics – to be guided always by the logic of the class struggle, and within that by the interests of the working class, including its "interest" in learning what capitalism is and what socialism strives to be and to achieve.

10. Shuffling the signposts

Capitalism broke down into protracted crisis, erupting into two world wars, between about 1914 and about 1950. Opportunities for the working-class to replace capitalist rule with its own rule did exist in "the epoch of wars and revolutions". But the working-class was defeated. And in a strange and unprecedented way. The victors in the defeat of the working class and the destruction of Bolshevism presented themselves – and even thought of themselves – as representing the working class. They presented their system, in which the working class was enslaved more than in the typical capitalist states, as working-class socialism.

That confused all the maps and signposts. In Britain in 1940, when a German invasion seemed imminent, the road signs were removed so as to confuse the invaders. What happened to the socialists resembles that. The Marxist signposts have yet to be sorted out and re-erected. Capitalism revived after the mid 40s, and started to grow and develop again. Stalinism, in the mid-twentieth century, seemed to many to be the alternative to capitalism. It was still expanding into new areas at the start of the decade in which, at the end, the USSR collapsed from its inner contradictions. Then capitalism eventually overwhelmed, in economic, military and political competition, the aberrant, historically freakish and unviable Stalinist bureaucratic collectivism.

Yet the Orthodox Trotskyists continued to guide themselves by often garbled memories from the mid twentieth century crisis of capitalism. Thus the "evolutionary floor" which Marx and Engels gave to communism was knocked out of Orthodox Trotskyism. Socialist revolution became not a matter of the positive development and education of the working-class movement, but a quasi-mechanical consequence of the ever-present "crisis" as soon as general mass discontent and the building of a revolutionary-party "machine" should rise high enough.

The post-Trotskyist movement went through its own long "Third Period". Proletarian revolution was always imminent or in process. Strange and alien phenomena – in the first place, those of Stalinism – were misidentified as aspects of it. That was an aspect of reversion to utopianism. The Orthodox Trotskyists built on Trotsky's identification of the USSR as a "degenerated" workers' state and their own definition of the new Stalinist states as "deformed" workers' states to shed a core idea of Trotsky's: the idea that Stalinist Russia was an unviable freak social formation that would in the short term collapse, either before bourgeois onslaught or working-class revolution; and that if it were not, then it would have to be reconceptualised as a new form of exploitative class society. † They moved to an implicit acceptance of "socialism in one country" – the development of the USSR , and now other backward states of Stalinism, in parallel with and eventually outstripping, advanced capitalism.

They relegated Trotsky to the status of a posthumous utopian savant. The "word" was given. Thereafter in capitalism no progress was possible. Capitalism was unconditionally and universally reactionary. That then meant: reactionary against Stalinism – and has now come to mean: reactionary against no matter whom.

The power of the idea that capitalism was in its death agony to motivate and mobilise made it of great value to apparatus Marxists. Trotsky once recommended the idea for its mobilising powers – he did not mean, falsify reality so as to be able to use it! Our alternative to capitalism is a socialism that retains, spreads and deepens the conquests of bourgeois civilisation from the Renaissance and earlier onwards. These include rational, critical, realistic assessments of our world, of our alternative to capitalism, of ourselves. That too was often lost.

We need to remind ourselves of the fundamental ideas of Marxist socialism. For Marxists, socialism has become possible only because capitalism has created a mass proletariat and created means of production which, liberated of the drives and unreason of capitalism, can create abundance for all in the basics of life. We base our socialist program on this Marxist idea of the necessary evolution of capitalist society, of its forces of production, as the irreplaceable ground-preparer for socialism; on the social, intellectual and political preparation of the proletariat through both capitalist evolution and communist education and organisational work, to make it able to seize power in capitalist society.

---

† See The USSR In War, and Again And Once More On The Nature Of The USSR, both in In Defence Of Marxism.

The survivors of Atlantis

1. The Orthodox Trotskyists

When the Trotskyist mainstream, in the late 1940s, turned towards a more "positive" account of Stalinism, there was a big exodus from its ranks, already thin and sparse. The defeated and depleted Trotskyist current, always small, shrank in the 1950s to being very little, even minuscule. In Trotsky's time the gap between its ideological riches and its small forces had been one of this movement's most characteristics features. Now, in terms of its ideas, too, it shrank.

The Orthodox Trotskyist politics elaborated over the 1940s and codified at the 1951 congress were a mutation of the politics of Trotsky, a grafting onto it of antagonistic elements.

The major surviving Trotskisant current, the so-called Orthodox Trotskyists, organised in the "Fourth International" of James P Cannon, Michel Pablo, and Ernest Mandel, and its splinters, the Morenists, Lambertists, Grantites, Healyites, etc., sided with the Stalinist camp in the world polarisation into two blocs. They were "critically", but "unconditionally", for the "defence" of the Stalinist bloc against the other bloc. They were for all its full and partial replications and partisans all over the world. The expansion of the Stalinist bloc was, they insisted, the World Revolution advancing, though, to be sure, advancing in unexpected and uncongenial ("deformed") ways.

They identified Stalinism of various sorts with the "world revolution", and regarded the Stalinist states as "progressive". Automatically they took sides with the Stalinist bloc in its imperialist competition with capitalist imperialism and even in such an old-style colonialist enterprise as the Russian invasion of Afghanistan (1979). They backed China in Tibet in 1959, criticising the Maoists for tardiness in extending "the revolution" to Tibet.

The Orthodox Trotskyists came to accept the essential utopian idea behind "Socialism in One Country" by way of adopting the view that the USSR, and later the Stalinist bloc, were stable societies "in transition to socialism". Although Isaac Deutscher was not himself a Trotskyist – he insisted on that, and there, at least, he was telling the truth – he was greatly influential with the Orthodox Trotskyists. What he wrote about the prospects before the USSR, in for example his 1960 book *The Great Contest*, now reads like wild ravings.

Mao was proclaimed the political legatee of Trotsky, not Stalin.

Much scholastic ducking and weaving, conjuring and mystical hocus-pocus by such Orthodox Trotskyists as Ernest Mandel was devoted to "proving" that Stalin's "socialism in one country" had been refuted by the spread of "the revolution" – that is, of Stalinism – far beyond the borders of the USSR.

For the USSR and the East European satellite states these Orthodox Trotskyists advocated Trotsky's old program of working-class revolution. Following Trotsky, they called what they advocated a "political revolution". In fact what they, like Trotsky, advocated was a profound social revolution, the destruction of the Stalinist state power and its replacement by a working-class regime based on workers' councils. That meant a fundamental transformation in property, from ownership by the totalitarian state, which was itself owned by the Stalinist autocracy, to ownership by a democratic working-class quasi-state.

For the countries in which Stalinist guerrilla armies had won power in civil wars and made their own Stalinist states, the Orthodox Trotskyists tended to advocate not revolution but reform as the way to working-class democracy. Some of them, by way of "open letters" to the Chinese or Yugoslav "comrades", turned themselves into utopian-socialist would-be advisers of Stalinist ruling classes on how to abolish their systems.

In at least two senses this was not the "Trotskyism" of Trotsky. The Orthodox Trotskyists shifted from seeing Russian Stalinism as a freak phenomenon that could not survive – Trotsky's position – to seeing the USSR and new Stalinist states as stable social formations, "in transition to socialism". Socialism itself would be at the other side of working-class "political revolution" against Stalinist autocracy or – in China and other countries – radical democratisation; but this view implied an acceptance of the logic of "socialism in one country", of the idea that Russia could develop in parallel to capitalism and outstrip it. The fact of other Stalinist states coming into being had no bearing on the central reason for the falsity of this perspective: that it was utopian to imagine that a country, or even, in the new situation, a bloc of countries, could evolve from backwardness to compete with, overtake and overthrow and supplant advanced world capitalism.

This thinking was also a radical turn away from Trotsky's tentative conclusion that if Stalinist Russia survived the world war intact it would have to be radically re-conceptualised as a new form of bureaucratic class society.

On such questions the politics of the Orthodox Trotskyists were a hybrid of Trotsky's and those of the pre-war Brandlerite "Right Communists" or critical "liberal Stalinists", splinter from the Communist International, formed after Stalin took his "left turn" and purged Bukharin and others in 1929. Isaac Deutscher, though he had been a Trotskyist from 1932 until 1940, was after that a Brandlerite in his ideas about the USSR. Brandlerite politics and assessments suffuse his very widely read three-volume biography of Trotsky, and his biography of Stalin. For the last sixty years of the 20th century, most anti-Stalinists were of this Orthodox Trotskyist – or better, Orthodox Trotskyist/ Deutscherite – persuasion.

In their own inadequate and contradictory way, despite their belief that the advance of Stalinism in the world was the "deformed" advance of the socialist world revolution, nevertheless, they were comprehensively anti-Stalinist. At their worst, when calling on Stalinist ruling classes to reform their own system, they advocated radical reforms that, if they were realised, would not have left much of Stalinism intact. (That was a regression to utopianism in a different sense, socialism as appeals to the ruling class).

Their adaptation to Stalinism was never uncritical adaptation – those who ceased to be critical ceased to be even nominally Trotskyist. It was a misguided attempt at a revolutionary socialist "accommodation" to the fact of Stalinism, so as to promote the "full" Trotskyist program. It was never inner acceptance of it, never a surrender of the idea that the Stalinist states had to be democratised, transformed, revolutionised. Even at their most inadequate, the Orthodox Trotskyists were for a revolution against Stalinism.

But Ernest Mandel, for example, used his erudition and his intellectual talents to weave, from the ideas of Lenin and Trotsky, ideological clothing which could be draped on the expansion of Stalinism in order to identify it as part of the world revolution of the proletariat. Directly and indirectly, over the years, this Orthodox Trotskyism tied large numbers of anti-Stalinist militants into accepting, tolerating or half-justifying aspects even of Russian Stalinist imperialism.

As a truthful picture of Russia began to form out of the mist of wishes, fantasies, lies and falsifications – after say, the Russian invasion of Czechoslovakia, to put down the emerging "socialism with a human face" there – many CPers were disillusioned. Orthodox Trotskyists could not experience that sort of "disillusionment". We knew all the horrors of Stalinism already and had a theory – "degenerated and deformed workers' states" – to frame them in. So long as nationalised property existed the Stalinist state would be "progressive", anti-capitalist and worthy of defence; Trotskyists had to defend them on principle. So in 1979, when Russian invaded Afghanistan, every

Orthodox Trotskyist organisation in existence (with the exception of *Socialist Organiser*-Workers' Liberty) refused to oppose the occupation. There was a big minority in the French organisation LCR which wanted to call for the withdrawal of the Russian army, but some groups were very enthusiastic for the expansion of the "degenerated workers' state".

It was their assessment of the USSR, inherited from Trotsky but erected by themselves into a self-blinding dogma, that trapped the Orthodox Trotskyists into letting themselves be reduced, too often, to the role of mere satellites of the Stalinist bloc and its partisans in the capitalist states. That misidentification of the USSR was one pillar of a complex historical disorientation: the existence of the Russian degenerated workers' state and the coming into existence of other Stalinist states was seen as proof that this was "the era of wars and socialist revolution".

Almost everything "Trotskyist" in our early 21st century post-Stalinist world – including *Solidarity* and Workers' Liberty – has its roots in that Orthodox Trotskyist current. It was, probably, the ambiguities, self-contradictoriness, and politically protean character of that current which allowed it to survive, in many political variants and compounds.

2. One, two, three – many "Third Periods"

One of the most destructive experiences of the working-class movement was what the Stalinists called the "Third Period". It played a major part in letting Hitler take and consolidate power. The "Third Period" was called that because the Stalinists (in fact, Bukharin initially) divided the history of the world since World War One into three periods: the post-war revolutionary storms, then capitalist stabilisation and consolidation, and then the "Third Period".

The Third Period, which opened about 1928, was the era of a new revolutionary offensive, everywhere in the world. It was the era of the certain victory of the working class and its peasant allies, everywhere. Now. Or soon. In terms of what was going on in the world, it was raving nonsense. But it was the fixed doctrine of the Communist International and everyone it influenced. Events in the world had to be construed according to what they should be in the doctrines of the Third Period. The example most relevant to the politics of today was the way the Comintern construed events in Palestine in 1929, when it arbitrarily redefined what it had first described as a pogrom movement as a great anti-imperialist uprising.

Everything in the world was construed as what, in Third Period theory, it had to be, should be, but in cold fact was not. It was a form of political delirium. In the Third Period, when revolution was immanent and imminent, the main enemies of the Communist Parties were the "social-fascists" (social democrats), and other hyphen-fascists, such as the "Trotsky-fascists". The Stalinists sometimes allied against the "social-fascists" in Germany (the SPD, the biggest party based on the working class) with the, so to speak, fascist-fascists, the Hitlerites, breaking SPD-led strikes, backing the Nazi initiative to unseat the SPD state government in Prussia in an August 1931 referendum, competing with the Nazis as the best people to "liberate" Germany from the national oppression of the Versailles Treaty imposed in 1919, etc.

In part the Third Period doctrine reflected the turmoil in the USSR of the period of forced agricultural collectivisation and breakneck industrialisation.

The concept of "imperialism", as it was in left-wing discourse after 1945, had something in it akin to Third Period doctrine for the Stalinists, but also for the Orthodox Trotskyists. The epoch of imperialism was the last epoch of capitalism. The revolution was due, indeed already underway in the form of the various Stalinist seizures of power. This was the period of wars and revolutions. The time from 1948-50 was, for the Orthodox Trotskyists, one of frantic and sometimes borderline, or over-the-border, crazy construing of events to fit that picture. Anti-imperialism in the "Third World" was also, by definition, incipiently the socialist revolution, because it could become Stalinist bureaucratic revolution, and because it was deemed certain to ruin the old capitalist powers economically. "Imperialism" came to be defined as "what stood in opposition to the 'socialist' camp". Everything was read off from the theory, the formula, the blueprint. To a considerable extent the Orthodox Trotskyists had the same reality-confusing method as the Stalinists in the Third Period.

3. Utopianism central still

The great and prolonged crisis of capitalism in the mid twentieth century properly roused revolutionary Marxists to the idea that the eras of peaceful and progressive capitalist development were gone forever. "The point was to change it", to overthrow it now: that was all. The philosophers had interpreted History; and History had favourably pronounced on the philosophers with the seeming collapse of capitalism. The point was to change it – and that narrowed down into "Build the Revolutionary Party". This idea persisted long after the crisis that unleashed it was over, and long after History had taken unexpected turns, with the consolidation of Russian Stalinism, and the spread of Stalinism across one third of the globe.

The perspective of hopeless capitalist collapse was kept in place by the dominant Orthodox Trotskyist doctrine that the Stalinist states were "post-capitalist", the deformed embodiment of a still developing and expanding albeit distorted proletarian world revolution, and thus proof that it was still "the age of wars and revolutions". It persisted despite capitalist revival and prosperity in the most advanced countries, and fast capitalist growth in many poorer countries.

Long before the fall of European Stalinism, and Francis Fukuyama's thesis, derived from it, that we had reached "the end of history", Orthodox Trotskyists had applied a similar idea to capitalism.

History, they thought, had reached a point beyond which almost everything in advanced capitalism was reactionary. The SWP-UK had its own dialect of this idea, a core idea of its sectarianism – a thesis that when world capitalism became ripe for socialism, thereafter everything capitalist became reactionary. It was the method of the great utopian socialists – once the socialist idea has been invented, everything else is reactionary.

The "evolutionary" aspects of modern communism were, as we have seen, central to the contribution of Marx and Engels and their school of politics. They have largely been lost by the would-be left.

4. The other Trotskyists

There was another Trotskyist current – that of Max Shachtman, Hal Draper, Julius and Phyllis Jacobson, Herman Benson, Joseph Friedman, Albert Glotzer, Irving Howe, Stanley Plastrik, and the others who fought Trotsky in 1939-40 because they rejected any sort of "critical support" for the Russian Stalinist army in its war with Finland (from November 1939 to April 1940).

They went on to break, in 1940-1, with the idea that the USSR was any kind or degree of workers' state. In response to events, they elaborated a distinct strand of Trotskyism.

In the 1940s the Orthodox Trotskyists without Trotsky floundered politically in face of, first, the unexpected survival of Russian Stalinism, and then the eruption of Stalinist imperialism. Like Bible-fetish Christians, they read in the Big Book of "Trotskyist" "orthodoxy", where they themselves had written as immutable dogma an unrepresentative selection of Trotsky's works and phrases, especially on the USSR.

In contrast, the "other Trotskyists", the Heterodox Trotskyists, responded to the consolidation of the Stalinist autocracy and the rise of its empire to the eminence of second power in the world with accurate reporting and sober assessment of its meaning for the working class's socialist theory and its implications for the socialist working-class program. It can be argued (as I have argued, in detail and at length, elsewhere) that this heterodox Trotskyist current, in fact, despite its episodic dispute with Trotsky in 1939-40, continued the politics of Trotsky and applied them to the world, and specifically to Stalinism, in the way that Trotsky himself would most likely have done if he had survived into the 1940s. Be that as it may, they evolved a distinctive Trotskyist tradition and gave it life. For two decades and more, they produced a powerful literature that has for that period no equal, nor any near relative or rival. Ultimately, from the end of the 1950s, their tendency too fell apart.

Where the Orthodox Trotskyists saw the Stalinist states, which expropriated capitalism, as the advancing ("deformed") world revolution, the Heterodox Trotskyists saw Stalinist revolutions as the advance and spread of totalitarian slavery that they in fact were.

What they had in common, the two basic strains of post-Trotsky "Trotskyists", was the belief that capitalism was collapsing and dying. For the "orthodox", that gave them confidence that History was (sort of, in a "deformed" blood-thirsty way), on their side, and shaped the way they saw Stalinism. To the Shachtmanites, capitalism was sure to be replaced soon, one way or another – and the choice of replacement was either Stalinist "barbarism" or socialism. In the capitalist prosperity of the 1950s and 60s, they saw only a respite in the disintegration and death-decline of capitalism. The prosperity could not last, and, therefore, so it sometimes seems in their writings, it did not really exist, at least in terms of the long-term perspective. Shachtman wrote in 1961 of the "unarrested decline and helplessness of the capitalist world" (*The Bureaucratic Revolution*, p.3),

Stalinism was indeed expanding, and it would continue to expand for some years after Shachtman's death in 1972. Following through the line of thought that under bourgeois democracy, in sharp contrast to Stalinist totalitarianism, the working-class movement could function, and could prepare itself to create a socialist alternative to both capitalism and Stalinism, Shachtman and his close friends went over to the US-led bloc. They abandoned the socialist program of independent working-class politics, of the "third camp", and sided with bourgeois-democratic capitalist USA against the Stalinist bloc, seeing the US and its allies as the only halfway-viable alternative to Stalinism. They took that course for reasons that have much in common with those which led the Orthodox Trotskyists to back the Stalinist bloc (critically – but the Shachtmanites too were critical of "their" bloc).

Within the US-led bloc, they thought, working-class independent socialism could emerge; otherwise it would be crushed by advancing Stalinism. Shachtman became mired in the dirty politics of the Democratic Party. As a tendency, his co-thinkers evolved into born-again social-democrats. Shachtman himself never abjured support for the October Revolution, but some of his co-thinkers would, later (see Al Glotzer in *Workers' Liberty* 16).

Others in the heterodox Trotskyist tendency – Hal Draper; Phyllis and Julius Jacobson and a few others, who started the magazine *New Politics* in the early 1960s – rejected Shachtman's course and maintained independent socialist politics. But in their own particular way, they too moved very far from the politics of the tendency in its heroic days of the 40s and most of the 50s. They rejected the project of building a revolutionary socialist party. Draper repudiated and rejected what he called the "micro-sect" project of organisation-building. They became mere propagandists – with propaganda, to be sure, of a very high order.

5. What a Marxist party is and does

The working class, at high points of struggle, can and does improvise with great creativity, often forcing the Marxists to shake themselves up and re-think in order to "catch up" with the class. But a lucid overview of the mechanisms of capitalism, of the nature and relations of the social classes, of the long historic evolution of which working-class socialism will be the culmination, and of socialist strategy, cannot be improvised.

Broad labour movements can arrive at generally socialist hopes and aspirations, just as young people can arrive at angry rebellion against capitalism. Quick, seemingly miraculous, transformations in the thinking of labour movements have occurred and will occur. Why? Because the workers who accept capitalism are in a condition in which their interests and their desires as both workers and human beings are at odds with the ideas about society and the world they have been taught to accept. In times of big struggles, those ideas come into direct conflict with the experience of the worker, and start to totter. Once that begins, everything can change.

Scientific understanding of capitalism, of society, of the centrality of the working class and the politics of working-class self-liberation – in short, understanding of how we can map the way from capitalism neo-barbarism to human liberation – does not arise "spontaneously". It has to be brought into the struggle by those who have laboured for years or decades in advance to educate themselves and absorb the lessons of past struggles.

Marxism is a necessary part of this process. But it has to be the authentic Marxism, the real Marxism, of its best period. It is to make Marxist theory a living reality in working-class practice that socialist organisations do what they do.

6. The post-Stalinist "fetish-party"

The revolutionary party has as its central task to achieve the political and organisational emancipation of the working class, i.e. to help the working class learn to see capitalism and itself as they are. It needs the organisational sinews of a body of socialists organised for combat all the way from the struggle on a trade union level at the point of production through to organising an armed insurrection. But it is centrally, irreplaceably, and uniquely, the carrier of a system of ideas, a world outlook, a socialist program, a method of analysing the world and society which serves the interests of the working class. Its core activity and responsibility in history is as an educator of the working class, enlightening workers about the nature of capitalist society and about what the working class can and must do in history. The Stalinist "party of a new type" had an entirely different and antagonistic function, and a substitutionist relationship to the working class. Its purpose was a new purpose, a Stalinist bureaucratic one. The tragedy of the Trotskyist movement has been its general adoption of a Stalinist model of a machine party. Such a party cannot serve our goal of working-class liberation.

The cry "build the revolutionary party" is too often, among would-be revolutionary socialists, an expression of an unthought-through yearning for revolutionary socialist competence and adequacy; and too often it encapsulates a false idea of a "revolutionary party" as essentially a "machine", an apparatus. That conception of a revolutionary party has been dominant in Britain for many decades now. Avowedly Trotskyist writers have taken the Stalinist coinage, "party of a new type", as good Leninism. Cliff Slaughter, for example, in the 1960s the main writer on theoretical questions for what was then the biggest group of the revolutionary left in Britain, wrote of

"... the Leninist concept of leadership of the working class by a centralised party and Lenin's 'party of a new type'." Duncan Hallas, the writer who sought to give the SWP (IS) a literary "Leninist" makeover in the 1970s, wrote of "Lenin's emphasis on the necessity for a revolutionary party, a 'party of a new type' as the means through which the working class can rise to the level of self-rule", and stated that: "Our view of the party is different... The CPGB originally set out to build just such a party, a 'party of a new type'..." †

The cry for a "Revolutionary Party" often works against the revolutionary adequacy it has failed properly to anatomise and define. This fetish arises from misreading cause and effect: like the medieval architects who copied the appearance of ancient buildings but had no idea of how exactly the architects worked: they would make as mere decoration things like columns that had functions in the structures they tried to copy.

Adequacy, beyond sectist convenience and streamlining of decision-making, is unlikely to be the outcome of creating an infallible "party" Pope, and a college of Party Cardinals – what this project almost always does create, and has done in the history of the post-Trotsky "Trotskyists". Again: such a structure served the Stalinists in what they were really trying to do (as distinct from what they said they were trying to do), but cannot conceivably serve a genuine left-wing movement.

"The party" comes in practice to be seen as self-sufficient, and to have interests of its own that it can serve irrespective of the working class. This is a sectist caricature of the approach of the pre-1914 Second international. The apparatus comes to be seen as in practice more important than the working class. The history of the British Trotskyist movement in recent decades contains some terrible examples of this. The idea that the party is, or can be, counterposed to the working class, and can be set adrift from the core ideas of Plekhanov, Lenin, Trotsky, and others, is a source of endless ideological corruption in the would-be left. Any argument will do to win a point or sustain "a line", and never mind the political education of the working class. Agitation becomes autonomous from propaganda and program.

The Stalinist fetish of the revolutionary "party of a new type" was a by-product of the utopian project of building socialism in Russia,

---

† Slaughter, *What is Revolutionary Leadership?, Labour Review*, Vol.5 No.3, October-November 1960. Hallas, *Marx and Politics, Socialist Review*, No.83, January 1986; *The CP, the SWP and the Rank and File Movement, International Socialism 95*, February 1977.

China, etc. A recognisable descendant of that idea of a party continues in the ranks of the Trotskisant left today. Both the SWP-UK and the Socialist Party (Militant) are terrible examples of party fetishism and the intellectual, moral, and political self-mutilation that inevitably goes with it.

In 1984 the SP/ Militant found itself in the leadership of Liverpool's Labour city council and the Liverpool labour movement in conflict with the Tory government, during the miners' strike. Did it work to integrate its struggle with the greatest industrial action since 1926? The very opposite. It made a short-term deal with the Tories, which bought the council a year's time. It left the miners in the lurch – and guaranteed its own defeat when, with the miners beaten, the Tories and the Labour Party leaders came for Liverpool council, as they did in 1985-6.

Why did SP/Militant do that? It wanted to preserve their own "apparatus", its "party", and thought that was the way to do it. (Very foolishly, as it turned out).

Likewise, as the Tories, intent on crushing the working class, came to power in 1979, the SWP adopted the thesis that nothing could be done in the period ahead except build "the socialists" , i.e. the SWP (the "theory of the downturn").

Both these groups continued the Stalinist conception of the "party of a new type" – only rendered more absurd – and senselessly counterposed it, when they thought that would serve their interests, to the working class.

To see the revolutionary party only as a "machine" is radically to misunderstand its nature and its prime task – that of education. To go beyond that to the view that the apparatus can say and do anything that "builds the party", more or less irrespective of the effects on the consciousness of the working class, is a vicious and essentially Stalinist travesty of the idea of "building the party".

Often, by way of demagogy and the dominance of agitation-led activity to "build the party", this travesty works against the education of the working class. Only the conscious struggle of the living Marxists, reacting specifically and concretely, focusing and redefining Marxism, can make of Marxism a consistently revolutionary instrument for the working class, for separating out and maintaining scientific consciousness in the working class.

7. The bomb and the book

In the late 19th century, as far as the Tsarist authorities were concerned, the most fearsome revolutionaries in the Russian Empire were the Narodnik terrorists. They killed a Tsar in 1881. Lenin's brother Alexander, who took part in a plot to kill another Tsar, was hanged in 1887.

By comparison, the Marxists, with their doctrinal disputes, seemed relatively harmless. Some Marxist scientific literature was legally tolerated. Yet, Trotsky would write with perfect truth after the October revolution, it was not those who set out with guns and bombs in their hands who overthrew the Tsar, but those who set out with Marx's *Capital* and Plekhanov's *Our Differences* under their arms.

Of the Ulyanov brothers, it was not the heroic martyr Alexander but the book-worming Vladimir (Lenin) who posed the fundamental threat to the system. Marxism offered an alternative world outlook to that of the bourgeoisie and the landlords and those throughout society who supported them. It provided a theory of society and a method of extending and deepening that theory; it offered the perspective of a different type of society growing up within the capitalist class society, but dependent for its realisation on the revolutionary activity of the capitalist wage-slave class, the proletariat. The Marxist socialist movement was the memory of the proletariat.

The "fusion of science [Marxism] and the proletariat" created mass working-class movements that did, indeed, seem capable of carving out the future they proclaimed. The battle for Marxism against bourgeois and petty-bourgeois outlooks within the labour movement was understood to be itself a front of the class struggle – the "ideological front".

After the collapse of the Second International in 1914, Lenin and others felt obliged to dig down to the roots of the Marxism that had dominated the International, and worked to define the flaws, mistakes and corruptions of doctrine that had led to the International's collapse. Of the results of this work Lenin's *State and Revolution* is perhaps the best known. The Marxist "movement of the book" had to clean, shuffle, re-read and supplement its books. In Russia "science and the proletariat" had been fused as nowhere else – a raw, militant proletariat able to innovate new weapons like the mass strike and a Marxist movement forced to keep its intellectual weapons sharp and clean. A version of Marxism emphasising capitalism as progressive in history had been adapted by layers of the Russian bourgeoisie opposed to the backward Tsarist system, and other versions of basic *Das*

Kapital Marxism by the populists. The proletarian Marxists had to define and redefine themselves, the nature of the Russian revolution they worked for and their own role in that revolution. "Theory" was central.

Yet, though Lenin and Trotsky, Luxemburg, Plekhanov and Martov believed that there could be no revolutionary movement without a revolutionary theory, they made no fetish of "theory".

What distinguished Lenin's group from all the others was its capacity to pierce through the limits of its own theory and learn from the living working class, adjusting theory accordingly. There was a living, fructifying interaction between theory and practice. Thus, though Lenin and his comrades, like all the Marxists before 1905, believed that Russia needed and could not have other than a bourgeois revolution, they came in practice to differ from the others.

Using theory as blindfold rather than microscope, the Mensheviks were content to stay on the level of generalities and to draw conclusions not from life, but from the theoretical generalisations. A bourgeois revolution? Then obviously it will be led by the bourgeoisie.

A bourgeois revolution? Yes, said Lenin, in chorus with the others. But, he continued, no longer in chorus, what kind of bourgeois revolution? He insisted on examining the real Russian bourgeoisie as it was in life, irrespective of what theory said. He concluded that the Russian bourgeoisie could not lead a revolution and postulated that the workers and peasants would have to make the bourgeois revolution, against the bourgeoisie.

Focussing on the social realities, he thus concretised and deepened theory and laid the grounds for a revolutionary transformation of Marxist theory in the course of the revolution of 1917. The idea of fetishising "theory" in such a way that it blinkered perception and stifled concrete analysis and thought was utterly alien to Lenin. So was the idea that one could blame "bad theory" if, out of deference to "theory", one failed to keep concrete social, political and economic reality under constant review, testing and honing, and, where necessary, supplementing the theory in the process.

For Marxists there is no such thing as agitation that does not enlighten and educate the working class about the system as a whole. But if "building the party" is the self-sufficient goal, then almost any agitation that attracts interest can make sense. "Action" becomes all-important, irrespective of the conditions, and almost irrespective of what action.

8. The priorities of a Marxist party

If there is no irreplaceable ideological and educational task for the Leninist party, then there is no need for our party. Were it not for the ideological task of the revolutionary party of the working class, were it not for the peculiar problems of the proletariat in that respect, then the working class could be expected to improvise the necessary organisation for the seizure of power, as the bourgeoisie and petty bourgeoisie have done. If all the proletariat needs is an organisation, then the tightly knit revolutionary organisations are just sects, premature and almost certainly irrelevant. If what the proletariat needs is only a machine, then it does not need to have its militants labouring for decades in advance of the maturation of the situation where it requires an uprising. The consequences of this are that our party is in the first place and irreplaceably a selection of politically conscious militants committed to activity in the struggles for the party's goals. It must thus be selected on the basis of a minimum of political education and knowledge, and commitment.

If it is to be a party which is a living organ in the class struggle, then it must try to integrate itself in all the areas of the class struggle and in the actually-existing labour movement. If it is to be a party whose deliberations correspond to experience in the struggles of the working class, then it has to be a party of activists – of people with a minimum of commitment to the struggle. That commitment, under the direct control of the party, must be a condition of participation in the party's deliberations – that is, of full membership.

It has to be a party of the proletariat, but it is not identical to the proletariat: it must be capable of standing against the proletariat and of struggling within it when the mass of the working class is under the influence or domination of the ruling class or of pernicious pseudo-radical doctrines, be they Stalinist, Peronist, Christian or Islamic clerical-fascist, or any of the many variants of reactionary anti-imperialism. Its proletarian political character depends in the first place on its program and its historical relation to the proletariat. A proletarian character in the crude sociological sense is not sufficient and in some epochs may not be possible.

The proletarian party without a mass working-class membership organised at the point of production and deploying the power which the working class can have at the point of production, is impotent; proletarian militancy at the point of production devoid of the historical program of working-class socialism and perspectives for achieving it, is sterile and ultimately impotent.

If you place Gerry Healy's 1970s WRP at one end of the spectrum, the SWP at the other and the Socialist Party in the centre, you see important differences but also certain things in common which give the "Trotskyist" organisations of recent decades their character. They are organised as tight single-faction organisations. There is a pro-designated leadership, and a narrowly defined set of ideas which function as shibboleths and are not open to discussion. Internal dissent is not allowed, or is allowed only so long as it does not impinge on the cardinal doctrines of the group. Dissent in the public press is very, very rare, and for most such groups unknown. Minorities are allowed to form factions not at all, or only for limited periods. The possibility of a concerted challenge to the incumbent leadership really does not exist. It ceased to exist, for example, in the loosest and most nearly civilised of such groups in Britain, the SWP, years ago.

But there is more than the formalities and structures. There is also the spirit of these groups. It is the spirit of the narrow, persecuting religious sect. The feeling and emotions and commitment which are a necessary part of any sustained activity around the old socialist program of replacing capitalism by "the cooperative commonwealth" are all focused on the group, on its particular ideas and shibboleths, and on its own claimed identity as "the party", the Church of the Lord. It is that spirit – cultivated and cherished by the organisers of the groups listed above – which gives the final stamp to the groups' character as sects.

From the spirit flows intolerance, the transmutation of ideas supposedly based on theorising about an evolving and changing world into religious dogmas, believed on faith and separating the faithful and the saved from the sinners and deservedly damned. Such quasi-religious formations need intolerance, need a "party regime" that keeps an iron grip, need the typical internal atmosphere of an intense religious cult – or they disintegrate. They need certainties and dogmas and infallible leaders, and these can be sustained in place only when dissent is forbidden or limited and ritualised. In important part, that pattern has become part of the Orthodox Trotskyist tradition because the ideas of the various groups have been at blatant odds with reality.

A political culture in which every participant has the taken-for-granted right to disagree with the majority, to pose awkward questions about both ideas and individuals, and to express his or her opinions and proselytise for them in voice and writing would be anathema to the quasi-religious "Leninist" sects. Contact with that way of working would dissolve the pretensions of the leaders of such cults, dissipate the holy aura surrounding the ideas for which they function as a priestly caste.

For that reason such groups not only control or stifle elements of such an approach within their own ranks, but they also cultivate and foment extreme hostility and hatred for it when it comes from outside their own band. Instead of teaching their supporters to reason about the world, they teach them dogmas. Complicated theories are reduced to phrases packaging hopes and wishes about, for example, the Middle East or Ireland, which then fill the space that should be filled by a rational account of the world we have to deal with.

AWL has tried to learn the lesson of the awful fate of the people who try to be honest socialists but tragically fall back into the primitive semi-religious approach characteristic of the dawn of the labour movements in the last century and earlier. AWL conducts its discussions openly in the pages of our publications. There are no sacrosanct ideas or individuals that cannot be discussed or questioned, no religious awe around either our ideas or our activities.

We do not repudiate the tradition of Lenin and those who made the great working-class revolution in Russia in 1917. On the contrary, we believe that we defend that tradition as it really was.

That the outcome in history of the 1917 revolution was – by way of Stalinist counter-revolution – a negative and horrible outcome, was not the fault of Lenin or his "tradition", but of those socialists in the West who left the Russian workers in the lurch and made their peace with their own ruling class.

Rosa Luxemburg, who was in private a forceful critic of some things the Bolsheviks did as well as being their partisan †, said it all very well in 1918, in the course of criticising Lenin and his comrades. "Whatever a party could offer of courage, revolutionary far-sightedness, and consistency in an historic hour, Lenin, Trotsky, and the other comrades have given in good measure. All the revolutionary honour and capacity which western social democracy lacked were represented by the Bolsheviks. Their October uprising was not only the actual salvation of the Russian revolution, it was also the salvation of the honour of international socialism."

Insofar as post-Stalinist socialism will have to be rethought, and the elements of socialism recast, Lenin's tradition should and will be a central part of that socialist self-reconstitution.

---

† *She never published her criticism of the Bolsheviks in power. It was not published until after her death, in 1922, by Paul Levi, her lawyer, who had been expelled from the KPD for "losing his head" in the aftermath of the ill-advised "March Action" of 1921.*

Above: Labor Action 23 April 1945. Right: Daily Worker (USA), 27 June 1925

Imperialism and anti-imperialism in the making of the contemporary left

Who Is That You All Are Going to Whip, Mr. Legree?
—By Robert Minor

THE DAILY WORKER
June 27, 1925

Imperialisms and anti-imperialism

"Impartiality in the face of injustice is the virtue of a slave" – James Connolly.

"There is not, nor can there be, such a thing as a 'negative' Social-Democratic slogan that serves only to 'sharpen proletarian consciousness against imperialism'. A negative slogan unconnected with a definite positive solution will not 'sharpen', but dull consciousness, for such a slogan is a hollow phrase, mere shouting, meaningless declamation" – Vladimir Lenin

"We have to take strong measures against the abstract 'anti-fascist' mode of thinking that finds entry even into our own ranks at times. 'Anti-fascism' is nothing, an empty concept used to cover up Stalinist skulduggery. In the name of 'anti-fascism' they instituted class collaboration with the [French bourgeois] Radicals..." — Leon Trotsky †

Introduction

Conflicting answers to the questions, what is imperialism, and who are the imperialists, shaped and reshaped the left for most of the 20th century. Questions concerning imperialism and anti-imperialism now are central in the current malaise of the left.

"Imperialism" – in the generic, contemporary common-usage, sense, and the sense in which I shall use the word here unless otherwise qualified – is the drive by stronger states to enlarge their rulers' power and revenues at the expense of weaker states and peoples by threatening or deploying military, naval, and air power, or financial or diplomatic coercion. In the words of James Connolly, it is a system of "international brigandage". Opposition to imperialism is the sine qua non for consistent democrats and socialists. To be anti-imperialist is to be for elementary democracy and for peaceful, civilised methods in world affairs as in all others. It is to champion the people of all countries against every form of encroachment, robbery, bullying, and financial and military coercion.

There are many imperialisms in history, each with characteristics unique to itself and its historical context, each with different drives,

---

† *James Connolly, Workers' Republic, 16 October 1915; Vladimir Lenin, A Caricature of Marxism and Imperialist Economism, Collected Works 23 (28-76); Leon Trotsky, Bourgeois democracy and the fight against fascism, Writings 1935-6 p.242*

ways of operating, goals. The dominant imperialism of the first half of the 20th century, the imperialism of advanced capitalism in Britain, Germany, France, and the USA in that period – the imperialism analysed by Vladimir Lenin in 1916 – was different from other imperialisms in history. In Lenin's analysis (and in widespread usage at the time), the specific early-1900s imperialism was the interlocking coercive world system generated by a capitalism dominated by great monopolies, where financial and industrial capital had merged within each state. The world was divided between a number of colony-holding empires. They jockeyed with each other, and in 1914-18 fought each other for the division and redivision of the world. They did that again in 1939-45, in a more complex world. Advanced capitalist countries – Britain, France, Germany, and the Netherlands and Belgium – used their own colonies as more or less closed-in markets for goods and capital investment, and as their own preferred sources of raw materials.

In Lenin's judgement, that early 20th century capitalism was the highest and last phase of capitalism, the stage immediately before the working-class socialist revolution. Alas, it was not so. The workers were defeated. Capitalism survived and evolved.

In its economic structures and the typical behaviour of its subdivisions, international capitalism is no longer what it was in Lenin's day. The colonial empires no longer exist. The main capitalist states have ceased to be "imperialist", in the sense of Lenin's 1916 analysis of imperialism. Yet something like Lenin's conclusions about the condition of capitalism, his inferences, and his immediate perspectives, is still widely accepted on the left. Advanced capitalism is seen as more or less synonymous with imperialism. It is seen as comprehensively regressive and reactionary, as having reached the end of its historical rope.

More than that. The Second Congress of the Communist International in 1920 laid it down as a rule that the communists would support movements in the colonies and semi-colonies which took up arms against metropolitan rule, and in that it was right, I think. (The Communist International also made an explicit exception: pan-Islamic movements). On the ostensible left that rule has now, in a radically different world, devolved into an imperative to back smaller states and regional imperialisms (Iraq, Iran, Serbia…) in all conflicts with the greater capitalist states (the USA, the UK, the EU). It generates an absolute and unconditional opposition to advanced capitalism and to capitalist advance – to backing, against the capitalist big powers, more or less any of their enemies, whatever the issue in dispute is. "Anti-imperialism" means, in practice, now, anti-capitalism, not in the sense that all socialists are anti-capitalist, wanting to replace capitalism by working-class socialism, but in the sense that international opponents and rivals of the advanced capitalist powers are backed for the purely negative reason that they are against those powers. Here, "anti-imperialism" functions to rationalise, and to give moral fervour and a respect-worthy political genealogy, to siding with backward and reactionary regimes and political movements.

The governing idea has come to be that advanced capitalism, or the economically and military strong capitalist states, are imperialist and reactionary not as and when they do imperialist and reactionary deeds, and not because their ways of functioning correspond to early 20th century imperialism and Lenin's picture of what imperialist powers did (tariffs, arms races, a world divided into rival colonial and semi-colonial empires, etc.), but by virtue of an inner capitalist essence. "Imperialism" is advanced capitalism; advanced capitalism is imperialism, whatever it does, or does no longer.

The advanced capitalist states are reactionary as against their opponents, no matter who or what they are, or what the issue in dispute is. Any, or almost any †, challenge to them by states or political movements is by definition "anti-imperialist" and therefore good. It must be supported even where there is no element in it of a fight for liberation or for self-determination. That is so even when the opponent is entirely reactionary, as with political Islam. This version of anti-imperialism is an anti-imperialism cut adrift from Marxist politics, Marxist concerns, and Marxist historical perspectives. By analogy with what Marx and Engels in the Communist Manifesto called "reactionary socialism", this is best called "reactionary anti-imperialism".

The point here is not that the USA, or other great powers, never do deeds like those typical of the colonial imperialism of the first half of the 20th century. Episodically they do; and when they do, they should be opposed. But neither in the past nor now are the advanced capitalist states reactionary, or "imperialist", apart from what they are and what they do. Not everything they do is automatically reactionary.

The tight connection between the economic growth of monopolies and high finance, and high tariffs, arms races, division of the world

---

† *There are limits and doubts. Almost no anti-Stalinist left group has backed Assad in Syria (other than Counterfire, and then only equivocally and by implication); almost none has agitated to "Stop the Bombing" against Daesh in Mosul (as distinct from refusing to endorse the USA).*

into rival colonial empires, etc., which Lenin and Trotsky observed and analysed, no longer exists. It has not existed for decades. The analysis and the theory of "imperialism" cannot be, as it was with Vladimir Lenin and Leon Trotsky and the Marxists of their time, a matter of diagnosing and arguing that certain economic trends in advanced capitalism had led to a specific version of the colony-grabbing and looting typical of "imperialism" throughout history. Plainly, we are not in a period when capitalism has reached the end of its historical span.

The ostensible left, in its subservience to political Islam all the way back to the clerical-fascist Iranian revolution of 1979, disparages and pits itself against the achievements of hundreds of years of bourgeois civilisation, against achievements such as civil liberties, intellectual freedom, the freedom to be and proclaim oneself against religion and its apostles, the right to meet and speak and organise freely, the achievements of bourgeois civilisation on which socialism will be built. The ostensible left did that when it sided with Stalinism against advanced capitalism. It is doing it still today, with clerical-fascist and regional sub-imperialist regimes or movements. Even after China has abandoned most of its "socialist" masquerades, Chinese imperialism in Tibet is still supported by a big section of the ostensible left, those around the Communist Party and its daily, the *Morning Star*.

Worse in terms of generating confusion: in typical left-wing discourse, in its accounts of 20th century history, colony-grabbing and looting is not "imperialist" if it is done by other than advanced capitalist states. If those imperialist activities were carried out by what, for both all Stalinists and all Orthodox Trotskyists, was a progressive or "socialistic" state – Russia in Afghanistan, Mao's China in Tibet, or Tito's Yugoslavia in Kosova – then they were not imperialism. They were not to be opposed, and might be welcomed ardently.

To get our bearings, we need to go back and explore. There have been many different imperialisms, before the capitalist era and during it. We should start by reminding ourselves again: for Rosa Luxemburg, Karl Liebknecht, Leon Trotsky, and Vladimir Lenin around 1914, and still for Trotsky in 1939-40, the specific contemporary form of imperialism was the rivalry of blocs led by the great centres of monopoly and finance capital, for the division and redivision of the world and the annexation of territories to their own spheres of colonial control or influence.

Imperialism old and new

In the beginning, for the Marxists of Vladimir Lenin's time, were the deeds, the imperialist seizures, rivalries, army, navy and later missile races, and wars, of the great powers. What they did, and why they did it: that was imperialism. Then came the search for explanations, the theories, the attempt to fit the phenomena of 20th century imperialism into the general Marxist understanding of capitalism and its development; to locate it in the historical retrospective of previous imperialisms and earlier capitalistic imperialisms; to place it in the context of the stage that capitalism had reached, and what the new developments said about the prospects of a working-class revolution that would put an end to capitalism and its imperialisms.

Today, for the ostensible left, it is not a matter of deeds and then theories – theories which are further modified and refined by further experience – but the other way round. The whole question is turned on its head. In the beginning is the designation, definition, identification, and indictment of advanced capitalism as imperialism, the identification of advanced capitalism with imperialism. "Imperialism" is used as another word for advanced capitalism but also as the criterion for deciding what in any dispute or conflict are the good and bad sides. It is the criterion outside and beyond any question of the characteristic deeds of the imperialist powers of Lenin's time: holding colonies, using military and naval means to gain economic advantage, imposing unequal treaties on weaker states, etc.

The Marxist analysts of Lenin's time were agreed in dating the start of modern-capitalist, monopoly-capitalist and finance-capitalist, imperialism at roughly 1900. The British navy ruled the seas of the world. Britain and other European powers had great colonial empires. In 1898 Germany declared a new "Weltpolitik", or "world policy" ("we demand our own place in the sun"). The great naval race between Britain and Germany began; it would later spiral further into rivalry in building super-battleships, the "dreadnoughts". That race led straight to the Great War a decade and a half later.

1900 was also about the time at which the term "imperialism" entered common currency as denoting a world policy of building rival economically-integrated empires. In the decades before the 1890s, the term "imperialism" was more likely to denote a political system ruled by an "emperor", such as France under Napoleon III's "Second Empire", referring to his mode of rule within France rather than to his colonial ventures in Indochina or Mexico. †

"Imperialism", in the new meaning being given to it around the year 1900, was not only colonies and colonialism, though it included colonies. Britain had had an Irish colony in the 16th century, the Ireland England had had as vassal from the 12th century, reconquered and more intensely exploited. It had an American colonial empire from the start of the 17th century, and an extensive colonial empire in the mid 18th century. France and Holland, too, had old empires. In the mid 1700s, France, paralleling Britain, had control of a very large part of North America. Some of that immense territory, in Canada, was taken in war by Britain in the 18th century, and the rest would be sold by France to the USA in 1803 for the equivalent in today's money of $250 million.

The 17th and 18th century empires were "mercantilist": the colonies existed to serve the "mother" power and were restricted in what they did to what was either in the interest, or not against the interest, of the metropolis. Their trade was tethered, their right to build ships limited. Bilateral relationships with other than the "mother country" were prohibited. The empires were relatively closed-off, competing, international entities, each with the "mother country" and its interests at the centre. Britain's American colonies rebelled against that imperialism and their place in it; so did "the Protestant nation" in Ireland in 1782, peacefully and for 18 years successfully. The high-tariff imperialism of the 1930s and 1940s would look to many like a new edition of mercantilism.

The mercantilist system had operated by way of huge trading companies – like the British and Dutch East Indies companies – operating as independent state-like powers. The 18th century British conquest of India was directly the work of the British East Indies Company and its mercenary armies. Marx wrote: "The discovery of gold and silver in America, the extirpation, enslavement and entombment in mines of the aboriginal population, the beginning of the conquest and looting of the East Indies, the turning of Africa into a warren for the commercial hunting of black-skins, signalised the rosy dawn of the era of capitalist production. These idyllic proceedings are the chief momenta of primitive accumulation [of capital]. On their heels treads the commercial war of the European nations, with the globe for a theatre. It begins with the revolt of the Netherlands from Spain, assumes giant dimensions in England's Anti-Jacobin War, and

---

† For a period in the 1890s, "imperialism" was often defined in yet another way, to mean a specific project in British politics, the conversion of the British empire into an Imperial Federation with internal free trade and uniform tariffs against the rest of the world.

is still going on in the opium wars against China". (*Capital* volume 1). The first World War, though it was not called that, was fought in the years 1754-63 by France and Britain, each with its warring allies in America, India, and Europe.

In history, many, many imperialisms: Babylon, Carthage, Rome... An ancient Athenian empire, in which Athens forced tribute from other Greek states had lasted about 70 years, roughly as long as the second British colonial empire, and the Stalinist Russian Empire did. The Ottoman (Turkish) Empire conquered Constantinople in 1453, for a thousand years the capital of the Eastern Roman Empire, today's Istanbul. It spread to capture and control much of what is now Eastern Europe, West as far as Vienna, and into the Arab territories in North Africa, creating a great sprawling empire that was, increasingly the stagnant and rotting "sick man of Europe" and widely so-named. It survived until the First World War, by which time most of the peoples in Eastern Europe had liberated themselves and created their own states (Montenegrins, Greeks, Serbs, Bulgarians, in a protracted series of wars of liberation). There are many more instances of pre-monopoly-capitalist imperialism.

Imperialisms have varied in character and modes of operation, and have had a great range of relations between the core state and the subordinate, subjugated people and their territories. Empires expressed in one way or another the different economic systems in the imperial states; they served their drives, needs, aims. To some degree, at least, and sometimes completely, the conquered people, their social structures, their languages, and their institutions were remodelled in the image of the imperial states. The world-engirthing empire of the small offshore European island, Britain, was the bearer of a new mode of production and a new civilisation, that of capitalism and its commerce. Bourgeois democracy in India and other places, Ireland included, is a foster-child of the British empires. Empires evolved, broke up, recombined, and died for various reasons: conquest, slow decline, overwhelming decrepitude, moribund economies.

Many anti-imperialisms

As there have been many imperialisms, so also have there been many "anti-imperialisms", ranging from the war-making and hostile propaganda of competing empires to the elementary drives of subject peoples to throw off foreign yokes and the rule of foreign robbers foreigners. It is a characteristic of rival empires to tell some of the truth – about each other. That was so when England and Spain confronted each other in the 16th century, when Whig England of the 1688 bourgeois revolution fought the French absolute monarch Louis XIV, or when Bonaparte confronted the early edition of quasi-aristocratic bourgeois rule embodied in France's long-time opponent, Britain. †

The 20th century jingo song "Rule Britannia" was initially an 18th century glorification of British liberties as against the tyrannical monarchy of France, Britain's imperial arch-rival. The feelings for which "Rule Britannia" was a vehicle changed as realities changed. "Lillibulero", still an Orange, and (until 2014) BBC, anthem, was the popular song of the 1688 English Revolution. It was concerned with the threat of restored Stuart absolute monarchy, allied with absolutist France; its anti-Irish sentiments expressed, in the main, fear of James II's Irish Catholic ("Taig") army.

Empires championed and helped the victims of rival empires, often incongruously. England helped the Dutch in "the Lowlands" in the 16th century win freedom from Spain. Spain landed an army in Ireland to help fight the genocidal armies of Elizabeth I. The absolute monarchy of France, which itself controlled a large part of what is now the USA, sent soldiers to help the democratic American rebels against Whig England. The France of the Directorate sent soldiers to Ireland to rouse and help the people against English rule; the Kaiser's Germany sent guns to the 1916 Irish insurgents. British public opinion in World War One regarded Karl Liebknecht as a hero who, like Britain, was fighting Prussian militarism. A major part of the Nazis' campaign for power in Germany after its defeat in 1914-18 focused on liberating Germany from the oppression of the Versailles Treaty. Hitler's wartime Germany produced a number of films glorifying Ireland's struggles for freedom from Britain, and a film indicting mass murder and mass graves in concentration camps – the British camps for Boer civilians during the South African war of 1899-1902. (Many civilians died of dysentery in those terrible camps, but they were not designed to be death camps as the Nazi camps were).

When Arab wars of liberation against Turkish rule erupted during World War One, the Arab insurgents allied themselves with Britain, and Britain with them. Britain helped the resistance movements in the countries occupied by Nazi Germany, even the Stalinist-controlled Titoite forces in Yugoslavia.The Nazis tried to help the anti-British IRA. The West helped the fighters in Afghanistan in the 1980s resisting Russian imperialism. There have been many, many "anti-imperialisms". One of Lenin's central concerns in his 1916 pamphlet on imperialism was to establish a consistently Marxist critique of the imperialism of his day, and to distinguish the working-class and

Marxist critique of that imperialism from other anti-imperialisms. He wrote criticism of liberal and other anti-imperialisms. He regarded some of the "anti-imperialisms" as downright reactionary and regressive vis-a-vis the advanced-capitalist imperialism which they, and Lenin, opposed.

The Marxists and early 20th century capitalist imperialism

In the years around 1900 and after, the Marxists, who had opposed and fought the 19th century deeds of imperialist brigandage when they were being carved out, registered something new in contemporary history – a new "imperialism", in the first place a new bellicosity among the great powers. (So did some liberals). Their concern was then to discover and define what was specific, unique, new in this version of the centuries-old patterns of "imperialism", in the sense of big powers oppressing and exploiting weaker peoples. What was the new finance-capitalist, monopoly-capitalist imperialism, and what did it signify politically and historically? How did it differ from the many imperialisms in history – from the many different systems of conquest or intimidation and exploitation of states and peoples?

A new capitalist imperialism had emerged by about the year 1900. The new world system was dominated by competing monopoly-capitalist imperialisms. What should the policy of the Marxists be against it? What should they fight to replace it by?

Summarising and building on the work of Marxist writers since the late 1890s, notably Karl Kautsky and Rudolf Hilferding, Vladimir Lenin in 1916 analysed, in terms of the basic Marxist account of capitalism, its development and its contradictions, the distinctive new capitalist imperialism of the early 20th century that had led to the Great War of 1914-18. It had coincided with the latest stage of capitalism, the fusion of bank and industrial capital (finance capital) and the predominance of economic monopolies. Lenin argued that this imperialism had to be seen as a product of those economic trends. In the new era, after 1900, the world was already divided up into great colonial empires. In the Great War, states fought for re-division of the world and immediately for military domination in Europe and on the high seas, over which, since the Battle of Trafalgar in 1805, Britain had had unbreakable control.

To Lenin and other Marxists, this was a capitalism in which the spontaneous market mechanisms, free trade, etc., had in many respects atrophied and been replaced by the monopolisation of the means of production and circulation, and more-or-less free markets by the competition of cartels and conglomerates clustered round rival states. To Lenin, capitalism had already socialised, centralised, and concentrated the economy, and was now increasingly parasitic and regressive. Lenin, in his pamphlet of 1916 and in his 1920 introduction to a new edition of it, insisted that "imperialism is the eve of the social revolution of the proletariat"; that "a world-wide revolutionary crisis is arising which... cannot end otherwise than in a proletarian revolution". Karl Kautsky had made a similar pronouncement as early as 1909. Lenin's reasoning was rooted in his analysis of the place of this specific monopoly-capitalist or finance-capitalist imperialism in capitalist evolution: it was the highest and therefore last stage of capitalism. Or, it could be.

In a broader framework Lenin did not believe that capitalism had or could have a historical terminus. Only politics, and political and social working-class victory, would put an end to capitalist development. Capitalism would continue to grow and change unless a communist proletariat overthrew it and replaced it by workers' power and socialism. When he wrote of early 20th century imperialism as the eve of the socialist revolution, Lenin was not making platonic predictions: he was immersed in the work of preparing the working-class movement to make the "prediction", the imperatives and the potential he saw in the new situation, into political reality. Lenin wrote, against Kautsky's prediction of an "ultra-imperialism" in which the industrial powers would peacefully combine to annex agrarian territories: "Can it be denied... that a new phase of capitalism is 'imaginable' in the abstract after imperialism, namely, ultra-imperialism? No, it cannot. Such a phase can be imagined. But in practice this means becoming an opportunist, turning away from the acute problems of the day to dream of the unacute problems of the future". (*Collected Works* 22 (103-107)) Such dreaming meant becoming a "socialist" who accommodated to capitalism instead of concentrating on preparing the workers to overthrow and replace it. The world was "rotten-ripe" for the socialist revolution. What would that working-class socialist revolution do? It would replace capitalism by democratic control and planning. Socialist revolution would turn the big elements of planning and coordination that already existed between the cartels and the monopolies, and within individual cartels and monopolies, into full and comprehensive democratic planning and control of the whole economy, and thus greatly broaden and deepen democracy. It could do it on a world scale. It would eliminate the rivalries between cartels and their national governments which had brought humankind to the dead end of world war and the slaughter of millions. For Trotsky at the end, in 1940, capitalism seemed to offer a future of world wars which would be "the grave of civilisation". The proclamation in the Communist Manifesto that the working class had to win the battle of democracy took on a deeper, if not a new, programmatic meaning in the epoch of monopoly-capitalist imperialism. The Communists were the "consistent democrats", against the docked and limited bourgeois, or imperialist-bourgeois, plutocratic democrats.

It is important to understand that Lenin saw his theoretical work on imperialism as, so to speak, a provisional rough draft, far from full and definitive analysis and theoretical model for the new complexities of the world. In Lenin's view, "1900 imperialism" was the highest and last phase of capitalism, but his analysis of imperialism was not in his opinion the last stage of Marxism on the subject. Rosa Luxemburg offered a different economic account of early 20th century imperialism, but drew similar political conclusions.

Lenin's "imperialism", "1900 imperialism", was a world dominated by rival drives by military-political means to monopolise markets, sources of raw materials, and outlets for capital-export, and the conflicts between the competing great powers that resulted.

It was a worldwide predatory phenomenon and it was equated by the Marxists with advanced capitalism; but with Lenin this equation was part of a short-term perspective of a last stage of capitalism to which the revolutionary workers would soon bring an end. The workers would confront and overthrow imperialism. In the view of the Lenin-Trotsky-era Communist International, the colonial world, or some of it, would play an important part, its revolts allying with the risings of the metropolitan working class. The final confrontation would not be between metropolitan capitalism and the Third World, and not between the pioneering (backward) workers' state in the USSR and advanced capitalism, but fundamentally between parasitic capitalist imperialists and the working class of the advanced capitalist countries.

As it turned out, the communist workers were defeated and crushed. The Stalinist bureaucracy and the social system it elaborated became a very great force in the world. Capitalism mutated after World War Two, and the imperialism (in the generic sense) of capitalist states mutated too. Still, however, the ostensible left talked of imperialism as largely unchanged and synonymous with advanced capitalism. It identified advanced capitalism as being the last stage of a capitalism grown absolutely reactionary. In a world in which advanced capitalism was no longer characterised by the traits it possessed when it was analysed by Lenin, the identification of "imperialism" with "advanced capitalism" took on radically different meanings and implications for the left from what it had meant for Lenin in 1916, or 1920.

On the evidence of the first 40 years of the 20th century, Trotsky in 1940 saw the only possible capitalist future as one of world wars for the division and redivision of the world, of the decline of civilisation, and, maybe, a new class-divided and exploitative world-wide social system, "bureaucratic collectivism", radically different from capitalism or socialism, pioneered by the Russian Stalinist state. "The march of events has succeeded in demonstrating that the delay of the socialist revolution engenders the indubitable phenomena of barbarism – chronic unemployment, pauperisation of the petty bourgeoisie, fascism, finally wars of extermination which do not open up any new road. What social and political forms can the new 'barbarism' take, if we admit theoretically that mankind should not be able to elevate itself to socialism?... Fascism on one hand, degeneration of the Soviet state on the other, outline the social and political forms of a neo-barbarism". (Trotsky, *Again and Once More on the Nature of the USSR*, October 1939).

Not only one sort of imperialism

The overall character of the blocs in the 1914-18 war, of the war itself, and of the world-wide system of imperialism then, was determined by the competing great capitalist powers in the conflict and the world-wide interlocking system they dominated – Germany, on one side, Britain and France, and eventually the USA, on the other. But there was more than one sort of (generic) imperialism within each imperialist camp. In the era of monopoly-capitalist imperialism and finance-capitalist imperialism, other sorts of imperialism did not disappear. Different sorts of imperialism, each with its own characteristic aims, goals, and methods, existed side-by-side with the most advanced capitalist imperialisms, even though those latter gave the World War and the world system from which it erupted their overall character. Intertwined with the leading powers in each bloc, other imperialisms pursued their own specific and characteristic goals. They were subordinate partners, but still they had their own special modes and concerns, within the great imperialist blocs. And new imperialisms came into existence. Lenin himself noted: "Among the [non-European countries], new imperialist powers are emerging (e.g., Japan)". More importantly, the Stalinist Russian empire rose to become the great power in Europe after 1945.

Like geological stratifications in an upheaving earthquake, different sorts and stages of empire were jumbled together. Tsarist Russian imperialism, or Austro-Hungary in its conflict with Serbia over Bosnia that triggered the 1914 war, were not governed by the same economic drives for markets, for sources of raw materials, and for opportunities for the export of capital as Britain and Germany were. Japanese imperialism was not quite the same imperialism as the imperialism of the great world-bestriding economic powers; still less was Ottoman imperialism. The Turkish slaughter of about one and a half million Armenians during World War One had nothing to do with the dominant drives, in the war, of the dominant power in the imperialist bloc to which the Ottoman Empire belonged, namely Germany. Portugal, a long-time close ally of the UK, and in comparative terms a backward, stagnant, once-great power, had a big colonial empire in Africa and even enclaves in Asia (Goa in India; East Timor), yet it was only marginally involved in the war. The Netherlands, which ruled the Dutch East Indies, what is now Indonesia, and would fight a vicious colonial war there in the late 1940s †, was not drawn into the 1914-18 war at all.

The difference in levels, techniques, goals, and the special features of different imperialisms would continue to be of enormous importance. Even the leading European monopoly and finance capitalist states of the early 20th century combined within themselves different levels and aspects of society, and different sorts and elements of the imperialisms threaded through the previous centuries. The strong junker-militarist element within German monopoly-capitalist imperialism was no small part of the totality that led Germany into the First World War. The same with Japanese militarism and the remnants of Japanese feudalism and its "Bushido" ethos in World War 2. Again, in World War 2, the character of the Nazi regime, pursuing its own crazed geno-imperialism in lockstep with Germany's monopoly-capitalist economic needs and drives, had no small part in generating and shaping the events of the Second World War and its aftermath. Cultural autonomy, cultural inertia, played a big part, as it always does.

It was not even true that all the finance-capital-dominated imperialist states and blocs were fully identical. There were important distinctions between expansionary German militarism and British or

---

† *Against which there was a strong labour movement opposition in the Netherlands – something largely forgotten that should not be.*

124

French imperialism even in World War One. The "White Dominions" in the British Empire already had a large degree of self-rule: the Australian colonies and New Zealand from the 1850s, Canada from 1867, even South Africa, with its recently conquered territories, from 1910. The black African colonies, of course, did not. India only had minority representation for a few Indians, indirectly elected on a limited franchise (since 1909).

While Lenin was surely right to insist on characterising the early 20th century world imperialist system and the warring imperialist blocs by their dominant great powers, which had similar and symmetrical drives, the idea spun from that, that there was only one sort of imperialism, would come to be utterly misleading for the Marxist movement later in the 20th century.

In World War Two, as in World War One, there were, despite quasi-identical monopoly-capitalist economic structures, enormous differences between the British/ US bloc and that dominated by Hitler's Germany. The failure to understand this and to take it into political account disoriented the Orthodox Trotskyists †. They, for example, expected the British-US conquerors to be the same in Europe as the Nazis had been. When the Allies landed in France in 1944, the French Trotskyist newspaper had shouted in a front-page headline: "They're all the same", explaining that "Roosevelt's liberation is the same as Hitler's socialism" (*La Vérité*, 22 June 1944). But it wasn't.

World War 1 had led to the dissolution of the Austrian, Ottoman, and Russian empires and to the appearance of a cluster of new states, including some new imperialist states in Europe. The Marxists of the Lenin-era Third International, and Trotsky's Fourth International, characterised Czechoslovakia, Poland, and Yugoslavia as imperialist states because their boundaries contained unconsenting and often

---

† *Trotsky had begun to understand it. "When the small farmer or worker speaks about the defence of the fatherland, he means defence of his home, his family and other similar families from invasion, bombs, and poisonous gas. The capitalist and his journalist understand by the defence of the fatherland the seizure of colonies and markets... In the pacifism and even patriotism of the oppressed, there are... elements which we must know how to seize upon in order to draw the requisite political conclusions" (The Death Agony of Capitalism, 1938). "In the wake of a number of other and smaller European states, France is being transformed into an oppressed nation" (Writings 1939-40, p.296). "Without in any way wavering from our program we must speak to the masses in a language they understand. We Bolsheviks also want to defend democracy, but not the kind that is run by sixty uncrowned kings. First let's sweep our democracy clean of capitalist magnates, then we will defend it to the last drop of blood... The working class must learn military affairs in order to advance the largest possible number of officers from its own ranks..." (Writings 1939-40, p.104)*

oppressed peoples (Slovaks and Sudeten Germans in Czechoslo-vakia, Croats and Kosovars in Yugoslavia, Ukrainians and Jews in Poland, etc.) They were smaller versions of what the multinational Austro-Hungarian Empire, and Tsarist Russia, had been: conglomer-ates of different peoples and once and future nations. This patchwork would lead to terrible things after World War Two, when 12-14 mil-lion Germans were expelled from central and Eastern Europe and driven west into the ruined and starving Germany.

Vladimir Lenin's critique of "anti-imperialism"

Lenin denounced the "high imperialism" of his day, condemned it as having led inexorably to 1914. He also criticised the different sorts of anti-imperialisms, as Marx and Engels had criticised the different so-cialisms and anti-capitalisms in their day (in the Communist Mani-festo). "The bourgeoisie makes it its business to promote trusts [capitalist combines], drive women and children into the factories, subject them to corruption and suffering, condemn them to extreme poverty. We do not 'demand' such development, we do not 'support' it. We fight it. But how do we fight? We explain that trusts and the employment of women in industry are progressive. We do not want a return to the handicraft system, pre-monopoly capitalism, domestic drudgery for women. Forward through the trusts, etc., and beyond them to socialism!" (*Collected Works* 23 (77-87)).

"Imperialism is as much our 'mortal' enemy as is capitalism. That is so. No Marxist will forget, however, that capitalism is progressive compared with feudalism, and that imperialism is progressive com-pared with pre-monopoly capitalism. Hence, it is not every struggle against imperialism that we should support. We will not support a struggle of the reactionary classes against imperialism; we will not support an uprising of the reactionary classes against imperialism and capitalism" (*Collected Works* 23 (28-76)).

When we support national uprisings against imperial rule, wrote Vladimir Lenin in the passage quoted at the head of this chapter, that is not only because we are "against" imperialism, but because we are positively for national freedom. When Marxists, continuing the policy of the anti-imperialism of early twentieth century Marxism and com-munism, support even the most undeveloped victims of capitalism against their advanced capitalist-imperialist conquerors, would-be conquerors, maltreaters and exploiters – for example, the Ethiopians under the leadership of the feudal monarch, Haile Selassie against the Italian invasion in 1935 – we do not adapt to such forces and their dominant views of the world, and we do not idealise them. We do not champion such views against the typical world outlooks of advanced capitalism. We do what we do from our own class viewpoint on history, on advanced capitalism, and on what programmatically we fight for as an alternative.

Those who uphold reactionary anti-imperialism on the left today conflate that old communist policy with idealising and glorifying anti-US forces and accepting them, in fact if not in words, as possessing a viable progressive alternative to "imperialism", i.e. to advanced capitalism. For some of those who tried to build an anti-war movement in support of the Serbian regime of Slobodan Milosevic in 1999, "anti-imperialism" came to mean condoning attempted genocide because it was done by a "progressive" regime, i.e. a regime opposed by "imperialism" (equated with the NATO powers)... There was in that no support for an anti-imperialist liberation movement. There was nothing in Milosevic's Serbia for socialists to support, and in its imperialist-colonialist treatment of the Kosovars everything to oppose and condemn. When socialists supported feudal Ethiopia against Italy in the 1930s, it was not the feudalism that we supported, but Ethiopia's fight against being gobbled up by a predatory alien power. In 1999, over Kosova, support for Serbia could mean nothing except support for its policy in Kosova, the cause of the war.

The way that much of the Left today courts and flatters Islamic clerical fascism, painting up its "anti-imperialism", etc., is the clearest and most terrible example of what the ostensible left now is. The Communist International never did that, nor did the Fourth International of Trotsky. Nor even, for a long time, did the Fourth International after Trotsky, despite its partial political disorientation, and its putting "The Colonial Revolution" at the centre of its conception of an ongoing socialist revolution, Stalinist-led "for now". We never abandoned or subordinated our critical attitude to alien, non-working-class, criticisms of imperialism. We made political war on them.

1939-50: the world transformed

Trotsky in 1938 summed up what imperialism meant to Lenin and the other founders of the Communist International, and meant still to him:

"The formation of national states on the European continent occupied an entire epoch which began approximately with the Great French Revolution and concluded with the Franco-Prussian War of 1870-71... From 1871 to 1914 European capitalism, on the foundation of national states, not only flowered but outlived itself by becoming transformed into monopoly or imperialist capitalism. 'Imperialism is that stage of capitalism when the latter, after fulfilling everything in its power, begins to decline'. The cause for decline lies in this, that the productive forces are fettered by the framework of private property as well as by the boundaries of the national state. Imperialism seeks to divide and redivide the world. In place of national wars there come imperialist wars. They are utterly reactionary in character and are an expression of the impasse, stagnation, and decay of monopoly capital... The struggle of the oppressed peoples for national unification and national independence is doubly progressive because, on the one side, this prepares more favourable conditions for their own development, while, on the other side, this deals blows to imperialism... Imperialism camouflages its own peculiar aims – seizure of colonies, markets, sources of raw material, spheres of influence – with such ideas as 'safeguarding peace against the aggressors', 'defence of the fatherland', 'defence of democracy', etc... 'In our day ... it is silly even to think of a progressive bourgeoisie, a progressive bourgeois movement...' Since war is waged by both imperialist camps not for the defence of the fatherland or democracy but for the redivision of the world and colonial enslavement, a socialist has no right to prefer one bandit camp to another..." (*Lenin and imperialist war*, *Writings* 1938-9, p.164).

In line with that picture, Trotsky asked: "Just how is a military victory of decaying democracies over Germany and Italy capable of liquidating fascism, even if only for a limited period? If there were any grounds for believing that a new victory of the familiar and slightly senile Entente (minus Italy) can work such miraculous results, i.e., those counter to socio-historical laws, then it is necessary not only to 'desire' this victory but to do everything in our power to bring it about. Then the Anglo-French social patriots would be correct". (*Writings* 1938-9, p.210).

In 1939 the capitalist empires went to war again. Belgium, France, and Holland, each of which had a large colonial empire, were overrun and occupied by Germany. In the east, Czechoslovakia, Yugoslavia, and Poland were occupied, Poland in part by the USSR: the fate of the people conquered by the USSR was justly summed up by Trotsky in 1939 as Stalin "converting them into his own semi-slaves". In the eastern areas conquered by Germany, the systematic slaughter of Jews began in June-July 1941 and was soon being organised in factories built for mass murder and the burning of thousands and millions of bodies. The Nazis conquered Ukraine in 1941 and began applying

128

their doctrines of master-race and slave-races to the Slavs they conquered.

The tide of war turned against the Germans at Stalingrad in late 1942, and the Russians began a relentless advance to the west. Late in 1944 they crossed their borders of June 1941. They pushed into Germany. They took Berlin in May 1945 and pushed on to 100 miles further west. The Russians (and Stalinists who had come to power independently of Russian help – Yugoslavia and Albania) now controlled Poland, Czechoslovakia, Hungary, Romania, Bulgaria, Yugoslavia, Albania, a third of Germany, and North Korea. They had annexed the Baltic states in 1940 and now reconquered them. Russian troops would vacate Austria only in 1955, the Porkkala region of Finland in 1956, and northern Iran (under strong pressure) in mid-1946. In 1945, the Russians asked the UN to give them a mandate to rule over part of the former Italian colony of Libya.

The Americans and the British, who occupied most of Western Europe, restored the old European states. Even West Germany had got back self-determination by 1949, four years after the fall of Hitler's state. (The Allied occupation authorities retained some powers until 1955, but used them less and less). The Russia-conquered countries experienced full-scale plunder. The rape of hundreds of thousands of women was regarded by the army high command and Stalin, in fact if not in plain self-indicting words, as a natural right of the Russian "anti-fascist" conquerors. † Food, medical equipment, machinery, trains, railway lines, were removed to Russia. Many hundreds of thousands of captured German soldiers were used in Russia as slave labour. For Stalin they were a valued spoil of war: the Russian Stalinists looted people, as well as looting equipment, food, and factories. In the Russian-occupied states, coalition governments were set up, all with key ministries and control of the police in the hands of Stalinists put there by Russia. In effect they had state power. Trade relations with Russia were put in place on terms that plundered the economies of the satellite states. The Russians used what one of their satraps, the Hungarian Mátyás Rákosi, called "salami tactics", slicing away at the "partners" in government. By 1947-8 full-strength Stalinist dictatorships were in place. The last act in that transformation took place in February 1948, with the ousting from the Czech gov-

---

† "It is highly unlikely that historians will ever know how many German women were raped by Soviet soldiers in the months before and years after the capitulation... likely in the hundreds of thousands... even... up to two million" – Norman Naimark, The Russians in Germany, p.132-3.

ernment of all the non-Stalinist remnants.

With the exception of Czechoslovakia, the Stalinist parties had very little support in any of those occupied countries. The old Polish Communist Party had been dissolved by Stalin in 1938 and its members denounced to the Polish police state: the party was, so the Stalinists said, infested by Trotskyists and Luxemburgists. A new Communist Party of Poland was put together in 1942 to help Russia against Germany. Using police control, manipulation, persecution, coercion, and murder, Stalinist parties were cobbled and designed to be state-ruling quisling parties for Russia. New Stalinist state machines were constructed, using some people from the old state apparatuses. The East European states were now in economy, and soon in all society, structurally identical with Russia. It was impossible to see how, logically, to characterise the USSR as a degenerated workers' state and the East European countries as state-capitalist states and systems. Still, the Orthodox Trotskyists, at the Second World Congress of the Fourth International in April 1948, managed it, for a while. They defined the satellite states as bourgeois police states on top of state-capitalist economies, that is, as a species of fascist state. After a period of confusion, the Fourth International had in mid-1946 called on the Russians to withdraw from all those countries, Germany included. The signal for a radical and sudden transformation of the Orthodox Trotskyists' politics came with the unexpected excommunication from the Stalinist church of the Titoists of Yugoslavia, in June-July 1948. They proclaimed themselves independent Communists. That triggered a precipitate revision of the Orthodox Trotskyists' analysis, codified only a few weeks earlier at their Second World Congress. By late 1949 they had concluded that nationalised economy in itself was the new criterion for defining both Russia and its satellites as "workers' states". All the satellite states were "workers' states", "deformed" by their Stalinist origin, but workers' states nonetheless. Russia was a degenerated workers' state; these were *deformed workers' states*. The realities of the satellite states – totalitarian state repression, lack of civil liberties (free speech, right of organisation and assembly, freedom of publication), the prohibition of trade unions and the existence of state-run pseudo-unions of the Nazi "labour front" type, etc. – had led the Orthodox Trotskyists to classify them as in effect fascistic states. Those same characteristics, unchanged except in recently having been tightened up, did not deter them from deciding that these self-same entities, unchanged, were like Russia: they were deformed workers' states. The psychological blow of coming to the new conclusion, first for Tito's Yugoslavia in conflict with Stalin's Russia, and, within a year or so, for the other satellite states, must have been enormous. Inevitably it shattered and pulped their basic ideas on these questions. It was the psychological and political precondition for all that followed, such as the idea of a World War Three that would simultaneously be a Stalinist deformed working-class revolution.

Many Orthodox Trotskyists, including James P Cannon and Ernest Mandel, held out against some of these ideas for a while longer; but eventually they accepted them. They had to do that, or else jettison the idea that Russia remained any kind, or degree, or remnant, of workers' state. From then on, they saw a world divided between the Stalinist and the capitalist ("imperialist") blocs; and a world revolution that was "unfolding", "initially" under Stalinist leadership and control. The would-be adviser attitude they now took up to the Yugoslav regime was the beginning of an oft-to-be-repeated pattern. From the Korean war (June 1950 to June 1953) they swung into full-scale acceptance of Stalinist revolutions as the next stage of world progress, and the first stage of the world proletarian revolution.

The left – if you choose for the sake of argument to include the Stalinist parties, and non-party Stalinist supporters (a very large constituency), in the left – and the Orthodox Trotskyists, fortified with Trotsky's ideas of 1939-40 transformed into self-blinding dogma, managed the tremendous feat of not seeing Russia as imperialist, or the Russian empire as an empire, or the looting and slave-hunting in post-war Europe as any sort of imperialism. The idea that this was a spiralling socialist revolution, or, for the Orthodox Trotskyists, a great and progressive expansion on the model of the still "progressive" degenerated workers' state, defined away the fact that there was now in existence, confronting capitalist imperialism, a great new non-capitalist empire whose reality, for people in its maw, was as Trotsky had described it in 1939: semi-slavery.

In the two decades after 1945, while Russia consolidated (and, to help contain revolt in the mid-1950s, adjusted) its hold on its East European empire, the old European colonial empires which had survived the two World Wars dissolved (Portugal's African empire was the last to dissolve, in the mid 1970s). Some peoples won their freedom by insurrectionary wars of liberation, and some became independent with the agreement of the colonial powers. France fought prolonged colonial wars in Indochina (1946-54) and Algeria (1954-62). The Dutch fought a war in Indonesia (1945-9). Britain fought small wars in Malaya, Kenya, and Cyprus, but in the main the greatest colonial empire in the world dissolved peacefully, beginning in

1947-8 with the Labour government giving independence to India, Pakistan, Burma, and Ceylon. The USA, the economic and military superpower of the post-war capitalist world, did not need colonies, and it had a strong anti-colonial culture which combined the memory of its own origins with the anti-colonial self-identification of Irish, Jewish, Polish, and other Americans. The USA was a great force in dissolving the old European empires. In 1956, Britain and France, allied with an Israel trying to secure its existence in a hostile world, resorted to old-style imperialism to reclaim the Suez Canal from Egypt, which from 1882 to 1952 had been a British protectorate, host to British military bases. They invaded and occupied parts of Egypt. The US used financial pressure to force them to disengage. At exactly the same time Russia bloodily put down a rising in its empire, in Hungary, and threatened Poland with reconquest. A decade later it invaded Czechoslovakia to stop the regime liberalising itself and replacing the old Stalinist rigidity by "socialism with a human face".

As the old empires changed more or less out of recognition, for the left, "imperialism" came to be mainly defined as the power antagonistic to the Stalinist empire, as much as, and eventually far more than, by what the capitalist states did in the world. That changed and evolved, ceasing more or less to correspond to what the great powers had done in Lenin's time and in his model of imperialism. "Anti-imperialism" was primarily defined as siding with the Russian bureaucratic empire and with those who, for longer or shorter periods, were its allies or sought-after allies. An "anti-imperialism" that was pro-Russian-imperialism, or "soft" on it, became the norm where Stalinists or Orthodox Trotskyists had presence or influence. Oxymoronic anti-imperialism, pro-imperialist "anti-imperialism", was born, conquered the ostensible left, and spread across the world.

Facing page: Labor Action 2 April 1945

Bureaucratic Imperialism and the socialist revolution

133

"The driving force behind the Moscow bureaucracy is indubitably the tendency to expand its power, its prestige, its revenues... the element of 'imperialism' in the widest sense of the word which was a property in the past of all monarchies, oligarchies, ruling castes, medieval estates and classes" – Leon Trotsky, *Again and Once More on the Nature of the USSR*, October 1939.

Did Stalinist Russia after World War Two, surrounded by a large cluster of vassal states, constitute a new imperialist power? In light of the facts, it is a strange, even ridiculous, question to ask. It was asked. The wrong answer shaped and reshaped the Marxist left. The effect of the answer given then still shapes the left.

The contrast between the USA and Russia in Europe from 1944-5 onwards, in their relationship to the countries they occupied, was remarkable. The Russians looted and raped, slave-hunted, and held its European satellites in an iron grip. There was a qualitative difference between what the Russians did in Eastern and central Europe, and what the Americans did in western and central Europe. The Americans did not hunt, capture, and enslave as Russia did.

The independence of the West European states was quickly restored. Britain, with its Labour government, began to free the colonies – India, Ceylon, Burma in 1947-8. In 1948 the USA created the Marshall Plan, a vast system of credit and aid for the countries of Europe, an American capitalist attempt to restore a ruined Europe to health as capitalist states. It was called a variant of imperialism by the anti-Stalinist left. In overall terms of what it meant for the peoples of Europe it was – all qualifications granted – benign, supportive, and liberty-restoring.† The contrast with Russia's behaviour where it ruled was damning and should have been all-defining.

In short, the imperialists did not behave primarily like imperialists, in the sense of enslavement, exploitation based on force and superior strength, or plain nastiness. The "non-imperialist" Russians did, crassly and to a degree that is sometimes scarcely believable ††. The Orthodox Trotskyists faced this conundrum with ideological blindfolds over their eyes.

On the eve of the explosion into world power of an empire that was not capitalist, and not governed by the specific characteristics and drives of the finance-capitalist empires – Stalinist Russia – Trotsky had insisted on restricting the term "imperialism" to the states of finance-capitalism.

The Russian empires, both the empire of the Tsars and later Russian Stalinist imperialism, were empires in which the majority of the people were not of the dominant Great Russian nationality. The October revolution broke down the walls of that great prison of the peoples, giving independence to some (Finland, Poland, Latvia, Lithuania, Estonia), autonomy to the smaller peoples who remained within a common state with the Great Russians. Under Stalin, the bureaucratic rigidity and the subordination of everything to central Moscow rule had destroyed the autonomies of the component republics of the USSR and thus cancelled out self-determination for the peoples of the USSR. Stalin's Russia reverted to being what in Tsarist time it had been called – a prison-house of nations. For Ukraine, for instance. And Stalin deported whole small nations, the Volga Germans and the Crimean Tatars for example.

By the end of the Second World War, the Stalinist bureaucratic empire had become the greatest power in Europe, and the second great power of the world. World rivalry now came to be rivalry between the USA and the Western European powers, with their colonial empires, on one side and the new Russian Empire on the other. Radically different social systems; different imperialisms, and the USA almost without colonies. Their differences could not be characterised, as Lenin had characterised the dominant monopoly-capitalist imperialism on both sides of World War One, only in terms of differing from earlier capitalism by degrees of economic development, but also by the full panoply of economic, social, political, and intellectual characteristics of the competing societies. Each of the two blocs had a different drive, mechanism, modus operandi, immediate goals. They embodied different civilisations and different levels of civilisation. In

---

† *The historian J. Robert Lilly estimates a total of 14,000 women raped by US troops in western Europe: Taken by Force: Rape and American GIs in Europe during World War II. Some 900 US soldiers were put on trial for rape in Europe, and 29 hanged. 25 of the 29 hanged, out of 151 sentenced to death for rape, were African-American. The American military authorities also imposed conservative politicians as immediate post-liberation local authorities in place of grass-roots committees here and there. They censored the press, and actively colluded with the Stalinists in the mass expulsion of Germans from the east. They often looted domestic property and dismantled or restricted sizeable parts of German industry, continuing to do so even after the USA had begun to reverse the process by the Marshall Plan. They kept hundreds of thousands of Jews in detention camps. And so on. But all that was on a different scale from the brutality of the Russians in the east. See William I Hitchcock, The Bitter Road to Freedom: A New History of the Liberation of Europe.*
†† *So crassly that as late as 1955 some Marxists – Tony Cliff, for example – still saw a new world war looming because the primitive, plundering Russian imperialism would be driven to war by economic hungers and shortages and the consequent desire to loot. As far as I know, Cliff never tried to square this with the accounts of Russia in the first, 1948, or the second, 1955, version of his book.*

the strange USSR system even the Stalinist terror played an economic role, against bureaucratic inertia and against the bureaucratic economy congealing into stagnation and collapse.

If, in 1940, Trotsky still generally reserved the term "imperialism" for monopoly capitalism and states like Czechoslovakia, he did not "reserve" the anti-imperialist program for those states. He directed it also to the USSR. In putting national independence of the Ukraine at the political forefront of his revolutionary socialist concerns, as he did in April 1939, Trotsky implicitly characterised Stalin's Russia, in which the majority of the people were of submerged nationalities, as imperialist in the sense that Austria, Tsarist Russia, and Turkey had been, or as some second-tier European states were (Poland, Yugoslavia) or recently had been (Czechoslovakia). He said so, more or less plainly. †

This "degenerated workers' state" was ruled by an oligarchy which was governed by "the tendency to expand its power, its prestige, its revenues... the element of 'imperialism' in the widest sense of the word which was a property in the past of all monarchies, oligarchies, ruling castes, medieval estates and classes". In 1939-40 that bureaucratic "imperialism" was becoming a major characteristic of the Stalinist bureaucracy. In 1944-5 the new imperialism engulfed a large part of Europe.

In October 1939, Trotsky considered the possibility that "the Red Army tomorrow invades India and begins to put down a revolutionary movement", and wrote: "In every case the Fourth International will know how to distinguish where and when the Red Army is acting solely as an instrument of the Bonapartist reaction and where it defends the social basis of the USSR".

When Trotsky still, in 1939, insisted on reserving the term "impe-

---

† In a 1937 discussion with one of his Chinese comrades, Trotsky said: "we ask for an open proclamation from the Soviet bureaucracy that at the end of the war no part of China would be occupied...". The Chinese comrade asked, in surprise: "Do you then think that the Soviet Union could be capable of conducting an imperialistic policy?", Trotsky replied: "If it is capable of organising frame-ups, killing the revolutionaries, it is capable of all possible crimes" (SWP-USA Internal Bulletin, December 1937). But what would such a "proclamation" from Stalin be worth? Why would demanding the "proclamation" not mean inviting Stalin to lie and deceive, and later betray? Would it not mean lending him credence by making the demand as if he could and would fulfil it? This formulation by Trotsky may have influenced James P Cannon and the SWP-USA during World War 2, who made "demands" on Stalin which, in the circumstances, were preposterous and, for the Trotskyists, both disorienting and a by-product of their disorientation. See introduction to The Two Trotskyisms Confront Stalinism, pp.46-48.

rialism" for monopoly capitalism, and was asked for an answer to the phenomenon of Russian imperialism, he offered two answers. In one, he admitted, as above, that there was a Russian Stalinist imperialism, one of many in history, and he proposed an anti-imperialist program for Stalin's empire: self-determination for a soviet Ukraine, and implicitly for the other oppressed peoples in Stalin's territory. In the other answer, he fended off the question with a non-sequitur: it was not monopoly-capitalist, he said. At the end of his life Trotsky left the question in a state of vagueness and contradictoriness and reliance on special uses of important political words, or refusals to use them. The Trotskyist movement would pay a high price for this in political and historical disorientation, and confusion about Russian imperialism, for many decades to come, until the collapse of the USSR in 1991.

And the Orthodox Trotskyists at the end of World War 2? They had spent the years from the German invasion of Russia in June 1941 to the end of the war weaving strange fantasies about the "Red Army" as a friend of European workers' revolution (see *The Two Trotskyisms Confront Stalinism*). They began partially to sober up at the end of the war. What did they make of the new Stalinist imperialism?

If Trotsky had argued in 1939 that Stalinist Russia was imperialist "in the widest sense of the word, which was a property in the past of all monarchies, oligarchies, ruling castes, medieval estates and classes", in 1948 the Orthodox Trotskyists did not dare even to say that much. Yet for them the USA and Europe remained imperialist in the same sense as before, despite the liquidation of the old colonial empires in the post-war decades, and more or less regardless of what they might do, because they were advanced capitalism. The USA was imperialist despite the restoration of European independence, democracy, and industry after 1945, and despite its lack of colonies other than Puerto Rico and Hawaii (which became a full state of the USA in 1959). Russia was non-imperialist despite its occupation and looting of the East European countries. Real politics was replaced by political brand-names and fantasy, the analysis of deeds by the arcane diagnosis of class "essences".

At the end of World War 2, to the question: is Russia, which occupies half of Europe, imperialist? – the Orthodox Trotskyists replied: it is a degenerated workers' state, that is, they answered by responding to a different question (which they saw as the same question). They followed Trotsky in 1939-40, but in a different world in which victorious Stalinist Russia was the greatest power in Europe and one of the two great world-bestriding super-powers. Russia, they said, was not, could not be, imperialist: it was a degenerated workers' state. Therefore such deeds as Russian occupation and exploitation of Eastern Europe had to be seen differently from similar actions by capitalist powers. You had to take a dual, a double, two-visions, "dialectical" view in the world of the two great powers, one for each political and social hemisphere. Of the political ancestors of the present-day ostensible left, the Communist Parties saw the Stalinist expansion as historical progress and working-class power. The Orthodox Trotskyists, reluctantly and hesitantly and over several years of discussion, dissension, and large-scale desertions †, came to see it as a form of deformed working-class power, once removed from the actual working class

Before 1940, when and wherever diverse sorts of imperialist empires existed, the Trotskyists not only identified them as imperialist, but put forward a program of national liberation. We have seen that Trotsky proposed a similar program for Ukraine in April 1939, while refusing to call the USSR by the same descriptive name as capitalist imperialism. The post-Trotsky Orthodox Trotskyists eventually did the same thing for the East European states in the mid-1940s. †† It was their political salvation that most of them, most of the time, rose above their theoretical and political confusion and came out clearly for freedom for the peoples of Eastern Europe. Thus, despite the confusions, disorientations, and vacillations, they did not betray or definitively abandon the political fundamentals of Trotsky's movement. They criticised Stalinism in Eastern Europe. But see it for the imperialism it was, they could not.

Their theory of Stalinist imperialism was that it was a series of deformed workers' revolutions imposed by the Russian "degenerated workers' state" and by other Stalinist formations, such as Tito's Partisan peasant army in Yugoslavia and Mao's peasant army in China, taking Stalin's Russia as their model and ideal. They demanded freedom for the East European Stalinist states and Ukraine. But that, they thought, was a matter of sorting out problems within the ranks of the

---

† *The French Trotskyist group, second only to the SWP-USA in its influence and importance, went down from about a thousand members at its post-war peak to 150 at the time of its split in 1952.*

†† *After flailing in confusion for a while. At the end of the war and the commencement of Russian overlordship in Eastern Europe, they offered to the workers of the Russian-occupied countries the formula: "tolerate the presence of the Red Army only to the extent that it is a friendly proletarian armed force" but favour its defeat where it "opposes insurrectionary movements of the masses" – February 1946. The Two Trotskyisms Confront Stalinism, p.394.*

ongoing world revolution. Russia was not imperialist, despite the fact that an anti-imperialist program of national liberation had to be advocated and fought for against it in the countries it occupied, including Germany. In all conflicts with capitalist imperialism, the USSR was not a bureaucratic-imperialist rival to capitalism, but "the anti-capitalist camp". At least one of the Orthodox Trotskyists, some of the time, took this to outright political lunacy by defining the whole USSR as "part of the labour movement". †

If those beliefs about the world, fundamentally the idea that the USSR was some sort of workers' state, and that parts of the world were already post-capitalist and developing towards socialism – if any of that had been true, then advanced capitalism, which stood against the socialist world-revolution-a-building, was indeed by contrast entirely reactionary. Those who thought on those lines were led not only to devalue "for now" the achievements of bourgeois civilisation in history – democracy, civil rights, free thought, free speech, freedom to organise, rule of law, etc. – but also to give positive support ("critical" support, against capitalist imperialism) or tolerance, however reluctant, to terrible things.

Those horrors were seen as an unfortunate part of a historical combination which they had no choice but to accept as History offered it, because its main component was a "deformed world revolution". The horrors would in due time be sorted out, but meanwhile they were secondary or tertiary. The fact that Stalinist victory in any country would extirpate all democratic rights, including the right for labour movements to exist, could not be allowed to influence the attitude to the fundamental conflict between capitalism and the (deformed) "world revolution". That would be "subjective". That would be "sectarian".

In real history, of course, the bureaucratic USSR was not a progressive alternative to capitalism. It was not socialist in any sense, to any degree, or on any level. It was not "in transition to" socialism. It was indeed a rival to capitalism but a regressive and reactionary one. It was not "post-capitalist", but in important respects pre-capitalist, a

---

† *See for example James P Cannon, SWP Internal Bulletin 6 (10), November 1944, quoted in The Two Trotskyisms Confront Stalinism, p.601. This thought was probably rooted in the very misleading idea that the Soviet Union, as a degenerated workers' state, could be understood as an equivalent to a heavily bureaucratised or gangster-ridden trade union. This idea was here used as a literal equivalence. All notion of quantity and quality, of the difference between a totalitarian state power and bureaucratic or gangster trade-union leaders operating in a bourgeois-democratic system, was gone.*

system in all respects paralleling capitalism as a class-exploitative society and one in its methods worse than typical modern capitalism. All the events hailed as revolutionary working-class triumphs by so many socialists were in fact reactionary and regressive. The Maoist Chinese revolution was a historical regression. For more than a quarter-century it took hundreds of millions of people under arbitrary rule by totalitarian despots, some of whose plans and projects were borderline crazy, or over the border. The economic "Great Leap Forward" of 1958-62 cost the lives of something like 30 million people. Incredible as it might seem – like so much in the history of international Stalinism – one consequence of the "Cultural Revolution" of 1966-71 was to abolish higher education in China for a decade. And now, after Mao, the regime has imposed three decades of totalitarian rule combined with cut-throat market capitalism. Only people in the grip of delusion and wish-thinking scenarios, whose own "natural" criteria had in their eyes been discredited by unexpected events, could have seen Maoism and the Maoist revolution (and, later, the Maoist movements all over the world) as anything but reactionary.

Some of these attitudes, methods, mindsets have survived into the post-Stalinist era in the idea that advanced capitalism, defined as "imperialism", is unconditionally reactionary, so reactionary that almost any force that opposes it, or the capitalist great powers, thereby becomes "good".

Trotsky, though we can see, now, that he was mistaken, nevertheless had good reasons for insisting, then, and for then, as he himself saw it, on maintaining a distinction between monopoly-capitalist imperialism and the imperialism of the Stalinist state. What made clinging to Trotsky's formulation into the political catastrophe for Orthodox Trotskyists of denying the reality of Russian bureaucratic imperialism was their failure to register and draw conclusions from the fact that the bureaucracy, which Trotsky thought could not last more than "just a few years or even a few months" (*The USSR in War*, September 1939), had stabilised as a ruling class in a new form of society and expanded into a vast empire outside the USSR. They adjusted falsely to the emergence of the USSR as the greatest military power in Europe, with vast, newly conquered, territories and many, many peoples held in subjection and varying degrees of exploitation. Where Trotsky in 1939 had answered plainly that Russia was imperialist in the generic sense of the word, the Orthodox Trotskyists did the opposite, reluctantly and hesitantly defending what Stalinism did as, in its essence, the extension of the revolution.

"The colonial revolution" is socialist revolution?

Central to the formation of the ideas of the ostensible left on imperialism and anti-imperialism has been the fact that the Orthodox Trotskyists conflated working-class socialist revolution and the anti-colonial revolutions of the 1940s, 50s, and 60s, in what they saw as a variant of Trotsky's permanent revolution. What is "permanent revolution", as Trotsky expounded it? The French revolution had been a particularly radical bourgeois revolution against the remnants of feudalism in France. Tsarist Russia needed a similar revolution to establish civil liberty and a democratic republic. The bourgeois liberals in Russia were unable and unwilling to lead a bourgeois revolution like that of France against Tsarism. In Russia the working class, leading the peasants, did fuse two revolutions, the bourgeois-democratic revolution and the working-class revolution, into one continuous movement, one ongoing "permanent" revolution. They made the October 1917 revolution. In the 20th century many countries, China for instance, had not had successful bourgeois revolutions. Colonies and semi-colonies were occupied or controlled by imperialist powers. In many of those countries the bourgeoisie was even more feeble, and even more tied up with external imperialist interests and with the old landlord classes, than the Russian Tsarist bourgeoisie had been. The internal bourgeois revolution had to also be an anti-imperialist movement. Trotsky advocated that the working class, through the Communist Parties, should, as in Russia, take the lead in an anti-imperialist movement which the victorious workers could lead straight to working-class power.

In the Communist International's and the Fourth International's idea of permanent revolution, elements of a bourgeois revolution would be fused with working-class revolution by the workers' party taking the lead in societies with a combined and uneven development, and there would be no stable period of bourgeois rule in between. The workers would drive the revolution straight on, destroying all elements of imperialist and bourgeois rule.

The Communist International did not use the expression "permanent revolution". Its Theses on the Eastern Question of 1922 put the idea like this: "The Communist International... remains convinced that the oppressed masses can only be led to victory by a consistent revolutionary line that is designed to draw the broadest masses into active struggle and that constitutes a complete break with all who support conciliation with imperialism in the interests of their own class rule... The objective tasks of the colonial revolution go beyond the bounds of bourgeois democracy because a decisive victory for this revolution is incompatible with the rule of world imperialism... The struggle for influence over the peasant masses will prepare the indigenous proletariat for political leadership. Only when the proletariat has done this preliminary work in its own ranks and in those of the social layers closest to it can it challenge bourgeois democracy, which in the conditions of the backward East is even more inadequate than in the West..."

This was one version of permanent revolution, Trotsky's. The working class was the protagonist at the head of the farmers in nations trying to reconstruct themselves "under the leadership of the proletariat". In the 1920s and 30s, Trotskyists advocated working-class leadership of liberation movements in colonies and semi-colonies such as China and India. Such working-class-led revolutions happened nowhere. Stalinists in Yugoslavia, China, Vietnam – in all cases, peasant movements led by de-classed and militarised "Communist Parties" – led anti-colonial revolutions. The working class played no important part in those revolutions. They created totalitarian regimes modelled on Stalin's Russia.

In the 1950s and 60s version (partially excepting Algeria), "permanent revolution" came to mean Stalinist revolutions that would end not in working-class rule and freedom, but in tight Stalinist bureaucratic dictatorships like, for instance, China's. These eliminated the possibility of an independent working-class movement, let alone of the working class developing so as to be able to take power and exercise it.

In 1932 Trotsky had warned that the de-classed peasant-based Mao-Stalinists might confront the working class as a hostile, alien, enemy force: they "will incite the armed peasants against the advanced workers". † That they did.

The Stalinists in power did not do as the working class would do in Trotsky's formula for permanent revolution, and did in Russia, bring two revolutions together, winning liberty and a democratic republic and simultaneously seizing economic power from the bourgeoisie and the landlords. All the things central to Marx's and Trotsky's permanent revolution – civil rights, working-class freedom, self-rule – were eliminated. The society went straight to full-blown Stalinist totalitarianism. This was not so much fusing the bourgeois-democratic revolution and the working-class revolution as bypassing both. It was something else entirely.

---

† *Peasant War in China and the Proletariat, Writings 1932, p.192ff.*

The Orthodox Trotskyists' theory of Russia as a degenerated workers' state was adapted to explain the East European Stalinist states – in the first case, Yugoslavia – as *deformed* workers' states. Before the Orthodox Trotskyists could do that adaptation, and as an essential part of it, they had to elaborate what was in fact, despite their claims of Trotskyist orthodoxy, a new theory of Russia as a degenerated workers' state. They did that by shedding all of Trotsky's framework for seeing Russia's nationalised economy as the empirical evidence that Russia was still a workers' state – its origin in the workers' revolution, its uniqueness in the world, the unstable and transitory character of the Russian system as Trotsky saw it. For Trotsky his conclusion was very much pro tem: "Might we not place ourselves in a ludicrous position if we affixed to the Bonapartist oligarchy the nomenclature of a new ruling class just a few years or even a few months prior to its inglorious downfall?" For the Orthodox Trotskyists, from the mid-1950s, the USSR and the other Stalinist states were stable systems "in transition to socialism". The concept of "transitional" in Trotsky's writings, carrying connotations of transient or transitory, was given a meaning which it could not have had for Trotsky.

The Orthodox Trotskyists made their shift by amending Trotsky's theory of the Russian degenerated workers' state so that the sole criterion of such a state came to be nationalised property. In that scale the satellites too were workers' states – "deformed workers' states".

Stalinist victories were seen as victories for permanent revolution. This "permanent revolution Mark II" might be called "totalitarian permanent revolution", except that it had nothing to do with socialist "permanent revolution", or with working-class rule, other than in being their stark opposite.

Between the 1940s and the 1970s, the Orthodox Trotskyists saw the revolts in the colonies and semi-colonies as a segment of an unfolding "world revolution". Where the anti-colonial revolts were Stalinist-led movements, their victory would also be a victory against capitalism and for "socialism": deformed workers' states would be created. The world socialist revolution would be making progress. The Orthodox Trotskyists supported anti-colonial movement not only for their fight against the colonial overlords – though of course they did that – but also for their attributed anti-capitalism, even in the Stalinist version created by movements such as Tito's, Mao Zedong's, and Ho Chi Minh's.

The Orthodox Trotskyists worked out schemas according to which colonial wars of liberation, if they developed their full potential, must produce socialist revolutions modelled on what had happened in Yugoslavia, North Vietnam, and China, that is, in reality, Stalinist revolutions. By the 1960s, after the Cuban revolution, they had extended their revolutionary anti-capitalist expectations beyond Stalinist-led colonial revolutions, like China and Vietnam. They came to believe that only a socialist revolution could be the result of the eight year long Algerian war of liberation against France, which was not led by Stalinists. Some, with extra nonsensicality, would extend this scenario even to the Provisional IRA war in Ireland. Thus anti-imperialism, meaning conflict with the capitalist big powers, was, per se, also anti-capitalist, or sure to become so as the struggle "developed and deepened". Had to become so. Could not but become so.

This was a variant of Trotsky's permanent revolution, they said. In fact, for all the Orthodox Trotskyists, "permanent revolution" was implicitly (at best) transformed into its opposite, into a notion of walled-off stages. First there would be the creation of a Stalinist "deformed workers' state" – or, in Cuba, they thought, a less-deformed workers' state – and then, eventually, once the Stalinists had created an advanced economy, the workers' revolution (called "political revolution"). Some Orthodox Trotskyists – Ted Grant for the crassest example – came to see the first, Stalinist, stage as part of the program they advocated.

The Communist International had seen and proclaimed an important distinction between those anti-imperialist nationalists who organised militant and military activity against their overlords and those who did not. The Communists could combine with the "revolutionary nationalists". Lenin explained at the Second Congress of the Communist International, in 1920: "The imperialist bourgeoisie is doing everything in its power to implant a reformist movement among the oppressed nations too... Very often... the bourgeoisie of the oppressed countries, while it does support the national movement, is in full accord with the imperialist bourgeoisie, i.e. joins forces with it against all revolutionary movements and revolutionary classes... We, as communists, should and will support bourgeois-liberation movements in the colonies only when they are genuinely revolutionary, and when their exponents do not hinder our work of educating and organising in a revolutionary spirit the peasantry and the masses of the exploited". The Orthodox Trotskyists merged that distinction between "revolutionary nationalists" and pliant bourgeois anti-colonialists into an idea that all such militant revolutionary nationalist struggles were incipiently permanent revolution, and to be identified, now or soon, with socialist revolution.

The "colonial-revolution-is-permanent-revolution" mutation of Trotsky's theory, the belief that all anti-colonial movements were or could be a variant of socialist revolution, was contradicted by unfolding reality over decades. The intense overvaluation of national-liberation movements remained – the pulping and blending of basic Marxist ideas and qualifications into a populist-nationalist pastiche.

How "anti-imperialism" became regressive anti-capitalism

Over many decades of the 20th century, the Communist Parties, the large Stalinist-influenced Labour and socialist left, and those influenced by Orthodox Trotskyism, did not recognise the greatest, the most brutal, the most oppressive empire in the world, Russia's, as an empire. Not even when its imperialist character loomed gigantically across the world. Not even when they felt themselves obliged to propose an anti-imperialist program of national self-determination for its victims. That was because they saw Russia and the Russian empire as progressive and "socialistic", and therefore felt obliged to back them, however critically, in their conflicts with the capitalist-imperialist states, in the first place the arch-imperialist USA.

If advanced capitalism and imperialism are the same, more or less, and you apply anti-imperialist negativism to advanced capitalism as such, in abstraction from particular imperialist actions and relationships, then you adopt an ahistorical, "absolute anti-capitalist" attitude to capitalism that goes back to before the Communist Manifesto.

The post-Trotsky Orthodox Trotskyists therefore faced the world after the end of World War Two with five fundamental attitudes on the question of imperialism.

First, a stubborn belief that all imperialisms were equally aggressive and predatory, and, in consequence, that the US-British occupation of Western Europe would be as terrible as the conquest by Nazi Germany had been. Only slowly and reluctantly, and long after facts had contradicted their expectations, did they register European reality on any generalised level. The Orthodox Trotskyists continued to see "imperialism" (redefined as "advanced capitalism") as uniquely warlike because of its antagonism to the USSR, and in contrast to a USSR judged less warlike.

Second, the belief that capitalist imperialism was a society at the end of its possibility of development. Imperialism was capitalism in its phase of rot and decay. The idea that capitalist imperialism was moribund capitalism was a dogma of the Stalinists and a framing idea of their picture of the world outside the Stalinist-ruled territories.

145

The Orthodox Trotskyists took it over (and, essentially, the Heterodox Trotskyists too went along with the idea that advanced capitalism was in hopeless decline). †

Third, that this was moribund capitalism whose rulers, on questions such as war, had little choice on how to behave. They were caught in an automatic logic, even on a question like war in the era of nuclear weapons. They could not manoeuvre, they could not make intelligent choices.

Fourth, the belief that "imperialism" in their epoch could only be the imperialism of finance and monopoly capital, and a refusal to characterise Russia and China, even when Stalinism ruled one-third of the world, as imperialist.

Fifth, the belief that the colonial wars and uprisings against imperialism all over the world were the "permanent revolution", and even, in fact especially, those led and controlled by Stalinists would organically lead to socialist revolutions unless blocked in their logical and natural development.

Anti-imperialism and anti-Americanism

"Today US imperialism is humanity's worst enemy, and its global hegemony poses the greatest danger to humanity's future" – Moshe Machover. ††

A major part of Russia's strategy against its opponents after World War Two was to divide them. The Stalinist system had survived World War Two because the capitalist imperialist powers were divided and fighting each other, the British-American-led bloc on Russia's side and the German-led bloc on the other. Russia tried to recreate equivalent situations, this time with the older capitalist-imperialist powers, Britain, France, etc., against American imperialism.

War between the UK and the USA had been expected by Marxists such as Trotsky in the 1920s: they thought Britain would not peacefully accept the rising hegemony of America. From the late 1940s, the Stalinist CPs of old-imperialist Europe focused much of their pro-Russian propaganda and agitation against American imperialism, American bases, American soldiers, etc. The Communist Parties were

---

† *Some of the more "intellectually challenged" Orthodox Trotskyists, the Lambertists, contented themselves with the observation that capitalism was developing the means of destruction, not of production – as if arms production and civilian production were, in modern conditions, mutually exclusive.*

†† *Israel, the Palestinians, and Iran: a debate between Moshe Machover and Sean Matgamna. 2008.*

nationalists of their own peoples, albeit only for so long as that might serve the USSR. They presented their pro-Russian core politics in terms of what could be construed as the enlightened best interests of their own countries. They were, everywhere, anti-American pseudo-patriots and Yankophobe pseudo-nationalists. America was the great warmonger, the main "enemy of the Soviet Union", with military bases throughout the world, and the ally of Germany's restored-to-power semi-"Nazis". The French and British parties were virulently anti-American, presenting themselves and great-European-empire-holding Russia as above all wanting peace, and the USA as the obstacle to peace. This was a time when Trotskyists had to oppose the presence on demonstrations of placards and chants such as "Yankee bastards go home", and dispute anti-German agitation conducted in terms of identification of West Germany with Nazism.

Attempts to exploit French and British resentment of the USA remained central in Stalinist-defined working-class politics for decades. It was an example of "absolute anti-capitalism". The more advanced the capitalism, the more reactionary. This anti-Americanism is still a big factor in much addled-left absolute anti-capitalism.

The three root confusions

The confusions and misunderstandings on the contemporary left about imperialism and anti-imperialism with which we are concerned here thus have three fundamental causes.

1. The first is that the imperialist world described and analysed by Kautsky, by Lenin, by Trotsky, by Luxemburg, and by other Marxists, and by honest liberals of their time, has changed fundamentally over the last hundred years. That imperialism isn't there any more. Colonies are no longer in existence, or only small remnants exist now.

2. The second is, that the typical left, the predominant left, both the Stalinist left and the Trotskisant left, over many decades, did not recognise Russian imperialism as imperialism. No matter what the USSR did, because of its "socialist" or "workers' state" nature it could not be imperialist. Opposition to the Russian Empire came to be seen as one of the key defining features of advanced capitalist imperialism. Being antagonistic to Russian Empire was one of the central things that defined advanced capitalism as "imperialist".

3. The third is a misuse of Trotsky's term "permanent revolution" and the conflation of colonial independence movements and working-class revolution. For much of the left, for much of the 20th century, the "colonial revolution" was construed as a version of socialist

revolution or incipient socialist revolution and as part of the world revolution whose "fortress" was the USSR. To be anti-imperialist was to be pro-USSR and to champion the colonial countries that were expected to become Stalinist.

The idea, central to the anti-imperialism of the Communist International and the Fourth International, that the alternative to imperialism was socialist revolution in the advanced world coupled with anti-colonial movements in the less advanced, has been turned upside down. The "operationally" direct anti-capitalism has been defined as a colonial revolution that could bypass capitalism and link up with the Russian revolution in its "degenerated workers' state" shape. In fact, radical anti-colonial movements led to Stalinist states. There, "socialism" was redefined as an alternative mode of economic development, rather than as workers' power. The ostensible left used dogmatic juggling with words and ideas to prove that those movements were "really" working-class and that the revolutions they made were "really" working-class revolutions, even if deformed.

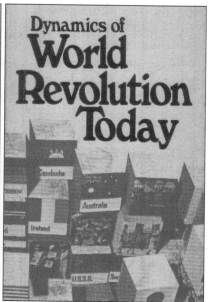

Between the early 1950s and the 70s, and with increasing doubts into the 80s, the Orthodox Trotskyists described world events as an ever-advancing process of "world revolution", manifested for the time being in Stalinist and statist-nationalist victories in poorer countries. Left, a book produced for the 50th anniversary of 1917; right, the Orthodox Trotskyists' summary of their perspectives in 1963.

148

Imperialism and the left: twenty case histories

1. Korea

During World War Two the Orthodox Trotskyists had fervently backed Russia and developed freewheeling fantasies about the "Red Army" triggering and maybe helping working-class revolutions in the countries it entered. They had vacillated around the call for the withdrawal of Russian troops from the countries which they had conquered in 1944-5. (See *The Two Trotskyisms Confront Stalinism*, pp.564-6). In the Korean war of 1950-3, the Orthodox Trotskyists attached themselves (still often critically) to the new Russian imperialism and its allies and client states. The Russian army invaded Japanese-controlled north Korea at the very end of the war, in 1945. The Russian's "sphere of control" in Korea became, like the East European satellite states, a Stalinist police state. In June 1950 the North Koreans invaded South Korea with Russian agreement, if not on Stalin's orders. They were on the point of overwhelming the feeble South Korean resistance when US, British, Australian and other soldiers entered Korea under the banner of the United Nations to stop that happening. (Russia had temporarily withdrawn from the UN Security Council, and so was not in a position to veto the UN decision). From December 1950, large Chinese armies fought side by side with the North Koreans against the American and UN forces. This, for Russia, was a proxy war.

For a month after the outbreak of the war on 25 June, the American SWP, the most important of the Orthodox Trotskyist organisations, hovered on the brink of a "third camp" position, refusing to back either side. They had too sharp an awareness of what Stalinist rule brought to peoples and to working classes not to be inhibited in backing Russia's proxy North Korea in its attempt to conquer South Korea. They were only just bringing themselves to accept the idea, which they had at first resisted, that the Stalinist satellite states in Europe were "deformed workers' states". After a month and four near-Third-Camp issues of their weekly paper, *The Militant*, in the 31 July issue they came down solidly on the side of North Korea.

How did they square that with their earlier condemnations of Korean Stalinism? They ignored what was specific to Stalinist societies and regimes, and redefined and rechristened Korean Stalinism and the North Korean Stalinist state as "the colonial revolution" in the Korean peninsula.† The American Trotskyist leader James P Cannon wrote an open letter to the President and Congress of the USA. He demanded that they stop their attack on the "colonial revolution" in Korea. The "Korean revolution" was an "anti-imperialist" revolution. What was it positively? On that the SWP were silent. They made atrocity propaganda against the South Korean regime and were silent about obnoxious things the North Koreans and Chinese did. They had adopted the Stalinist method – used for "anti-fascism" – of negativism and silence on the existing realities and alternatives. The "anti-imperialism" here was used as a mask for pro-Stalinism, for shamefacedly taking sides with Stalinism.

The new approach allowed the SWP-USA to square the political circle, and to deal with Stalinism in Korea by ignoring it. Stalin had photographs doctored to remove such people as Trotsky from the visible historical record. Cannon and his comrades did something like that for contemporary world politics with their portrayal of Korea; and not only for Korea. Stalinism as a force (in fact, the dominant force) was airbrushed out of many parts of their picture of the reality around them, as Trotsky and others were excised from old photographs of the revolutionary years in Russia. "Anti-imperialism" was fused with partisanship for Russian and other Stalinist forces. As a political line it worked up to a point; as an account of the world

---

† In doing so, they stepped into line with the Orthodox Trotskyists in Europe. The French paper La Vérité, close to the Paris-based Fourth International leadership, also responded at first coolly, with no call to back the North Koreans (La Vérité 256, 2nd half of June 1950). As well as old-Trotskyist hostility to Stalinism, enthusiasm for the Tito regime in Yugoslavia would have been a factor here: Tito denounced the North Korean invasion and Stalin's role in triggering it. But the European Orthodox Trotskyists soon came out strongly for North Korea (International Secretariat of FI statement 1 July 1950, in Quatrième Internationale May-July 1950; La Vérité 257, 1st half of July 1950). The fate of Korea since then is history's brutal verdict on that. North Korea survives. It may be the most completely totalitarian state that has ever existed. Its people are regimented and stifled, and many starve. The country is now ruled by the third priest-king of the Kim Il Sung dynasty. Claims made for the god-kings include the story that one of them was born of a virgin mother. Another does not defecate. The middle Kim, the present monarch's father, looked to European fascists like Hitler for inspiration as well as to Stalinist Russia, but the regime is still based on the order imposed by Russia in 1945-6. It is an unspeakably regressive, exploitative regime, without parallel anywhere on earth, or possibly anywhere in history. The unfavourable contrast with capitalist South Korea, whose society has all the faults of capitalism everywhere, is enormous – as if to leave no strand of plausibility for the idea that the Stalinist revolutions embodied historical progress as against capitalism.

150

it was a piece of fiction. That sort of fiction, that sort of, so to speak, photo-doctoring, would from now on be an integral strand of the Orthodox Trotskyist world outlook.

2. World War is Revolution and Revolution is World War

What they said about Korea was an aspect of a new world view that the leaders of the Fourth International had worked out from 1950-51. World War Three was imminent. It would be an international class war. This war would simultaneously be a revolution. The mass Communist Parties of France and Italy and the other CPs would rally to the invading Russian "Red" Army, which would quickly sweep through Europe to the Atlantic. The imminent world war was immanent working-class revolution; the working-class revolution was the imminent war. †† The "colonial revolution" which was also the (deformed) socialist revolution was part of that tissue of bleak political fantasies. This visionary, millenarian politics would last until the mid 1950s. Major aspects of it would last for decades, minus the cataclysmic centrepiece of the Third World War-Revolution. This was Orthodox Trotskyism's "Third Period". The world was experiencing an unstoppable process of permanent revolution. This was not a working-class revolution as it had been understood previously. It was a revolution led by Stalinists ("at this stage"). World War Three would be one of its instruments. The Orthodox Trotskyists, like the Stalinists during their "Third Period", now looked around the world and everywhere saw or construed proof of the view they brought to analysing it.

3. The Israeli-Arab war of 1948

In November 1947 the United Nations proposed that Palestine, where, under British rule, Jews and Arabs were engaged in simmering guerrilla warfare against each other, be partitioned into a Jewish and an Arab state. Previously, in 1937, the British Peel Commission had also proposed a partition: the Palestinian Jews accepted the idea,

---

†† *This was a variant of the idea that they had had in World War Two about the "Red" Army playing the role of detonator, and being friendly, or not hostile, or not effectively hostile, to working-class revolution when it entered countries such as Germany. But that earlier idea was one in which the working class would be the decisive force, the protagonist. Now the Russian Army and the Kremlin controlling it were seen as the protagonist, and the local working classes as a subordinate and Stalinist-controlled part of the process.*

but Britain abandoned it because of Arab opposition. The British formally relinquished control of Palestine in May 1948. The Jews proclaimed the independent state of Israel in the UN-allocated territory. The surrounding Arab states, Egypt, Iraq, Transjordan, which were under British influence or quasi-control, immediately invaded. Some of their officers were seconded British soldiers. They joined with the Palestinian Arab forces that had already been at war with Palestinian Jews. Against most expectations, the Haganah (the Jewish militia) defeated the Arab armies and drove them back. A lot of Palestinian Arabs followed the Arab armies or were driven out. The UN-proposed Palestinian Arab state disappeared, with most of its territory taken by Jordan and Egypt and some by Israel.

The Orthodox Trotskyists had not yet hammered out the ideas that would shape them politically in the decades ahead: of "the colonial revolution" as the leading sector of the world revolution and indeed, where Stalinists controlled the anti-imperialist movement, as one of the roads to workers' states. Those would come after the Russian-Yugoslav split (June 1948); the Maoist victory in China (1949); the Orthodox Trotskyists' conclusion that the East European Stalinist states were a variant of not-quite-adequate workers' states, species of a new category, "deformed workers' states", which they had invented; and the start of the Korean war. The Orthodox Trotskyists' Second World Congress was held in April 1948, only weeks before the Israeli-Arab war started. With the possible exception of a handful of people in South Africa, no Orthodox Trotskyist, in Palestine or outside it, backed the Arabs.

The Palestinian Trotskyists, in a document of January 1948 published by the official Fourth International magazine in June-July 1948, declared: "By its racial war against the Jews of Palestine, the Arab League wants to... prove to imperialism that it is a factor that can serve it even better than Zionism... It is interested in... using this chauvinist war... to crush the Arab working class and all the left groups... to heighten racial hatred against minorities". The June-July introduction to the document denounced the May 1948 invasion and demanded "full national minority rights for the Jewish community".

4. Suez, 1956. Israel and the British-French invasion of Egypt

Egypt was in the vanguard of the Arab-nationalist politics of the Middle East. It had been under British hegemony, with varying legal formulas, for seven decades until an army officers' republican coup d'état in 1952 deposed the King and began to untie the British fetters on the country. Britain withdraw its troops in October 1954. In July 1956 Egypt nationalised the Suez Canal, built and owned by British and French capital. In 1956 Britain still had a grip on both Jordan and Iraq. To Arab nationalists, Israel was the great enemy.

Britain and France invaded Egypt and seized Port Said in November 1956. Their pretext was to stop an Israeli-Egyptian war which, with the collusion of Britain and France, Israel had started a few days earlier. The Egyptian state could not withstand the invaders. But the USA could and did. President Dwight Eisenhower put an end to the British-French-Israeli adventure by withholding credit from Britain and France. Financial weapons were used against the military weapons of the British and French, and they were superior. It was a game-changing moment in the history of post-World-War-Two imperialism.

After seven weeks in occupation of Port Said, the British and French, dollar-whipped, withdrew. The British prime minister, Anthony Eden, was forced out of office. Israel withdrew to its pre-war borders. A United Nations garrison was established at Sharm El Sheikh to keep the peace: it would remain in place until 1967, when Egypt forced it out in preparation for an attack on Israel (which Israel would pre-empt in the Six Day War).

The Trotskyists everywhere condemned the British, the French, and the Israelis. The Trotskyists were strongly on the side of the Arab nationalists, against both the European powers and the Arab kings. None of the Trotskyists drew sweeping condemnations of Israel from its role; certainly no-one yet questioned its right to continue in existence. A small pamphlet, *Stop the War! Hands off the Arab people!*, by Gerry Healy, published at the start of the British-French invasion, encapsulated the mindset, delusions, and historical perspectives of the Orthodox Trotskyists then.

"The Arabs instinctively fear Israel because it is a Capitalist State which they feel is a threat to their desire for freedom... The Imperialists have, in Israel, succeeded in the creation of a state which can lead to a bloody holocaust that will make Hitler's crimes seem a tea party... The Jewish working people everywhere must denounce Israel's stab in the back to the Arab people. The future of Jewry lies through a socialist solution and not through a Capitalist Israel. A socialist solution demands a real solidarity with the Arab people. In Israel this means unity in action against the common Imperialist enemy between the Jewish and Arab poor peasant and working class. Any other road spells a terrible end for Jewry". Healy was cruder than others might have been, but the crudeness has its own value for understanding the processes by way of which Orthodox Trotskyist attitudes to Israel would evolve.

5. The Algerian war of independence

Vietnam in the 1960s came a decade after an earlier shaping experience for the modern left, the Algerian war of liberation against France (1954-62). On that, the revolutionary left tried to exercise political judgement as between two Algerian organisations, the MNA and the FLN, which were engaged in a bloody rivalry. Many backed the "left wing" of the national liberation movement, the MNA, led by Messali Hadj. Messali was understood to have had links with the early Communist International and had support in the Algerian trade union movement and among the many Algerian trade unionists in France. The Independent Socialist League (Shachtman); the Cannon segment of the split Orthodox Trotskyist world movement; the Lambertists in France; the SWP-UK's predecessor Socialist Review; and the Healy group in Britain, which published a pamphlet with a portrait of Messali Hadj on the cover – they all backed Messali, against the more recently emerged and formally more right-wing and purely nationalist FLN. The Pablo-Mandel Orthodox Trotskyists backed the other nationalist organisation, the FLN, the eventual rulers of Algeria. They would spin more explicit fantasies around the FLN once it assumed power in July 1962.

It became known that the MNA was putting up much less of a fight than the FLN, and eventually, around 1958, that in some areas (under tremendous physical pressure from the FLN drive to destroy it) it had arrangements of coexistence with the occupying French forces. There are perhaps parallels with the rival anti-German forces in early-1940s Yugoslavia, Stalinist and Chetnik-Royalist, and with the two IRAs of the 1970s, the Stalinist led "Official Republicans" and the initially right-wing breakaway, the "Provisional IRA". In the polemical war between the different Trotskyists, the Pablo-Mandel group won hands down against the champions of the MNA and Messali. I know of no balance sheet drawn up by any of the Messalists, the pro-MNA Trotskyists. The others never drew adverse conclusions from the fact that after Algerian independence the FLN regime became a quasi-Stalinist state (though one on bad terms with Russia); it eased up after 1989 but by then was also very corrupt.

The anti-imperialist politics that seemed to triumph then, of unconditional solidarity with those leading the anti-imperialist fight irrespective of politics, dominated the left thereafter. This experience was silently fed into the anti Vietnam war movement by Trotskyist groups influenced greatly by their experience over Algeria, and by the IS organisation, the future SWP-UK.

For the Orthodox Trotskyists, Algeria established the absolute supremacy of the idea that the most militant and combative anti-colonial force was the one that deserved backing. The idea that judgements and choices should be made as between the political programs of anti-imperialist forces was seriously discredited.

6. Indochina

One of the greatest of the anti-colonial, and then Stalinist-capitalist, wars of the 20th century began to take shape as World War Two was drawing to its end. France had ruled Indochina since the 1860s. Japan established military bases there from 1940, and took over the administration in March 1945. With the collapse of Japan later in 1945, the British took control, and then handed Vietnam back to France.

An old-style war of colonial conquest and resistance to it between France and the Stalinist-led Viet Minh peasant movement began in 1946 and continued until a great military defeat of the French at Dien Bien Phu in March-May 1954. An internationally brokered agreement signed in Geneva in July 1954 ended the war by dividing the country into the North, a new Stalinist state, and the South, a capitalist state, also independent.

South Vietnam was a typically corrupt bourgeois state of that time and region. Civil war and infiltration by north Vietnamese soldiers started in the early 1960s. The USA got drawn into the war in the belief that if South Vietnam fell to "communism" it would create a domino effect in Thailand, Indonesia, and other countries. Increasingly, it became an American war with North Vietnam to stop Vietnam and the rest of Indochina "going Communist". The US withdraw, defeated, in 1975.

This was now a war not of the old colonial type, but one between the two world systems, capitalism and Stalinism. Unlike the French after 1946, the USA did not want to make Vietnam an old-style colony. The social and political program of those fighting the USA, and their state in North Vietnam, were those of a typical Stalinist totalitarian movement.

From 1965, the ending of certain draft exemptions for some students lit the fuse for a great explosion of protest against the American war in the USA, and then in other capitalist countries. Vietnam was the first war from which TV cameras nightly beamed terrible images, uncensored, into living rooms all over the world. People responded with proper horror and unqualified hostility to the USA and its war.

Orthodox Trotskyist critics had believed that the Geneva deal in 1954 had been a Stalinist "sell-out", and that the Stalinists could have taken all of Vietnam for "the revolution" if they had not, under USSR pressure, made peace. They supported the anti-war movement and took centre place in organising mass demonstrations in a number of countries, including the USA and Britain.

The US ruling-class opponents of Stalinism were willing in Indochina to "destroy it in order to save it" (as one American commander infamously said of a Vietnamese city). The Orthodox Trotskyists were right to oppose the Americans in Indochina and to support self-determination for the peoples there. The political tragedy in Indochina was that the Stalinists had won the support of so many people; but the American alternative was worse than victory for Stalinism. No cause could justify what the Americans were doing to the peoples of Vietnam, and eventually Cambodia and Laos, inflicting on them the heaviest bombing operations in world history.

But the Orthodox Trotskyists, and others, as in Korea after 1950, failed to tell the full story.† They told the story as a simple one of im-

---

† In the USA, the fact that victory against the USA would also be victory for expanding Stalinism led some generally respect-worthy socialists, in the first place Max Shachtman, effectively to side with the American government against both the Vietnamese Stalinists and the anti-war movement. Their thought was that Stalinist victory in Vietnam would cauterise the country politically, wipe out the possibility of a labour movement developing there, and thus extinguish all possibility of socialism, as anti-Stalinist Marxists understood it. Although their stand discredited Shachtman and his comrades, and their concerns were dismissed with contempt by typical leftists of that period, those concerns were not contemptible. Since about 1947, the Heterodox Trotskyists of the Workers Party/ISL had abandoned Trotsky's idea – which most of them had maintained in the early 1940s despite deciding that Russia was a new form of class society – that the USSR was historically unviable. Shachtman came to see it as a viable alternative to capitalism – indeed, to believe that it was winning in the competition with capitalism and inevitably would win if a working-class socialist revolution did not in good time replace capitalism. The battle between socialism and the looming threat of world Stalinism was what the old slogan "socialism or barbarism" now meant. If Shachtman was "revisionist" vis a vis Trotsky and the Marxist tradition upon which he stood, it was here not in seeing the USSR as a new class society, but in seeing it as able to defeat capitalism by competition from its periphery. (Trotsky in 1939 had rejected the idea that to consider "the system of 'bureaucratic collectivism' as a theoretical possibility" was "a complete revision of Marxism". "This is an apparent misunderstanding", Trotsky responded. "The Marxist comprehension of historical necessity has nothing in common with fatalism" – Again and Once More on the Nature of the USSR, October 1939).

perialism and anti-imperialism, of war between good and evil, between "the people" and the great technology-heavy American imperialist slaughter machine. It was that; but that Stalinist victory would be a victory for totalitarianism was also part of reality and its possibilities, though no part of the Orthodox Trotskyists' picture. †† It was the same approach as in Korea. By now, the Orthodox Trotskyists had got used to the idea of Stalinist-controlled anti-colonial revolutions.

In Britain the revolutionary left emphasised our all-out anti-imperialism – in contrast to those like the Communist Party who wanted "negotiations" – with the slogan "Victory to the NLF". The whole anti-war movement of the late 1960s and early 70s, even when it criticised the USSR, as it did, for not doing more for North Vietnam, was saturated with illusions in Stalinism, at least in those Stalinists who "made revolutions". The Orthodox Trotskyists, like the Stalinists, believed that victory over imperialism was identical to defending and expanding the Vietnamese "socialist" or "deformed workers'" state. Most of the Orthodox Trotskyists did not advocate a working-class revolution against the North Vietnamese regime. They did not believe that a "political revolution" was necessary there as in the USSR and the East European Stalinist states.

In the Orthodox Trotskyist left †††, reshaped by opposition to the Vietnam war, reinvigorated by "1968" and the big influx of politically raw new young activists around that time, there was always a powerful strain of reactionary anti-imperialism. The Vietnam campaigns were a redefining experience, saturated as they were with expecta-

---

†† *Vietnam was one of only three countries in which a mass Trotskyist party had been built (Ceylon/ Sri Lanka and Bolivia were the others). In the mid 1940s the Trotskyist organisation had much working-class support in Saigon. Politically, they opposed the British and then the return of the French, while for a period the Viet Minh, for reasons of international Stalinist realpolitik, muted their "anti-imperialism". In 1946 the Stalinists killed hundreds of Trotskyists, the cadres of the movement, and effectively wiped it out. A similar massacre occurred in Greece around the same time.*

††† *This writer amongst them, too. The predecessors of AWL did argue that a new anti-Stalinist "political" revolution was necessary in North Vietnam. When the Stalinists won in 1975, we immediately wrote: "The new regime in South Vietnam will not be a revolutionary workers' democracy. Far from it. Any forces in South Vietnam fighting for such a program will find the regime an enemy rather than an ally" (Workers' Fight 95, 3 May 1975). But we too let anti-imperialist militancy determine our operational politics on Indochina. Even those of us who knew and were troubled by the fact that a NLF Vietnam would be a totalitarian Stalinist Vietnam emphasised our militant anti-imperialism by sloganistically siding with the Stalinist political movement. Anti-imperialism and militancy came first in our hierarchy of political values. We were gripped in a massive contradiction, with our anti-Stalinism and our simultaneous militant siding with Stalinist anti-imperialism.*

tions for the victory of the socialist revolution, soon, across the world. For the Orthodox Trotskyist ancestors of the present left, there was much of political indifferentism about Stalinism: "don't confuse my anti-imperialism with your complexities".

7. Israel, the left, and the 1967 Six Days War

On 5-10 June 1967, in six days, Israel defeated Egypt, Jordan, and Syria. The Egyptian government had been threatening war against Israel; on 19 May it had expelled UN forces from Sinai and Gaza (there since the war of 1956); and on 22-23 May it had closed the straits of Aqaba connecting Israel to the Red Sea.

Israel struck first, and suddenly, destroying the Egyptian, Jordanian, and Syrian air forces on the ground and quickly overrunning and occupying Jordan's West Bank, Egypt's Gaza, and Syria's Golan Heights. Militarily, it was a tremendous coup. The pre-1948 entity of Palestine was reunited, but under Israeli control and with the area designated for a Palestinian state in 1947 becoming effectively a colony of Israel.

On 19 June Israel proposed a general peace agreement to the Arab states; Israel would evacuate the occupied territory except the Syrian Golan Heights and East Jerusalem in return for recognition by the Arab states and "normalisation" of their relations with Israel. None of the Arab states recognised Israel, or had diplomatic relations with it. In September a conference of Arab states resolved that there would be "no peace, no recognition and no negotiation with Israel". Things again settled into a tense armistice that would last until October 1973.

On the Jewish festival of Yom Kippur, October 1973, Egypt and Syria suddenly struck against Israel. Israel was taken by surprise. Egyptian forces advanced quickly, and for a while it looked as if Israel might be overwhelmed. Israel rallied, and the Egyptians and Syrians were driven back. Five years later Israel and Egypt would sign a peace agreement. Egypt recognised Israel, and Jordan would follow in 1994. Even today they are the only Arab states to have recognised Israel.

1967 was the start of, so far, 50 years of Israeli colonial rule over the Palestinians of the West Bank. In 1967, the international left was vehemently pro-Arab and consequently anti-Israel – "Israeli-defeatist". Though the Orthodox Trotskyists did not necessarily understand that, this "defeatism" could not be what socialist "defeatism" had been in say, Britain, or France, or the USA in World War One. Defeat for those states did not mean destruction of the country and the society. Defeat for the tiny land of Israel would necessarily mean that, unless there was speedy outside intervention on Israel's side.

The general attitude of the left before June 1967 was broadly summed up in the formula of the Pablo-Mandel Fourth International: for a socialist federation of the Middle East with full autonomy for national minorities such as the Kurds and the Israeli Jews. In fact defeatism for Israel in 1967 already contradicted that. Autonomy after Arab conquest begged the question: what would be left to be "autonomous"? And why would the victorious Arabs want to make terms with a defeated and conquered Israel? The 1967 and post-1967 line emerged straight out of the left's belief in the "Arab Revolution" as part of the "colonial revolution" – the colonial revolution that was also, for the Orthodox Trotskyists, a possible socialist revolution and certainly part of the struggle of the two great power blocs in the world, US "imperialism" against Russia and China, designated as non-imperialist. †

It was the time of the great demonstrations against the Vietnam war in cities across the world. The habit of intense and uncritical partisanship for Vietnam which had established itself, and of editing out such details as the NLF's Stalinism, spread to other issues, and to Israel and the Arabs. Vietnam had made "anti-imperialism" the defining characteristic of the putative left. The movement against the Vietnam war brought a new generation into left-wing politics, but it was also a great political school teaching support for revolutionary

---

† *We have seen that for Gerry Healy in 1956, the Arabs were already socialist and anti-capitalist. By 1967, in response to events, that idea had spread widely. The precise "class character" of the leading Arab nationalist states was in dispute among Orthodox Trotskyists. Ted Grant of the Militant (now the CWI, then the Revolutionary Socialist League and the British section of the Mandel Fourth International) had pronounced in mid 1965 that Syria was a deformed workers' state, like the Stalinist states in Eastern Europe, China, etc., though Syria was ruled not by Stalinists but by the Ba'th party in symbiotic partnership with the military caste. Burma, so Grant thought, was also a deformed workers' state. There were others in the Fourth International who came very close to arguing that Nasser's Egypt was a workers' state. In 1965, the Mandelite Livio Maitan wrote that a workers' state could "emerge" in Egypt "in a relatively cold way, without the active revolutionary intervention of the masses at the crucial moment of the qualitative leap" (Hansen, The Workers' and Farmers' Government, Education for Socialists bulletin 1974, p.6). In Egypt the Nasserist state had expropriated the bourgeoisie, leaving them a stock exchange on which to trade the entitlements given them in compensation. The difference inside the Fourth International was between those who asserted that the Egyptian state, as it was, could become a deformed workers' state without upheavals, and those who argued that for that to happen there would have to be a "mobilisation of the masses" of some sort.*

Stalinism. It made "anti-imperialism", identified as anti-American-ism, an absolute value, the great measure of opposition to all the evils of the capitalist world. Much of the way the left related to Israel in 1967, at the time of the Six Day War and the occupation of the West Bank and Gaza, was on the same "anti-imperialist" pattern, with the Arab states in place of the Vietnamese and the Israelis as the imperi-alist embodiment of all that was bad. No part of the blame for the plight of the Palestinians was allowed to lie with the Arab states who rejected Israel's offer to withdraw from the West Bank and Gaza in return for Arab recognition of Israel, and who had kept the Palestini-ans ghettoised in refugee camps as a political hard fact to use against Israel. Israel was seen as the antagonist of the Arab Revolution, of its "permanent-revolutionary" workers' state reality or potential, and of the Russian bloc with which Egypt and Syria had friendly and col-laborative relations. The Egyptian Communist Party had dissolved into the Nasserist state-apparatus "party". Israel was also seen as the ally of the reactionary forces in the Arab world – the sheikhs and Saudi Arabia – which were closer to the USA. It was in that context, as part of that world viewpoint, that "revolutionary perspective", that a new attitude to Israel was worked out.

In 1967 and immediately after the Trotskyists did not declare for the destruction of Israel. They called upon Israel to evacuate the Arab territories seized in the Six Day war. The Palestine Liberation Organ-isation in the build-up to the 1967 war had been under the effective control of Egypt and fronted by Ahmed Shukeiri, still shouting as in 1948 about "driving the Jews into the sea". The PLO became a far more independent and politically sophisticated body in the wake of the defeat of the Arab states. In 1969 the PLO raised a new program-matic slogan, for a secular democratic state in all pre-1948 Palestine, with religious rights for Jews. This could be seen, and was widely seen, as a reasonable proposal to Israel. In fact it was used as an an-swer, an alternative, to the Israelis' offer of land for peace. But the new proposal could only "work" if Israel voluntarily agreed to dis-solve its state into a common entity with its antagonists and enemies of the previous half-century. There was never a possibility that Israel would do that. In practice, "secular democratic state" implied the conquest of Israel and the destruction of Hebrew self-determination.

Many who started off favouring the "secular democratic state" for its seeming reasonableness, its desirability, its seeming allocation of something like equal rights (though not national rights) to Jews, eas-ily evolved to favouring the conquest of an unreasonable Israel in order to win that "secular democratic state". Secular democratic state" was a variant, or close relative to, the old policy of the Arab states, finessed into a semblance of reasonableness and acceptability for those who did not start out hostile to Israel or Jews as such. That was the policy which for Orthodox Trotskyists replaced commitment to "autonomy" for the Israeli Jews. It was a policy unique, unprecedented: that the Israeli state should abolish itself, or, failing that, be abolished by force and conquest which should be backed, morally and politically, by the anti-imperialist left.

You could, and many of us did, choose not to see that the "conquest of Israel" was implied by the "secular democratic state". Faced with Israel's often brutal colonial rule in the West Bank and Gaza, and the stalemate between Israel and the Arab states, the "anti-imperialist" left turned into an advocate, in effect, of the conquest and wiping out of a nation which was deemed unworthy of existence because of its so-recent origins and its ill-treatment of the Palestinians in the occupied territories. Yet the situation in the West Bank and Gaza was shaped after the June 1967 war, as after 1948, at least as much by the intransigence of the Arab states – Arab states within some of which Palestinian refugees were kept in limbo as refugees by refusal to let them work or gain citizenship – as by any Israeli policy at that stage to annex the West Bank. †

After the Israeli victory in 1967, Israel formed close ties to the USA (for the first time), and the whole question became part of the general opposition to world "imperialism" whose traits and characteristics have been explored above. Thus by the time of the Yom Kippur war of 1973 the left was uninhibited and full-throttle for Egyptian victory and the defeat and destruction of Israel.

8. Cambodia

The Stalinist-but-also-very-strange Khmer Rouge had fought their way to control of Cambodia by April 1975. American bombing had

---

† *The greatest atrocity against the Palestinians driven out or fleeing in fear in 1948 was the Arab states' refusal to let them build normal lives where they now lived. The greatest massacres of Palestinians were also the work of Arab states or factions: Jordan, Syria, and the Lebanese Maronites in 1982. Three quarters of a million Palestinians were refugees in 1948. A big part of that three-quarters of a million will, in the course of nature, be no longer alive 70 years later. The assertion, commonplace today, that there are six million Palestinian refugees is a straight ideologically-tailored lie. It relies on the idea that the grandparents (or in some cases great-grandparents) of people scattered across many countries can pass on to them a right that is greater than the rights of Israeli Jews to go on living where they and their parents and in many cases their grandparents were born and have lived their lives.*

done tremendous damage to the country and its people. But by Orthodox Trotskyist reckoning Cambodia was now, or was becoming, a deformed workers' state, paralleling the expansion of the Vietnamese Stalinists to control of all Vietnam.

The Khmer Rouge were social engineers, social sculptors in the Stalin and Mao tradition, willing to use mass murder to reshape the population of Cambodia. One of the first things the new rulers did was to empty the cities, driving the people out into the countryside. By systematic terror and starvation they imposed a horrendous grip on the people, killing vast numbers in the process. They worked systematically to kill off certain segments of the population, the intellectuals and even the literate, as well as members of the old ruling classes.

In the Khmer Rouge's Nazi-like policy of killing off whole categories of the country's people, around 1.7 million people died, over one-fifth of the whole population. Their rule was brought to an end by a Vietnamese invasion in early 1979. The Khmer Rouge were driven back into the forests, where they fought on for years. Long after the truth about their regime had become widely known, the Khmer Rouge continued to receive backing from the US and the UK under Margaret Thatcher, for whom the main enemy was the Vietnamese allies of the USSR.

Like the Khomeiny revolution and its reactionary horrors in Iran, the Cambodian revolution and its worse horrors posed hard to-be-or-not-to-be questions for those who had supported the Khmer Rouge against the Americans. Was this unspeakable Nazi-like regime, which had emerged from the revolution whose supporters had marched through the streets of Europe and America, a deformed workers' state, like Vietnam and China – or what was it?

The SWP-USA and its co-thinkers in the Fourth International pronounced that Cambodia was no deformed workers' state. The Mandel segment of the Fourth International said yes, it was; and even though the Vietnamese invasion put an end to the mass murder, they deplored it: war between two workers' states! Others argued that Cambodia was a Stalinist state, essentially in its basic nature like Mao's China and Stalin's Russia. Those who said yes, it was, if China was, thereby faced up to the general issue posed by the Cambodian reality. Those who said it wasn't, tried to duck the issue. The Chinese Maoists had committed atrocities against the people of China, in the cause of social engineering, no different in principle from what the Khmer Rouge did. Tens of millions had died in senseless social and economic experiments imposed by force on the people, for example the Great Leap Forward after 1958. The Khmer Rouge terror was in principle an intensified, speeded-up version of the Great Leap Forward and of previous Stalinist deeds such as the USSR's forced collectivisation in 1929-33. Three million or more Ukrainians had died in that piece of social engineering by way of the bayonet and mass starvation.

Yet the Khmer Rouge's grotesque revolution did not inhibit us from hurray-ing for the Khomeiny clerical-fascist revolution only a little later. The attitude to the Khomeinyists and their mass of followers was a straight transcription from the policy of supporting revolutionary Stalinists. Cambodia sobered some anti-imperialists on the left; but the world enthusiasm for the Khomeiny revolution showed how small an impact it made.

9. Iran: the counter-revolutionary revolution

The alliance of the kitsch left with Islamic clerical fascists since 2001 is a continuation of the way the left related to the clerical fascists in Iran in 1978-9. The Iranian revolution of January 1979 was a major event in world history and in the formation of the present-day left. It faced left anti-imperialists with the stark fact of a reactionary revolution, more akin to the Nazi "revolution" of 1933 and after than to a progressive anti-imperialist overturn.

The USSR, in partnership with Britain, had occupied the northern part of Iran from August 1941 to May 1946. Britain, occupying the south, had withdrawn in March 1946; at first the USSR refused, and it withdrew only under heavy international and especially American pressure. There was an Iranian Stalinist party, the Tudeh party.

In 1953 the Shah of Iran was returned to full power by a CIA-helped coup against a reforming nationalist prime minister, Mohammad Mosaddegh. Between 1953 and the fall of the Shah in 1979, the state, an adamantine military-police dictatorship, did much to modernise the country. It was socially progressive on such issues as women's emancipation from Islamic restrictions. It developed close ties and military alliances with the USA.

The Shah's regime, which had its own reasons for conflict with Arab regimes, collaborated with Israel. It was the sub-imperialism of its region, intervening militarily for example in Oman (1972-5). As in other countries, before and after that, modernisation bred religious reaction, and a melding of that religious reaction with social discontent. By the mid 1970s, the religious reaction was a growing force, led by the Islamic clergy. Organised hierarchically, the Shia clergy were in effect a structured religio-political Islamic party.

Mass rebellion raged through 1978, involving many millions. It included large working-class actions. Some women, in their traditional religious garb, were prominent. The insurgents said that they advocated democracy against the military-police dictatorship. They did, but they didn't, or their decisive leaders didn't, mean by it what ignorant well-wishers wanted them to mean. By "democracy" they meant giving control to the mullahs and their Islamist mass movement.

There was a vast wave of sympathy and support outside Iran for the anti-Shah revolutionary movement. It was anti-imperialist and anti-West. Many currents combined in that movement. Democrats rebelling against dictatorship tended to cast the Shah as embodying dictatorship, and the mass movement hegemonised by political Islam as representing democracy. †

Stalinists and Orthodox Trotskyists saw the movement as directed against the Shah's western alliances and therefore to the benefit of the "defence of the USSR". Among some Orthodox Trotskyists, politics had become so hazy and unfocused that they hoped that "the Iranian revolution" would go beyond capitalism and inaugurate a socialist Iran. The great swirling movements of millions of roused-up people – demonstrations, strikes, mass meetings – were an intoxicating spectacle to see and respond to, especially for revolutionaries who had learned not to ask awkward questions of any revolution that presented itself for their consideration. †† The Orthodox Trotskyists had first, in the 1940s, reluctantly accepted Stalinist revolutions that created economic equivalents to the USSR. Then there was active support for the North Koreans, and more-or-less uncritical support for the Vietnamese and Cambodian Stalinists. Now there was great enthusiasm for a clerical-fascist-installing revolution as a movement which might evolve to, or engender, socialist revolution. It would be hard to invent a starker expression of profound political and historical disorientation.

The movement, decisively led and controlled by organised Islamic clerical fascists, soon showed itself in power for what it was: repressive Islamic totalitarianism, and the large-scale murder of others in

---

† The forerunner of the AWL took that attitude too, though there was opposition inside the organisation to the group's support for the Islamist movement.
†† The secretary of the British Mandelites (IMG), Brian Grogan, visited Iran and enthusiastically joined in the chants of "Allahu Akhbar" (Grogan, Insurrection in Teheran: An Eyewitness Report, 1979, p.2) When the Fourth International fragmented and the IMG broke apart in 1985, he would become an SWP-US-backing Castroite.

Iran who had taken part in the mobilisations against the Shah. Iranian women were driven out of many jobs and forced to wear Islamic religious garb: they were thrown back many decades. So, in general, was Iranian society. This was a revolution – it rose against an unpopular regime and replaced it – but a profoundly reactionary and socially regressive revolution. Backing that revolution was not much better than backing Hitler's "German liberation" (from Versailles) would have been in 1933.† (The German Stalinists, of course, had backed the Nazi Germany-needs-to-be-liberated line before 1933).

Clerical-fascist Iran was a vast encouragement to political Islam everywhere. Nearly four decades later the clerical fascists still run Iran, and the international reverberations of the Iranian revolution are still thundering around the world.

10. The Iran-Iraq war, 1980 to 1988

In 1980 Iraq seized the chance offered by the turmoil created by the Islamic revolution there to invade Iran. This was a war between two regional "strong powers", between Shia (Iranian) and Sunni (Iraqi) Islam, and between a theocratic Iran and the quasi-secular militarist sub-imperialism in Iraq. It was, like the First World War, though it lasted twice as long, a war of prolonged stalemate, with trench warfare, poison gas, and enormous casualties, maybe as many as a million.

The Orthodox Trotskyists, with the exception of the forerunner of the AWL, sided with "the Iranian revolution" against the Iraqi invaders. In a war of two regional imperialists, that meant backing the one embodying a clerical-fascism against a quasi-secularist one. The SWP-UK was in the same political territory as AWL until 1987, when they came out in support of Iran, explaining their change after almost seven years of war by the discovery that Iraq had some degree of US backing...

11. The Russian invasion of Afghanistan

Afghanistan's Stalinist "Great Saur Revolution", in April 1978, and the Russian invasion of Afghanistan that flowed from it 20 months

---

† *During the Hitler-Stalin pact, some Stalinists, Rajani Palme Dutt in Britain for instance, began to reconsider Germany in the light shed on it by its "capitulation", as they saw it, to the USSR. It was even true that there were "left-wing", anti-bourgeois Nazis, such as Gregor Strasser, who wanted to go on to a "second revolution". They were slaughtered in Hitler's "Night of the Long Knives", June-July 1934.*

later, at Christmas 1979, were two of the most important events of the second half of the 20th century. The invasion led to the so-named Second Cold War. Their failure to subjugate Afghanistan in a nine-year colonial war was one of the things that shattered the self-confidence of the Russian Stalinist bureaucracy, and contributed to its downfall.

The April 1978 revolution was a freakish event – an army and air force officers' coup controlled by the People's Democratic Party, the Afghan Stalinist party. † The PDP was itself a tiny town-based middle-class organisation with perhaps as few as two thousand members, but in any case only a few thousand, in a country then reckoned at about 18 million people. The symbiosis between the PDP and the Air Force and Army officers was like that between the Ba'th and the Syrian and Iraqi armies. It had came into existence in the previous quarter century, during which Russia had equipped and trained the Afghan air force and army officers. Afghanistan's neighbour and rival, Pakistan, had the patronage of the USA. These army and air force officers took the USSR as their model for modernising Afghanistan. It was a coup, not a revolution, not even a Stalinist-style revolution, that they made in April 1978. In China, Vietnam, Yugoslavia, Stalinist revolutions had been led by organisations at the head of mass movements. The PDP had no such base. It had only the officer corps. The army and air force soldiers in these organisations obeyed the officers in the traditional military discipline of command and obedience. The military hierarchies remained intact.

A gap of centuries of social and intellectual development divided the towns and their educated elites from rural Afghanistan. Having very small support in rural Afghanistan, the new regime had only force to rely on. They used military and airborne terror to enforce revolutionary decrees for which there was little or no support in rural Afghanistan – land reform, for a surprising example. Within a couple of months of the coup, the regime was at war with much of rural Afghanistan, and soon with almost all of it. The Stalinists in power found themselves using the typical techniques of colonial war against the people they were trying to force-march into the 20th century. Villages were napalm-bombed, crops destroyed in the fields. By the end, an estimated six million people, one third of the population in 1978, had been killed or driven over the borders into Pakistan and Iran.

The PDP had been divided between two very hostile factions, Khalq and Parcham. They united under Russian pressure to make

† *See accounts at http://archive.workersliberty.org/wlmags/wl102/Afghanistan.htm and http://www.workersliberty.org/taxonomy/term/1352*

the coup. But not for long. Soon the Stalinists in power started killing each other. Within a year of the coup so many officers had been killed or jailed that a large number of Russian air force pilots had to be brought in so that the air force could continue to function. Russian pressure to take things more slowly had no effect on the ruling faction, Khalq.

Their policy was to slug it out with the peoples of Afghanistan. By that time they probably had little other choice if they were not to let themselves go down before the hostility of rural Afghanistan. Russia invaded at Christmas 1979, shot the leaders in power, had the leaders they put in their place retrospectively invite them to invade Afghanistan, and got bogged down in the last great colonial war of the 20th century – Russia's Vietnam war.

What attitude should socialists take to the Russian annexation of Afghanistan? This question immediately divided the international left. All the "Orthodox Trotskyist" organisations † either backed the invasion enthusiastically or took the line that, the Russians being there, they could not now condemn the invaders or call upon them to withdraw. This was an offprint of what the Trotskyists had said about Russia's occupation of part of Poland (the Nazis occupying the rest) 40 years earlier, in 1939, in a radically different world. After six months or a year many of the Orthodox Trotskyists sobered up and stopped supporting Russia's colonial war. Others †† backed Russia through a decade of savage colonial war in Afghanistan. A lot of labour movement people, including some Labour MPs, backed Russia in Afghanistan. An odd thing in the response of the ostensible left

---

† *Except what is now AWL. The invasion of Czechoslovakia had been widely condemned in the West, and Russian Stalinism had been discredited. That situation had prevailed until Afghanistan precipitated the so-named Second Cold War, a new upsurge of anti-American "anti-imperialism" on the left, and a new crop of delusions that Russia was connected to socialist revolution.*

One of the rowdiest labour movement meetings I've ever attended was a debate I had in Edinburgh soon after the Russian invasion with a pro-USSR Labour MP, Ron Brown. It was a Saturday afternoon at the end of some miners' gala or conference, and a big proportion of the large meeting were miners, many of them bevvied-up. The meeting was overwhelmingly pro-Russian and very hostile to those who denounced Russia's invasion of Afghanistan. Most of them would have been Labour Party people. To the loud approval of much of the meeting Brown praised the Russian leaders for sending tanks to Kabul. I attracted fierce abuse and much interruption when I argued that we should condemn the invasion and call on the Russians to get out of Afghanistan. "The Yanks are against the Russians, so is Margaret Thatcher, so is the CIA – and so are you".

†† Militant (now Socialist Party/ Socialist Appeal), the Spartacist Tendency, Workers Power...

to the invasion was that, in contrast to the Orthodox Trotskyists, some Communist parties refused to back the Russians. For example, the Communist Party of Great Britain condemned the invasion. Jack Woddis published factually honest accounts of what was happening in Afghanistan, and condemned it. These were Stalinists turning themselves into bourgeois liberals, but they had learned something from their experience, and in this case behaved as serious political people.

One consequence of the invasion and the second Cold War which it triggered was that many leftists were driven by the logic of their position on Russia and other Stalinist states to rally to Russia. Since the invasion of Czechoslovakia in 1968, Russia had been in bad odour on the left – even the British Communist Party had criticised it then – but now that changed for many Trotskyists and others. In the eyes of some Trotskyists, the fact of the invasion of Afghanistan itself spoke for Russia – it had "gone to the aid of a revolution". In the world polarisation, Orthodox Trotskyists rallied to what they saw as the "working-class camp", at the heart of which was Russia.

12. The Falklands war and the breakthrough to full-fantasy anti-imperialism

A major experience in the formation of today's addled left "anti-imperialism" was the British-Argentine war of 1982 over the Falkland Islands. This minor event, in world-political terms, generated an "anti-imperialism" based entirely (not almost entirely – entirely, exclusively, 105%) on fantasy and strange and ridiculous constructions on events. It was element-pure fantasy anti-imperialism: none of those involved, not even the UK, was in reality playing the role ascribed to it in the gammy-left fantasy-scenario.

The war was a freak event. It was part of no larger conflict; no issue other than possession of the islands was involved. Both Argentina and Britain were bourgeois states. Argentina was a regional sub-imperialism. Neither of them oppressed the other. Neither of them was trying to conquer the other, or likely to, as a result of the war. The Falklands Islands were not a base from which Britain oppressed others in the region, and never had been that. The only issue between Britain and Argentina, the cause of the war, was the fate of the Falklands Islands and their inhabitants.

Any Argentine claim to the Falklands can be based only on relative geographical proximity (about 400 miles across the South Atlantic). Any historic claim rests on the brief possession of the then long-uninhabited islands for a few years (1829-33) by modern Argentina's ancestor state. Argentine possession of the islands in 1982 would "liberate" the people who lived there, who were and are by their own choice British in language, culture, and identity, from self-determination: it would liberate nothing and no-one else. It would not indirectly liberate peoples against whom the islands were being used as a base for hostile British operations: there were no such operations, and never had been. There may be oil riches in the seas surrounding the islands, but no serious plans exist to exploit them.

The war opened with an Argentine invasion, that is, by the seizure of the islands by a regional sub-imperialist state. The faltering military junta that ruled Argentina invaded when they did and as they did in an effort to annex to their regime the forces of Peronist chauvinism (which included a vocal element of 1940s-style antisemitism, issuing slogans like "Kill a Jew a day"). A transfer of sovereignty over the Falklands (for Argentina, the Malvinas) from Britain to Argentina might have been negotiated, on the basis of some sort of continued Falkland Islanders' self-rule, on the model of Hong Kong, perhaps. The sudden invasion and seizure ruled that out. It was a political ploy to boost the junta, and an act of unilateral imperialist-style brutality against the conquered islanders.

Thatcher's Britain went to war briefly to regain control of the islands. Some on the left, including the majority of the AWL's predecessor, opposed Britain's war but naturally refused to take sides with Argentina. That time round, the SWP-UK was on the side of rational politics (and Militant/ SP confirmed its place at the head of all other contenders in the annals of kitsch-Trotskyist absurdity and bizarrity by proposing, instead of the war, an immediate socialist federation of Britain, the Falklands, and Argentina).

The main forces of Orthodox Trotskyism, in the first place the Fourth International then combining those around Ernest Mandel with those around the SWP-USA, reacted with extravagant proclamations that an "anti-imperialist" war of liberation was being waged by Argentina against British imperialism. In Argentina, the biggest left organisation, the "Morenist" PST, tried to ride the chauvinist wave by full-voiced support for the junta's military adventure. The basic criterion for authentic anti-imperialism – some element of the liberation of peoples, and the winning by them of democratic rights to self-determination – was entirely absent. Indeed, Argentina was depriving the Falklanders of self-determination.

It was the time of the so-called "Second Cold War", triggered by Russia's invasion of Afghanistan in December 1979, and many social-

169

ists experienced the world as an intense polarisation between "anti-imperialist" and imperialist "camps". They wrote the regional-imperialist enterprise of the fascistic Argentina junta into the script as an imagined anti-imperialist action that was going on nowhere outside their heads.

The scenario which the would-be Trotskyist supporters of Argentina wrote about the South Atlantic war had nothing to do with what was happening in the world around them. The fact that they were knowingly falsifying reality was neatly summed up in their reportage. The Fourth International press, trying to prove the correctness of a political line from its popularity with the Argentine "masses", reported on a gigantic demonstration in Buenos Aires in support of the seizure of the Falklands and the subsequent war with Britain. The vast demonstration, the Fourth International press told its trusting readers, as if that settled all debate, had chanted "Malvinas Argentinas". You had to go to the serious bourgeois press, *The Economist* for example, to get a proper report of the demonstration and its slogans. There had been chants of "Malvinas Argentinas", but also, as the second part of the chant, "The people are Peron's".

This "anti-imperialism" was such a nonsense that it could not tolerate, without collapsing, even accurate reporting. The whole episode was a piece of pseudo-politics, pseudo-anti-imperialism, with the self-aggrandising Argentine regional imperialism cast in the role of the anti-imperialist which it was nowhere near being, in the Falklands or anywhere else. It was pure unalloyed fantasy. † Irresponsible fantasy that testified to political bankruptcy.

13. Serbia's war on Kosova and NATO's war on Serbia, 1999

The SWP had been on the sane side of left-wing politics in the Falklands war of 1982. In 1987 they made a lurch towards kitsch-left anti-imperialism. That was the beginning of a new era for them.

The keynote was struck by their announcement that now, seven years into the Iran-Iraq war, they were switching to support for Iran, because the USA favoured Iraq.

---

† *The minority in the AWL's predecessor organisation, led by Alan Thornett, now a member of the Mandelite Fourth International, declared that Argentina was in "our", the USSR-led, "class camp", and advocated an "Argentine defencism" that ruled out hostile working-class action against the junta so long as Argentina was at war with Britain. It was self-indulgent make-belief. It was possible for the Thornettites to say what they said because they didn't know the ABCs of the politics they dogmatised about and, at root, didn't care.*

The confusionist politics of the would-be left on "imperialism" stretches way back, and, as we've seen, is rooted in the selective anti-imperialism of the Stalinist movement and in the Orthodox Trotskyist method of purely negative anti-imperialism, ignoring the question of what, positively, was being supported. But something new emerged during the Balkans war of 1999.

When NATO bombed Serbia to stop a drive to kill or drive out Kosova's ethnic Albanian people (93% of its population), most of the left did not just refuse to endorse NATO (as AWL did), but positively backed Serbia. To see Serbia as "anti-imperialist" was as pure a piece of fantasy as it had been to see Argentina's war over the Falklands as anti-imperialism. But here the fantasy involved siding with an active imperialism, or sub-imperialism, and, implicitly, with what it was doing in Kosova. It was not comic-opera nonsense, as supporting "anti-imperialist" Argentina had been, but full, all-out partisanship for a regional imperialism attempting genocide in Serbia's colony, Kosova. It was the immediate prelude to the ostensible left's alliance with political Islam after 9/11. By way of campaigning "against the war", NATO's war, and "against imperialism", that is against the NATO powers, making a police-action war to stop genocide in Kosova, the kitsch left actively sided with the primitive Serb ethno-imperialism of Slobodan Milosevic and worked to whip up an "anti-war movement" in support of those engaged in a war to kill or drive out the Albanian population of Serbia's colony, Kosova.

Some did this because they had not quite got rid of the idea that the Milosevic regime, the most Stalinist of all the successor regimes in the former Stalinist states, was somehow "still" progressive, or even "still" socialist. (For instance, Arthur Scargill's Socialist Labour Party talked about the regime's "workers' state" tradition). Others – the SWP-UK – simply thought that a big anti-war movement on any basis would rouse young people to action and thus help build up the forces of the SWP. So the British crowd came in response to their demagogic agitation, they cared not what came to the Kosovar Albanians... Yet others were one-sided pacifists, or old style Neanderthal anti-Germans, like for example Tony Benn.

They spent the war re-enacting a foolish parody of the Stalinist antics that had over decades destroyed independent working-class politics and corrupted the collective mind of the ostensible left. The state of the British left at the start of the 21st century was most terribly depicted in the demagogic, one-sidedly pacifistic "anti-imperialism" which it deployed to build that pro-Milosevic "stop the war" movement in April-June 1999. The central "demand" of the anti-war move-

171

ment of 1999 was for NATO to stop the war before it had secured its immediate objective of forcing the Serbs in Kosova to desist and withdraw their troops. Translated into real-political-world terms, that meant: let the Serbs get on with it!

14. Afghanistan, 2001

In 2001, after the 9/11 Al Qaeda attacks in the USA, the USA and Britain invaded Afghanistan, which was harbouring Al Qaeda terrorists and refused to repress them or hand them over to the USA. The left, including AWL, opposed the invasion and the US war that followed. Many on the left went further, giving explicit or implicit support to the Taliban. *Socialist Worker* undertook even to defend the Taliban's treatment of women. The Taliban forced women into seclusion only "as a means of protecting them", because they "feared that their soldiers would behave as some previous mujahedeen groups had on taking a city" (SW, 6 October 2001). The SWP had also refused to condemn the attacks on New York on 11 September 2001. Those attacks had been, so they implied, good or at least well-intentioned anti-imperialism. They would develop such notions until they overshadowed and reshaped everything for them.

15. The Iraq anti-war (and anti-Israel) movement

Three years after the Balkans war, the same people in Britain who had backed genocidal Serbian imperialism in Kosova recycled their "Stop the War Coalition" and expanded it. The Iraq anti-war movement of 2002-3 consisted of a number of very large demonstrations. Vast numbers of people came out, † to proclaim that they did not want the invasion or occupation of Iraq. A smaller number came out to protest against Israel in the Israel-Hezbollah war of August 2006.

The ongoing campaign, between demonstrations and long after they had passed, consisted of a group of people with politics that were not necessarily those of the marchers: the Communist Party of Britain, the Socialist Workers Party, the Muslim Association of Britain (which proudly proclaimed its links to the Muslim Brotherhood), George Galloway, and others. These gave the campaign its slogans and rallying cries and, so to speak, constituted the face and voice of the anti-war movement. They also (the SWP mainly) provided the many thousands of placards, with their chosen slogans, distributed

---

† *As, of course, did the AWL.*

to marchers. They took on the colours of the Ba'th Party – George Galloway MP on the platforms proved that – and after the occupation of Iraq, of the "resistance" which they supported there, made up of Sunni supremacists, Al Qaeda, and other clerical fascists, including, on and off, the Shia-based Sadr movement. They determined that the demonstrations had a markedly Islamist and anti-Israel dimension, demanding the destruction of Israel in such slogans as "Palestine shall be free – from the river to the sea", often carried by young people who most likely had not grasped the implications of such slogans.

Although, when it had first taken shape in 1999 in relation to Kosova, its SWP core had made it into a murderously anti-Muslim movement, now, after 2002, it became a very Islamic "anti-war" movement. The SWP-UK's "Respect (George Galloway)" party (so-named on ballot papers), rooted in the anti-war movement, campaigned in the 2004 Euro-election as "the best fighters for Muslims". The chameleon political quick-change antics would denote utter political disorientation even without any of the "anti-imperialist" extravagances that in fact went with them. The new "anti-imperialists" of the SWP even issued a statement offering a political rationale for the 7 July 2005 London Tube bombers, who never themselves supplied one, apologised publicly for having once backed Salman Rushdie and his right to publish the novel that got him fatwa'd by the Iranian regime, explicitly dropped support for secularism in schools, etc. ††

16. "Anti-imperialism" and European unity

Long-time, widespread, and deep left-wing opposition to the EU is an aspect of the addled left's "anti-imperialism". The initial "left-wing" opposition came from the Communist Party, concerned to stop "imperialism" strengthening itself against the non-imperialist Russian degenerated workers' state. The Orthodox Trotskyists eventually fell into mimicry of them.

There are two basic lines of possible working-class socialist policy in relation to the European Union, as to all major developments of capitalism. The first advocates building on what the bourgeoisie has created and uniting the working class across the EU to fight the bourgeoisie for democratic and social reform and, in the course of doing that, by way of educational work in the labour movement, building towards socialist transformation by working-class revolution on a

---

†† *See further the section in this book, "The warmongering anti-war demonstration".*

European scale. Such an approach does not imply backing what the dominant capitalists and their servants do, or the way that they do it. It counterposes working-class measures on a European scale to the bourgeois system. It does commit us to European unity, in the first place working-class unity, and to opposing politically all those who advocate the break up of the European Union and, in real-world terms, to advocate the restoration of the old, long-bankrupt, European bourgeois nation-state system out of which erupted two World Wars in the first half of the 20th century.

The alternative response to the bourgeois character of the existing process of European unification is to advocate regression to the era of competing and sometimes warring European national states – to an outlived earlier stage of bourgeois rule. Despite some of its advocates' concern with working-class self-defence, this is a reactionary policy. It is a break with the best traditions of the working-class movement and the real traditions of Marxism. It is the same fantasy politics as with those who responded to "1900 imperialism" by wanting to turn the historical clock back to an earlier epoch. It is, as Lenin argued in his critique of the petty-bourgeois anti-imperialism of his time, regressive economically and politically.

The unification of Europe was a policy of the working-class left long before any sort of union became the policy of the ruling bourgeoisie. Trotsky raised the call for a United States of Europe in the middle of the First World War. In 1923, at the time of the French occupation of the Ruhr region of Germany, the Communist International adopted the slogan for the Socialist United States of Europe.

It took the Second World War, the destruction of large parts of Europe and the long-term threat of USSR conquest in western Europe before bourgeois quasi-unification became practical politics. Because of the successive series of defeats the working-class movement has suffered we do not have the Socialist United States of Europe advocated by revolutionary socialists, but the quasi-democratic bureaucratic European Union of the bourgeoisies. Socialists now start from that. We cannot start from anywhere else.

Historically the knitting-together of peoples and states is one of the great progressive works of capitalism. But, as with "globalisation" now, progressive capitalist development proceeds unevenly, inhumanely, destructively – in short, in a bourgeois (and therefore also a bureaucratic) way. The bourgeoisie industrialised much of Europe in the 19th century. In the long term, they were creating the precondition of socialism – a high level of labour productivity and thus the possibility of abundance for all and the elimination of ruling classes and class exploitation. In the lives of many millions they created industrial hell-holes and foetid slums. They tore down all the old defences of the working people. The pioneer new technology, that of the British cotton industry, made it profitable for the cotton kings to get the raw material to feed machines, run by the child and woman wage-slaves in the cotton mills, by way of black slavery in the USA. It was the union of the bourgeois technological vanguard with an American version of primitive forced labour.

Some early working-class rebels, and good-willed bourgeois and aristocratic sympathisers with capitalism's wage-slaves, wanted to "rescind" industrialisation and the rampant rule of the markets and go back to an earlier historical stage. Describing such ideas as "reactionary socialism" in the Communist Manifesto, Marx and Engels proposed instead that the working class should in the short term organise to protect themselves, and in the longer term aim to win political power and take over industrial society, humanise it and use what the capitalist era in history had achieved as the basis on which to build a socialist society. There was no other way to build a humane working-class system, except on the basis of the economic achievements of capitalism: socialism is in history the child of advanced bourgeois society. No other socialism is possible. If the experience of Russian Stalinism seemed for a long time to put into question this basic postulate of revolutionary Marxism, its collapse confirms both its truth and its centrality in Marxist politics.

The Communist Manifesto established the basic working-class approach to bourgeois society and its development – simultaneously to fight it for working-class self-defence and betterment, and in the longer term to supplant it and build on its achievements.

Socialists in Marx's tradition fight the bourgeoisie within their system. They conduct the working-class struggle for trade union and social rights, for the fullest democratic rights and procedures, and ultimately for the overthrow of capitalism and its replacement by socialism. We know only one viable anti-capitalism: the conquest of political power by the working class and thereby the transformation of advanced capitalism into the beginning of socialism. Anything else is reactionary anti-capitalism, in the muddled form of a utopian drive to go back to stages capitalism has outgrown or superseded.

Fundamentally the same issues arose at the start of the 20th century. The new imperialism bestrode the world. Great trusts and cartels united with powerful states to fight other states and their industries for markets and colonies. In response, there arose a bourgeois and petty-bourgeois movement against these "unacceptable" manifestations of capitalist development. Proposals were made to break up the giant industries, to unscramble and undo what the organic evolution of capitalism was doing. In America, such ideas were made law, and Standard Oil was broken into parts – most of which then developed into giant corporations... It was, even if desirable, simply not possible to roll the film of capitalist development backwards. Lenin, Luxemburg, Trotsky and that whole generation of Marxists mocked at the ideas (and actions in the USA) of the "trust-

---

† *The expulsion of the nucleus of what is now AWL, the Workers' Fight group, from the SWP-IS was triggered in 1971 by the combative opposition of Workers' Fight to IS's precipitate change of line to one of opposing the EU. Chris Harman defended that change with the argument that EU entry "aimed to rationalise and strengthen capitalism. It is an attempt to solve certain of capitalism's problems by capitalist methods. There was a time when revolutionaries could regard certain such measures as historically progressive... Today, however... rationalisation of the system means strengthening it at a time when we as socialists argue that revolutionary change alone offers mankind any future. We have to oppose such measures..." (International Socialism 49, August 1971). Tony Cliff of the SWP-UK had written in his book Russia – A Marxist Analysis (chapter 6): "capitalism, wherever it exists is reactionary... today...". A "conclusion as regards the reactionary character of Russia state capitalism, notwithstanding the rapid development of its productive forces, can be refuted only if one could prove that world capitalism has not prepared the material conditions necessary for the establishment of socialism". This was Cliff's way of avoiding, ducking, the conclusion which implicitly saturated his own version of state capitalist analysis of Stalinism – that the Stalinist economic system, presented by him as better-developing than "western" capitalism, was therefore relatively progressive. His picture of Russian Stalinism paralleled that developed by the Orthodox Trotskyists. It was, beneath the name "state capitalism", one of its dialects of the Orthodox Trotskyist account. (Ted Grant, in 1949, and Hal Draper, in 1956, from different angles, argued that Cliff's argument was really a version of the claim that the USSR was bureaucratic collectivist: www.marxists.org/archive/grant/1949/cliff.htm and http://www.workersliberty.org/node/15556.*
"The bureaucracy", Cliff wrote, "has earned as much tribute as Marx and Engels paid to the bourgeoisie. 'It has been the first to show that man's activity can bring about. It has accomplished wonders far surpassing Egyptian pyramids, Roman aqueducts and Gothic cathedrals'..." (chapter 1). When he finally arrived in 1963 at a general theory of state capitalism which supposedly unified his radically different theories of state capitalism in Russia and in China, it was that state capitalism was the only way that backward countries could develop. The role of state capitalism in underdeveloped countries was analogous to the role of the bourgeoisie in the development of ordinary capitalism in Europe. It was progressive? Yes by the logic of what he wrote, and by the logic of his historical analogies. But he avoided that conclusion with the cancelling out statement that because world capitalism was ripe for socialism, therefore this state capitalism, though it was developing the means of production in a large part of the world, could not be progressive. It was reactionary. The conclusion was entirely arbitrary. See further "Cliff's state capitalism in perspective", http://www.workersliberty.org/node/21345.

busters" and denounced their program as a petty-bourgeois utopian aspiration to "devolve" capitalism back to a stage it had long passed and could never return to. Lenin saw the gigantism of capitalist organisation as a potentially progressive work of social integration and organisation: the answer to its exploitative and brutally capitalist character was for the working class to win political power, and by expropriating the bourgeoisie take over the economy and put it under rational, humane working-class control.

To say, as some do, that because socialism is now possible, therefore capitalism is completely reactionary and must be opposed in everything, including in his work to unite Europe, is entirely arbitrary and a-historical. † It is also both foolish and sectarian. Capitalism does not come to a dead end: for example, the microchip revolution over recent decades is a tremendous capitalist-era addition to humankind's power over nature and potentially over its own social affairs. These and other contemporary technological advances will be taken over by the working class, which develops and changes with capitalism and within it and its constantly changing technologies. Capitalism continues to develop and, in its own bourgeois way, continues to socialise production. It continues to create the material basis for socialism.

Yet for decades a large part of the ostensible left has made opposition to a capitalist European Union a central policy, indeed a principle. The predominance of demagogy and shallow agitation-led politics is striking here. "No to the Bosses' Europe – Yes to the Socialist United States of Europe", the slogan of the Trotskisant left, in practice it means – in the absence of immediate prospects of a European working-class revolution, it must mean – supporting the continuation or re-erection of barriers between capitalist countries in Europe. For the pioneers in this question, the Communist Parties and their sympathisers, and the USSR which guided them, that is what they wanted it to mean. Their de facto advocacy of the continued "Balkanisation" of Europe, flowed from their opposition to that which gave the movement to a united Europe much of its impetus – Europe as an effective opponent of new USSR expansion.

In the 1960s and 70s, anti-Europeanism took root in the Trotskisant left in Britain, for whom it never made any political sense higher than keeping in with the "big battalions" of the pseudo-left. Socialists and the labour movement cannot be consonant with our own history and oppose the unification of Europe, even by the bourgeoisie, when the immediate and short-term alternative is the old bourgeois state system. Within the bourgeois moves to unification we can only advocate our own program – working-class unity across the fading frontiers, the fight for democratic structures and procedures.

The way forward is a working-class campaign to democratise the EU, and a Europe-wide working-class campaign for a Socialist United States of Europe. We seize the chance to unite the European working class; we propose that the working class should set as its goal the creation of a fully democratic Europe, the overthrow of the bourgeoisie and the creation of the Socialist United States of Europe.

17. East Germany, 1953

In June 1953, three months after the death of Josef Stalin, a big illegal workers' demonstration in East Berlin, initiated by building workers, met with the bullets of the East German police, backed up by the occupying Russian army. Revolt spread across East Germany.

The first internationally visible uprising against Stalinist rule, it combined a national anti-imperialist movement and a strong working-class revolt which spearheaded it. The capitalist great powers respected their post-war agreements with Russia and did not intervene. The Communist Parties around the world, still high-gear Stalinist, denounced the rising as "anti-Soviet", "anti-socialist", "Nazi", etc. The Trotskyist Fourth International supported the rising but divided, in part, over different responses to it.

The Fourth International had long before declared for the withdrawal of the Russian forces from East Germany and the other Russian-occupied satellite states. † Despite making it an article of faith that Russia was not imperialist, they advocated an anti-imperialist program against Russian occupation. They were better as practical politicians against Russian imperialism than as Marxist analysts.

Now they came to what that meant in practical application. This was eight years before the wall dividing East and West was built across Berlin, and movement between east and west Berlin was easier. The Orthodox Trotskyists had for three years been preaching that the Third World War, which more or less everyone in the political world took to be inevitable, would be a great revolutionary war in which the Russian army would sweep across Europe. It would be greeted with the uprising of the Communist Parties of Western Europe. Together they would destroy capitalism and create states like

---

† *In June 1946: Fourth International 7 (8), August 1946.*
†† *Murry Weiss, The Militant, 13 July 1953; Ernest Mandel, Le soulèvement ouvrier en Allemagne orientale, Quatrième Internationale, July 1953.*

those in Russian-controlled East Europe: "deformed workers' states".

East-West tension had begun to ease immediately after Stalin's death. The Korean war had been in stalemate for two years, and was about to end (July 1953). That was part of the easing of tensions. Now, instead of seeing the West European workers rising to greet and ally with the "Red" Army, the Orthodox Trotskyists saw an uprising spearheaded by the working class against the Russians and their not-at-all-Red army. The "Red" Army was shooting down German workers in the streets.

The Russians shouldn't be there anyway, so just demand that they get out? But in the Europe of Stalinist and capitalist blocs, to say that the Russians should get out was to advocate a vacuum into which the American, British, or French armies might move. The solution? Call on all foreign troops to get out of Germany. One segment of the Orthodox Trotskyists (tardily) raised the call for Russian troops out; the other called for *all* occupation forces to withdraw: British, French, US, Russian. ††

Focusing on *all* foreign troops in Germany was what Trotskyists called a "centrist evasion". It was a siding with the "Red" Army at one remove, so to speak. It was the Russian occupiers' "Red" Army, backing the East German police, that was shooting Germans in German streets, propping up a totalitarian East German regime. West Germany was a functioning bourgeois-democratic regime. The British, American, and French armies were there, now, by consent, and in any case were not playing a role in West Germany remotely comparable to that played by the Russian occupying force in East Germany. To call on everyone to withdraw was to evade the point. It was the "Red" Army that was the oppressor in Germany, and it was now fighting the workers and other East Germans in a vastly unequal confrontation of tanks and guns against stones and petrol bombs.

One side let itself be guided by their more or less fantastic theorising; the other, by the fact that German workers were being shot down on German streets. A segment of the Fourth International around the SWP-USA, backed by British and French Trotskyists, would eventually call the politics of the International's Secretariat, around Michel Pablo and Ernest Mandel, a "capitulation to Stalinism". There were other engines of division at work in the Fourth International as well as the East German uprising; but the East German question opened up a clear political divide, in 1953, on Russian imperialism.

18. Hungary, 1956

The "thaw" after Stalin died – that is, the relaxation of state terrorism against the people – and then Khrushchev's "secret speech" (which was far from secret) at the 20th Congress of the CPSU in February 1956, in which he denounced Stalin as a murdering, paranoid tyrant, destabilised Eastern Europe and the ruling Stalinist parties.

In the late 1940s and early 50s the "Communist Parties" of the satellite states had been purged at leadership and basic cadre level, in a drive to weed out potential Titos. Leaders of the parties, especially those who had been in the underground at home during the war, rather than in Moscow, were accused, forced to confess, tried, and hanged or jailed. Those of them who were of Jewish origin were denounced as part of a "Zionist" world conspiracy against Russia. László Rajk, the secretary of the Hungarian party, and Rudolf Slánský, secretary of the Czechoslovak CP, were hanged; Wladyslaw Gomulka in Poland and Imre Nagy in Hungary were jailed. Rajk, whose reburying in 1956 was the occasion of a gigantic anti-Stalinist demonstration in Budapest, shouted "Long live the Party!" as he was being hanged.

In June 1956 Poland's workers erupted, starting what soon became a network of workers' councils across Poland. Resentment at Russian occupation and national oppression created mass opposition movements in Poland and Hungary, and stirrings in Czechoslovakia. In all of these there were strong seams of political Catholicism. Intellectuals, including elements of the ruling parties, began to organise discussion clubs. The oppositions did not challenge "socialism", but wanted to win reforms and cleanse the state and society of Stalin's legacy. Things threatened to get out of Russian control.

The Poles had a great nationalist tradition, and had had a stronger resistance movement than any other in Nazi-occupied Europe except Yugoslavia. They had, in the Warsaw Ghetto rising of 1943 and the general Warsaw Rising of 1944, a recent history of revolts. With that history, and with its workers' councils, Poland seemed the most likely to explode into an assault on the Russian occupation forces. In fact it was Hungary that exploded. In October the Russian leader Nikita Khrushchev visited Poland and let the new CP leadership of Wladyslaw Gomulka, recently out of jail, convince him that they could control Poland. In Hungary, the political police opened fire on a demonstration in Budapest and the country ignited. Stalinist police were lynched in the streets and defeated in gun battles. The insurgents armed themselves with petrol bombs and guns captured from their opponents, and soon controlled much of Budapest.

The newly installed reformist government of Imre Nagy declared that Hungary was leaving the Warsaw Pact, the Russian-controlled military alliance, equivalent of NATO. The Russians invaded. They met with fierce resistance. Some troops were affected by the insurrection and, being seen as unreliable, were withdrawn. It looked as if the Hungarian insurgents had won. But no, fresh Russian troops were launched against Budapest, and the rising was defeated. Many refugees stream across the border to Austria, from which Russian occupation troops had been withdrawn only in late 1955.

After the military victory of the Russians, the Hungarian workers went on a general strike, and the Russian reconquest took the form of myriad battles for control of the factories, the "means of production". The government leaders Imre Nagy, Pál Maléter, and others were captured; 18 months later it was announced that they had been hanged.

In 1956-7 the previously monolithic Communist Parties across Europe and the USA were badly shaken by this succession of shocks, from the 20th Congress, where Stalin was denounced and seemingly repudiated, to the very Stalin-like suppression of the Hungarian Revolution. Large numbers left the Communist Parties: in Britain, 7,000 or so out of a membership of about 35,000. † Khrushchev's revelations included an account of Stalin's antisemitism, and that set the many Jewish party members in political ferment.

On Hungary, the Orthodox Trotskyists, though now divided into the ISFI (Pablo, Mandel) and ICFI (SWP-USA, Healy in Britain, Lambert in France) were in agreement. They denounced the Russian armies of occupation and sided whole-heartedly with the Hungarians. That what Russia was doing in its satellites was imperialism they denied explicitly; but they advocated an anti-imperialist program of national liberation from Russian overlordship and endorsed those who fought that overlordship. The Orthodox Trotskyists recruited CPers; the British group of Gerry Healy, hundreds of them. Some of them were book-educated intellectuals, which was new.

One of the subgroups that had sided with Pablo and Mandel in the 1953 dispute over East Germany, the band in Britain led by John Lawrence and Hilda Lane, backed the Russians and drew closer to

---

† A story circulating among dissident CPers at the time went: when Stalin died, he left a little box labelled "to be opened in time of trouble", with inside it a message: "If things get bad, blame it all on me". He also left a smaller box labelled: "To be opened if things get much worse". In October 1956 they opened the smaller box, and read the message inside it: "Do as I did". They did.

the Communist Party. They would join the CP in 1958. A subgroup in the SWP-USA led by Sam Marcy also backed the Russians and split to become the semi-Maoist Workers World Party, which still exists.†

19. Czechoslovakia, 1968

Czechoslovakia and East Germany were the most industrially advanced of the Russian satellite states. Czechoslovakia had a strong independent communist tradition before World War Two. The ratio of the membership of the CP to the country's population was the highest outside Russia. The last stage of tightening Czechoslovakia into a fully totalitarian Stalinist state, early in 1948, had been staged as a parody of a workers' revolution, Stalinist orchestrated and controlled: workers demonstrated in factories, marched and "demanded" (supported) what the Stalinists wanted to do. Czechoslovakia then experienced an all-pervasive Stalinist totalitarian regime.

Twenty years later, Czechoslovakia took up where Poland and Hungary left off in 1956. The economy had become stagnant, with little growth. The CP leadership split into two groups over how to resolve the economic difficulties. Perhaps because there was such a strong real communist tradition in Czechoslovakia, not the hatred of "communism" in most of Russia's satellites, they took their differences to the working class. The leaders went to speak and debate the issues at mass factory meetings. That was new, and tremendously important. The Stalinist old guard led by Antonín Novotný were de-

---

† *Paradoxically, some Shachtmanites, in the ISL in the USA, took Hungary as a signal to recoil from the idea, dominant since 1946-7 in the ISL ranks, that Russia and the other Stalinist states were stable class societies capable of replacing capitalism on a world scale. They gravitated towards the Orthodox Trotskyists and the theory that the "deformed and degenerate workers' states" were unstable non-class societies and that there was no Stalinist empire. A group of them joined the Orthodox Trotskyist SWP-USA. The international Spartacist cult of today is a Stalinoid-Cannonite splinter from that 1950s grouping.*

†† *All the Orthodox Trotskyists opposed the invasion, though not all of them without ambivalences and differences. As far as I know, the sole exception was a tiny Irish organisation, the League for a Workers' Republic, which had connections with the forerunners of AWL. The LWR leaders decided that they were obliged to back the Russians because a counter-revolution against nationalised property was occurring before the Russians put a stop to it. They were soon persuaded to change their "position". In Britain the Socialist Labour League's Newsletter raised two slogans, no to Stalinism and no to the restoration of capitalism. Even the Warsaw Pact invaders had not spoken of capitalist restoration.*

feated by the reform faction led by Alexander Dubcek, the son of old communist militants of the pre-war movement. Czechoslovakia experienced a tremendous liberalisation, casting off its Stalinist chains, inhibitions, and paranoias. The Dubcek CP was loosening and evidently intent on abandoning its monopoly of politics and communications, and criticising the Stalinist past. Dubcek proclaimed the need for "socialism with a human face". The experiment embodied an attempt at a socialist renewal and a final break with Stalinism.

On 20 August 1968, Russia and its Warsaw Pact satellite powers sent their armies into Czechoslovakia to put down the half-born human-faced socialism of Dubcek and his comrades. Via a "letter of invitation" which they got old-guard people in Czechoslovakia to send, they said plainly that they were going in to suppress the liberalisation and to restore CP monopolies. "The overall political management of society [has] gradually eluded the control of the Party's Central Committee… elements hostile to the Party have begun to take part in the political life of our country". The Czechoslovak leaders did not mount an armed resistance. They knew they would be too outmatched to prevail and survive. Crowds accosted the soldiers, trying to talk politics with them. In the end Moscow prevailed. For the first time in its 48 year history, the British CP disagreed with Russia and refused to defend the invasion.††

One of the recurrent paradoxes of the Orthodox Trotskyists was that they cited any turmoil in the Russian empire in Eastern Europe, not excluding invasions and massacres, as "proof" that Russia was not an empire: it was not stabilised, it was encountering difficulties, it was "in crisis". The SLL launched a loud, bitter, mendacious, incoherent campaign against the IS organisation of Tony Cliff (today's SWP-UK) and against the idea that there was such a thing as Russian imperialism. The SLL hotly denied that fascist-like behaviour by the Russian state had anything to do with imperialism. Russia was a degenerated workers' state: it *could not* be an imperialist state.

20. Anti-imperialism and the Provisional IRA war

Northern Ireland, where the "anti-imperialist" Provisional IRA began its military campaign in early 1971 with the killing of three British soldiers lured to a sex-baited trap in a Belfast flat, presented the "anti-imperialist" left with a complex problem, which it was in no state to unravel, understand, and respond to coherently.

The basic problem in Ireland is that the people are divided into two distinct national-communal identities, expressed also in religious differences. Each of those has for centuries defined itself by opposition to the other.

On top of that age-old division, the 1920-22 partition of the island created a new, artificial minority, the Catholic-nationalist population of the "Protestant-Unionist" Six Counties state, about a third of the Six Counties population in 1922 and well over 40% today. (The 2011 census showed 40.8% Catholic, 41.6% Protestant, and 17.7% of other, no, or unstated religion). The Catholic-nationalist population is and always was a bigger minority in the Six Counties than the Protestant Unionists were in all of Ireland in 1922. Instead of a rational and democratic modus vivendi between Unionist and nationalist Irish people, there was a "settlement" imposed by military might on the nationalist people of Ireland, and specifically the nationalists of the six counties of Ulster. (Three of Ulster's nine counties are in the 26 Counties state). A central reason why it developed like that was that both nationalists and Unionists in Ireland had patrons in British politics, the Liberals for the nationalists and the Tories for the Unionists, and each Irish side believed that it could rely on its British allies to coerce the other Irish. In the event, the Tories stood by their Irish allies, and the Liberals deserted theirs. The alliances, and the belief on both sides that they could rely on coercion of the other Irish by their British allies, sapped any will that might have developed for an agreed and democratic intra-Irish settlement. A strange variant of that sort of thinking was, as we will see, at the heart of the later phase of the Provisional IRA's military campaign and the strategy of its leaders.

Now a majority of the population even of Belfast, the nationalist people of Northern Ireland are a majority in a large part of the territory of the Six Counties sub-state, in the parts that are contiguous with the 26 Counties state. Derry City, for example, Northern Ireland's second city, where the nationalist-to-Unionist ratio is three-to-one (2011 census), is two miles from the 26 Counties border, but on the "wrong" side of it, inside the "Protestant state for a Protestant people". "British-occupied Ireland" was an anti-partitionist name-tag for Northern Ireland; in fact, unless the will of the Six Counties Unionist majority counted for nothing, occupied Ireland was only the territory along the Border.

II

One of the mysteries of modern Irish history is why the architects of partition chose to incorporate into their "Protestant-Unionist" state such large nationalist majority areas adjacent to the border. Three possible models of an Irish Unionist sub-state (or territory administered from London, not Belfast, as was intended before World War One) were in play around 1914: four, or six, or nine countries to be excluded from a Home Rule Irish state. Four would have given the Unionists an impregnable majority. Six gave them a two-to-one majority. Nine, all of the province of Ulster, would have given them a bare and precarious majority.

In part, the answer lies in how Irish Protestants saw their "nation" – as a second Irish nation, scattered across the island, and only secondarily the compact Unionist majority in Ulster, which was a fallback territorial base for the Unionists, from which they could threaten to opt out of a Home Rule Dublin Parliament. They wanted not partition, but to stop Home Rule for any part of Ireland. Some Unionist leaders were not partitionists.

The nationalist writer Frank Gallagher tells the remarkable story that the Unionist leader Edward Carson proposed to the nationalist leader John Redmond that he should agree to exclude nine countries from Home Rule because that would mean partition would not be permanent (*The Indivisible Island*, 1957). The Unionists, with their "nation" scattered through the island, felt entitled to take as much as they could get.

All proportions guarded and all qualifications made, an imperialist system of the sort that existed in inter-war Poland, Czechoslovakia, and Yugoslavia, with their large oppressed national minorities, existed also in Northern Ireland. The Six Counties state, designed by the people who had shaped the Europe of the Versailles Treaty, incorporated against its will a one-third Catholic minority. In fact they designed a state rendered unviable in the long term by its character as a little Orange empire. It would last half a century, until 1972, when Britain would put an end to Six-County majority self-rule.

The Anglo-Irish Treaty of 1922 had provided for a "Boundary Commission" in which all the parties were represented; in a few years it would redraw the boundaries between the 26 and Six Counties, and allow the transfer of the Six Counties Catholic areas to the "Free State". In 1925 the Six Counties government refused to take part in the Boundary Commission. The others met, and it was agreed to pay the 26 Counties government a sum of money in compensation. The Dublin government spokesman pronounced this "a good bargain". The border remained where it was, as did all of Northern Ireland's Catholics. In 1922, when the Irish Free State was set up, the Catholics along the border had been militarily pinned down by the British army and an Orange state militia, the Special Constabulary. The

Unionists fiddled with the borders of local government electoral districts so that, for the most notorious example, Derry City, with a two-to-one Catholic majority then, had a council in which the Protestants were a two-to-one majority over the Catholics. Votes went with houses, and therefore Catholics were discriminated against in public housing. Jobs were scarce, and therefore they were discriminated against in scarce employment. They were second-class citizens, subject to the rule of Orange bully-boys and cops and thuggish Special Constables. It became the convention that the British Parliament would not discuss internal Northern Ireland affairs, though there were Six Counties MPs at Westminster.

From 1922, the 26 Counties had Dominion status, like Canada and Australia, far more than the old Home Rule schemes had offered. 26 Counties leader Eamonn De Valera adroitly transformed that status into real independence, while the 26 Counties remained in the Commonwealth. The last move in that 1930s transformation was the negotiated removal of three remaining British naval bases, in 1938. That gave the 26 Counties the possibility of being neutral in World War Two. And it was.

If Northern Ireland quickly became a Protestant-sectarian state, Protestant Unionists lording it over the Catholics, the 26 Counties just as quickly became a Catholic theocratic state, with its democratic institutions not much more than glove-puppets for rule by the bishops. In the 26 Counties the whole education system was controlled by the Church (and in Northern Ireland it was the Catholic Church that insisted on separate Catholic schools). Priests and priests' nominees ruled in public affairs. In the early 1950s a rudimentary health service for mothers and their new-born babies was, notoriously, vetoed by the bishops, and the minister foolhardy enough to resist, Dr Noel Browne, had his ministerial career ended. Laws in the 26 Counties were moulded to reflect Catholic doctrines irrespective of the opinions of the Protestants, Jews, and others, with the abolition of divorce in 1925, for instance. Northern – and southern – Protestants saw their sloganised fears that "Home Rule is Rome Rule" come to life in the 26 Counties state.

In recent decades revelations about the extent of the violence inflicted on children in schools by nuns and Christian Brothers (a celibate monk-like teaching order), rape by priests of institutionalised children, murderous ill-treatment by nuns of "illegitimate" babies (consigned to unmarked mass graves) – all those have greatly undermined the Catholic Church's authority. Ireland, which for many decades sent shoals of missionary priests and nuns all over the world, does not have enough priests-in-training now to replace aged priests at home: the average age of Catholic priests in Ireland is now approaching 70. These horror stories might have come straight out of such old sensationalist Protestant anti-Catholic pamphlets as the notorious *The Awful Disclosures of Maria Monk*. In the mid 20th century the two Irish states looked at each other with jaundiced eyes, and each saw part, at least, of the truth about the other. Catholics in the North had, after the 1940s, far better, British, levels of welfare-state benefits, and British education standards. Catholics, including those who were not rich, had access to higher education. The contrast with Catholics in the "Catholic state", which until the 1970s turned out shoals of semi-literate youngsters for mass export to the British labour market, was tremendous.

Observers believed that the welfare state had reconciled the Catholics to living in the Partition state. There was some truth in that.

III

In the mid 1960s, Northern Ireland Catholics started to move, demanding "civil rights" – "one man [sic], one vote, one man, one job, one man, one house". They identified with the US black civil rights movement of the time, singing some of its songs such as "We Shall Overcome". The Wilson Labour government was sympathetic to them. Some of its ministers had as MPs campaigned against the Unionist sub-state.

Sectarian fighting broke out in Derry in August 1969 and spread to Belfast. The Six Counties state had begun to break down into sectarian-political civil war. In Derry and Belfast, barricades were erected to wall off the Catholic areas from attack by pogromists and sectarian policemen. On 14 August the British army took control of the streets in Derry to stop the fighting, and on the 15th they did the same in Belfast. The army provided a necessary scaffolding of military force to prop up the crumbling Six Counties political entity. They would play that role for 38 years after 1969. Legislation was quickly rushed through Westminster, granting all the demands of the civil rights movement. It was now not nearly enough. The basic civil right the Northern Ireland Catholics lacked was national self-determination. Everything else in the previous 50 years had flowed from that. Now it came to the fore.

Large numbers of young people had been radicalised in the civil rights campaign in 1968-9. What would they do now? What could they do? The IRA, reviving quickly, offered them an answer. Republican-Stalinists like Cathal Goulding and Sean Garland had won control of a depleted rump IRA. By the mid 60s they had turned the Republican movement substantially from militarism to politics. The Republicans had, it was widely agreed, been very inadequate in defending the Northern Ireland Catholic areas in August 1969. Many blamed that on the IRA's turn to politics. In December 1969, the IRA split. The secessionists became the Provisional IRA. Within 15 months they were in a position to launch a guerrilla campaign.

There had been other IRA actions since the 1920s – a smattering of attacks on customs posts along the Border, and bombs in Britain, in 1939-40, and then the "Border War" of 1956-62. That was a series of raids into the North from the South, with at most passive Northern Ireland Catholic support. From 1971, it was war from inside the Six Counties. Within one year of starting the military offensive, the Provisional IRA had won the only substantial victory they would win in their 23 year war. The British abolished Protestant Home Rule in Northern Ireland. In March 1972 they abolished the Stormont Parliament.

IV

The rationale for the Six Counties entity had been that it allowed Protestant-Unionist self-rule. That self-rule had also been sectarian-political misrule over the Catholics. Now, in response to a year of Provisional IRA shootings and bombings, the British took it away. The Protestants, since before World War One, had had a veto on an all-Ireland parliament. Now the Catholics had won a veto over Protestant-Unionist majority rule in the "Protestant state for a Protestant people".

A Six Counties referendum on a United Ireland, with Britain pledging to respect the result and to act on it, was held in March 1973. On a 59% turnout, with nationalists boycotting the poll, 99% voted for partition. Unionists and nationalists had different ideas of what the unit for majority and minorities should be. For the Unionists, it was the UK, and then the Six Counties. To nationalists, the choice of the Six Counties as the area within which such things could be decided guaranteed the result. The Catholics were corralled into a sub-state within which, short of a demographic revolution, they could never be the majority. Majorities and minorities in that unit were to them invalid.

The Protestant Unionists, fearful of being forced into a united Ireland, formed a militia, unofficial but legal, the Ulster Defence Association, which would be 40,000 strong at its peak, the equivalent in proportion to population of 1.5 million in Britain. They organised a partially successful general strike (27-29 March 1972) against the abolition of Stormont. Then some of them started assassinating Catholics picked at random. The Provisional IRA declared a truce in June 1972, but it broke down quickly (in July). The war resumed and intensified. London and Dublin now worked out a new "constitutional settlement" for Northern Ireland – compulsory power-sharing (with an ultimatum: either that or never again Belfast self-rule) – in the Sunningdale Agreement of November 1973. The Provisional IRA, and the Protestant ultras whose voice, and personification of their prejudices, was the Rev Ian Paisley, rejected it. With some Unionist political trickery, a majority was found in the Northern Ireland Assembly which had been elected in May 1973 to work the Sunningdale Agreement. A Belfast government was set up, with Unionist leader Brian Faulkner as "Chief Executive" and Gerry Fitt of the Social Democratic and Labour Party as his deputy. In terms of electoral strength, the SDLP was the most important element in it. The Paisleyites – betrayed, they said, and with some justice even if one thought it a good thing to "betray" them – created uproar in the Assembly.

Then a snap British general election was called in February 1974, and eleven of the twelve Northern Ireland MPs returned to Westminster were enemies of compulsory power-sharing and of the power-sharing government in Belfast. The Assembly and the power-sharing executive lost all authority. A Protestant general strike on 15-28 May – this time a very powerful general strike – brought down the government. The Protestants had smashed Britain's plan to reform the Protestant state for a Protestant people on a new basis of compulsory power-sharing.

Britain now decided to set up a Six Counties Constitutional Convention, in which elected deputies would thrash out a constitution for Northern Ireland acceptable to both Protestants and Catholics. The Convention met for a little less than a year (May 1975 to March 1976), during which time the Provisional IRA called off its military campaign. Amidst bitter intra-Unionist clashes, the Convention failed to reach any agreement. In rejecting compulsory power-sharing, the Protestants saw themselves defending the very principle on which Northern Ireland had been erected: Protestant-Unionist self-rule, and rule over the Northern nationalist minority. A similar "Irish Convention", for all Ireland, set up in 1917 after the 1916 Rising, had also failed to produce an agreement. London continued direct rule in Northern Ireland; the Provisional IRA resumed its campaign.

The British government then decided to "sweat it out" – or that the people of Northern Ireland would – as long as necessary. In early

1977 the Labour government became dependent on Liberal and Ulster Unionist support in the House of Commons. That gave the Ulster Unionists new political leverage. The Labour government deprived IRA and other prisoners of the de facto political status they had had since 1972. That started a long and grim struggle between prisoners and the government which, under Thatcher's Tory government, culminated in the hunger strikes of 1982, in which ten men starved to death.

In 1985 a new Anglo-Irish Agreement was signed, giving Dublin a treaty-bound say in how Northern Ireland was governed, though Britain retained all executive power. The Thatcher government faced down mass Protestant outrage: an attempt at a general strike failed. The Provisional IRA campaign continued until the ceasefire of 1994. That ceasefire held in Northern Ireland even when the IRA bombed Manchester and the London Docklands in 1996.

V

In the 18 years of war, from 1976 to 1994, the IRA won nothing that was not available in principle to the Catholics in 1973, from the Sunningdale Agreement. The important difference with the Good Friday Agreement which came in 1998, after the ceasefire, was that an accord between political extremes was now necessary for power-sharing coalition government between those who won majorities in the two contending communities. It set up intricate, bureaucratically-managed, "balanced" sectarianism. A constitutional nationalist, Seamus Mallon, said what needed to be said about the IRA's war from 1976 to 1994: the Good Friday Agreement was Sunningdale for slow learners. What had the IRA been fighting for? A united Ireland. They called on the British to be "persuaders" to the Unionists for a united Ireland. But the limits of Britain's powers of persuasion with the Protestant Unionists had been shown again and again in the years after 1969, especially in the Unionists' defeat in 1974 of power-sharing government. Meanwhile the IRA war targeted Northern Ireland's Protestants, whose agreement or at least acquiescence was necessary for any united Ireland. Essentially British "persuasion" here could only mean financial or physical coercion of the Protestants into a united Ireland. By the end, in the early 90s, the Provisional IRA was shooting workers – in theory any workers, but in practice Protestant workers – who did building work or fixed a broken latch on a lavatory door at a police station. The gigantic contradiction in the IRA's campaign was that everything militaristic they did outraged the Protestant Irish whose consent they needed to win for a united Ireland. The whole IRA campaign was, and implied, an attempt to co-erce of the Protestant-Unionists into a united Ireland. Who would or could coerce them? The IRA? The Catholics of all Ireland, embarking on a war of conquest? The Provisionals squared the circle with the fantasy that Britain could be made to coerce ("persuade") the Protes-tants into a united Ireland. The IRA waged a 16-year war to coerce the British into "persuading" (coercing) the recalcitrant section of the people of Ireland! It was a preposterous nonsense. †

Coercing the British into coercing the Orange people into a unitary Ireland, was impossible, as well as undesirable. They were in an im-passe. The truth was that the Provisional IRA had been soundly de-feated both militarily and politically. The world climate after 9/11, the antagonism of the US government towards "terrorists", faced them with a loss of Irish-American help and money. The Provisionals settled for a variant of things that been on offer since 1973.

In 1981 the deaths on hunger-strike of ten Republican prisoners – seven Provisional IRA, three Irish National Liberation Army – had brought a great surge of sympathy and support to the IRA. Bobby Sands, a hunger striker near death, was elected MP for Fermanagh and South Tyrone.

Thereafter the Provisional IRA developed a new political strategy. They would triumph, they said, with "the ballot box in one hand, and an Armalite in the other". After the ceasefire they became a political movement North and South. They entered the Northern Ireland gov-ernment in 1999. Martin McGuinness became deputy First Minister (in fact co-equal with the First Minister) in 2007. Like other Republi-cans turned conventional politicians – Fianna Fail, Clann na Poblachta, the Stalinist Official Republicans who became the Work-ers' Party – they are now simply bourgeois politicians. They have ac-quitted themselves respectably in opposing anti-black racism in the South (opposing the 2004 constitutional amendment, carried by a 79% majority, to deny citizenship to "foreign" children born in Ire-land), but that was just being halfway-decent liberals.

VI

The responses, commentaries, proposals, slogans, analyses of the ostensible left, British, Irish, and international, through all those

† It was a late offshoot of the policy of the pre-1914 Home Rule Party, which had looked to a Liberal government to coerce the Northern Ireland minority. It was a direct continuation of the approach of De Valera's "constitutional Republican" Fianna Fail: they tended to look to the British overlord for a solution to the intra-Irish division, not to rapprochement with the Northern Ireland Unionists.

decades, is a political atrocity story. In 1968-9 the Irish supporters of the SWP (then called IS) in People's Democracy, Eamonn McCann, Michael Farrell, and Bernadette Devlin (McAliskey) were wildly ultra-left, identifying the main enemy as the reforming Unionists around Northern Ireland prime ministers Terence O'Neill and James Chichester-Clark. They helped exacerbate communal tension to open clashes – and then in August 1969 called for British troops to be sent in. Then, separating from the British IS/SWP group, they became left-flank propagandists for the Provisional IRA in the 1970s and 80s.

Worse than that, the international Marxist left wallowed in fantasies that Ireland had to be seen in a "permanent revolution" perspective in which the "national struggle" would grow over into socialism. Ireland would become a West European offshore socialist island, a Cuba. The British Mandelite magazine of the time, *International*, appeared in May 1969 with a front cover proclaiming: "Permanent Revolution Reaches the UK" – and that was the nonsense-keynote struck right at the start. In what became the conventional left-wing account, the Provisional IRA was fighting a more-or-less pure anti-imperialist war, of the type that the Comintern had discussed in 1920, and the nationalist Irish had fought between 1919 and 1921. The Protestant Unionists were classified not as a national minority but tagged politically, as just a politically reactionary grouping; and their concerns and their existence were dismissed as beneath consideration as, when the Provisional IRA went at them, were their persons.† Even though no halfway sane socialist would have advocated or voted for the military campaign launched in 1971, it did bring down Protestant-Unionist sectarian government in Northern Ireland. For the Catholic nationalists it won a veto against its restoration. After the events of 1974-6, when the Constitutional Convention was dismissed in March 1976, the Provisional IRA's resumption of the war made it, as has been said, a war to coerce Protestant Unionists into a united Ireland, or to coerce the British into "persuading" the Protestants, that is, into coercing them. The objectives were unachievable (and, for socialists, undesirable), and therefore the war from 1976 to 1994 made no political or military sense. Until 1981 the Provisional IRA played with an inadequate and underdeveloped notion of a federal united Ireland. They abandoned it in November 1982.

The British left, as distinct from the international "Trotskisant" left, had responded to the beginning of the IRA war in 1971 and the start of the bombing campaign in Britain in 1973 with panic-stricken cries of dissociation.†† When, after the hunger strikes, the Provisional IRA turned to politics, they achieved widespread support in Britain, even from MPs such as Tony Benn, who had been in the government which sent in the British troops and again in the government that withdrew political status from IRA prisoners and started the struggle which led to the hunger strikes. In truth, the idea that the Provisional IRA's was simply an anti-imperialist struggle lost all its very limited meaning with the resumption of the Provisional IRA campaign in 1976. "Permanent revolution" here became a licence for chameleon political adaptation to the Provisional IRA and for the ultimate betrayal of Wolf Tone Republicanism: denial that the Protestant Irish minority, the Protestant Unionists, have sovereign rights. †††

---

† *The ignominy to which some of the would-be Trotskyists reduced themselves was best summed up in the public advice offered by the Lambertist-nationalist Paddy Healy to the Provisional IRA on how to make shooting Northern Ireland workers who fixed the plumbing or a broken window in a police station acceptable to Southern trade unionists.*

†† *Some of us, the British Mandelites, the forerunners of some of those who now produce the LRC Labour Briefing, the original group of the AWL (Workers' Fight), and a few others, felt obliged at the start to defend the Provisional IRA's right to fight British imperialism. That came to be indistinguishable from backing their war. The predecessors of AWL continued to do that, with decreasing conviction, through the 1970s. In Ireland, the Trotskyists (Fourth International) backed the IRA, spinning fantasies about the war in the North triggering an Irish "Permanent Revolution", that is, evolving into a socialist revolution. For almost all the ostensible left, criticism of Sinn Fein and the IRA was ruled out. None of them denounced the post-Good-Friday-Agreement IRA/ Sinn Fein for a sell-out, which is what their previous line indicated and implied. Their silence on the Provisional IRA's sell-out of the "Irish revolution" shows how little they took it seriously.*

††† *In addition to all the discussions surveyed here as "case histories", there were discussions among Trotskyists, during World War Two and after, on the national question and the resistance movements in the great colonial powers, France, Belgium, and Holland, conquered by Germany; and on Russia and its conquered and occupied East European satellite states. Those are very big subjects in themselves. They will be discussed in the forthcoming Fate of the Russian Revolution Volume 3.*

Hitler Is Gone; Fight For Freedom Begins!

By ALBERT GATES

Il Duce Is Dead!
Bravo! Italian
Partisans

By SAM ADAMS

HE WAS NOT ALONE

TOO BAD, MR. CHURCHILL, TOO BAD—

UPPER CLASSES TREMBLE A LITTLE

THE PEOPLE VERSUS THE STATESMEN

NEXT WEEK'S FEATURES:

COMPLETE STORIES ON THE RISE AND FALL OF THE FASCIST

REGIMES IN GERMANY AND ITALY—A STUDY

IN CAPITALIST REACTION

LABOR ACTION

MAY 7, 1945 — A PAPER IN THE INTERESTS OF LABOR — ONE CENT

CUTBACKS HAVE BEGUN; UNEMPLOYMENT RISES

How the 'Father of Fascism' Died

By WALTER WEISS

Employment in Detroit Area Decreased by 107,000 Workers

By MARTIN HARVEY

LABOR OFFICIALS 'FIGHT'

I. The Working Class

(Continued on page 3)

(Continued on page 3)

Frisco Parley Opens Big Three Power Fight

SAN FRANCISCO

SHADOW BOXING

(Continued on page 3)

Labor Action 7 May 1945: how revolutionary socialists greeted the fall of Hitler

Iraq and the "liberal interventionists"

"The attempt of the bourgeoisie during its internecine conflicts to oblige all humanity to divide up into only two camps is motivated by a desire to prohibit the proletariat from having its own independent ideas. This method is as old as bourgeois society, or more exactly, as class society in general. No one is obligated to become a Marxist; no one is obligated to swear by Lenin's name. But the whole of the politics of these two titans of revolutionary thought was directed toward this, that the fetishism of two camps would give way to a third, independent, sovereign camp of the proletariat, that camp upon which, in point of fact, the future of humanity depends." – Leon Trotsky, *Writings Supplement 1939-40.*

"No matter what the good intentions of the British parsons, or of sentimental Kautsky, may have been [the result]… is a most reactionary method of consoling the mass… distracting their attention from the sharp antagonisms and acute problems of the present era, directing it towards illusory perspectives." – V I Lenin, *Imperialism*

"The sharp knife of Marxism was the instrument by which the bourgeois intelligentsia cut the Populist umbilical cord, and severed itself from a hated past. It was this that accounted for the swift and victorious spread of Marxism during the latter years of the last century. As soon as Marxism had accomplished this, however, it began to irk this same intelligentsia. Its dialectics were convenient for demonstrating the progress of capitalist methods of development, but finding that it led to a revolutionary rejection of the whole capitalist system, they adjudged it an impediment and declared it out of date. At the turn of the [19th/20th] century, at the time when I was in prison and exile, the Russian intelligentsia was going through a phase of widespread criticism of Marxism. They accepted its historical justification of capitalism, but discarded its rejection of capitalism by revolutionary means" – Leon Trotsky, *My Life*, chapter 10.

Why we fight capitalism even when it is progressive

On D-Day, 6 June 1944, an armada of ships and planes launched British, American and Commonwealth soldiers into a full-scale invasion of Hitler-ruled mainland Europe. Though pluto-democratic capitalism rules Europe still, it is a fact that those armies did in 1944-5 liberate Europe. The bourgeois-democratic legal rights which today's labour movements utilise in their work, and without which they could not exist except as small persecuted underground movements, were restored by the victories of those armies, aided by risings which the invasion triggered in Hitler-controlled Europe.

The struggles of the working class and others against their native reactionaries in the years after 1944-5 secured the bourgeois-democratic rights that exist now. But the starting point for all that was the assault on Nazi power launched on 6 June 1944. Before then German fascist armies controlled most of Europe, excepting only Sweden to the north, Switzerland in the middle, the offshore islands of Britain and Ireland to the west, and Spain and Portugal, where "native" fascist regimes ruled. Stalin's totalitarian armies, advancing from the East, controlled the rest of it. Everywhere in that Europe, excepting only the four bourgeois-democratic states, the old labour movements had been broken up, outlawed and destroyed, their militants conscripted into armies or labour armies, jailed, or killed. On the day Stalin's assassin struck Trotsky down, 20 August 1940, the work of a century of building labour movements in Europe had been all but wiped out. Only underground fragments of it survived. Some of those did work which international socialists have a right to be proud of, like the strike by Marxist-led Amsterdam dock workers in protest at the rounding up for deportation of Holland's Jews, and the publication in France of the underground Marxist paper *Arbeiter und Soldat*, which French Trotskyists and German soldiers produced for the workers in uniform of the German army. The strongest underground fragments of the labour movement were Stalinist mutations, armed with the program of creating their own totalitarian states.

The states whose armies fought their way up the Normandy beaches on 6 June 1944 had done terrible things in the British colonies; in the USA, where tens of thousands of Japanese-Americans were rounded up and put into internment camps; and in the bombing, before and after D-Day, of German civilians. Fourteen months after 6 June 1944 they would atom-bomb the Japanese cities of Hiroshima and Nagasaki. Even so, against the Nazi rulers of Europe and the militarist rulers of Japan, they carried bourgeois democracy on their bayonets. They promised liberation to the peoples of Europe, they were greeted as liberators, and ultimately it was liberators they proved to have been.

Inside months they had begun to restore to the peoples of Europe democratic and social rights and freedoms which it had taken the more advanced of them decades and centuries of working-class and popular struggles to win. In Japan, the conquering US army – the army of the same criminal government that had atom-bombed Hiroshima and Nagasaki – carried through a bourgeois revolution from above – land reform, and the installation of a bourgeois democracy hitherto unknown in Japan. Both Japan and West Germany had their sovereignty largely restored within a decade.

These liberating armies did not deliver socialism. They did not free the peoples of Europe – or of the US and Britain – from capitalist exploitation. In other words, they were bourgeois. But the bourgeois-democratic parliamentary systems they helped create allow the working class to think about its affairs, express its politics, and organise to fight for socialism. Looking back, it is impossible from a socialist or working-class point of view to refute the judgment that the invading armies of 6 June represented progress against reaction. The strongest counter-argument against the idea that the British and Americans – despite their bourgeois ideas, standards, aspirations and methods – embodied progress against historic regression, and civilisation against geno-imperialist Nazi barbarism, is the fact that they were allied with Stalinist Russia.

I paint this picture in true but deliberately strong colours in order to bring into focus the thing that concerns me here – the attitude which socialists took to those who represented progress and bourgeois-democratic liberty in 1945. We did not "support" them. We did not pretend they were something other than what they were – exponents and practitioners of bourgeois exploitation, and imperialists motivated fundamentally by imperialist rivalry with Germany.

The Trotskyists in Britain † proclaimed the war against fascism to be a war the workers had a life-or-death interest in winning. But they preached distrust of the ability – and in many cases the will – of the capitalist ruling class to win the war against fascism. They demanded freedom for Britain's colonies. They proposed such things as union-controlled training schools for working-class officers. They advocated that the working class push the ruling class aside and seize power,

---

† *The Revolutionary Socialist League – a small minority of the Trotskyists in Britain, though it was the official section of the Fourth International proclaimed in September 1938 – was straightforward "revolutionary defeatist" and denounced the others as "defencists". In the USA the Workers Party was "defeatist" and the Cannonite Socialist Workers Party had a policy like the majority in Britain, the Workers International League/Revolutionary Communist Party. But the political situation in the USA was not the same as in Britain. The workers of the USA were not faced with fascist invasion and conquest.*

and continue to prosecute the war against fascism to victory. That would have been the best outcome. The second best outcome was the victory of bourgeois-democratic capitalism over the Nazis. The biggest ostensibly revolutionary socialist organisation in Britain, the ILP, supported, in fact though sometimes not in plain words, the war, while calling on the workers to fight in Britain immediately for socialism.

There was much that was unclear and incoherent in what the Trotskyists and the ILP said. Many who think that what they did was right would reject the idea that their policy was a variant of "revolutionary defencism", and the Trotskyists of the 1940s would have indignantly rejected that description, but in my opinion that is what it was. Nobody on the anti-Stalinist Marxist left had anything like a pro-Hitler or a pro-Hirohito policy. Even the outright "defeatists" towards the British ruling class had no overt "softness" on Hitler in their arguments. They would have denounced, and did denounce, those who made such propaganda as poisonous enemies of the working class and of socialism.

Neither the "defeatists", nor those who were de facto "revolutionary defencists", thought it their business to counter the – often hypocritical – anti-Nazi propaganda of the British state by defending or "explaining" Hitler. The idea that the Trotskyists or the ILP might have done that would have been regarded by all of them as either the product of a deranged mind, or of a malicious slanderer. Such misrepresentation was, of course, put into circulation by the biggest proclaimedly Marxist organisation, the Communist Party of Great Britain, which denounced them as fascists and (unsuccessfully) called on the workers to "treat a Trotskyist as you would a fascist".

But what of their mirror image, the socialists who drew exactly the same conclusion about Britain and America from the vile nature of the Saddam Hussein regime in Iraq as some socialists in the 1940s (George Orwell, for example) once drew from the nature of Hitler's Germany? Those who supported Bush and Blair? They were as unbalanced and nonsensical in their own way as those who had a policy in relation to Iraq following the model of the CPGB's in relation to Nazi Germany during the Stalin-Hitler pact.

Grant, for the sake of argument, that the US neo-conservatives had with the invasion of Iraq launched a drive to install bourgeois-democratic regimes in the Middle East, intending to do there something like what the invaders of June 1944 did in Europe – and that we could estimate that they would probably would succeed. In fact, it was by no means so simple and straightforward, but let us pretend it was.

Then socialists would be glad of the progress they made – as we were glad to see Saddam Hussein brought down. But even if they had played the role of "bourgeois revolutionaries" from above in the Middle East, the American and British bourgeois states would not thereby have ceased to be what they are – states that protect and promote, under bourgeois-democratic political systems, a never-ending capitalist exploitation of the workers at home and abroad. The system as a whole remains what it is even if something "progressive" is being done in one of its parts – in this case, the Middle East. Even if they had played an entirely progressive role in the Middle East by creating bourgeois-democratic regimes where there had been air-tight dictatorships, nothing in the socialist criticism of capitalism would thereby be cancelled out, because nothing of the socialist alternative to capitalism which we fight for would be thereby achieved.

Indeed, the more the societies in the Middle East became open and nakedly marketist – the USA planned for Iraq to be a case in point – the more plain, obvious, and logically incontrovertible would become the crying need for the socialist alternative to capitalism.

When the "anti-imperialist" pseudo-left justified their support for a Milosevic (in 1999) or Saddam Hussein by pointing out how many millions of people die needlessly each year as a result of the international capitalist system which Britain and the USA maintain and promote, it was an obscenity because the argument is being used – as it was used in 1939-41 to justify Hitler – to justify regimes of repression and mass murder. But it is also a truth. It stands between us and any notion that the bourgeois system is not so bad after all.

It is, even in the best conditions, a system of brutal exploitation, of socially and culturally corrosive commercialism, and of grotesque ecosystem-destroying waste. We must replace it by socialism.

Inverting the kitsch left

Over Iraq, after the 2003 US invasion, the left was disoriented not only though by-then-traditional kitsch "anti-imperialist" responses, but also by a mechanical inversion of those responses into critical support for the US and UK occupying troops.

Iraq was occupied by those troops. The political and military arrogance, the brutality, the reckless use of power and fire-power, and the naked rapacity of the USA – their plans to sell off Iraqi state assets, their insistence that reconstruction contracts go to foreign, mostly US, corporations – cut against the possibility of a democratic system developing.

In fact only a quarter-democratic system has emerged. It has elections and some civil liberties, but no sound legal basis for the activity of the still-harassed trade unions. The government is dominated by Iran-linked Shia Islamists and so corrupt and sectarian that in mid 2014 the Sunni ultra-Islamist group Daesh rapidly conquered big areas of northern and western Iraq, and is still, in mid-2017, only gradually being pushed back.

The US government had said it would eventually retire into the background, and hand power to a self-governing Iraq. The USA signed an agreement to withdraw in 2008, and completed withdrawal in 2011, though it has sent some forces back to help the Iraqi government fight against Daesh.

From soon after the 2003 invasion, and especially in 2005-7, there was a simmering civil war in Iraq, with many thousands of deaths. The main forces of the so-called "anti-imperialist resistance" were thoroughgoing reactionaries, whose concern was to prevent democratic reform and the loss of power by the old ruling Sunni elite minority. Daesh is the continuation of a major strand from that resistance. There were also Shia ultra-Islamist "resistance" forces.

The Iraqi labour movement, long suppressed by the Saddam regime, saw a renaissance after 2003, but was and is still weak, and probably could not survive the victory of any of the "anti-imperialist" resistance forces, let alone an unrestrained civil war between the Sunni and Shia Islamist "resistance" forces. In 2005-7 especially, the occupation forces, with all their brutalities and follies, also sustained the conditions in which the Iraqi labour movement was starting to rise to its feet.

The demagogue "reactionary anti-imperialists" – "Respect", the SWP, George Galloway, etc. – backed the anti-working-class, reactionary, mostly Sunni-supremacist, "resistance". But there was also their mirror-image. For those mirror-image people, it was not enough to have an attitude to the IFTU (the biggest trade-union group in Iraq, led by the Iraqi Communist Party) like we had to the Solidarnosc labour movement in Poland in the 1980s: unconditional support for its right to exist, and all-out support against the Polish state, combined with criticism where necessary of its politics.

They insisted on support also for the politics of the IFTU, which critically supported the 2004-5 government of Ayad Allawi, installed by, propped up by, and operating as a front for the US occupation. They claimed that there is no difference in practice between political criticism of the IFTU, and the attitude of the reactionary anti-imperialists who condemned the IFTU for refusing to commit hara-kiri on the altar of the "anti-imperialist" clerical fascist "resistance" – the attitude that led to the shouting down of the IFTU representative at the European Social Forum in October 2004.

They took the hope that – as in Germany and Japan after 1945 – out of the US-British victory against Saddam Hussein would come a bourgeois-democratic system in which a labour movement can develop; and they transmuted it into positive support to the USA, Britain, and their allies and stooges, and thereby took political responsibility for them and for their military and economic policies.

Their D-Day, our 1945

We have already seen that, as it turned out, good did come from the post-Second World War US occupation of Germany and Japan – after they had buried the dead, reconstructed the economies, and begun to rebuild the cities levelled in such atrocities as the fire-bombing of Tokyo and Dresden and the atom-bombing of Hiroshima and Nagasaki.

And therefore? We have to conclude that the Second World War did not come from imperialist rivalries, and that the victors were not (bourgeois-democratic) imperialists? We forget that later in the 1940s the US occupiers helped the Japanese bourgeoisie crush the militant wing of the new Japanese labour movement, though without extinguishing that movement altogether? We conclude that no purpose was served, and could have been served, by the efforts of revolutionary socialists who fought for a wider democracy and for socialist redress, against the Stalinists, against the residual pro-Nazi resistance in Germany, but also against the US occupiers?

That the result, bourgeois democracy in Japan and Germany and Western Europe, wipes out the fact of imperialist rivalries, and imperialist methods like the bombing of Dresden or Tokyo? Or that because we hope for a qualifiedly good outcome in Iraq, we must deny that it is an imperialist occupation? That we had to refrain from being "nasty", avoid saying true but unpleasant, debunking things? That we must not name and define for what they are the characteristic brutality of the US military, and the USA's crude, bungling, rapacious, imperialist methods in Iraq?

Suppose we led or influenced working-class anti-fascist partisan forces in France or Italy at the end of the Second World War, and found ourselves on the same side as the invading armies of the US and Britain. If we "worked along with" the invading armies against a common enemy, that would be informed by the certainty that we would soon or simultaneously come into conflict with those armies and with their French and Italian allies, supporters, and stooges, and that we must prepare and fight out that conflict by honest and independent criticism. †

Kornilov and Kerensky

Other historical examples are relevant. When the Bolsheviks fought against Kornilov's attempted coup in Russia in September 1917, Lenin wrote:

"Even now we must not support Kerensky's government. This is unprincipled. We may be asked: aren't we going to fight against Kornilov? Of course we must! But this is not the same thing; there is a dividing line here, which is being stepped over by some Bolsheviks who fall into compromise and allow themselves to be carried away by the course of events. We shall fight, we are fighting against Kornilov, just as Kerensky's troops do, but we do not support Kerensky. On the contrary, we expose his weakness. There is the difference". (*Collected Works* 25 (289-293)).

It is easy for a new-fledged realpolitiker philistine to dismiss this as just Lenin playing with words. After all, the Bolsheviks fought Kornilov, and thereby in fact "supported" the Kerensky government against those who tried to overthrow it.

Lenin was concerned that there should be no blurring of distinctions, no hint or talk of "supporting" Kerensky in any positive or political sense, no suggestion of the Bolsheviks "softening" their hostility to the government besides whose forces they were fighting to defeat a common enemy that threatened both the Kerensky government and the labour movement.

If the Bolsheviks "supported" the Kerensky government in the sense of fighting on the same side against Kornilov, they did not – and that is what concerned Lenin – subordinate to it. They did not endorse it. They remained mortally hostile to it. The Bolshevik refusal to "support" Kerensky was a pledge for the future, which they re-

---

† *Discussion in Solidarity of the possibility that the US invasion of Iraq might leave behind a more-or-less functioning bourgeois democracy, as the 1940s US occupations had done in West Germany and Japan, may have helped generate some of the "Marxist neo-con" nonsense of Alan Johnson and the "Labour Friends of Iraq". But what divided them from us was their abandonment of an independent working-class, Third-Camp, stance in relation to Blair and Bush – their moral, political, and intellectual collapse before Blairism and capitalism. None of that necessarily followed from even the most optimistic surmises about the US-British occupation of Iraq.*

deemed when they chased Kerensky out of St Petersburg on 7 November 1917.

The Spanish Civil War and voting for the Republican budget

Another valuable illustration here is Trotsky's discussion with Max Shachtman in 1937 about the Spanish Civil War. † Trotsky reprised this discussion in January 1940 (*From a Scratch to a Danger of Gangrene*):

"On September 18, 1937, Shachtman wrote me: 'You say, 'If we would have a member in the Cortes [parliament] he would vote against the military budget of Negrin [the Republican prime minister].' Unless this is a typographical error it seems to us to be a non-sequitur. If, as we all contend, the element of an imperialist war is not dominant at the present time in the Spanish struggle, and if instead the decisive element is still the struggle between the decaying bourgeois democracy, with all that it involves, on the one side, and fascism on the other, and further if we are obliged to give military assistance to the struggle against fascism, we don't see how it would be possible to vote in the Cortes against the military budget... If a Bolshevik-Leninist on the Huesca front were asked by a Socialist comrade why his representative in the Cortes voted against the proposal by Negrin to devote a million pesetas to the purchase of rifles for the front, what would this Bolshevik-Leninist reply? It doesn't seem to us that he would have an effective answer'.

"This letter astounded me. Shachtman was willing to express confidence in the perfidious Negrin government on the purely negative basis that the 'element of an imperialist war' was not dominant in Spain.

"On September 20, 1937, I replied to Shachtman: 'To vote the military budget of the Negrin government signifies to vote him political confidence... To do it would be a crime. How we explain our vote to the anarchist workers? Very simply: We have not the slightest confidence in the capacity of this government to conduct the war and assure victory. We accuse this government of protecting the rich and starving the poor. This government must be smashed. So long as we are not strong enough to replace it, we are fighting under its command. But on every occasion we express openly our non-confidence

---

† *Shachtman responded that he had been "entirely wrong" on the issue; but his letter to Trotsky had been in the name of Cannon and others as well as himself: The Two Trotskyisms Confront Stalinism, p.452.*

in it: it is the only one possibility to mobilise the masses politically against this government and to prepare its overthrow. Any other politics would be a betrayal of the revolution'."

In the Spanish Civil War we were revolutionary defencists on the Republican side. 100% and 150% defencists. Trotsky's text sums up our position in all situations in which we want victory for one side, but pursue the politics of mortal class and political enmity towards those in power on that side.

A Trotskyist deputy in the Cortes would indeed have wanted the Republican militias to have guns and the best possible military equipment. (More than once I have encountered otherwise intelligent people who think that Trotsky's point was that we didn't want the Stalinists to have guns. But it wasn't). The voting in the Cortes was part of a political, not a military, process. In voting against the budget we would express not opposition to arming the anti-fascist fighters at the front, but our opposition to those in political control.

Such a thing seems hopelessly self-contradictory. It is only so if such incidents as voting are detached from the connecting chain of which they are part – and detached from socialist perspectives – and treated in isolation. If Trotskyist votes in the Cortes against the military budget would in practice lead to no money for weapons, then we would be in a situation not of voting to express no confidence in the government, but of challenging it for power.

But we will never get to that situation of challenging for power if we are not prepared to start by using our votes and voices to express intransigent hostility to the rulers.

Trotsky expressed this approach in an article of 1939: "The policy that attempts to place upon the proletariat the insoluble task of warding off all dangers engendered by the bourgeoisie and its policy of war is vain, false, mortally dangerous. 'But fascism might be victorious!' 'But the USSR is menaced!' 'But Hitler's invasion would signify the slaughter of workers!' And so on, without end. Of course, the dangers are many, very many. It is impossible not only to ward them all off, but even to foresee all of them. Should the proletariat attempt at the expense of the clarity and irreconcilability of its fundamental policy to chase after each episodic danger separately, it will unfailingly prove itself bankrupt... The workers will be able to profit to the full from this monstrous chaos only if they occupy themselves not by acting as supervisors of the historical process but by engaging in the class struggle..." (*A Step Towards Social Patriotism*, 7 March 1939).

The slave trade

Take another example from the history of the suppression of black slavery. Even though the activities of the British navy to stop the slave trade (after 1808) were an aspect of Britain's drive for dominion on the world's seas (this was in the middle of the wars against Napoleonic France), it was none the less right, good, progressive, and to be endorsed and supported, that the slave trade should be stopped. Someone who was hostile to British domination of the seas – rightly so, from our point of view – and who therefore, was concerned purely with that aspect of reality, denounced British ships stopping the slave ships of other, sovereign, nations on the high seas and freeing the slaves, would have been a malign fool.

But someone supporting the British drive to suppress the slave trade would have been a different sort of a fool to ignore the facts that slavery continued in the British colonies, until 1834. That the great British cotton industry, which exploited children in Britain, depended for its raw material on the labour of American black slaves who were being worked to death, on average, in seven or eight years. That the British ruling class exploited large parts of the world – India, Ireland, the West Indies, etc. That suppression of the slave trade meant the growth of "slave-breeding farms" in the USA: that is, farms that bred human beings with no rights, for exploitation, from childhood, as other farms bred sheep and cattle.

Or to feel that it would be a betrayal of the fight against the slave trade even to mention such things…

In the late 18th century Britain was the most advanced bourgeois society in existence. The bourgeoisie ruled there. Its civil liberties inspired liberals and reformers everywhere. Yet in its wars against the French bourgeois revolution, and then against the Empire which Napoleon Bonaparte erected on the social advances of the revolution, bourgeois Britain allied with the deepest and dirtiest reactionaries in Europe, with kings and tsars, bishops and medieval-minded aristocrats. When the French war ended in 1815, the political settlement of post-revolutionary Europe was shaped by the so named Holy Alliance of Austria, Russia, Prussia, dominated by kings, emperors, aristocrats, and Christian witchdoctors. They entrenched reaction in power, everywhere, placing a giant tombstone over progressive Europe. It took decades, and many revolutions, for that reactionary work to be undone. Though Britain acquiesced in the post-war Holy Alliance system it did not join the Holy Alliance. The pressures and exigencies of war gone, Britain for a while in the 1820s pursued a far more progressive foreign policy. It supported the independence of Greece, submerged for centuries in the Turkish Empire, whose patriots, by way of revolutionary war, created the first Greek state in modern history, in 1829. It supported the self-liberation of the peoples of South America from Spanish rule.

In a sense, the bourgeois social nature of Britain manifested itself in, as Marx put it, "England's mission to promote constitutionalism" (as against despotism) internationally. Its great power nature and interests soon reasserted themselves and led to decades of supporting the repressive Turkish Empire, in order to prevent Russia aggrandising itself at the expense of the Turkish "sick man of Europe'.

That the pluto-democratic USA, free of the long struggle against Russia, might after 1991 adopt a "mission to promote constitutionalism", was by no means impossible. The USA announced similar plans both after World War One, under Wilson, and after World War Two, under Roosevelt and Truman. Both quickly ran aground, but they were serious plans. They were more serious than George W Bush's similar talk around 2003, which ran aground even faster and more comprehensively.

Bismarck

In the 1848 revolution in central Europe – in the first place, in Germany – the bourgeoisie proved unable to carry through "its own" revolution, in part for fear of the proletariat. Afterwards, over decades, parts of the bourgeoisie's social program, and some elements of a welfare state, were introduced under Bismarck by those who in the revolution had defeated the bourgeoisie.

Bismarck's reforms were necessarily alloyed with regressive and reactionary Junker (landlord) elements, whose interests Bismarck also served. They included something recognisably like the bourgeois-democratic revolution aspired to by the revolutionary democrats in the defeated revolution of 1848 – but also, and especially from the point of view of the working class, something radically different. Lenin commented, in retrospect: "Can anyone in his right mind deny that Bismarck Germany and her social laws are 'better' than Germany before 1848?... Did the German Social-Democrats... vote for Bismarck's reforms on these grounds?" (*Collected Works* 23 (262-270)).

Russian Marxists and the liberals

In Russia, when all Marxists, as distinct from the populist agrarian-socialists, believed that the only possible revolution was a bourgeois-democratic revolution that at best would lead to a bourgeois-democratic republic, they debated the question of how they should relate to the bourgeois democrats, the liberal bourgeoisie, the right-populists, etc. The different answers to that question defined and shaped the political formations in Russian Marxism in the 20 years before 1917.

To simplify it a great deal, the Mensheviks said that since it was to be a bourgeois revolution, the bourgeoisie would have to lead it, and therefore the working class should avoid doing anything that would frighten the bourgeoisie. They accommodated to the bourgeois political formations, whose political goal came to be a constitutional monarchy. They educated the workers they influenced in such a spirit.

The Bolsheviks took a radically different approach, even though until 1917 they too believed possible only a revolution that would end in bourgeois power.

The most important liberals in pre-1917 Russia took the Bismarckian model of "reform from above" as their own desired "bourgeois revolution" for fear of both the workers and the peasantry.

The Bolsheviks taught the workers they educated to aim for a radical "Jacobin" revolution in the style of the French revolution of 1789-93, led by workers and peasants, that would level all the institutions of the old regime and clear away all the debris of the past. In making such a revolution, in alliance with the peasants, the working class would educate itself in the best way possible and to the highest possible degree to fight for its own working-class interests against the bourgeoisie in power.

They thought it certain that the end result of the anti-Tsarist revolution, for a considerable time ahead, would be a bourgeois-democratic regime, under the bourgeoisie. But they advocated independent and revolutionary tactics so that the working class would best be educated, and the historical epoch of bourgeois rule possibly foreshortened, especially in the event that the radical bourgeois revolution in Russia helped trigger working-class revolutions in European countries which were "ripe" for socialism.

It did not work out like that. The Tsar defeated the revolution of 1905, and when the Tsar was overthrown in 1917 the Bolsheviks steered towards a working-class seizure of power, believing that the

First World War would trigger working-class revolutions in the west, to which worker-ruled Russia would then become an economically underdeveloped appendage.

The Bolsheviks adopted the politics expressed in the old slogan coined in mid 19th century Europe to define the tactics of working-class organisations fighting side-by-side with bourgeois revolutionaries against royal and feudal reaction: "march separately, strike together".

In its early political manifestations, Stalinism broke with that approach. Among the consequences of that was the very bloody defeat of the Chinese working class in 1927 (which has a great deal to say both to the "reactionary anti-imperialists" – and to the democratic pro-imperialists!)

The Left Opposition and Stalin's "left turn"

An example from the history of Stalinism will shed further light on the question of the attitude we take when alien, anti-working-class forces, are, or seem to be, doing work we want done, and would like to be strong enough to do ourselves, in our way.

In the mid 1920s, Trotsky and the Left Opposition, and then the United Opposition (with Zinoviev), advocated a program of industrialisation for the USSR. Their opponents, the Stalinists and the Bukharinites, scoffed at this idea.

Then in 1928-9, faced with some resistance by rich peasants (the "kulaks"), the Stalinists, who controlled the state, broke with the Bolsheviks' "right wing", the Bukharinites, wiped out the kulaks, and forcibly drove the peasants into collective farms, wreaking vast destruction in rural Russia. Simultaneously, they launched a powerful drive to industrialise the USSR.

Their state waged a brutal one-sided civil war on most of the people over whom they ruled. They turned Russian society upside down. In the Ukraine they created an artificial famine and used it to break the resistance of the peasants, three million or more of whom died.

The Trotskyists had been finally defeated in December 1927, and many hundreds of them, including most of those who had led the Bolshevik revolution, exiled to Siberia and similar wilderness places. From there they saw the Stalinists beginning to industrialise the USSR, at a furious pace and with murderous recklessness.

Some of the exiles began to ask themselves, and each other: isn't this our program which Stalin is carrying through? A cruel, crude, wasteful caricature of it, indeed. The Stalinists are what they are, but, even so, it is a version of our program that they are implementing. Don't we want to see done what they are trying to do? Putting our "factional" feelings aside in the interests of the revolution, don't we want them to succeed? And if they are defeated in their struggle with the peasants, will that not lead to bourgeois counter-revolution, to the final destruction of the October Revolution? Aren't we, as serious people, obliged to do whatever we can to help them? So many of the defeated Oppositionists began to think. Some of them were demoralised and wanted only an excuse to give up the fight. Many of them were sincere. They began to resent Trotsky, Rakovsky, and the other irreconcilables. In that mood, hundreds of them capitulated to Stalin in 1928 and 1929.

Abandoning their own politics, they served the Stalinists. Some, Pyatakov for example, took leading positions in the construction of the new industries. In the purges of the mid-30s, almost all of them, including Pyatakov, would be shot or imprisoned.

Against these self-depoliticised ex-Bolshevik "social engineers" and would-be "administrators of the historical process", what did Trotsky and his comrades say? Trotsky insisted that, quite apart from specific criticisms of what the Stalinists were doing – and he was highly critical – the fundamental thing for revolutionary socialists was not only what was being done, but who was doing it, how, and why.

Lenin, expressing the same idea in general, says somewhere that the most fundamental issue in the politics of class society is who? whom? Trotsky now posed the same basic question to the capitulators: who? whom?

Trotsky too believed that, fundamentally, what the Stalinists were doing was historically progressive, despite all that had to be said against their methods. He believed that the pressure of the Opposition and its program had played a big part in determining that the Stalinists, when their old pro-kulak policy broke down, turned on the rich farmers and on the Bukharinite right wing of their own party.

But Trotsky refused to blind himself to the difference between the program of the working-class Left Opposition and what the bureaucracy was actually doing "on the ground".

Both the Trotskyists and the rightists around Bukharin had wanted to retain the market framework which had been introduced in 1921, with the "New Economic Policy". The Stalinists shattered it entirely and created a regime in which the totalitarian state used mass terror as the instrument for enforcing its own arbitrary and subjective economic and social decisions, recognising neither economic nor human nor any other restriction or restraint.

Where the Left Opposition had coupled proposals for industrial-isation with proposals for raising working-class wages and improving working-class conditions, the Stalinists in their drive to industrialise cut wages, severely worsened working-class conditions, destroyed the trade unions as workers' defence organisations, and created pseudo-unions to regiment the workers on behalf of the state and its objectives. They turned the working class of the USSR into something closer to a class of slaves than to a free proletariat. (Trotsky registered as much in 1939-40).

The result was needless chaos, waste, starvation, deprivation, famine, and the death of millions.

They did however industrialise the USSR. To this day you will find academics to argue that Stalin carried out the industrialisation program of the Left Opposition – that the Left Opposition had first advocated the policies that Stalin eventually carried out. In fact Stalin's was a different industrialisation, serving different objectives, and, for the working class and society as a whole, producing radically different results. Who? whom? proved to be the all-defining questions. Means shaped ends, the "who" determined the "what" and the "how".

Looking back with hindsight, we can see what Trotsky did not so clearly see, that the difference between the program of the Left Opposition and the seeming variant of it being carried out by the Stalinists was a class difference. Both the Left Opposition and Stalin were for "industrialisation", but they represented different class programs of industrialisation.

What Trotsky did see clearly in 1928-9 was that socialists who had undertaken to organise and lead the working-class struggle for emancipation had to distinguish between the industrialisation of the bureaucracy and the sort of industrialisation, administered by and serving the working class, that the Opposition had advocated. He saw that the Opposition had to maintain their own political program. They had to criticise the bureaucracy and its methods from the point of view of its working-class victims, and continue to counterpose their working-class program to that of the bureaucracy.

They had to defend the working class, and help the working class to defend itself from the bureaucracy. Whatever it meant for the tempo of the bureaucracy's version of industrialisation, the immediate material interests and well-being of the working class had to be championed and secured – just as, under capitalism, whether its work was considered progressive or not, the Marxists put the organisation, education, and self-assertion of the working class before everything else.

The Trotskyists did not identify with bureaucratic industrialisation. They did not politically support Stalin. In short, they refused to join their ex-comrades who chose to betray the interests and the cause of the working class and go over to the "progressive" bureaucracy.

The argument would be beside the point that Bush and Blair, representing free-market pluto-democracy, are not to be compared to the totalitarian Stalin. The analogy is between the Left Oppositionists who saw Stalin carrying through what looked like a variant of their industrialisation program, and socialists now who see Bush's and Blair's attempt in Iraq to realise, in their own way and for their own reasons, a bourgeois-democratic regime that for us is both desirable and, when the working class is not yet ready to make a socialist revolution, necessary.

The analogy is between the politically demoralised and politically deracinated ex-Trotskyists who thought that the best contribution they could make to securing the interests of socialism was to go over to Stalin and commit political and moral suicide – and those who thought that the best contribution they could make to progress in Iraq was to become cheerleaders for Blair and Bush and their Communist Party allies in Iraq.

The Third Camp

Some of the critical supporters of Blair and Bush still thought of themselves as Third Camp socialists. But they had introduced a small "correction" into what were our common politics. Third Camp politics were fine, but they would become "operational" only in the future. They were mañana Third Campists!

For the present they consoled themselves and others with the illusory perspective that everything was all right for democracy, the Iraqi labour movement and the fight against clerical fascism and other forms of reaction in Iraq – Blair and Bush are on the job! All socialists – especially Iraqi socialists – could do is back them, help to "hold up their hands", until they succeed.

"Tomorrow", promised the Blairites-For-The-Duration, they would again be Third Camp independent socialists. Tomorrow would belong to the "Third Camp", working-class political independence and socialism. But today – that belonged to Blair, Bush, and their allies in Iraq!

As Vladimir Lenin wrote about Karl Kautsky:

"In short, any number of promises to be a Marxist in another epoch, not now, not under present conditions, not in this epoch! Marxism on credit, Marxism in promises, Marxism tomorrow, a petty-bourgeois, opportunist theory – and not only a theory – of blunting contradictions today... In practice this means becoming an opportunist, turning away from the acute problems of the day to dream of the unacute problems of the future. In theory this means refusing to be guided by actual developments, forsaking them arbitrarily for such dreams..." (*Collected Works*, 22 (103-107)).

Or, in this case, to give up – "for now", of course – the "dream" of building the "Third Camp" of an independent working-class left and attach oneself to the powers that govern the affairs of the world.

Though labour movements exist in many countries, what does not exist is a strong international "Third Camp" in Trotsky's sense: a politically independent labour movement, in which the working class acts as a "class for itself" in politics, counterposing itself to all the other camps and in the first place to the bourgeoisie of its own state.

From where we are to that, we have a long political way to go. Though great transformations may happen in a relatively short time – "twenty years in a day" – a strong organised "Third Camp" does not yet exist.

In this situation, our basic approach is the one Max Shachtman expounded when explaining his opposition to the Korean war.

"We have no intention or desire, no right and no need, to abandon the fight for socialism in this way or in any other. The Third Camp does exist. It is nothing but the camp of the workers and oppressed peoples everywhere who are sick to death of insecurity, exploitation, subjection and increasingly abominable wars, who aspire to freedom, peace and equality.

"We never promised that we would be able to organise them into an independent movement, packed, wrapped, sealed and delivered by a specified date. We did say that unless they are organised into a movement independent of capitalism and Stalinism, the decay and disintegration of the world would continue, as it has. We did say that the forces of the Third Camp of socialism and liberty, are here, and it is our sworn duty to help organise them into an independent movement. The only way we know how to do this is: tell the truth about capitalism and Stalinism; help make those we can reach conscious of the problem of society today and how to solve it, and increase the clarity of those who are already partly conscious of it...

"Our opposition to the war does not mean support of Stalinism, in Russia or elsewhere. Only ignorant or mendacious people say that.

The best that can be said for such people is that they are so completely sceptical about the ability of the masses to attain socialist independence freedom and peace, that in their obtuseness they conclude that the only way American imperialism can be opposed is by helping Stalinist imperialism. We will try to teach the ignorant better; and we will answer the mendacious as they deserve to be answered.

"Our opposition to Stalinist imperialism is not one whit less uncompromising than our opposition to American imperialism. We do not need any instruction on how to fight the latter so that the former is not the gainer thereby. We do not oppose American imperialism so that it may be defeated by Stalinism...

"The Social-Democrats, to whom the Third Camp is a joke because they long ago ceased to regard socialism as a real fighting goal, have naturally proclaimed their adherence to the cause of American imperialism in Korea. The Fourth Internationalists to whom the Third Camp is an incomprehensible and uncomprehended blasphemy because they regard Stalinist totalitarianism as part of the working-class camp, have just as naturally proclaimed their adherence to the side of the Stalinists in Korea.

"The voice of socialist independence and internationalism is stilled in those movements or reduced to a whisper. In our movement, it will remain clear and firm. It will be heard, and it will be echoed". (*Socialist Leader*, 30 September 1950).

Or, as Trotsky put it:

"We are not a government party; we are the party of irreconcilable opposition... Our tasks... we realise not through the medium of bourgeois governments, but exclusively through the education of the masses through agitation, through explaining to the workers what they should defend and what they should overthrow. Such a 'defence' cannot give immediate miraculous results. But we do not even pretend to be miracle workers. As things stand, we are a revolutionary minority. Our work must be directed so that the workers on whom we have influence should correctly appraise events, not permit themselves to be caught unawares, and prepare the general sentiment of their own class for the revolutionary solution of the tasks confronting us." – The USSR in War.

Top: platinum miners at Marikana, S Africa, 2012. Below: Hong Kong dockers' strike, 2013

Top: Solidarnosc and the Gdansk shipyard workers, 1980. Below: strikes and protests in France, 2016: "No to the [new] labour law. We are not cattle".

The revaluation of values

The end of the colonial revolution, that is, of colonialism, by the 1970s, left no anti-imperialism other than direct anti-capitalism. Since then, what was "anti-imperialism" in Lenin's sense – working-class revolution combined with colonial revolution – has been replaced on the ostensible left by absolute negation of advanced capitalism (and *especially* of *advanced* capitalism) and identification with the reactionary "anti-imperialism" of smaller predatory powers. The left's alliance with Islamic clerical fascism and such states as Iran is an example.

The mutation has developed in a world where the former semi-colonial and colonial victims, China and India, are world powers; where once-colonial Africa is covered by independent states; where, US militarism notwithstanding, advanced capitalism operates chiefly through economic means and strengths; where some of the "anti-imperialist" powers are in some or all senses reactionary and regressionist, and some of them regional imperialisms; where the only progressive anti-imperialism, the only anti-imperialism in the spirit of Lenin, Luxemburg, and Trotsky, is now inseparable from working-class anti-capitalism and socialist revolution.

The mutant anti-imperialism is not working-class socialist anti-imperialism. It is reactionary anti-imperialism. And it is far worse in its consequences than any of the reactionary petty-bourgeois anti-imperialist strands which Lenin condemned and denounced. For the anti-imperialists of the ostensible left, it is not enough to criticise the great powers, tell the full truth about their goals and methods and activities – in Iraq, for the pertinent example. They believe that "Leninism" and anti-imperialism demands that they side explicitly with the enemies of the big powers – any of the enemies, no matter how reactionary what they counterpose to the big powers may be.

II

As there are many different sorts of imperialism in history, so also of anti-imperialism. Up to the middle of the 20th century, and in some cases beyond, the world was divided into great colonial empires – British, French, Belgian, Dutch, Portuguese, Russian. Russia waged the last of the old-style wars of colonial conquest for the decade after it invaded Afghanistan, in 1979. That colonial imperialism has gone out of existence, as a result of revolt against the rulers, or because the

214

rulers found continued occupation unprofitable. To an important extent the repression of peoples that was a routine part of colonial imperialism continues now as the work of the successor states, many of them bureaucratic administrative units, not nations, created by colonialism to contain "alien" segments of the state's population. Against old colonial imperialism, the Communist International advocated a fight for national independence, led by "revolutionary" nationalists or by a Communist Party, or both in alliance. This was seen as part of the movement towards world revolution and the global removal of capitalism, in which the working class, especially the working class of the advanced countries ripe for socialism, would be the protagonist and leader of the rest of the plebeian population. The proletarian revolution in the advanced capitalist countries was the central anti-imperialism.

The theses of the Second World Congress of the Communist International noted in 1920 that the unequal weight of different independent countries is as natural a consequence of market relationships as is inequality in wealth between formally equal citizens within a bourgeois democracy resting on wage exploitation.

The idea of seeking the economic equality of countries under capitalism was dismissed as the world-politics equivalent of seeking the equality of the millionaire and the worker under capitalism: "An abstract or formal posing of the problem of... national equality... is in the very nature of bourgeois democracy. Under the guise of the equality of the individual in general, bourgeois democracy proclaims the formal or legal equality of the property-owner and the proletarian..."

Inequalities can perhaps be ameliorated in both cases, but then they pile up again. It is like hacking down grass that is densely seeded and abundantly watered: the effect is soon undone by nature, so long as seeds and roots remain in place.

III

One of the worst traits of post-World-War-Two Trotskyism is that we responded to colonies gaining independence (with non-Stalinist regimes) by saying: this isn't real independence. As a reference to the limited economic and political weight of most of the ex-colonies in a world market dominated by the big powers, "not real independence" was all right as a casual description, and as far as it went. But it was and is confusing and obfuscating. The description was very often used as an intellectual prop for denying, in our positions and responses, the manifest facts that "imperialism" was ceasing to be colonial imperialism, or anything like it, and that it had ceased to have

215

many of the defining characteristics which Lenin anatomised and Trotsky summed up in his 1939 drawing-of-distinctions between "'imperialism' in the widest sense of the word" (which covered and included Russia) and "imperialism" as defined in "contemporary literature, at least Marxist literature" (which did not).

Too often, the description was used to pretend, in a world of tremendous change, that nothing had "really" changed, or (contradictorily) that "the colonial revolution", especially when led by Stalinists who would use Stalinist Russia as a model, was dealing mortal blows to world capitalism. And there was sleight of mind in it. Imperialism is the use of force and extra-economic means to rob, constrain, dominate certain countries; for ex-colonies not "really" independent because of their relative weight in international commerce, it was a matter of market economic relations, not of "imperialism" as it had been. †

Against colonial imperialism, the democratic and socialist program of anti-imperialists is clear: self-determination and independence. Drive out by as much force as necessary the colonial power, its political control, its armies, its local agents. The duty of socialists in the metropolitan countries is actively to back the colonial freedom fighters. At the Second Congress of the Comintern in 1920, the British

---

† *Lenin wrote, in a polemic with other Bolsheviks, Bosch, Bukharin, and Pyatakov: "Big finance capital of one country can always buy up competitors in another, politically independent country and constantly does so. Economically, this is fully achievable. Economic 'annexation' is fully 'achievable' without political annexation and is widely practised. In the literature on imperialism you will constantly come across indications that Argentina, for example, is in reality a 'trade colony' of Britain, or that Portugal is in reality a 'vassal' of Britain, etc. And that is actually so: economic dependence upon British banks, indebtedness to Britain, British acquisition of their railways, mines, land, etc., enable Britain to 'annex' these countries economically without violating their political independence". (A Caricature of Marxism and Imperialist Economism, 1916: CW 23 (28-76)). He was contending that political independence was not impossible even in an era of world-ranging giant concentrations of capital which made "economic independence" impossible; he was arguing against comrades who said real political independence was impossible in the era of imperialism, and therefore it was not worth advocating or fighting for it. When, today, for example, weaker states borrow from banks centred in the big capitalist powers, and are forced to agree in advance that disputes about repayments will be settled by US or British courts, that is not just "the market" in the abstract. But this subjugation is generally not subjugation to a particular alien power (of the type Lenin described for Portugal and Argentina); rather, it is subjugation to the general rules of all the big centres of capital. No amount of political independence will mend it. International working-class solidarity can alleviate it, and only socialist revolution will mend it. Here too there is no meaningful anti-imperialism other than working-class struggle against capitalism and to replace its world system by working-class socialism.*

delegates were told by Karl Radek, a leading Bolshevik, that: "The International will not judge the British comrades by the articles that they write... but by the number of comrades who are thrown into gaol for agitating in the colonial countries".

But what when ex-colonies become politically independent, while still a very great deal less than economically self-determining, even in the very limited sense that the great powers are self-determining, or "independent"? Still very much less than economic equals of the big powers? †

After the liquidation of old colonialism, "imperialism" is primarily, the workings of the capitalist world market, in which the rich and advanced countries have great advantages. What, now, is anti-imperialism? It is the working-class anti-capitalist revolution! Against the "imperialism of free trade, and economic might, and military clout", of the USA now, the only feasible, serious, real, "anti-imperialism" is inseparable from working-class anti-capitalism.

IV

Against colonialism and military occupation, the anti-colonial struggle for self-determination has definable, reachable, achievable, self-limited objectives. The anti-imperialism which denounces ineradicable aspects of the relationship of capitalist states in a world where the market is God – which condemns inequalities of wealth and what goes with them, which denounces state egotism and self-aggrandisement – is, if translated into the realities of our world, denouncing capitalism, in a confused way. Populist anti-imperialism, as distinct from working-class anti-imperialism, denounces capitalism in a mystified and mystifying, and fundamentally confused and incomplete, way. It does not propose to overthrow capitalism, and hence it has no serious anti-imperialist program.

The program of driving out the colonial power becomes meaningless in the old progressive sense. But there can be a new sense: eco-

---

† *The thought that economic inequality makes political independence irrelevant can lead to very reactionary conclusions, as the case of Palestine shows. It is said that a separate Palestinian state, side by side with Israel, would be economically unequal and therefore its political independence would be worthless. Implicitly that thinking dooms the Palestinian people to nothing but what they have now, or worse, until they are able to conquer and eliminate Israel. (And even then? An Arab state covering the whole area between the Jordan and the sea would still be tiny and short of natural resources). This line of thinking is a variant of what Lenin, polemicising against Bosch, Bukharin and Pyatakov during World War One, called "imperialist economism", a devaluation of politics or a substitution of economics for it.*

nomic nationalism, the drive to become economically self-sufficient, as nearly autarkic as possible. And there can be eruptions of backward-facing cultural-religious national and racial chauvinism. The Iranian revolution is a terrible example, but the clearest.

V

A strange thing on the ostensible left now is what might be called posthumous, after-life, or amputee Stalinism. It is to be found mainly in and around the *Morning Star*, a Communist Party paper. †

The *Morning Star* still sides with the Russian and Chinese regimes in international affairs and in its report of their internal affairs. It is an aggressive supporter of Chinese colonialism in Tibet, and tends to side with Putin in Ukraine. It is as if the *Morning Star* thinks that the Stalinism they used to support in those countries has not ceased to rule (in Russia) or changed radically (in China).

The *Morning Star* used to think that Stalinist Russia and China were "socialist". Now? They cannot possibly think the same of Putin's Russia or Xi Jinping's capitalist-nurturing, openly anti-working-class, China. Yet their political attitudes now, in relation to Russia and China, are not far from the attitudes they had to the old Russian and Chinese Stalinist states. †† Some of the ideas and attitudes of the would-be left now are not only Stalinist in origin, but also in their present form more irrational than were the similar ideas in their old Stalinist form.

Ideas that made their own sense when the supposedly socialist or in-transition-and-travelling-towards-socialism USSR was at the centre of a world view – for instance, the absolute hostility to advanced capitalism, and more-or-less automatic support for the "camp" in conflict with it – are utterly nonsensical now that the USSR has vanished into history, now that there is nothing even notionally better than the advanced capitalist countries. No socialist can even for a moment think that Iran or Taliban-ruled Afghanistan or the Daesh "Islamic State" show a desirable future to humankind, or a hope for a better future, or an alternative to capitalism, as the devotees believed

---

† *Published daily since 1930 (except for 18 months from January 1941, when it was banned for making pro-German propaganda); for its first 36 years it was called the Daily Worker.*

†† *In fact, at one period the Morning Star and the Communist Party were sometimes more critical of the old Stalinist states than they are now of Russia and China. As we've seen, the Morning Star criticised the Russian invasion of Czechoslovakia in 1968, in the CP's first public word of dissociation from Russia in 48 years. In 1979-80, the Morning Star condemned Russia's invasion of Afghanistan.*

Stalinist Russia was. No-one can see them as the Orthodox Trotskyists saw the "degenerated and deformed workers' states", as a progressive step beyond capitalism and in transition to socialism.

For 30 years after the 1949 Maoist conquest of all mainland China, the Communist Party of China ruled a system repeatedly disrupted, at a cost of tens of millions of lives, by arbitrary economic experiments made possible by the absolute power of the Maoist state over the people. Early in the 1930s, Trotsky said of Stalin's forced-march industrialisation and agricultural collectivisation that the thinking behind it was "bureaucratic raving". "The rejection of 'objective causes'… represents the 'theoretical' ravings of bureaucratic subjectivism" (*The Degeneration of Theory and the Theory of Degeneration*, April 1933). That was Mao, too, and perhaps more so.

In the last 35 years the Chinese Stalinists in power have cultivated an old-style capitalist economy, and ruled on behalf of a new capitalist ruling class intermeshed with the CP bureaucracy. In the changed circumstances of a civil society, and of an economy not subject to their old hands-on control, they have maintained, as well as they are able to, a totalitarian political regime that holds down the working class and the other working people for rampant capitalist exploitation. Simply to describe this system – the working class exploited by myriad capitalist enterprises and held in an iron dictatorship on behalf of the capitalists – is to described a fascist or fascistic regime.

True, Chinese Stalinism under the present dispensation is less comprehensively reactionary than it was in the Mao period. But that people who in Britain and in relation to most of the world side with workers against their exploiters should back either the Russian or the Chinese regime is in socialist, or consistent-democrat, terms, incomprehensible. The political rulers of China call themselves "communists"? Facts about China freely available in the West, and scarcely disputed, show that claim to have nothing to do with the social and economic realities, or the future prospects, of China.

It is said that amputees sometimes experience pain where their lost limb used to be. These strange socialists and communists who back or half-back Putin and Xi Jinping still feel for Russia and China something of the same sort as they used to feel for the old Stalinist Russia and China, long after history has lopped off the old Stalinist realities. These are "amputee socialists". Their need for something to "support", cheer on, ally with against the great capitalist powers is such, and their old habits of mind are such, that they are now governed by wilful political make-believe and unreflecting nostalgia and by the old negativism towards advanced capitalism. They are in the

grip of a malign cultural inertia. It is as strange, and of the same nature, as the Argentine delusion of so much of the left in the 1982 Falklands war.

VI

Nameless, class-less, anti-imperialism, specifying only what it is
against; or an anti-imperialism repeating phrases that were true to
the reality of 1920 as if the same conditions hold today – these are
dominant characteristics of the aspirant left now. Despite their loud
hostility to "imperialism", their anti-imperialism is only as progressive or otherwise as the "anti-imperialist" forces it aligns them with.
Anti-imperialism is, so to speak, politically translucent. Positively, it
becomes a form of political chameleonism. Pure and simple negativism towards the USA and the advanced capitalist countries can
and does lead those "anti-imperialists" – people operating by emotion, positive but above all negative, without a map of the political
terrain in which they operate or a living conception of a socialist "des-
tination" – into self-righteous "anti-imperialist" alignment with political and social reaction.

Opposition to imperialism tends easily to become indistinguishable from a negation of advanced capitalism. It also negates many of
the conquests and achievements of bourgeois civilisation in history.
It can and does become endorsement of any movement away from
that bourgeois civilisation, even movement backwards, economically,
culturally, intellectually, socially, politically. Yet for us the precondition for socialism is the world economy created by capitalism. There
is no other viable foundation for socialism. Even though socialists
have often, and rightly, supported struggles against colonial or semi-
colonial oppression which have short-term economically-regressive
tendencies or disruptive effects on economic integration, in general
to disrupt the integration is regressive and reactionary.

Communists in certain circumstances have supported and do support less-developed or simply backward opponents of advanced capitalism, in conditions where peoples are threatened with colonial or
semi-colonial enslavement by a socially and economically more advanced country. They supported the Afghans, under the would-be
modernising monarch Amanullah, against British invaders in 1919.
In the 1930s they supported feudal Ethiopia under Haile Selassie
against the drive by Mussolini's Italy to conquer it. They backed the
Rifs of Morocco against France in the 1920s: the French Communist
Party led a tremendous campaign of support for them against France.
Trotsky penned a splendid account of communist attitudes in the

Manifesto of the Second Congress of the Communist International in 1920. "The Socialist who aids directly or indirectly in perpetuating the privileged position of one nation at the expense of another, who accommodates himself to colonial slavery, who draws a line of distinction between races and colours in the matter of human rights, who helps the bourgeoisie of the metropolis to maintain its rule over the colonies instead of aiding the armed uprising of the colonies; the British Socialist who fails to support by all possible means the uprisings in Ireland, Egypt and India against the London plutocracy such a Socialist deserves to be branded with infamy, if not with a bullet, but in no case merits either a mandate or the confidence of the proletariat".

The communists supported those underdeveloped peoples against those who would enslave them; they supported them for the element of self-liberation, of struggle for self-determination, in their conflict with more advanced civilisations. In similar situations today Marxists support the less developed against the more developed. The one precondition is that those in conflict with advanced capitalist powers represent some degree of progress, of seeking to escape domination and enlarge self-determination and freedom, or of opposition to historical and social regression.

Today's addled left take on the colour of the "anti-imperialists" they identify with (including real or aspirant lesser imperialisms, such as Iraq or Iran), and let themselves be politically defined by them. In our world, chameleon "anti-imperialism" signifies not so much support for residual struggles for national independence, as the anti-imperialism and anti-capitalism of political activists who reject everything socialists see as progressive in capitalism and liberal-democratic bourgeois society, everything on which we must build socialism, everything that socialists should defend as we once fought the bourgeoisie to win it.

In recent years, it has signified support for religious maniacs of the various currents of political and fundamentalist Islam, including the elaboration of political explanation and apologetics for terrorist attacks on civilians carried out by those people. Many of those fundamentalist currents consciously support regional imperialisms such as Iran and Iraq, and intra-Islamic sectarianism, Sunni against Shia, has also been a part of their program and motives for action.

When the Communist International codified its guiding principles on such things, the victory of "revolutionary nationalists" could be seen as a part of a general movement against imperialism spearheaded by the drive against capitalism of the Communist workers of the advanced world. Or as "anti-imperialist" movements in which communist working-class local forces, allied to, augmented and in part defined in their political character by their links with the world movement, could compete with reactionary "anti-imperialists" for political and social dominance, and shape the movement into a working-class-led anti-capitalist movement.

The Comintern did not expect that the colonies would become independent under capitalism – least of all in a world in which working-class communism had disappeared as a mass force. Today, "anti-imperialism" is often only a detached fragment of the program of the Communist International. The old political frame and the prospect of short or medium term working-class victory is no longer part of it, except in the heads of people who mutter, posthumously so to speak, about "permanent revolution" – not as a strategic orientation in which the working class can really fight for power, but as a magic mantra. It is a foolish mystification and in practice a mechanism for accommodation – and de facto political submission to – alien class and political forces. Forces whose ideals and goals are sometimes reactionary compared to a straightforward capitalist society, i.e. to what they call imperialism.

Iran, and its 1979 revolution, is the seminal modern experience here. Mussolini ruled for 21 years, Hitler for 12, Stalin for thirty. In Iran, the clerical-fascists have been in power 38 years as of early 2017, and they will rule for some incalculable time yet.

VII

Anti-imperialist populist nationalists at most aspire to "economic independence" – autarky – or attempt to create it. That too is limited in its possibilities, economically regressive in the main, and unsustainable. It was the policy of ruling Stalinists – Trotsky itemised as one of Stalinism's most reactionary aspects its policy of cutting off from the world market, as distinct from regulating and controlling relations with it. For decades populist nationalists in Latin American and other independent countries have been denouncing "Yankee imperialism". What can they do against imperialism, as populist "anti-imperialists"? Not a lot, and nothing fundamental.

That sort of "anti-imperialism" ruled in independent Ireland for the quarter century before 1958. It implied autarky, cutting off from the international division of labour. Behind high tariff walls, it created some native small industries, but they could not compete in the international market. The economy stifled in its own caul, haemorrhaging hundreds of thousands of people. From 1958, the same politicians who set it up, with the same individual in the lead, Sean Lemass, began to dismantle it. "Partial anti-imperialism" of that populist and nationalist sort is, in general, regressive and reactionary. It is of limited effectiveness and duration. In some cases it is possible for industry to grow up behind "nursery tariffs", as in its day 19th century German industry did; but generally the populist anti-imperialism does not even lay foundations on which the economy can build once reintegrated into the international division of labour from which it has withdrawn to one extent or another.

At best it proposes more or less serious interim ameliorations – protectionism, nationalisation of foreign owned industries, etc. It aims to strengthen "national" capitalism against "foreign" capitalism. These ameliorations may in themselves be worthwhile, play important roles in developing the economy of a given state for a period, in changing the relative places of developing states, but the depredations of the world markets will not in that way be overthrown.

VIII

Even when we think that the core of what the great powers are trying to do is desirable – as when NATO in 1999 stopped Serbia killing or driving out the Kosovar-Albanian population – revolutionary socialists in Trotsky's tradition do not endorse them politically or take political responsibility for them. Even when, as in 1999, we do not denounce or condemn outright, we neither endorse nor take political responsibility for them.

Some former colonies or semi-colonies are now regional or – China, for the great instance – even world powers. Saddam Hussein's Iraq was a regional imperialist power, or, if you prefer, a sub-imperialism. To approach its conflict with the USA and its allies, or any other such conflict, as if it were conflict between a colonial or semi-colonial people and "imperialism", that is, with your mind on past but now-transformed relationships, is to get lost politically.

Similar transformations of the role and relations of countries were made in Europe in the half-century before World War One. In the 1860s the First International proclaimed as one of its principles and active political goals the unification of Italy – and its freedom from oppressive Austrian interference. The Second International (1889-1914) had to come to terms with united Italy's transformation into an imperialist power (a weak one). German unification was the desire and goal of all enlightened European democrats in the middle of the 19th century. By the late 19th century Germany was a great imperial power. Today China and India, the ex-semi-colony and the ex-colony of the mid 20th century, export capital to Britain.

Of course the regional imperialisms, like Iraq or Iran, are not on the same level as the USA. So then socialists should behave towards the lesser, regional power, in conflict with the greater imperialism, as we did towards colonial peoples in conflict with colonial empires? Anyone who suggests that should at least raise that position to a coherent view of history. Applied retrospectively, that position would have involved supporting Japan and Italy, the weaker imperialist powers, against the USA and Britain in World War Two. Japan vigorously stimulated nationalists in a number of colonies, such as Burma and Vietnam, who then confronted the restored French and British colonial masters at the end of the war. I repeat: those who supported Saddam Hussein's Iraq or the mullahs' Iran would logically have to support Japan in World War Two.

And maybe even Germany. After all, as Stalinist propagandists insisted during the 22 months of Hitler-Stalin alliance, 23 August 1939 to 22 June 1941, France and Britain were the great colonial-imperialist powers who had conquered and possessed much of the world. And French and British imperialism had declared war on Germany, which was now allied with the Russian "workers' state". The central political leader of the British Stalinist party, Rajani Palme Dutt, argued that Hitler had "capitulated" to the USSR in the Nazi-Russian pact. Hitler was fighting France and Britain, wasn't he, and not the USSR? For the first nine months the Stalinists got a lot of labour movement people and organisations to listen to them. That changed when Germany overran Europe in May 1940 and a German invasion of Britain became a serious threat.

IX

To sum up: for Vladimir Lenin and the Communist International, anti-imperialism was, primarily and immediately, anti-capitalism, directed against the economically most advanced great powers. To imperialism it counterposed working-class socialism, working-class revolution. The colonies' struggle against metropolitan power was important in this, but subordinate. Events changed that. In positive terms, "anti-imperialism" came to mean, first, and for some only, what we called "the colonial revolution".

For that there were a number of reasons: defeats and setbacks for the working class in the advanced capitalist states; the fact of anti-colonial movements in India and China, the biggest colony and semi-colony of the period; the colonial wars of liberation elsewhere, political and military; the Russian turn (from late 1924) to "socialism in one country", which implied working-class revolution in no other country for the epoch it would take USSR to build socialism; the influence of the idea that the world's road to socialism lay not through workers' revolution but in the power which Russia's economic successes had over the imagination of the world.

Socialist revolution in the advanced countries was for all practical purposes removed from contemporary politics, except as an increasingly vague and unfocused aspiration. Hopes shifted to the colonial world. Wherever it could, the Stalinist Comintern promoted nationalism, even in the great colonial powers, Britain, and France, hoping it would hinder unity between the USSR's great-power enemies.

Anti-imperialism came to be primarily anti-colonialism. The central "anti-imperialist" focus of the Lenin-Trotsky Communist International, the working-class revolution in the advanced capitalist states, was pushed back and petrified. That was not done in one operation in the minds of the Moscow controllers of the Comintern, or done lucidly. It was done within a wild Stalinist period of bureaucratic ultra-leftism, 1928 to 1934-5, with the ultra-leftism deployed, with more or less cynicism, as a manipulative tool by the Russian autocracy, and intertwined with right-wing elements – the so-named "Third Period".

The loose threads of the piecemeal shifts from the anti-imperialist program of the Lenin-Trotsky Comintern were gradually pulled tight. The colonial anti-imperialist movements began to be seen, in the decades when Russia was confronted by Britain, France, and the other states with great empires, as *the* anti-imperialist movement. Anti-imperialism came to mean simply national struggles, including national struggles led by Stalinists.

There are no pure elemental seams to be found in the history of Stalinism. Side by side with the wild ultra-leftism, Stalin could and did talk of manipulating history by letting the Nazis take power in Germany so that Hitler would keep the great European powers, the enemies of Russia, occupied while he, Stalin, built socialism in one country. In the period of courting France and Britain as Russia's allies against Hitler (1934-9), anti-imperialism against the British and French empires was banked down, in so far as Moscow could bank it down.

In the 1930s and afterwards, "anti-imperialist" economic nationalism guided powerful movements. It shaped economic policies in countries as far apart as, for example, Argentina, and the 26 Counties Irish state. Of course, there can be progressive manifestations of "nationalism" in certain economic areas: Egypt's nationalisation of the

Suez Canal, for example. The nationalisation of primary resources like oil may be a legitimate expression of a drive for national independence. But as a general proposition, economic nationalism is regressive. Generalised economic autarky would plunge the world backwards to the conditions of the 1930s and 40s.

In his denunciations of fascism and in his analysis of Stalinism, Trotsky justly branded the drive for economic autarky, for cutting away as much as possible from the world market, as thoroughly reactionary. It was, he thought, one of the reactionary, retrogressive crimes of Russian Stalinism.

The same idea was there in all his own programmatic proposals for the development of the USSR – for instance, in *Towards Socialism or Capitalism?* (1925), in which Trotsky outlined his proposals for developing the USSR, his alternative to both the 1920s Stalin-Bukharin idea of "socialism in one country" "at a snail's pace" and to the later-imposed collectivisation of agriculture and forced industrialisation at a breakneck pace. It was there in his proposals in the early 1930s that the unemployed movements in the advanced countries should advocate economic recovery linked to trade with the USSR.

As for Karl Marx and Frederick Engels, in the Communist Manifesto, there was "reactionary" socialism as well as working-class socialism, so also there can be backward-looking as well as forward-looking "anti-capitalisms" and "anti-imperialisms". Lenin showed that in his critique – in the 1916 pamphlet *Imperialism: The Highest Stage* – of the petty-bourgeois anti-imperialists who implicitly, or more less explicitly, wanted to go back to mid-19th-century-level medium-scale capitalism and free trade.

What Marx and Engels, in the Communist Manifesto called "reactionary socialism" was the view of a section of the traditional right at the time of the Communist Manifesto. Strong strands of it can be found in political Islam, as in Catholic-Christian clerical fascism. It was and never entirely ceased to be an aspect of the Catholic Church.

The socialist who therefore would have looked to the Pope and his subordinates as allies would have been a self-certified political imbecile! † For the reactionary anti-capitalists whom Marx and Engels discuss in the Communist Manifesto, it was a matter of criticising modern industrial society and wanting to go back to a pre-industrial time, back to an idealised Middle Ages, to rule by enlightened kings and noblesse-oblige aristocrats. Its fundament was an incapacity to link their criticism of capitalist industrial society and its bourgeois rulers with a perspective of the development of the actual, real, evolving society which they lived in and criticised. They had a positive alternative to offer, though one historically, and in terms of social development, behind existing capitalist society, that is, reactionary. In part it was an imaginary older system they advocated – an utopia, based on idealisation of what they thought had once existed. So it is now with political Islam and its subtextual aspiration to go back to the 7th century. They were radical critics of capitalist society too alienated to do much about it. Thomas Carlyle was a critic of capitalism, but a thoroughgoing political reactionary, an anti-black racist, a defender of slavery, an admirer and advocate of historical "supermen". Hitler is said to have kept Carlyle's account of Frederick the Great by him, even in the bunker at the end.

The addled left has, by way of accommodation to "anti-capitalists" like clerical-fascist Islam, taken over this reactionary, critical, alienated, impotent role of the reactionary socialists of the 19th century. Does it have an "ideal"? Nothing so worked out as that of the "back-there-somewhere" reactionary socialists or the Islamic clerical fascists. The severe rejection of utopianism by Marx and his followers restrains the elaboration by would-be Marxists of blueprints for ideal societies. So the alternative is defined only negatively. And that opens the way for even clerical fascism to be embraced – or at least to be held hands with – on the basis of the single cardinal virtue of being against "imperialism". But, aside from and as well as the effects on it of accommodating to reactionary anti-capitalist or "anti-imperialist" forces, the kitsch leftists are made into sterile critics like the "reactionary socialists" by a too-all-cutting-off negativism towards capitalist society – the society in which and on which, in the Marxist perspective, we must build to erect our socialism. This is one of the preconditions of their accommodation to Islamic clerical fascism.

If for Lenin and Trotsky and Luxemburg and Liebknecht, imperialism was first what imperialism did, in Stalinist and Orthodox Trotskyist discourse all that was stood on its head. Imperialism was not what the great powers did, not what the Stalinist power was doing,

---

† For example, even the pro-fascist Pope Pius XII, whose church in Europe was complicit with Croat Ustashe and other murderous fascists in the Second World War, and after the war organised a network of escape and temporary refuge for them – even Pius XII, in his Christmas message for 1942, called for "legislation [to] prevent the worker, who is or will be a father of a family, from being condemned to an economic dependence and slavery which is irreconcilable with his rights as a person. Whether this slavery arises from the exploitation of private capital or from the power of the state, the result is the same..." He also, as other parts of that statement show, was one of the legion of those then who thought that capitalism was coming to an apocalyptic end.

227

not what a number of smaller entities across the world, amongst them former colonies and semi-colonies, were doing. Imperialism came to be a name reserved for monopoly-capitalist powers, whatever they did or didn't do or no longer did. Starting from the supposed "class differences" between Russia and the West, the definition became less and less concerned with indicative deeds, and more with the ascribed inner essences of the powers, their "class nature". The prohibition on defining Russia as imperialism, when its deeds were a representative re-enactment of all the imperialistic horrors of history, from enslaving captured prisoners of war through looting to mass rape, pushed the whole issue nearer to concern with metaphysical essences than to re-alities. The "class nature" of the bourgeois states was palpable social, economic, political, and ideological fact. The "class nature" of the Stalinist states? The "workers' state" and non-imperialist character of Russia was something ascribed, on the basis of reasonings about the secret and hidden seer-defined inner content of the totalitarian-state-owned industry, though flatly contradicted by all the visible re-alities.

This was an "essentialist" approach which held to faith-saturated and delusion-saturated dogma, defended by word-juggling; which refused to judge and categorise by deeds, that is, by manifest reality. Stalinist Russia was not imperialist, whatever it did, because it was not capitalist, because it was a degenerated workers' state. Of the two blocs, socialists identified with the regressive, backward, reactionary bloc, and took much of it as representing a progressive alternative to capitalism. If you hold to the idea that the greatest and most oppres-sive imperialism is not imperialism; and that the once-great empires remain imperialist in the same sense as before after they have di-vested themselves of colonies and semi-colonies; and if a political ten-dency does that decade after decade, then it does something to its ability to make sense of the world.

The idea of Russia as a workers' state, and Trotsky's theory about that, could not, after the changes in World War Two, be true according to Trotsky's reasoning in 1940. Likewise, if the advanced capitalist powers were imperialist after the end of their colonial empires, then they were not that in Lenin's sense or the Communist International's sense or Trotsky's. The 1939-40 distinction, held to for decades, that the advanced capitalist powers were imperialist, and the USSR was not, separated presumed essences from deeds. When two powers be-haved similarly, or the "good" "non-imperialist" imperialism be-haved worse, it was nonetheless the "better" power because of reasonings about whether it was capitalist or not.

What follows from this in politics may appear banal, but is greatly and often fatally lacking in the addled left: that we examine each situation concretely and in terms of its specifics, and that we approach no situation as if we are still in the world of the old colonial imperialism, and the program that properly went with it can be applied automatically. We approach no international conflict with the automatic assumption that the more advanced countries are ipso facto "imperialist" and therefore a priori in the wrong, and a less advanced antagonist is ipso facto "anti-imperialist" and to be supported, its ideological reflections automatically given a respectful hearing. Where old-style colonialism or the threat of it exists, the old anti-colonial program of national struggle for independence and self-determination shows us what our attitude should be. But to approach episodes like the NATO interventions in Kosova or Libya to stop massacres with the assumption that support is mandatory for whomever opposes the great powers is like trying to find your way around the comparatively hygienic London Underground with a map of the Moscow sewers.

Other than the proletarian revolution no anti-imperialist program exists except reactionary ones, more or less reactionary according to the degree of regression to economic autarky and degree of social regression (both Mao's China and clerical-fascist Iran have been enormously regressive for their societies). We live in a world where the most important victims of imperialism in the time of Lenin's and Trotsky's Communist International and Trotsky's Fourth International, India and China, are becoming super-powers... In which Iran, occupied as late as 1946 (by Britain and Russia), and Iraq, a British protectorate until fifty years ago (1958), long ago grew to be competing regional imperialisms, and spent most of the 1980s locked in a World War One-style regional imperialist war of attrition, with horrendous World War One-level casualties on both sides

In this world, the residual elements of "anti-colonialism" will be auxiliary and subordinate to working-class socialist anti-imperialism. Otherwise "anti-imperialism" becomes a siding with anything else against the dominant capitalist powers, and comes to include siding with lesser, weaker imperialisms and regional imperialisms, like Iran or Iraq.

We are against imperialism as such, on the lines sketched by the Second Congress of the Comintern? Yes, but the point is that "anti-imperialism" cannot be effective outside of context, or outside of the concrete truths of world politics. The Comintern theses themselves made a modification, an exception, insisting on "the need to combat pan-Islamism and similar trends, which strive to combine the liberation movement against European and American imperialism with an attempt to strengthen the positions of the... mullahs, etc."

Placards on left demonstrations today routinely denounce not only the Israeli government's real misdeeds, but Israel, as such, as the world's hyperimperialism

The anti-imperialism of the fools

How Israel came to be the world's hyper-imperialism

"For the... Arab-chauvinist logic, we need look no further than the [second] main 'world Trotskyist' group, the International Workers' League. They want a 'democratic, secular and non-racist Palestine' – but with no rights for Jews! An article by... Nahuel Moreno argues against the slogan of a constituent assembly even after the destruction of Israel. '[This] is precisely the shameful manner to support the Zionists and justify their presence, giving a 'democratic' veneer to their fascist usurpation. If you want to insinuate that this assembly would be made with non-Zionist Jews... these imaginary inhabitants do not exist' (Correo Internacional, March 1988). Moreno puts forward the slogan, consequently of unambiguous meaning, 'Zionists out of Israel', and goes on to say: 'Tomorrow [we will also oppose] Arab racism. But tomorrow, not today. Because today Arab racism against Israel is progressive'." – Clive Bradley, *Workers' Liberty* 10, May 1988

In June 1967 Israel occupied that part of pre-1948 Palestine which the United Nations partition plan of 1947 had designated for an independent Palestinian state, to exist side by side with Israel. That Palestinian territory had been occupied and annexed in 1948-9 by Jordan and Egypt, and a small part of it by Israel. Now all of pre-war Palestine and Gaza was under Israeli control. Various Israeli offers to vacate the newly conquered territories in return for peace and recognition by the Arab states were rejected. Israel's occupation of that Palestinian-majority territory has so far lasted half a century. It has turned Israel into a regional imperialist power (in the sense that Marxists had called the pre-World-War-2 Czechoslovakian, Polish, and Yugoslav states imperialist: they ruled over minority peoples repressed to various degrees by the Poles, Czechs, Serbs). Israel has been a grubby and brutal imperialist power in its treatment of the Palestinians. As with any other imperialist occupation, Marxists have demanded that the occupying power, Israel, get out of the Arab-majority territories and allow the Palestinians to have their own state there. That there were special problems is not to be denied, but those cannot justify Israel's policy towards the Palestinians.

Israel is a regional imperialist power, allied to the USA since 1967. To the Palestinians in the West Bank and Gaza it is a vicious imperialist power in its own right. The only consistent democratic response to that is to demand that Israel vacate the Palestinian-majority territory and allow the Palestinians to set up a sovereign independent state alongside Israel; to support the Palestinians in their demand for a state of their own; and, politically, to judge everything by how it relates to those principles.

But that is not how it is seen on the ostensible left. Israel has a singular and tragic history. Its power to evoke obsessional hostility to itself is one of the most remarkable things in late 20th century and early 21st century politics. In its strength and duration it is unique. Most of the ostensible left is in the grip of anti-Israeli hysteria.

For decades, from Israel's June 1967 Six Day War and with renewed energy after the 1973 Yom Kippur Israeli-Egyptian war, hostility to Israel has been a major, and seemingly ever-intensifying, force in the labour movement. Some of that is a proper hostility to Israel's treatment of the Palestinians in the West Bank and Gaza. But there is more than that. In fact, in the denunciation of Israel there is often indifference to the living Palestinians, for whom an independent state of their own alongside Israel would be a tremendous liberation. There is often a blatant antisemitism.

Israel is seen as the world's hyper-imperialist power, Israeli nationalism as pure racism, Zionism as akin to Nazism. Israel is put in the same foul category as Hitler's Germany. Zionism is depicted as a near-demonic force in history, a force that, in its time, was able to control and use Hitler's massacres of Jews in order to further its political goals. Israel is a historically illegitimate state: nothing less than the destruction of this state, and the forcible removal from the Hebrew nation in Palestine of the right to have a state of their own, will suffice to rectify history's mistake in creating Israel. Destruction of Israel is the dominant policy on the added left. That policy is pursued even at great cost to the Palestinians, postponing any redress for them until after Israel has been destroyed.

Palestine was for centuries a mere sub-section of the province of Syria within the Ottoman (Turkish) empire. The territory always had a Jewish minority. The notion of restoring or recreating, after so many centuries, a Jewish state in Palestine was developed in the late 19th century by Theodor Herzl in a Europe rank with competing nationalisms, and in direct response to the Dreyfus case. That was a startling eruption of mass antisemitism in the country which had emancipated Jews to common French citizenship during the great revolution of 1789-94. A Jewish army officer, Alfred Dreyfus, was wrongly convicted of spying for Germany, and, as that became widely known, France divided for and against admitting that the army had made a gruesome mistake and releasing Dreyfus from his prison on Devil's Island. This left-vs-right, egalitarian-vs-antisemitic division of France would continue into the time when Vichy France would round up Jewish children, women, and men and deport them to the Nazi murder-camps.

Herzl concluded that Jews would never be accepted as common citizens in a world where they had no state of their own. Thus the idea of creating a Jewish state in Palestine took shape as a modern idea.

In November 1917, a few days before the Bolshevik revolution on the eve of the British conquest of Palestine from the Turks, Arthur Balfour, the British Foreign Secretary, wrote a letter to Walter Rothschild, a prominent Jewish banker, declaring that a victorious Britain would look favourably at the project of creating a "national home for the Jewish people". (Balfour did not write of a Jewish state in Palestine). To a degree that letter was a by-product of the Russian Revolution of February 1917, an attempt to win the sympathy of Jews in Russia, and also of Jews in the USA, for Britain in the war. Strangely, Balfour seems to have thought that the declaration would endear Britain to the socialists of Jewish background in the ranks of the anti-Zionist Russian revolutionaries and maybe incline them to help Britain in the war.

Zionism evolved as a practical project of persuading and organising Jews to go to Palestine under the whips and spurs and goads of 20th century European antisemitism, and then of the Nazi-created ghettoes and death camps. A big migration of Jews from Poland in the 1920s, fleeing severe ill-treatment there; another from Nazi Germany in the 1930s; and then an influx of survivors of Nazi genocide from all over Europe in the 1940s, created a Jewish nation in Palestine. Some hundreds of thousands of refugees driven out of Arab countries in the late 1940s, the 50s, and the 60s went to Israel.

A benign British attitude to Jewish migration to Palestine lasted no more than a decade, and then began to change under Arab pressure. By 1930 Britain was restricting Jewish landownership and moving to limit Jewish migration.

Palestine had been a backwater economically and socially, and sparsely populated (about 700,000 people in 1917, about 8% Jewish,

11% Christian, 80% Muslim). Jewish immigration changed that. The economy quickened and grew. Much waste land was reclaimed by the Zionists and put to use. One consequence of the quickening economy was Arab migration into Palestine (at least 40,000 between 1922 and 1945), in parallel with the Jewish incomers. Arab peasants in Palestine were evicted after Jewish land purchases. All such things are hurtful. But the numbers were smaller than those of peasant evictions in many "normal" cases of capitalist market-forces – "several thousand families were displaced... between the 1880s and the 1930s", that is, in 50 years. †

Chronic conflict between Jews and Arabs soon became a feature of the changing Palestine. Jews had been tolerated for centuries, but as inferior beings, despised non-Muslims, paying a special tax (as Christians also did). Jews coming into a territory in which Britain under a League of Nations mandate now ruled over both Jews and Arabs, and Muslims no longer ruled over Jews, attracted cultural, religious, and then political hostility.

The basic units of effective Jewish colonisation at that time were the kibbutzim, agricultural entities run as collective socialistic enterprises. On principle they did not hire and exploit Arab labour: they were instruments of Jewish national settlement. They practised strict equality, including equality between men and women. The women of the Jewish communities, dressing for convenience in shorts and shirts, were especially offensive and resented. The incomers' way of life outraged the watching Muslims. This clash of cultures and of ways of living was and would be a major factor in the evolving Jewish-Arab conflict. And then there was political opposition to the Zionist project of building up a Jewish nation, especially on the part of the Palestinian Arab elite.

Jewish-Arab clashes started as early as 1919. In 1929 a strong surge of Arab attacks on Jews set the alarm bells ringing in London. It was a pogrom movement. It was not focused on British rule: one of the mobilising slogans was "the British are with us". The minority Labour government, in the person of Lord Passfield, the Fabian so-

---

† Benny Morris, *Righteous Victims*, p.123. *The Palestinian Jew and adaptive Arab chauvinist Tony Cliff put the figure at "three to four thousand Arab tenants" over the whole period of Zionist colonisation: Socialist Appeal, December 1946. More than that were evicted by landlords in Ireland in many single years clustered around 1848 and again around 1880: 104,000 evicted in 1850 alone, for example, and evicted into a ruined world in which starvation and cholera had recently killed a million people, one in eight of the population, and many hundreds of thousands were fleeing to Britain and America.*

cialist Sidney Webb, set up a Commission of Enquiry, and Britain then began moves that by the end of the 1930s, on the eve of the World War and the Holocaust, amounted to rescinding the Balfour Declaration. With war looming in 1939, Britain turned to placating the Arabs. The Jews were not going to side with Hitler's Germany; the Arabs might, and most politically aware Arabs did. Britain resolved to end all Jewish immigration within five years, and to limit it to a total of 75,000 over those five years, i.e. about 15,000 a year. Nonetheless it failed to win over the Arab leaders. The main Palestinian Arab leader, Amin al-Husseini, the Mufti of Jerusalem appointed by the British, went to Germany and in the war organised a force of Bosnian Muslims to fight for Germany.

In the traditional judgement of international socialists and consistent democrats, revolutionary nationalists have in principle a right to use their immediate enemy's enemy to help win their own freedom. This was more than that. It was an alliance based on a common murderous hostility to the Jews and a desire to destroy them. Husseini had close links with leading Nazis such as Adolf Eichmann and very likely knew all about the Nazi death camps. Had Germany occupied Palestine, even temporarily, during the war, the Arabs whom Husseini influenced would have helped the Germans kill all the Jews, as did antisemites in European countries such as France.

Those – Trotsky, for instance – who rejected the Zionist project as an answer to the threat that Nazism posed for the Jews of Europe had argued that Palestine could turn into a giant ghetto for the Palestinian Jews in which they would be trapped. That "ghetto", had the Nazis and Husseini won control of Palestine, would then have been emptied straight into Nazi death camps, as were the Jews penned in the Nazi-imposed ghettoes of Europe. †

Two of every three Jews in Europe died at the hands of the Nazis and their collaborators in occupied countries, approximately six million people, between June 1941 and April 1945. At the end the Allies ignored requests that they bomb the railways to Auschwitz. For all the time the great slaughter of Jews was going on, the British patrolled and blocked the sea-paths of entry into Palestine for Jewish refugees from Europe. Shiploads of Jewish refugees sank in the Mediterranean, as shiploads of "illegal" migrants to Europe sink now.

---

† It should go without saying, but it doesn't, and so needs to be said plainly: such things as the Mufti-Nazi alliance, and what might have come of it had Germany occupied Palestine, do not and cannot detract from the right of the Palestinian people to self-determination in their own state. They should inhibit the poisonous kitsch-left equation of Zionism and Nazism, but they don't.

The British rounded up Jews who landed "illegally" and put them in internment camps in Cyprus.

The "Revisionist" Zionists inspired by Zeev Jabotinsky – unashamedly nationalist, anti-Arab, and anti-socialist – in 1944 started a small guerrilla war against the British in Palestine. After the World War, Britain continued to exclude all but a small quota of Jews from Palestine. More than 250,000 Jewish survivors of the death camps were now living as stateless "Displaced Persons" in camps in Europe. Jews going back to where they came from were victims of a pogrom in Poland and antisemitic riots in Paris. In Britain, in 1947, during the British-Jewish conflict in Palestine, anti-Jewish pogromist riots fomented by the Mosleyite fascists erupted in Liverpool, Leeds, and Manchester. In the Jewish part of Manchester, Cheetham Hill, windows were smashed and mobs attacked people in the streets. Conflict between the British and the Jews in Palestine, and between Jews and Arabs, escalated steadily. In February 1947 Britain announced that it would withdraw in 1948, and on 29 November 1947 the United Nations resolved to partition Palestine into a Jewish state and an Arab state. Russia voted for that. Desultory inter-communal guerrilla war escalated into a simmering Jewish-Arab war, priming for the struggle after British withdrawal.

On 14 May 1948 Britain officially relinquished its League of Nations mandate in Palestine, and the Jewish community declared Israel a sovereign, independent state in the part of Palestine allocated to them in the UN plan of partition. Europe's "Displaced Person" Jews now came to Palestine: for them, the declaration of the Jewish state in far-away Palestine spelt liberation. Immediately, Egypt, Jordan (Transjordan), Syria, Lebanon and Iraq invaded Israel. Azzam Pasha, secretary of the Arab League, declared: "It does not matter how many Jews there are. We will sweep them into the sea". †

The Arab armies of Jordan and Iraq were in part officered by British soldiers. The Israelis lacked both weapons and enough fully-trained professional soldiers, though some of them had served in the British or US armies during World War Two. The widespread anticipation was that the Jews could not defend themselves, and that Britain would go back in and resume control as "peace-keeper" between Arabs and Jews. In fact the Jewish citizen army, the Haganah, defeated the invading armies and the local Palestinian-Arab armed forces which, naturally, had rallied to the invading armies. Peace in the form of an uneasy truce was established in 1949. No Arab state

---

† *Benny Morris, 1948: A history of the first Arab-Israel war, p.187*

or entity recognised Israel, and to this day, in 2017, only two of them do, Egypt and Jordan. In the course of the war between Israel on one side, and the Arab forces on the other, some 750,000 Palestinian Arabs fled. Some were driven out, some chose to flee. The Revisionist-Zionist Irgun militia had slaughtered some 254 men, women, and children in the Palestinian Arab village of Deir Yassin on 9 April 1948, as a way of terrorising Palestinians to flee. Five days later some 78 people from a contingent of Jewish medical staff and their escorts were slaughtered. In the next years and decades about 600,000 Jews in Arab countries fled or were driven out to Israel, their property seized.

In the 1948 war, the territory allocated by the UN for an independent Palestinian state was incorporated into Jordan, and small parts of it into Egypt and into Israel.

Both the USA and Russia stood godfather to the new Jewish state. Stalin wanted to make trouble for Britain in the Middle East, where, though declining, it was still the chief foreign power. This was a sharp turn for Russia. Stalin had backed the Arabs both in 1929 and in 1936. The Communist International first defined the 1929 rising as an anti-Jewish pogrom – which it was, or was primarily – and then decided that it had been a great manifestation of anti-imperialist rebellion. In 1936 and after the members of the Communist Party of Palestine, Jews and Arabs, were instructed to participate in terrorist acts against the Jews. The international Stalinist organisations began a worldwide and typically Stalinist propaganda campaign against Jews in Palestine.

Yet in 1947 Russia voted at the United Nations for partition of Palestine and for a Jewish state. More than that, Russia, by way of its satellite Czechoslovakia, provided guns for the Haganah, breaking an international arms embargo which in practice worked against Israel, since the Arab states already had guns, as states do. Soon after that, Stalin switched again. He launched a great campaign against "Zionism". Old Communist Party leaders in Russia's satellite states of Jewish background were tried, jailed or hanged, and denounced, as part of an international Zionist conspiracy. The world Stalinist press ran a full-scale "anti-Zionist" campaign. It was in that campaign that the now-common stories and constructions about the collaboration and inner affinity between Zionists and Nazis were put into world circulation and began to gain wide acceptance. After the Stalinist fashion, these ideas became dogmas, articles of faith, in the Stalinist world. And much of what the Trotskisant left now says against "Zionism" was elaborated in that anti-Zionist campaign by the Stalinists. When Stalin died in 1953, preparations were being made for an "anti-Zionist" show trial in which the main defendants would have been the Jewish doctors who had looked after the health of the residents in the Kremlin.

That trial would have been the signal for deporting Russian Jews to Siberia and for the slaughter of unknowable numbers of them, in a smaller version of the Great Terror of 1934-8, but now focused on Jews. That Stalin might have completed Hitler's work must be judged a serious possibility. After his death, Stalin's successors cancelled the trial. For two decades after the declaration of Israeli independence, the Trotskyist press had little to say about Israel. The Stalinist campaign against Zionism petered out in 1953, with Stalin's death. Israel's right to existence was not questioned on the left. No-one on the left openly advocated that Israel be abolished and destroyed. Not even the Stalinists did. The pronouncements of Ahmed Shukeiri, head of the then Egyptian-controlled Palestine Liberation Organisation, who stuck to the old slogan, "drive the Jews into the sea", were seen as an embarrassment, and as something entirely alien to the left. The left was aware of the plight of the Palestinian refugees, but no-one put the sole blame for that on Israel. Israel said that "the Palestinian state" was Jordan, which had seized almost all the territory allocated to the Arabs by the UN in 1947. That was true, except that the Palestinians did not rule in Jordan and would suffer mass slaughter there in "Black September" 1970.

Outside of Arab countries, there was no talk of reversing the 1948 "settlement" in Israel-Palestine, not until in 1967 Israel acquired control of the whole of pre-1948 Palestine. Then, demands for Israel to withdraw from the territories occupied in 1967 were subsumed in the new Palestine Liberation Organisation policy, declared in 1969, of a "secular democratic" Arab state (with religious rights for Jews) in all of pre-1948 Palestine. That slogan won widespread support on the left. As has been said, its immediate political effect was to delegitimise Israel, defining it as a state which should never have come into existence and therefore had no right to go on existing. It delegitimised Israeli nationalism, which was redefined as "anti-Arab racism". The old Stalinist equation of Zionism with Nazism was there in the repertoire to be dug up and put front-stage, and it was. Indignation at Israel's continued occupation of the West Bank and Gaza gave autonomous life to the "nice", "secular democratic state", version of abolishing Israel, that is, in practical terms, conquering it.

After 1967, Stalinist states, notably Poland, revived their old "anti-Zionist" themes from 1949-53. A forerunner of AWL commented: "One of the worst signs of the regression in Poland... has been a very thinly disguised eruption of antisemitism... Under the banner of anti-Zionism the Partisans [harder-Stalinist faction] play the anti-Jew tune blatantly, playing also the Polish nationalist tune – in this country which saw its millions of Jews leave few survivors as they vanished into Auschwitz only a generation ago". †

Indignation over Israel's invasion of Lebanon in 1982 helped generate the strange idea that Israel is the hyper-imperialism, the epitome of imperialism, the imperialism of imperialisms. Left-wing campaigners came, more and more, to pillory "Zionism" not as one of the competing nationalisms in the Middle East but as an absolute evil. Picking up on the shameless Stalinist obscenity of the late 1940s and early 50s, they branded Zionism as a sibling of Nazism. For form's sake, the Stalinists had said that not all Jews were Zionists – that there were many socialist (Stalinist) Jews. But the 20th century experience of the Jews of Europe had meshed Jewish identity with Israel and with Zionism. The equation of Zionism and Nazism, branding Israeli nationalism as racism, and Zionism as pure evil, as the epitome of imperialism, the most extreme reaction, the most virulent racism – that could not but imply a comprehensive hostility to the big majority of Jews who to one degree or another, critically or fondly, support Israel.

The Trotskyists had resisted the demonisation of "Zionism" (as distinct from political opposition to it) from its first appearance in 1929. Max Shachtman, speaking for the whole US Trotskyist movement, published an article in *The Militant* (1 October 1929), which declared that: "Not every movement led by spokesmen of an oppressed nationality is a revolutionary movement. It is a lamentable fact that at the present time the Arab movement is directed by unconcealed reactionaries... They are against all Jews as Jews. They set up the reactionary demand for the 'restriction of the Jewish immigration into Palestine'...". It denounced the way in which for the Stalinists "the magic wand of the 'Third Period'" had transmuted this reactionary movement into a "national revolutionary uprising against British imperialism". The American and other Trotskyists continued during the war to advocate an open door in Palestine (and in America, of course) for Jewish refugees. ††

After the war, some Trotskyists backed the Jewish guerrillas against the British, defining their struggle as an anti-imperialist

---

† *The present writer as "Stan Lomax", Workers' Fight 8, August 1968.*
†† *The US Orthodox Trotskyists sometimes fudged the issue and implicitly counterposed "Open the Doors of the USA" to letting the Jews into Palestine.*

movement (Felix Morrow in the USA, some in France). The Shacht-manite Workers Party USA backed Israel's right to independence and its right to defend itself, though they also deplored the partition of Palestine, a political entity which had existed for a mere 30 years. It would have been impossible for the Trotskyists of that period to see Israel as a representative, surrogate, or tool of "imperialism". As we've seen, arms supplies to it were embargoed by all the big powers except Russia, and certainly it was not a tool of Russian imperialism (which in any case the Orthodox Trotskyists did not recognise as an imperialism).

The Trotskyist press had denounced the Stalinists' antisemitic campaign in 1949-53. In the mid-1950s, when Nikita Khrushchev de-nounced Stalin, there was widespread further comment in the Trot-skyist press about Stalinist antisemitism, and this around the time when Israel invaded Egypt in alliance with the British and French, as part of a British-French operation to reclaim the Suez Canal.

The kitsch-left way of seeing the problem, like the Islamist cleri-cal-fascist way, is not only anti-Jewish, but also anti-Palestinian. It rules out any redress for the Palestinians this side of the destruction of Israel, and the setting up of an Arab or Islamic state in all of pre-1948 Palestine, including what is now Israel.

That left routinely equates Israel with apartheid South Africa, an equation that does not stand up. The Jewish population of Palestine has never depended on the exploitation of Arab labour, and the treat-ment of Palestinians in Israel has never been remotely like that of black and "coloured" people in apartheid South Africa. There is, how-ever, a "parallel" between Israel and South Africa that the serious left would do well to remember. Britain seized the Cape of South Africa during the Napoleonic wars, and began to put pressure on the Boers who had been there since the 17th century.

Starting in 1835, many of the Boers went off inland and founded new states. Eventually British expansion from the Cape caught up with them. The Boer War of 1899-1902 followed. Everywhere Britain was disliked. People backed the Boers. So did socialists. There was mass opposition to the war in Britain, from the socialist left, from Lib-erals and even from future Prime Minister Lloyd George. Britain's war was denounced by much of the anti-war "movement" as "a Jew-ish war" – a war for the interests of "Jewish financiers" and on behalf of Jewish settlers in South Africa. Though it is now half-forgotten, that was a large component of the case against the war made in Britain – and perhaps elsewhere: I don't know – by the anti-war cam-paign, and it was a big, vigorous, raucous campaign.

The Boer republics had denied equal political rights to new settlers, and that fact was used as an ideological weapon to justify Britain's war. What settlers? "Jews", said much of the anti-war movement. (Including some leaders of the British Marxist organisation, the SDF, Henry Hyndman and Harry Quelch. Hyndman's use of anti-semitism in anti-war agitation was part of the bill of indictment which the British followers of Daniel De Leon, and James Connolly, who split from the SDF in 1903 to form the Socialist Labour Party, drew up against him. Hyndman was far from being alone in the SDF on that). Such people as the Liberal J A Hobson, whose study of imperialism Lenin would draw upon during World War One, also denounced the war as one for Jewish settlers and for international Jewish finance.

The "Jewish settlers" were the "Israelis" in the war; "international Jewish finance" was the world Jewish (or, today, "Zionist") conspiracy or quasi-conspiracy, and, for some, hegemony; and Britain was what the USA is today, the chief backer of "the Jews". The campaign against the "Jewish settlers" and Britain was a campaign on behalf of the Boers – who were the foulest anti-black racists. †

At the beginning of the 20th century, those who fulminated against "the Jews", unlike the kitsch left today, had no inkling that they were feeding a fire that would engulf two out of every three of Europe's Jews.

The policy of eliminating Israel – not of stopping Israel ill-treating the Palestinians, and of winning for the Palestinians their own state, on the land where they are the majority or were the majority in 1967, but of conquering the Hebrew nation in Israel, depriving them of self-determination, killing an incalculable proportion of them – that policy is, in and of itself, a fully tooled-up species of aggressive antisemitism. The attitude of wanting to eliminate an entire nation is, on the left, unique to Israel. Israel's treatment of the Palestinians naturally and justly provokes hostility and condemnation, and sharpens the desire to help the Palestinians. The desire to see the Hebrew nation conquered and destroyed, coupled with positive support for any and all forces attacking Israel, ranging from suicide-murder bombers from the clerical-fascist Hamas to any Arab or Islamic state committed to destroying Israel – that is a form of self-generating and

---

† No, I am not arguing that it was wrong to oppose the Boer war, any more than deploring the politics of the anti-war movement in 2002-3 makes me think it was wrong to oppose the invasion of Iraq. But serious socialists try to learn from history – not to relive past errors, as the "absolute anti-Zionists" now are doing.

self-sustaining antisemitism. In the real world it is not an expression of concern for the Palestinians, though of course most of those who go along with it think it is. It is hostile to the needs and interests of the Palestinians on whom it battens.

By making any redress for the Palestinians dependent on the conquest and destruction of Israel, it rules out redress in the calculable future. A Palestinian state, however, is still not unachievable. It could be and should be imposed on Israel by international pressure and coercion. Tardiness in setting up such a Palestinian state is allowing the Israeli chauvinists to work towards making it impossible by way of the expansion of settlements on Arab-majority land.

One segment of Israeli leaders is, it seems, reconciled to the program of an Israeli state, covering all pre-1948 Palestine, within which there will be a vast hostile Palestinian minority at odds with the Jewish Israelis and therefore subject to "preventive" ill-treatment as now for an indefinite span of history. Such a one-state "solution" would continually reproduce a hellish situation for both Palestinians and Israeli Jews, as would its mirror-image, an Arab-Islamic state in all Palestine with conquered Jews as a minority.

Those who advocate or pursue a one-state policy serve neither Jewish Israelis nor Palestinians. Leaving aside whether it is right or wrong, justified or unjustified, for practical purposes the demand that the Palestinians renounce self-determination in their own territory, until the destruction of Israel at some indeterminate but far distant date, is an anti-Palestinian policy too. The pseudo-left advocates of this policy are in the grip either of "anti-imperialist" fantasies which see Israel as the world's hyper-imperialism, as the metaphysical essence of imperialism, or of God-will-find-a-way, other-worldly Islamists in whose picture of realities and likely future realities, the Palestinians as living human beings matter not at all.

The Palestinians are not well-served by their kitsch left champions and advocates, who follow their own agendas and fantasies, not the needs of the Palestinians or the possibilities of serving them. The kitsch left in Britain votes down Palestinian-serving two-states propositions at meetings.

The basic fact is that both the Islamic clerical-fascists and the "anti-imperialist" left, though they make full use in propaganda of Israeli's ill-treatment of the Palestinians and sometimes exaggerate it, are much more hostile to Israel than they are friendly to the Palestinians. Fundamentally, they are anti-Israelis, not pro-Palestinians. In practical politics their obsession with destroying Israel makes them poisonously anti-Palestinian, too.

On the level of policy and advocacy of policy, the candid answer of properly self-aware absolute anti-Zionists to the charge that they are antisemitic is: "so what? Our attitude is justified. It is antisemitic, but what of it?" Hostility to Israeli policy and Israeli actions against the Palestinians is just and necessary. Many Israelis disagree with their government's policies and actions. Is hostility to those Israelis, too, justified? Yes, would answer the candid absolute anti-Zionists: those people too are *Israelis*, they do not support the abolition of Israel, they are Zionists. Not their political opinions, but their existence is their offence, and the warrant for treating them as enemies to be disarmed and made helpless, destroyed, or driven out. And what of Jews across the world who back Israel's right to go on existing? Zionists, too.

The "anti-imperialist" hostility to "Zionists" – who, if "Zionism" is support for Israel's right to go on existing, include most Jews alive – is on some levels as strange as the old antisemitism was when it identified Jews with money. It was not that there were no rich Jews, no Jewish financiers, as rapacious as other financiers, no Jewish small-scale gouging money-lenders. The poisonous twist was the identification of all Jews with usurious wealth.

So now there is Israeli colonial imperialism in the Palestinian-majority territories. To go from that to identifying all Israeli Jews, and all Jews across the world who have affinity with Israel, with "imperialism", is the strange thing. Israel becomes the super-imperialism. Imperialism must be wiped out, and Israel is the epitome of imperialism, the imperialism of imperialisms, as Jewish capitalists were the money-capitalists of money-capitalism. *There* is imperialism. *That* is where imperialism lives – in Israel.

On one level this attitude is possible only to people who no longer see imperialism as primarily a system of state actions, but rather as an "essence" which they track to its worldly lair. Israel has all the real and alleged sins of all imperialism, and of advanced capitalism, loaded on to it, and all the hostility to imperialism focused against it. As gold is the universal equivalent commodity in which the values of all other commodities are expressed, so Israel is the universal equivalent of imperialism. It is not far along that trajectory to the idea of Jews everywhere being the embodiment of imperialism because of their typical identification with Israel. The article on Paul Foot and Tam Dalyell in this book (page 314) records a rare public example of the workings of the mind of one who knowingly substitutes "Zionist" for "Jew" to rationalise hostility to Jews.

Confronting the old antisemitism which identified capitalism with

243

Jews and Jews with capitalism, the German Marxist August Bebel famously said that it was "the socialism of fools". Wipe-out-Israel "anti-imperialism" is the anti-imperialism of the fools.

These cartoons portraying Jews in traditional antisemitic images were published not in the Nazi but the in the Stalinist press – in fact, the Jewish Stalinist press. They appeared in the Communist Party USA's Yiddish daily Freiheit on 4 September and 3 October 1929. It was the time of the anti-Jewish pogroms in Palestine which the Stalinists, after first denouncing them as pogroms, then hailed as an upsurge of revolutionary anti-imperialism.

The left in disarray: ten polemics

1. The warmongering anti-war demonstrations

The demonstrations all over Britain since the Israeli offensive on Gaza began on 27 December [2008] have been heavily fuelled by raw, justified, outrage at the human cost to the Palestinians of what Israel is doing.

Israel's offensive in Gaza is in the tradition of the US-British slaughter of Iraqi conscript soldiers retreating from their occupation of Kuwait at the end of the first Gulf war in 1991. An American soldier described that as "like shooting fish in a barrel". So too in Gaza now.

Israel has immense technical superiority over Hamas. And the Hamas "fish" swim in the "waters" of a densely-packed civilian population. At least a third of the casualties, maybe far more, have, inevitably, been "civilians".

The disproportion between the damage being inflicted on Israel's people and what Israel is doing to the Palestinians of Gaza makes it seem beside the point that this is a two-sided war, that Hamas is waging war on Israel too. The slaughter in Gaza cancels out awareness of everything else.

The coverage in the press has focused heavily on the slaughter, on the horror, and on the number of civilians being killed in Gaza. So have the nightly images on the TV screens.

Thus the *Guardian* and other media have done most of the work in conjuring up the feelings and the outrage that fuel the demonstrations; and the "left", especially the SWP, have done much of the organising for the demonstrations.

But the *politics* of the demonstrations have been provided by the Islamic chauvinists. In terms of its dominant politics – support Hamas, support Arab and Islamic war on Israel, conquer and destroy Israel – the big demonstration on 10 January [2009] in London was politically an Arab or Islamic chauvinist, or even, to a horrifying extent, a clerical-fascist, demonstration. *Their* slogans, *their* politics, *their* program, echoed, endorsed, and insisted upon by the kitsch left, have provided the politics of the demonstrations, more or less drowning out everything else.

The clerical fascists have been allowed to hegemonise the politics of the demonstrations to an astonishing degree. Despite the intentions of most of the demonstrators, these have not been peace demonstration, but pro-war, war-mongering, demonstrations – for Hamas's war, and for a general Arab and Islamic war on Israel. On Saturday 10 January [2009] in London many placards portrayed Arab heads of state, depicting them as traitors for not going to the aid of the Palestinians.

In their political slogans and chants, the dominant forces on the demonstrations have been not only against what Israel is doing in Gaza now, but against Israel as such, against any Israel – against Israel's right to exist. Opposition to the Gaza war, and outrage at it, only provide the immediate justification for flaunting and propagating the settled politics of organisations that seek the root-and-branch extirpation of Israel and "Zionism".

Such politics have long been a central theme of "anti-war" demonstrations, but my strong impression is that they are bolder, cruder, more uninhibited, and more explicit now than they have been.

On 10 January SWPers on loudhailers chanted: "Destroy Israel". This chant was pervasive: "From the river to the sea/ Palestine will be free" – demanding an Arab Palestine that includes pre-1967 Israel – was pervasive. Placards called for "Freedom for Palestine", which, for Arab and Islamic chauvinists and addled left alike, means Arab or Muslim rule over all pre-1948 Palestine. It implies the elimination of the Jewish state, and since that could be done only by first warring against Israel and conquering it, the killing of a large part of the people of Israel.

Placards equated Israel with Nazism, and what Israel is doing in Gaza with the factory-organised systematic killing of Jews in Hitler-ruled Europe. Placards about "60 years since the Nakba" [the Arab term for their defeat in 1948] – though not many of those – complemented the chants about "Palestine... from the river to the sea" and pointed up their meaning.

The dominant theme, "stop the slaughter in Gaza", understandable in the circumstances, could not – in the complete absence of any demands that Hamas too stop its war – but be for Hamas and Hamas's rocket-war on Israel. In so far as the placards and chants gave the demonstration its political identity, it was a demonstration for more war. Even the talk of "the massacre", though all too accurate, subsumed Hamas into the general population, and was one variant of implicit solidarising with Hamas, its rocket war, and, inescapably, its repressive clerical-fascist rule over the people of Gaza. The SWP in 2007 had welcomed Hamas's takeover in Gaza.

Talk of "genocide" in Gaza implied an absolute equation of the people of Gaza with Hamas, and absolute solidarity with Hamas.

Even the identifiable Jews on the Saturday 10th demonstration –

Neturei Karta, a Jewish equivalent of Hamas, whose people for religious reasons want to put an end to Israel – fitted into the general clerical-fascist politics.

On the January 3rd demonstration, a group of political Islamists near me, some with faces covered by scarves or balaclavas with only eye and mouth holes, pointedly raised their fists and started to chant Allahu Akhbar (God is great) as we passed the Houses of Parliament.

Platform speakers on Saturday 10th nonsensically but with demagogic effectiveness equated Israel – pre-1967 Israel too – with apartheid, and told us that Israel could be eliminated as white rule was in apartheid South Africa.

The "left" and the ex-left were heavily represented on the platform on Saturday 10th. Andrew Murray of the Communist Party of Britain (chairing), Tariq Ali (the rich "fun revolutionary" of long ago, all suffused in a grey-white tinge as if he had been dug out of the freezer, the ghost of anti-war demonstrations past!), Tony Benn, Jeremy Corbyn, and George Galloway spoke. The SWP's Lindsey German, convenor of the Stop The War Coalition, wore a vivid red coat, but that was the only thing red about either her or the platform.

No criticism of the Arab or Islamic chauvinism or Islamic clerical-fascism of so much of the demonstration, nor even any distancing from it. No support for Arab and Palestine Liberation Organisation demands for a Palestinian state alongside Israel. Only one-sided anti-war war-mongering – pro-Hamas, demanding, in different degrees of boldness and clarity, war to put an end to Israel. Craig Murray, a former British diplomat, made the most clear-cut demand for the rolling-back of 60 years of history and the elimination of Israel.

There was no criticism of the Arab and Islamic regimes other than for their "treason" to the Palestinians in not making war on Israel. A genuine peace march would at least have had some degree of criticism of the refusal of most of the Arab governments to make peace with Israel. And no reference whatsoever to the Israeli working class or to the idea that the Arab and Israeli workers should unite (even if in the not-near future).

Thus, the "left" on the demonstration, its main organisers, were entirely hegemonised and hypnotised by the politics, slogans, and program of Arab and Islamic chauvinism and, explicitly, of the clerical fascists of political Islam.

The feelings expressed in the demonstration had had a six to seven year build-up, during which that "left" has promoted the politics of Islamic clerical-fascism, and even its organisations, the British Muslim Initiative and the Muslim-Brotherhood front, Muslim Association of Britain. Hamas is an offshoot of the Muslim Brotherhood.

The "left", from outside the mainly-Muslim communities in Britain – it is still very much outside: the evidence of the demonstration is that the SWP has gained very few recruits of Muslim background from its half-decade of accommodating to Islam and posing as the best "fighters for Muslims" – has done all it can to push the youth of the Muslim communities behind Islamist political and religious reaction. It has courted and promoted the forces of political, social, and religious reaction within those communities.

Instead of advocating and building working-class unity on ideas and slogans such as "black and white – Muslim, Christian, Jewish, Hindu, atheist – unite and fight", the kitsch-left have made themselves into communalists, the best "fighters for Muslims". On the political basis of Muslim communalism, no working-class unity could conceivably be built.

Instead of helping secularising, rebellious youth in the Muslim communities to differentiate from their background, instead of using the anti-war demonstrations to give them a focus broader than their starting point, the kitsch-left has "related" to the communities as such, and to the conservative and reactionary elements within them – including clerical-fascists – and that has helped those right-wingers to control, and the political-Islamist organisations to recruit, the youth, including women.

Instead of organising anti-war movements on the basis of secular, democratic, working-class, socialist politics, it has organised an "anti-war" movement that advocates a general Arab-Islamic war on Israel.

Two seemingly contradictory things dominated the demonstration. The politics of Islamic chauvinism, clerical fascism, and hysterical hostility to Israel gave it its political character – an Islamic chauvinist demonstration in which the forces of the addled left sunk their identity, rather as the crazily ultra-left Stalinist German Communist Party in the two or three years before Hitler came to power sunk its own identity into fascist-led concerns with "liberating" Germany from the Treaty of Versailles.

And... it was a heavily a-political demonstration. A large part of the demonstrators, the majority I guess, have not sifted through the politics of the Israeli-Arab conflict, considered the options, studied the implications of slogans, and made deliberate choices, but react "raw" to the horrors of the Israeli offensive in Gaza, and many take the slogans, ideas, and programs stamped on the demonstrations by the Islamists and their "left" allies as things given.

For instance, "Freedom for Palestine", for many of the marchers, does not mean that they have thought about and understood what the slogan means to those who raise it: Arab and Islamic rule over all pre-1948 Palestine, slightly encoded. "Free Palestine", to such people, probably means freedom for the Palestinian-majority areas – Gaza and the West Bank.

That the clerical-fascists can politically dominate on the demonstrations is in part a result of this political underdevelopment. The precondition for it – for making people who react "raw" into demonstration-fodder for clerical-fascism – is the politics of the addled left vis-a-vis political Islam.

The demonstrations have also been undisguisedly antisemitic, more so than ever. Placards equating Zionism and Nazism and about Israel's "Holocaust" against the Palestinians all have implications way beyond Israeli politics and Israel itself. Calls for a boycott of Israeli goods, understandable enough on the face of it, were pretty much central. The main argument against such a boycott is that it is an indiscriminate weapon against all Israelis, and that it would quickly become a targeting of Jews everywhere, in Britain too. A small event on 10 January illustrated the point: a Starbucks café was attacked by some of the demonstrators seemingly because some people thought that it is owned by Jews.

The 10 January demonstration shows that political Islam now has a serious political presence in Britain. Nor can socialists and secularists draw comfort from the experience in the first half of the 20th century when superstition-riddled Jewish communities quickly assimilated and generated large-scale left-wing commitment by secularising Jews. The Islamist politicisation of the Muslim communities is not something specific to Britain, nor is it simply a movement of oppressed people.

Those politicised sections of the Muslim communities are part of a world-wide movement which includes powerful states and some of the richest people on earth (in Saudi Arabia, for instance.) This world-wide movement is, in political terms, very reactionary. It is not likely that any sizeable part of it will soon shed its present reactionary character.

The serious left has to find ways of supporting the Muslim communities here against racism, discrimination, and social exclusion, without accommodating politically or socially to their reactionary traits, and without falling into the politically-suicidal idiocy of pandering to Islamic clerical-fascism by way of adopting its slogans and goals. Involvement of Muslim workers and youth in the labour movement, combined with militant labour-movement commitment to defending the communities against racism and discrimination, has to be our chief method here.

Our keynote politics have to be of the type of "black and white, unite and fight", not the adaptive Islamic communalism that has reigned on the left for the last decade. Within that general approach we must fight Islamic clerical-fascism and help its opponents in the Muslim communities.

The kitsch-left has a lot to answer for over the last decade. There is no way of measuring exactly what could have been done to wean sections of Muslim youth away from political Islam, but if the "left" – in the first place the SWP – had maintained a principled working-class socialist, secularist stand, and combined that with defending Muslims against racism and discrimination, for sure more people of Muslim background could have been won to socialism. The clerical fascists would not have had the virtually unchallenged political ride they have had on the back of an accommodating addled left, and are still having.

It has to be said again that the flood-tide of world-wide political Islam has worked and is working against separating large forces of youth from Islamic reaction. The predominant form of "rebellious-ness" there seems to be against assimilating, "moderate" forces, and for political-Islamist militancy.

Even so, much could have been done. Instead the addled left has committed political hara-kiri, coloured itself Islamic green – and done its best to help reinforce the domination of conservative, reactionary, Islamic-chauvinist politics in the Muslim communities.

It has done everything it can to boost Islamic clerical fascism, pro-mote it, and render it politically respectable in the labour move-ment. We are probably far from seeing the full consequences of the politicisation of sections of the Muslim communities under cleri-cal-fascist hegemony that has taken place and continues now.

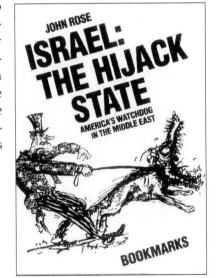

An SWP-UK pamphlet cover presents Israel as the USA's watchdog, and also the mad dog dragging the reluctant USA into aggression.

251

2. Is there a socialist quintessence in Irish nationalism? Ireland and the theory of Permanent Revolution

May 2015.
Charles: The shogun of the murdering anti-Crown IRA scum, I presume?

Adams: The bloody Prince and future King of the bastard English nation, I presume?

I

"We do not regard Marx's theory as something completed and inviolable; on the contrary, we are convinced that it has only laid the foundation stone of the science which socialists must develop in all directions if they wish to keep pace with life" – Vladimir Lenin, *Collected Works* 4 (211-2)

Revolutionary Marxism is a way of looking at the world, analysing it and changing it. It embodies certain key basic ideas (the ultimate priority of the mode of production in shaping society, including its ideas; the class struggle; the centrality of the working class in modern history). Marxism deals with an ever-changing reality. There is no rest, no finality. Reality moves, permutes, is transformed. The best texts of Marxism "age" and become progressively divorced from the evolved reality whose ancestor, so to speak, they captured. There can be no "sacred texts". To treat any of the texts of Marxism, the past judgements of Marxists, as embodying supra-historical truth. is to break with the heart of Marxism and to transform attempted works of science into quasi-religious objects of veneration. To the degree that such texts are worshipped instead of being critically reviewed, used, worked over, they lose whatever power they had to illuminate reality and thus help us in the work of changing it. We kill or fail to develop the capacity in ourselves to use the tools of Marxism.

The Marxists whose work we now venerate worked differently. Marxism was a method of analysing concrete reality. Previous Marxist attempts to analyse the same or antecedent reality offered guides, models, ideas, comparisons for the working, thinking, living Marxists. In truth, of course, everyone thinks about the world, even the religious text-worshippers, except that their cogitations do not go further than the thought that Marx or Lenin or Trotsky – or Stalin or Mao – was infallible and could tell you about your world, though it may have come into existence after they were dead. What the dogmatist usually does in practice is pragmatically and impressionistically take an attitude on current events and then find the right quotes to dress it up. Marxism as a method of analysing reality atrophies.

Ireland shows at its worst this process of atrophying and of dead "Marxism" being filled with alien content. Marx and Engels analysed Ireland. They died; Ireland changed. Partial analyses of aspects of Ireland's evolution were made by later Marxists influenced by Marx and Engels. Ireland evolved into two bourgeois states. And there, frozen at the point when the Communist International died as a Marxist, working-class organisation, "Marxism" on Ireland stopped.

Comments and analyses of Marx and Lenin (Lenin's radically wrong at the start: see "Marxism and Ireland" and "Why Lenin got Ireland wrong" in *Workers' Liberty* 22 and 23) became timeless truths of the Stalinist church and gained wide influence by merging with left-wing republicanism. "Trotskyists" who thought they had done their duty as Marxists if they re-labelled what the Stalinists called "completing the bourgeois revolution" and straight Republicans called "reunifying Ireland", calling it "Permanent Revolution" instead, have been a part, and not the least influential part, of this process. Nobody who knows both Irish reality and Trotsky's theory of Permanent Revolution could believe "Permanent Revolution" has any bearing on Irish politics. I have never in many decades of debate found anyone able to argue for it seriously. But they "believe" it. It is the common dogma, functioning as a licence for playing the chameleon to petty bourgeois nationalism.

Marxists, if they are Marxists, draw from life, not from the dead or half-dead reflection of ever-changing life in old texts.

II

For many years, self-indulgent socialists have woven political fantasies around the Provisional IRA / Sinn Fein, that is, around physical-force republicanism.

Their basic idea is that there must be an Irish national revolution – and they mean by that, that the political unification of the island must be won: that's all it can mean – and that in the winning of that nationalist, "bourgeois-democratic" revolution against "Imperialism" the Irish working class, North and South, Protestant and Catholic, can be roused, mobilised and educated in "the struggle" to go on "uninterruptedly" to make the Irish socialist revolution.

For the duration of the Provo War, "Permanent Revolution" served to rationalise socialist accommodation to the Provisional IRA: up to the Good Friday Agreement, there were always "Trotskyists", and not by any means only in Ireland, to argue that, any day now, the Provo war would start to "develop" into the Irish workers' revolution.

Let us discuss the theory of Permanent Revolution. † History knows a number of classic bourgeois revolutions against feudalism – that of the Dutch republic in the 16th century, the English Cromwellian revolution of the 1640s, and the "supplementary" revolution in 1688, and the great French revolution against the king and

---

† *See also account of it in the section on imperialism in this book.*

the entrenched aristocrats, in 1789 and after.

These revolutions won freedom for developing bourgeois societies from old feudal and church-state constraints, restrictions and interference. They won civil liberties – in England such things as habeas corpus, no pre-publication censorship and, above all, the rule of parliament – with very limited suffrage – instead of that of the king. In the Netherlands they won self-determination.

In France the lower orders, the "sans-culottes", made the revolution and put their own radical stamp on it before losing power to the bourgeoisie.

But what of countries in the era of modern capitalism where bourgeois-democratic revolutions still need to be made, and where a set of unrealised bourgeois-democratic tasks, necessary for the development of society, overlap with, abut on, working-class socialist revolutions or revolutionary movements? "Permanent revolution"?

Theories of permanent revolution concern themselves with the relationship of the working-class socialist revolution to still-ahead bourgeois revolutionary social tasks in underdeveloped countries, where feudalistic and other pre-capitalist institutions need to be overthrown – freedom for market economic development, civil liberties and a democratic republic need to be won. That includes colonies and semi-colonial countries during their struggles for bourgeois-democratic freedom against colonialism and imperialism, and in the first place for self-determination.

There are a number of theories of permanent revolution. They can be divided conveniently into pre- and post-October 1917 theories.

After the defeat of the bourgeois-democratic revolution in Germany in 1848, Karl Marx talked of the revolution "in permanence", and he roughed out working-class tactics for such situations: the workers would join with bourgeois revolutionaries against reaction, would strike the common enemy together with them, but would "march separately" – maintain working-class political independence and serve working-class goals. It would be a continuous process, up to the working-class conquest of power.

Marx soon faced up to the fact that capitalism had survived and entered into a long period of more-or-less stable expansion. Central Europe evolved differently from any "permanent revolution" scenario. In Germany, Bismarck, the servant of the junker landlords and the monarchy, carried out most of the bourgeois social – as distinct from political – goals of the 1848 revolution, in his own way and from above, without dislodging the junker class or the monarchy, indeed strengthening and enhancing them. When the radical bourgeois political tasks posed in 1848 were realised in 1918/19 – the monarchy overthrown, the democratic Weimar Republic set up – it wasn't as part of an ongoing working-class-led permanent revolution: it was counterposed by its leaders, the right-wing social democrats, to the German proletarian revolution. You could say it was inverted "permanent revolution". For the working class it was a counter-revolutionary bourgeois-democratic revolution. (It was the starting-point for the disorientation on the question of democracy which still sometimes skews the revolutionary left).

III

The pioneer Marxists in Russia, like the Marxists of other socially and politically backward countries, advocated a revolution like that of the French revolution, as a necessary stage in social evolution towards the possibility of a socialist revolution. The Russian Marxists, Plekhanov above all, took their stand against Russia's predominant Narodnik populists, who hoped that history would spare Russia the experience of capitalism, that there could be, so to speak, a jump into socialism rooted in the peasantry. Plekhanov insisted that capitalism already existed in Russia and was developing irreversibly. Following Plekhanov, Vladimir Lenin did that too, in a long book, *The Development of Capitalism in Russia*. Inevitably, capitalism would continue to develop. In Russia too, socialism would be made by the industrial proletariat. But what exactly did this mean in Russia – in concrete Russian social and political conditions?

On this two basic Marxist schools of thought emerged in the 1905 revolution and after, both based on the premiss that increasingly capitalist but immensely backward Russia was socially ripening toward a revolution like that which England and France had had. These were the Bolshevik and Menshevik schools.

I'll put it very schematically. For the Mensheviks, including the great pioneers Plekhanov and Axelrod, this bourgeois revolution would be led by the bourgeoisie. One task of the Marxists was to make sure the bourgeoisie weren't frightened off doing that by an over-assertive working-class movement. Lenin in 1905 and after (indeed, until he died, in January 1924) agreed that socially Russia was ripe enough only for a bourgeois-democratic revolution like that of France 100 years earlier. But, analysing the social and political relations in Russia, including those of the bourgeoisie to the landlords on one side and to the already powerful working-class movement on the other, he concluded that the Russian bourgeoisie could not, would not, lead an anti-tsarist revolution: they were tied in too closely by financial and other ties to the landlords and too afraid of the militant socialist working class to do that. At best they would work to modify the Tsarist regime, with post-1848 Germany and the English Whig settlement of 1688 as their models.

Lenin's paradoxical conclusion was that the bourgeois revolution in Russia would be led by the workers and peasants, in something like equal partnership. The workers and peasants would in that revolution play the role that the plebeian sans culottes had played in the French revolution, who had, before the Jacobins were overthrown, driven the revolution far deeper and broader than the bourgeoisie wanted. The "bourgeois revolution" would in that sense also be a revolution against the big bourgeoisie. It would be bourgeois in what it could achieve – a republic, democratic rights – but the bourgeoisie could not lead that revolution.

Vladimir Lenin postulated a "democratic dictatorship of the proletariat and peasantry". "Democratic dictatorship" was not a piece of political oxymoronism. Dictatorship did not mean what Stalinism would make the word mean in the 20th century. Lenin had in mind plebeian democracy: it would be mass dictatorship in the sense that the workers and peasants would overrule and destroy the laws and entrenched rights of the old rulers, physically suppressing those who served them and, in general, would act "dictatorially" in that sense. The force that would do it would itself be a democratically self-ruling mass movement.

It was, Vladimir Lenin argued, in the interests of the working class that as much as possible of the old feudalistic debris be cleared away, and replaced by a democratic republic in which all political and social relations were transparent and stripped of mystifications: these would be the best conditions for the working-class struggle for socialism in the decades after the bourgeois revolution had reached equilibrium.

Trotsky made pretty much the same assessment as did Lenin, but he disagreed with Lenin's political conclusions and the perspectives he built on them. In 1905 he analysed Russian social conditions and postulated that the Russian anti-tsarist revolution would be led by the working class which would go on interruptedly to take power for itself and make a working-class revolution. It would be one continuous process. Trotsky advocated "permanent revolution".

Yes, said Trotsky, to Lenin's democratic dictatorship of the workers and peasantry: the workers and peasants will make the bourgeois revolution, but not as in Lenin's conception as more or less equal partners. The revolution would culminate not in the establishment of a bourgeois-democratic republic but of a workers' republic: the permanent revolution would go in one uninterrupted movement, led by the workers, at the head of, not in equal partnership with, the peasantry, to working-class power.

The peasantry, argued Trotsky, can play no independent role in making the socialist revolution: they will, as in history so far the peasantry always have, follow, be led by, one of the town classes – either the bourgeoisie or the proletariat.

The workers, backed by, at the head of, the peasantry will make the revolution. The workers will take power – not democratic dictatorship of the workers and peasantry but dictatorship of the proletariat (again, dictatorship meaning not the meaning Stalinism has given it in modern history, but as above: it would be a mass popular dictatorship against the old ruling class and their institutions and their servants, smashing their power and institutions – taking those institutions by storm). And what will the working class do in power?

Pass a self-denying ordinance and not look out for their own working-class interests – for example, not pass eight-hour day legislation? No, Trotsky argued, the workers in power will act in their own class interests. Make Russian socialism? No. That was impossible. It was too backward, economically and socially. Here Trotsky did not differ from either the Mensheviks or Lenin that socialism could not be built in Russia.

This would be a working-class revolution in social conditions that were greatly unripe for the creation of socialism – where Marxists believed socialism was not yet socially possible. What would happen after the Russian workers had taken power and set up a workers' republic? That would be determined by the fate of the working-class revolution in Western Europe, where social conditions were ripe for the creation of a socialist society.

After the workers' revolution, Trotsky concluded, either the workers' dictatorship would be overthrown in Russia, as the Jacobins had been in France in 1794, or the revolution would spread to Western Europe and the countries where, once in power, the workers could begin to make a socialist society: on the international plane, the Russian revolution would, if that happened, be able to compensate for its backwardness, and Russia would take its place as a backward working-class-ruled segment of a European working-class state, which was driving towards socialism in the advanced countries.

For Trotsky, there would be an uninterrupted sequence of bourgeois-democratic revolutionary-socialist tasks, led by the working class at the head of the peasantry, and in that sense, a fusion of the two revolutions, bourgeois and proletarian.

But the defeats in the west – in Germany, the inverted counter-revolutionary permanent revolution – left Russia isolated. The Russian Stalinist counter-revolution was the result.

IV

What happened in 1917? The February revolution made a clean sweep of Tsarism, discredited by the war and its catastrophes. In Lenin's absence the Bolshevik party in Russia, led by Kamenev and Stalin, settled into supporting the new regime which, in fact, procrastinated over such "bourgeois" tasks of the revolution as the distribution of land to the peasants. Now, basing himself on the great militancy of the working class and, as always, guided by concrete realities, not by dogmatic abstractions, Lenin grasped what Trotsky had grasped already in 1905 – that the Russian revolution would either be a working-class revolution, or it wouldn't happen: counter-revolution would roll things back. The bourgeois and proletarian revolutions would have to form a continuous sequence. (In 1918, in *The proletarian revolution and the renegade Kautsky*, Lenin described the bourgeois-democratic revolution in the first period after the working class had taken power in the October revolution.)

So the difference between democratic dictatorship of the workers and peasantry and Trotsky's permanent revolution were of no importance? Lenin got there too, in his own step-by-step way? Lenin got there, but he had a struggle to reorient the Bolshevik party, to turn it away from support for the post-February revolution bourgeois regime and direct it toward taking state power. No one else but Lenin could have changed the role of the Bolshevik party from the role it played for a few weeks under Kamenev and Stalin to that of the party that led the proletarian – and thus also the bourgeois-democratic – revolution half a year later.

Suppose that Lenin had died in exile in January 1917. Then the "democratic dictatorship of the workers and peasantry" would not have been, as it was, a corridor to permanent revolution and Lenin's policy that culminated in working-class power after October 1917. It would have been interpreted as Stalin and Kamenev interpreted the old party line before Lenin returned to Russia and won the day for permanent revolution at the April conference of the Bolshevik party. If Lenin hadn't been there, or failed to win over the Bolshevik party, then Trotsky's "permanent revolution" would be known to us as the utopian fantasy of a Russian Marxist who blurred the distinction between the Marxist idea of the revolution and that of the socialist populists, as the Narodnik-populist Socialist Revolutionary Party did.

Without Lenin – without his ability to focus on evolving reality and not be confused by a previous, now outmoded, inadequate or incomplete theoretical scenario – the old Bolshevik commitment to a democratic dictatorship of the workers and peasantry would have led the Bolshevik party to play the role of saboteur of the working-class revolution that some Mensheviks played †.

There was a parallel between Trotsky's holding on to the formula that Russia was a degenerated workers' state, in the late 1930s, and Lenin's position on the democratic dictatorship of the proletariat and peasantry. The formula might be provisional and doubtful, but so long as it allowed adequate practical politics – on Stalin's USSR, in the first place, advocacy of a "political" revolution against the bureaucratic autocracy – it would not matter too much if the formula had to be jettisoned later on. Trotsky also spelled out the considerations that would lead him to discard the formula. They included: if Russia survived the looming world war.

At the end of his life, he moved steadily, step by step, away from the degenerated workers' state theory. In his last writing on the subject, on the eve of his death, *The Comintern and the GPU* [Stalinist secret police], he defined the Communist Party leaders all over the world as aspirants to the social role which the totalitarian bureaucracy played in Russia. He redefined the Russian system as only "provisionally" progressive. And then he died, leaving his followers to flounder around the degenerated workers' state theory, rather as Kamenev and Stalin had, without Lenin, floundered around the democratic dictatorship of the proletariat and peasantry early in 1917. What the Orthodox Trotskyists made of the theory of Permanent Revolution – see below – was rooted there: in the hames they made of the degenerated workers' state theory.

The Stalinists would turn Trotsky's ideas, and Lenin's 1917 ideas, on their head from the Fifth World Congress of the Comintern (mid 1924), imposing on communists in colonial countries (and even in Ireland) what in 1917 had been the Menshevik dogma: first must come the bourgeois revolution and then, at a later stage, a socialist revolution.

---

† *A pernicious, subterranean conclusion is often drawn from this episode, in and around the Trotskyist movement: Lenin's Bolshevik party made all the difference; that party was built on false political perspectives and then reoriented; so the task is to build the party and not to worry too much about the politics. Thus the SWP approach – "apparatus Marxism"*

V

In 1928 Trotsky wrote a book-length polemic against Karl Radek – *The Permanent Revolution*. He generalised the permanent revolution for colonial and semi-colonial countries. Essentially, it was the pattern of Russia – the bourgeoisie could not lead the struggle for national independence: the proletariat would have to, and combine that with making its own revolution. He summed this up as a process of "the reconstruction of the nation under the leadership of the working class".

Trotsky's permanent revolution was a perspective of action by the working class, led by working-class communist parties. Its protagonist was the working class, led by a revolutionary party. Nowhere in any of the allegedly working-class, in fact Stalinist-totalitarian, revolutions in third world countries, in the 1940s and after, was the proletariat the protagonist: in Yugoslavia and China peasant/déclassé communist parties took power. The workers played little part and no politically independent part. In China, for instance, the proletariat immediately felt the repression of the Stalinist regime.

The working-class communist movement in the earlier Chinese revolution had been massacred in 1927. The remnants of the Communist Party, led by Mao and Chu Teh, relocated to the countryside, abandoning the working class. The Japanese invasion of 1937 pulverised the coastal cities where the proletariat had been mainly based destroying much of the old proletariat. Trotsky in 1931 had raised the idea that the communists like Mao who had moved to the backward regions might evolve into an anti-working-class force. They did.

The Orthodox Trotskyists had to face the reality that Stalinist revolutions in Yugoslavia, China and Vietnam were anti-capitalist revolutions: they used the theory of the permanent revolution to rationalise accommodation to Stalinism, which was both anti-capitalist and anti-working-class, and in no sense bourgeois-democratic.

Isaac Deutscher did the same rationalisation in terms of Trotsky's theory of permanent revolution for a mass audience in his Trotsky trilogy. The whole sleight of mind here depended on identifying such things as the Communist Party of China (CPC) and the peasant armies with the proletariat – of reading backwards from the conclusion that China, for instance, was a deformed workers' state.

The Mandel-Pablo Fourth International did not think a political revolution necessary in China for 20 years after the Maoist consolidation in 1949! They interpreted the events of the revolution theory as a variant of Trotsky's "permanent revolution". In Trotsky's the working class had been central. In this new so-called "permanent revolution", the proletariat was not the protagonist but at most a bit-part player. The CPs were substituted for the proletariat. This Stalinist "socialist revolution" resulted in the rule of a primitive bureaucratic ruling class over the workers – over workers held in a tight, totalitarian grip. The bourgeois-democratic element – the bourgeois-democratic freedoms won in western Europe and other places – which had been a central dynamic in Trotsky's version of permanent revolution (as indeed in Lenin's approximation to permanent revolution, the democratic dictatorship of the proletariat and peasantry), was non-existent here.

Even if you identified the peasant movement with the bourgeois-democratic element of the bourgeois-democratic revolution, the fact of a totalitarian state radically changes all the values and meanings. The peasant movement leading to the expropriation of the landlords developed under firm Stalinist control. After the establishment of the Stalinist regime the peasants, like the workers, were at the mercy of the totalitarian state.

Stalinism in power negated almost all the gains of society in bourgeois-democratic history. In place of the "bourgeois-democratic" element in this revolution came a totalitarian Stalinist rule which Leon Trotsky, and even the Second Congress of the Fourth International as late as 1948, said differed very little from fascism.

In Volume 1 of his trilogy on Trotsky Isaac Deutscher asks how it was that Trotsky's prediction of collapse and defeat of the Russian proletarian revolution if it didn't spread quickly to Europe had not happened. He answered: Trotsky had not anticipated the power of a totalitarian state – the Stalinist state. As an observation that was true. Its implicit identification of the workers' "permanent revolution" with the totalitarian Stalinist state was a pernicious nonsense.

The point that concerns us here is that permanent revolution in Orthodox Trotskyism is radically different from Trotsky's permanent revolution. It is Trotsky's permanent revolution formula emptied of its central class content – working-class activity and working-class socialist revolution.

It is simply a formula to allow confused Trotskyists to reconcile themselves to revolution-making third-world Stalinism.

The proper formula for what this Stalinist "permanent revolution" was in reality would be not Trotsky's formula of the reorganisation of the nation under the leadership of the proletariat, but the reorganisation of the nation under the totalitarian dictatorship of the Stalinist bureaucracy put in power by civil war, based on peasant armies. Trotsky's profound theory was bowdlerised and relegated to a fond and stupid rationalisation for these Stalinist totalitarian revolutions.

I know only one case in the 20th century after 1917 where the formula about reconstructing the nation under the leadership of the working class described reality. That was in Poland between 1980 and 1989. There the whole movement for the emancipation of Poland from Russia's imperialist rule was led by the working class and its organisation Solidarnosc. The Polish nation reconstructed itself around the core movement originating in the Gdansk shipyards in 1980.

Permanent revolution? If you insist. Except that it was the reorganisation of the oppressed Polish nation by way of a revolution against the Stalinist and Russian overlords that created not a socialist but a bourgeois Polish society. It was bourgeois-democratic liberation winning tremendously important liberties, not least the liberty for the workers to organise freely; but it led not to working-class power and socialism, but to a new bourgeois Poland. Better by far if the Polish workers had transformed the property of the Stalinist state into real social property. Even so, bourgeois democracy is better, and against Stalinist totalitarianism, historically progressive.

VI

English-Scottish colonisation in Ireland came to be of two types: a thinnish upper-class layer across the island and, in north east Ulster, a colony like those of America where a whole British class-stratified society was transplanted and the natives replaced or driven to the margins.

Radical 19th century English critics – Richard Cobden and John Bright, for instance – called the Irish land system, and the relations between the tenants and the landlords, feudalism. So did the late 19th century Irish radical and socialist Michael Davitt; he called his 1905 book on the "Land War" of the 1870s-1880s, *The fall of feudalism in Ireland*. Certainly it was a system in which relations of power and politics, not bourgeois commercial market relations, were decisive.

The revolution against "feudalism" in Ireland was spurred on by radical agitators and organisers, Davitt and his comrades, but carried out by British governments, Liberal and Tory, over decades. The "Three F's" – fair rent, free sale, and fixity of tenure – were legislated by the Liberals in 1881 in an attempt to transform the Catholic Irish peasants into something like English and Ulster tenant farmers. The Anglican Church was disestablished (ceased to receive tithes) in 1869: it was the third church in Ireland, a small-ish minority religion, there being many more Catholics and more Presbyterians than Anglicans.

At that time, Marx, optimistic as always, thought disestablishment would end religious sectarianism. After 1870, the British government was ready to lend money so that tenants could buy out willing land-lords. This move, on the initiative of John Bright, was of great impor-tance in principle, but at first of little practical impact. The tenant had to put up a high percentage of the price.

A long series of British government initiatives, Land Acts in 1881, 1885, 1887, and 1895, changed the conditions, culminating in the Wyndham Land Act of 1903, the legislative result of an agreement reached by tenants and landlords at a conference in 1902. From 1885 Britain would advance all the money for a tenant to buy from a will-ing landlord. In social terms, this, organised from above, was the Irish bourgeois revolution. Protestant small farmers in Ulster benefited greatly too. By the time of the political revolution, in 1922 – political near-independence – Ireland was a land of mainly peasant propri-etors.

Of course, it is easy to conjure up alternative histories of Ireland. Some of Cromwell's republican soldiers refused to go to Ireland to reconquer its people. Suppose the radicals had won in the struggle within the anti-Royalist camp in the 1640s. Suppose the revolution of 1688 had been a radical bourgeois-democratic revolution and not what it was, one led and "owned" by a bourgeoisified layer of aris-tocrats, the so-named Whigs. The effect of England's bourgeois-democratic revolution might then not have been to push the Catholic people down into generations of helotry.

Or suppose the English Chartists had won in the 1840s. Then the English and Scottish and émigré Irish working class might have led the Irish peasants in a radical revolt. Karl Marx expected that inde-pendence for Ireland later in the 19th century would lead to an agrar-ian revolution in Ireland that would spark a revolution against landlords in England and Scotland too. For the 1870s and 1880s, one could sketch possibilities if the Ulster Protestant working class – the concentrated working class in Ireland then – had allied with or taken the lead in such movements as the Land War, from whose outcome a lot of Ulster Protestant small farmers benefited greatly. The conflict of sectarian or national identities ruled that out entirely.

Alternatively, in theory, the British working class could have taken the lead in organising the Irish farmers against the British and Irish ruling classes. But history is what it has been. In any case, all such scenarios were rendered obsolete by the Tory-organised bourgeois revolution on the land. And then by the political revolution which was triggered by the revolt of Protestant Ireland (with Northern Ireland's Protestant workers among the most determined) against being incorporated as a minority in a Catholic-majority Home Rule system. That led to the 1916 Rising, and, after the Anglo-Irish war of 1919-21, to the creation of the Irish Free State and a Northern Ireland state.

VII

In Ireland, permanent revolution has functioned as a rationalisation to allow some people to pretend that the Provo war would somehow evolve, self-transform, into an Irish proletarian revolution uniting Catholic and Protestant workers.

Insofar as anything definable and even remotely coherent is described in the Irish context by the formula "permanent revolution", it is the notion that the Irish national struggle is incomplete, and that Ireland's national struggle can only be completed under the leadership of the working class. But every single premiss of this idea is so false that the assertion is simply ridiculous.

Ireland is, in terms of society and economy, bourgeois. It is far freer from what might (misleadingly) be said to be feudalistic elements, than is Britain, with its House of Lords, the monarchy with its vested reserve powers, etc. Protestant Ireland had its bourgeois revolution in 1688. The history of the two countries is so intertwined way back into the early Middle Ages that you get in Ireland reflections and emanations from the various moves in British society toward modern capitalism, but in a very distorted fashion. The core Irish bourgeois revolution was made in the 19th and early 20th centuries by the British bourgeoisie from above (under tremendous pressure from Irish social revolt, certainly).

As we've seen, Michael Davitt named his book of 1905 about the struggle for the land between peasant and landlords *The fall of feudalism in Ireland*. Arguably the system before the reforms starting in 1869-70 really was a sort of feudalism, or first cousin to it. The landlords simply confiscated the work, land improvement, capital invested in changes on the farm, etc., by the tenant, thus expropriating every beginning to capitalist accumulation of the sort that Britain had experienced long ago. The immediate practical consequences of the provision made in principle, in 1869-70, for state assistance to peasants in buying out landlords willing to sell were negligible. Gladstone's Liberals, committed to low state expenditure, were in their basic approach and principles, willing only to provide state aid to tenants who could themselves put up a large part of the total price. Only the very well-off tenants could benefit; and in fact few tenants did at first benefit.

It is worth underlining that it was the Tories who carried out the full land revolution in Ireland. The Tories, in the succession of acts of parliament, simply gave the Irish peasants the land of landlords willing to sell – as indeed, by then, many were – substituting a state mortgage for the rent, usually for a lesser annual payment than there had been in rent. Over a number of decades the farmer would become the sole owner of the land. This was done in waves, the greatest being the Wyndham Land Act of 1903.

After the "political revolution" of 1918-23, the Free State Land Act of 1923 added an element of compulsory sale, but all that did was tidy things up a little bit: the British bourgeoisie had carried out a profound revolution in the land system in Ireland and in Irish society. In a sense, it was a very late extension of the British bourgeois revolution. This radical bourgeois social revolution, organised by the British ruling class from above, exchanged the old landlords for their petty peasant spawn. The winning of the Free State in 1922 and, in the dozen years afterwards, the extension of 26 county state autonomy to full and real independence, was a sort of – very important – political afterword.

One of the aspects of the land reform that is sometimes ignored was how important it was in Protestant Ulster, to the Ulster Protestant descendants of the 17th Century settlers. A large number of Protestant Ulster smallholders – who had had English style rather than Irish Catholic tenant relationships with their landlords – benefited greatly from the Tory Land Acts.

Ireland, I repeat, is a bourgeois society, north and south. There is no bourgeois-democratic development to win except maybe in certain Catholic areas along the border, whose majority population are in the six counties against their will and therefore lack self-determination.

All permanent-revolution-for-Ireland fantasists base themselves on the ideological lie that Britain is just a colonial power in Northern Ireland, that if the Northern Ireland people wanted them to go Britain would refuse to go, that the British are still manipulating the Protestants to their own advantage. But by this time of the political day you have to have turf-dust for brains, or subscribe to a mythical transcendental nationalism, to hold that view.

The opposition to Irish unity comes from Irish people – Irish Protestant/ Unionists who describe themselves as British. If talking of "British occupied Ireland", as distinct from Protestant-unionist-Irish-occupied north-east Ulster, has any meaning at all it is only in relation to the Catholic majority border areas of the six counties. Substituting vague talk of "imperialism" for the specific proposals and definable goals of a real bourgeois-democratic revolution is simply to mystify things. In reality the underlying logic of all talk about British occupied Ireland is to simply target the Protestant Irish people in north east Ulster. To my knowledge, no republicans state that clearly, or consciously want it. In practice, however, that logic worked its way during the IRA's long war in attacks on Irish Unionists, dubbed traitors for "collaborating" with Britain. That came to be a central part of the IRA campaign.

In Ireland north and south there is no way to go beyond what exists socially and economically except by way of a proletarian revolution – the Workers' Republic.

One of the self-consolations of post-Trotsky Trotskyism faced with a world taking shapes we never expected it to take was the response to things such as the liberation under bourgeois regimes of colonies and the abandonment of the old colonial systems – under American pressure – after 1945. Orthodox Trotskyists asked the question: but are they really free? They are not economically free, we said; they are caught in a worldwide web of imperialist economic rule.

True. But this is to amalgamate and confuse distinct things. Whereas it is possible to fight colonial-type imperialism physically, to drive it out of a colony, and thus to put an end to its robberies and to win freedom from predatory restraints and for development, it is not possible to win by that sort of struggle against the pressures of the world markets and of worldwide advanced-capitalist hegemony. That hegemony does not depend on occupation and colonisation.

The answer to this impossibility opted for in some third world countries has been economic autarky, self-cutting-off from the world market. It is in reality a retrogressive step. And yet this drive to autarky is – short of a worldwide working-class revolution – the only logical alternative to economically weak countries being immersed in the world economy. It is a reactionary populist-national blind alley.

Whereas a particular measure of third world state nationalisation of imperialist controlled assets may be progressive in terms of filling out national independence, the only completely progressive way out of the current situation for less developed countries and weaker economies is the proletarian revolution, in those countries and in the advanced capitalist countries.

Theories such as permanent revolution were pressed into service to explain post-colonial developments, as they had been used to rationalise Stalinist revolutions in Third World countries, but to do it in such a way that simultaneously denied or half-denied that "real" decolonisation had actually happened. Thus you had tremendous mystification. This is important for the Irish experience.

Ireland, of course, is not and, calculably, never will be the economic equivalent of Britain. Economic independence? In a number of countries certain nationalist regimes have tried to do something like that, cut off as much as possible from the world market – in Argentina, for example. And in Ireland.

Between 1932 and 1958 Ireland attempted to make itself as economically independent as possible. It did this behind high tariff walls. People who wanted to become manufacturers of goods sold in Ireland had merely to ask the government to put on a high enough tariff against the importation of such goods to make it economical for Irish manufacture to replace them.

It led to the creation of jobs. It perhaps served Ireland well in the Second World War. But after the Second World War Ireland was caught in a stifling system in which its goods could not compete overseas. Economic stagnation led in 1958 to the abandonment of that system (by the same governing party, Fianna Fail – and even the same minister, Sean Lemass – who had brought it into being in the first place).

In the politics of post-Trotsky Trotskyism the notion that the ex-colonies are not economically independent served to blur the distinction between working-class politics and national populism of various sorts, including third world Stalinism. It does that in Irish politics now.

It is not a matter here of supporting or not supporting an ex-colonial state's seizure of foreign-owned basic assets. Trotsky supported the Mexican state seizure of the foreign owned old fields as an aspect of Mexico's exercise of self-determination. It is a matter of explicitly or implicitly substituting for the program of the working-class revolution a program of national-populist economics and a drive to autarky as a way forward for ex-colonial countries – and even for an advanced bourgeois country like Ireland.

Nowhere should this be clearer than in independent Ireland, where governments operated such a policy for a full quarter of a century. There is only one national liberation or bourgeois-democratic task in Ireland that – in any theory of "Irish permanent revolution" – can be conceivably assigned to the proletariat – unification of the island.

VII

The problem is that the root of partition is the division in the Irish people. How might "permanent revolution" "work" to change the real Irish conditions? The people are mobilised by a working-class based party on the demand for unification. The roused workers ally with an equally roused peasantry – to do what? Invade the north? Resume the Provo war inside the north? Hope that such a Southern mobilisation for unification would evoke a similar movement among Protestants in Northern Ireland? Again, to do what? What would such a movement do, what could it hope to do?

In fact a mass mobilisation for unification in Northern Ireland by a majority – it would have to include a proportion of the Protestant Unionists – would achieve it quickly and easily. Britain would have no reason to resist it. Short of the whole situation radically changing, Britain would certainly not resist it.

And how would such a popular mobilisation for unification go over from its initial form – a movement for political unification of the island – into a working-class revolution? Or even into a movement for working-class revolution? Certainly it would not be out of the working class being the most consistent fighters for unification, while the upper classes would, as upper classes in third world countries did, drag their feet. Certainly not because British resistance would radicalise the movement and lead it in self-defence to take over British bourgeois property in Ireland.

In fact of course it is simply inconceivable that a mobilisation for unity would include most or even a lot of Protestant unionists. The experience of the Provos' war and its impact on the south shows that there would not be a mobilisation of anything like the majority of Catholics even in the South.

In any such mobilisation, the Protestant majority in north-east Ulster would inevitably be the target against which the unification movement would organise and unite. It would be against Britain only in so far as Britain defended them and refused to leave Northern Ireland without their agreement.

There was no Catholic mobilisation for unity, but even if there had been what would it have done? Invaded the north? With what goal? To conquer the Protestants, in alliance with the northern Catholics? In the name of what? Physical unification! And afterwards? Hold them against their will in a united Ireland as the Northern Ireland Catholics in the border areas were – and still are – held against their will in the six counties after 1922? Why? For what conceivable national or republican, socialist or democratic objective? This could make no sense other than as a rabidly chauvinist Catholic-nationalist project. And in the real Ireland it would make no sense even as that.

Of course – thank God! – there was no such mobilisation. The attempt by Republicans to send a few busloads over the border in August 1969 was a small political farce. If it had been other than that it would have been the beginning of widespread civil war.

The volunteers who got involved in the north † were negligible in number. The boasting of the then leader of the IRA, Cathal Goulding, that the IRA was mobilising to move north served only to help the Ulster leaders line up the Protestants behind their 6 County government. There was some movement in the south after Bloody Sunday 1972 – the British Embassy was burned in Dublin – and around the hunger strikes. It was always feeble and narrowly nationalist ††. The main effect of the Provo war was to polarise even more intensely northern society between Catholic and Protestant. I repeat: a sizeable southern involvement would have led to full-scale Catholic-Protestant civil war.

The Provo war had as its objective to beat down the Unionists and compel Britain to coerce them – "persuade them" was the doubletalk way of putting it – into a united Ireland. Politically the whole project was simply preposterous. As of 2017, there were 109 "partition walls" in Belfast and elsewhere in Northern Ireland, separating Protestant and Catholic districts, three times as many as there were at the point of the Provo ceasefire.

Arguably, if the Provos hadn't fought their war, a peaceful evolution towards Irish unity would by now be well advanced, bringing voluntary unity closer. And the permanent revolution Trotskyists in all this?

Irish socialists have been parasitic – politically, emotionally and intellectually parasitic – on the republican movements for many decades. The truth is that permanent revolution has had no political bearing on Ireland except in providing ideological rationalisation and glosses on what the Provos were doing. The socialists who talk of

---

† *I was one of them.*

†† *As I have established in a series of articles on the left and the Irish crisis in 1969, http://www.workersliberty.org/node/10010, the advocates of mobilisation and of opening the southern arsenals to the republicans, etc., to help the northern Catholics, `were either raving demagogues who didn't care what they said – for example, some writers in Socialist Worker at the time – or people who knowingly advocated that the existing states, including the independent Irish state, should stand back and let Catholic-Protestant civil war rip. Such a war might have redrawn the Northern Ireland borders. It would not, could not, have unified Ireland.*

"permanent revolution" are the mystics of Catholic nationalism! Not of republicanism in Wolfe Tone's sense or Connolly's or even Pearse's, but mystics and would be alchemists looking for the fifth essence of Irish nationalism, for a magical and golden transformation which will be revealed in time as socialism. In practice they have acted as political outriders and propagandists for the Provo war.

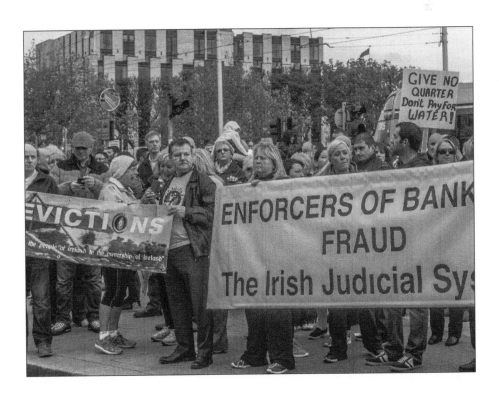

Irish protest in the wake of the collapse of the country's big banks following the 2008 global credit crash, and the government's adoption of a punitive EU adjustment program

271

3. Real and invented differences on political Islam

Ms German replies to critics of the Stop the War Coalition's links with political Islam

"The British are... doing all in their power to foster the Moslem Brotherhood, a clerical-fascist organisation in Egypt... [the Moslem Brotherhood] refused to participate on 21 February, 1946, 'Evacuation Day' as this was a real anti-imperialist movement and not a communal one... Slogans of solidarity among Moslem, Christian and Jewish workers were shouted throughout the demonstrations, and the fascist leader Ahmed Hussein, who tried to worm his way into the demonstration, was howled down and not allowed to speak."
– Tony Cliff, A New British Provocation in Palestine, *Fourth International* 7 (9), July 1946

Under the headline "A badge of honour", and the strapline, "The left doesn't have to compromise any principle to defend and work with Muslims – on the contrary", the most subtle thinker in the SWP leadership, Lindsey German, undertook in the *Guardian* (13 July 2004) to reply to critics of the SWP's political bloc with Islamist clerical reaction. In fact, she evades the issues. She deploys ideas that are common to the SWP and to ourselves, *Solidarity* and Workers' Liberty, in order to hide what is distinctive in what the SWP is doing. †

Of course international socialists are for freedom of religion, including Islam. *Of course* we defend Muslim people, immigrants and those born in Britain, from discrimination, scapegoating and racist attack. *Of course* we defend them physically and champion equality. *Of course* we work to draw immigrants and their children into the labour movement. *Of course* we try to explain to ignorantly self-righteous, non-Muslim people how Muslims come to have the ideas and practices they have. *Of course* we have stood and will no doubt again stand side by side against racists with Muslim priests and others we define as reactionary – that is, with people against whose influence on Muslim workers we fight, and against whom within the Muslim communities we support their progressive opponents. *Of course* we do not make any of these things conditional on Muslims' abandoning

---

† *Lindsey German has since (in February 2010) quit the SWP, and now is part of the SWP-splinter organisation Counterfire. The parting of the ways was not over the issues discussed here, and the SWP has not changed its approach on those issues.*

their religion and their sense of a distinct identity. *Of course* revolutionary socialists understand that drawing Muslims or Catholics, or whoever, into action is a more important, and also a more productive way of educating them away from religion, than playing would-be anti-religious schoolmaster to them. *Of course* we do not raise religious questions in a way that disrupts or makes impossible the involvement of religious people in a progressive struggle.

So far, the SWP says nothing we do not say. And, as a matter of fact, others on the left, including *Solidarity* and Workers' Liberty (and its predecessor *Socialist Organiser*), have a rather better record in defending Muslims from racist attack than the SWP has. On an infamous occasion the SWP took its people off to an Anti-Nazi League carnival instead of defending Brick Lane in East London against a projected fascist march through the Bengali area, at the same time as the carnival. The fascist march was, they proclaimed, a "provocation". Indeed! Against the Bangladeshis in Brick Lane? The fascist march on Bengali East London was, the SWP insisted, a provocation – against the Anti-Nazi League carnival. Notoriously, the SWP refused to side with the Muslims in Bosnia in the mid-1990s, when they were being massacred by Christian communalists; refused to help those of us who campaigned against the arms embargo that left Bosniacs defenceless against the well armed Serbs.

For the Left it must be one of two things. Either, while fighting racism and discrimination against Muslims and Muslim communities, we will find a way to combine that defence of vulnerable people with opposition to them where they are champions of intolerance, bigotry, and petrified, age-old sanctified ignorance, in short, of political, cultural, and civic reaction, trying to spread it from the large areas in the Muslim world where it is the norm, into the bourgeois democracies of the West. Or, we will ourselves cease, for practical purposes, to be socialists, secularists and democrats. The strapline on German's article says: "The left doesn't have to compromise any principle to defend and work with Muslims – on the contrary." Indeed, we don't "have to", but the SWP has and does. The SWP does and says things which no self-respecting socialist, secularist or decent liberal would be seen dead doing or saying! In German's strange *Guardian* article, for example.

Marxists are for "freedom of religion", but we do not champion any religion or assume the role of, so to speak, its "godparents". Even when we explain to the ignorant how things with Islam came to be what they are, we do not endorse, recommend or justify the religion and its doctrines, or its practices. We do not help reactionary priests

273

reinforce their hold on the minds of those brought up in their religion. When we ally with religious people in a common struggle, we do not disrupt that work by pushing their religion and our irreligion to the forefront. Indeed. But neither do we laud their religion, nor appeal for their votes by describing ourselves as the "best fighters" for Muslims (or Catholics, Jews or whoever), as "Respect (George Galloway)" – that is, the SWP under its strange, new hat [of 2004-2007] – did. Socialists cannot emancipate people sunk in religious communalism inside ghettoes where imams and the rich have a very strong grip if, minimally, they do not maintain their own identity, and work to break young Muslim people from their religious background. I repeat: even when we explain "strange" religious practices to backward non-Muslim workers, we do not endorse them, or appear to endorse them, or pretend that their beliefs are not as abhorrent as some of the beliefs of, say, fundamentalist Christians. We convey to Muslims, by our behaviour as well as by our words, respect for them as people, not respect for their religion and its political ideas: we are for the singer, but not for the reactionary song. We act as honourable, self-respecting people, who take our own secular ideas and traditions seriously. We are honest and candid with our temporary allies, treating them with the respect they deserve as thinking people. As people fully our equals – not as people to be soft-soaped, condescended to and manipulated.

Serious socialists do not, like the SWP, side with or defer to the establishment in the Muslim communities, with "The Mosque". Other than during the physical defence of a Muslim area under immediate attack, socialists would never enter into political partnership with clerical-fascists, like the Muslim Brotherhood. If we point out that Muslim fundamentalists are no worse in their beliefs than, say, Christian or Jewish or Hindu fundamentalists are in theirs, or point to the absurdity of the fascist degenerates of the brute BNP denouncing Muslims for their beliefs and practices, it is not to pretend, as German does in the *Guardian*, that, therefore (!) Muslim fundamentalists and Islamist clerical fascists aren't so bad after all. German's apologia is as gamey as SWP practice. She notes the new "politicisation amongst Muslims" as a result of recent wars and the Israel-Palestine conflict. She thinks it is a "badge of honour" that Muslims "should look to organisations like the Stop the War Coalition to help defend them" and that "the overwhelming majority of those so politicised do not turn to fundamentalist groups but to socialists, trade unionists and peace campaigners." That would be good, if it were true. Ms German "forgets" that the STWC prominently involved the oldest Islamist organisation in existence, the Muslim Brotherhood, through its British off-shoot, the Muslim Association of Britain (MAB). It would be hard to find a place to pin the "badge of honour" on Ms German's chest, already covered as it is with the badges of shameful surrender to Arab and Islamist chauvinism. But don't run away with the idea that Ms German is simply a blustering ignoramus. She knows what she knows. She admits that "some Muslims" hold views on "some issues" that are "more (!) conservative (!) than (!) those of the socialist and liberal left". Those who would persecute and kill gays, compel women to veil themselves, and impose Islamic clerical Sharia rule on society – the Muslim Brotherhood – are indeed a little bit "more (!) conservative (!) than (!)" most socialists and labour movement people! But we must not be "sectarian". She asks: "Would a campaign for gay rights, for example, insist that all those who took part share the same view of the war on Iraq?"

Indeed, it wouldn't and it shouldn't. But, Ms German, didn't the SWP and the Muslim Brotherhood/MAB impose on the February 2003 march against the war on Iraq the Arab-Islamic-chauvinist slogan on the Israel-Palestine conflict, "Freedom for Palestine" (meaning all of pre-1948 Palestine, including Israel – the elimination of Israel)? You insisted on writing it up on banners and placards alongside the slogans against the war. Wasn't that "sectarian"? Didn't that exclude almost all anti-war Jews? That, by the way, is palpable proof that the SWP functioned not as working-class socialists with an independent voice and independent democratic program for solving the Jewish-Palestinian problem but as vicarious Islamic-Arab chauvinists.

German is outraged at the charge that there was anything anti-semitic in the STWC: "Charges of antisemitism, support for terrorism, homophobia and sexism abound, as in the attack on Yusuf al-Qaradawi and the Muslim Association of Britain in recent days." Defending itself, the SWP is committed now to defending all things Islamic – here, Qaradawi. For all things Islamic are now holy to the SWP, amen! Qaradawi thinks Muslim states should jail and kill homosexuals, that women should know their place, that human bombs killing Israel civilians are a legitimate weapon against Israel: is he, therefore, homophobic, sexist, Hamas-supporting? Don't be ridiculous! The subtle Ms German knows what she knows. He is not a clerical-fascist reactionary – only more (!) conservative (!) than (!) Ms German and her comrades.

And "just because women wear the hijab, for example, does that mean that they are more oppressed than other women?" Of course not. Don't be ridiculous! She cites young hijabi Muslim women

275

speaking at meetings to prove it: these articulate, educated young women – some of them supporters of the Muslim Brotherhood – you are meant to understand are typical of Muslim women in Britain and elsewhere. Of course, they are nothing of the sort. And even if they were, it would not prove her point. Militant women reactionaries played a noticeable part in the regressive and reactionary Islamic revolution in Iran. Political idiots – ourselves among them – could point to that as proof that the Islamists were for women's equality. But Ms German is impervious to facts, historical or contemporary.

"Those who argue that the MAB are fascists... are dangerously wide of the mark." But the Muslim Brotherhood admits that MAB is its front! What does the SWP actually think of the MB, who in some countries are reactionary terrorists, and in all Islamic states stand for an authoritarian regime imposing sharia law? (The Muslim Brotherhood also wants to restore the pre-1918 Turkish empire, the Caliphate.) The Muslim Brotherhood is not clerical-fascist? What then should we call an organisation that advocates and fights for authoritarian Islamic regimes in the Islamic world and eventually, they intend, all over the world? How does she get around the fact that many of her readers – and thinking SWPers – know what the MAB/MB is? No problem: she insists that the BNP's views on gays are as bad as those of Qaradawi. The BNP are akin to those who "wanted to destroy democratic and working-class organisations in the interests of a German imperialist super-state", whereas "British Muslims are struggling to uphold their rights and culture in an environment of pervasive racism". And? And that should recommend tolerance of the views of Qaradawi (who lives in Qatar, not Britain) and those of the Muslim Brotherhood to socialists? If the rules of logic still apply to the leaders of the SWP, that is what she seems to say.

But why stop there? Surely the coupling of Qaradawi and the BNP works the other way around too? Why not lend a sympathetic ear to the BNP itself? After all, properly understood and interpreted, the viciously reactionary ideas and practices of the BNP are only a misguided and perverted form of revolt against our capitalist society by young, mainly working-class people. If we excuse the MAB/MB leaders, why not extend that tolerance to the poor misguided fools with real grievances against capitalist society who look to racist scapegoating and the BNP for a solution? Why not? Because "the clerical fascism" of the oppressed is not as bad as the fascism of an oppressor people, like the native white English, Welsh or Scottish? German doesn't say that, but what she says implies that. That way, beginning as Ms German does, lies political lunacy and moral and political suicide. German reminisces that the German Nazis "scapegoated" "gays, trade unionists, gypsies, socialists and above all Jews... in the interests of a German imperialist super-state". Well, as a matter of fact, Ms German, they did not "scapegoat" socialists or communists. We – working-class international socialists – really were the mortal enemies of everything they cherished, defended and aspired to. Weren't we? (And some of us still are...) They scapegoated Jews, etc., but against socialists and communists they fought the class struggle of the bourgeoisie to suppress the labour movement, which really was their enemy. Ms German's point? "British Muslims... are struggling to uphold their rights and culture in an environment of pervasive racism – a racism used to uphold the policies of the new imperialism." You follow that? They are, we should understand, the victims of the new... Nazis? They "struggle" in these conditions to "uphold their rights and culture". Note the coupling here: "rights and culture". Of course, socialists and democrats are automatically and unconditionally for Muslims' equality as citizens. But that does not mean we champion, endorse, defend or approve of their "culture" or say it's as good as any other culture (including our secular, socialist culture?). There are many things in their culture we, on pain of ceasing to be ourselves, must despise and fight against. For example, we are for the existing bourgeois state repressing and severely punishing those who mutilate the genitals of young girls. This practice is not confined to Muslims, but it is part of the culture of some Muslims. We are against bigoted Muslim, as against bigoted Christian attitudes to gays, to women, etc. Aren't we? Isn't Ms German? Isn't the SWP, any more?

With this virtuously "anti-racist" nonsense, German lines herself and the SWP up with the worst of the woolly, guilty, middle-class, "tolerate anything", *Guardian* liberals. We live in a world in which social workers who had some idea of the ill-treatment of little Victoria Climbie by her religious – Christian – aunt, who tortured and eventually killed her, did nothing to stop it because they "respected" "cultural differences". Such "tolerance" is no part of serious Marxist, or even serious liberal, politics. On certain things we are, and must be, vigorously intolerant. Ms German's message is that Islamic reactionaries are alright, really, when you compare them to the new imperialists who are... akin to the old Nazis? In fact, of course, the picture she presents is grossly exaggerated. The "old" imperialists needed racism, because they believed in the rule of master races and practised it... The idea that the "new imperialism" – which wants to set up native rulers in Iraq – needs "racism" of that sort is downright nonsensical. She presents the attitudes of the bourgeois state to the Muslim community as if they come not from a typically crude and brutal and, yes, racism-infected state response to real threats from Islamist terrorism – a real threat, for example, to commit indiscriminate mass murder on the London Underground – but from an intrinsic "racism". To question that is to invite the epithet "racist".

International socialists fight specific injustices that are inevitable products of this situation. We do not pretend that Islamist terrorism is not a real threat to ordinary working-class people, whose defence from terrorism we favour, even by the existing bourgeois state. German's exaggerations serve to justify the SWP's politics. They play the same role for the SWP as the notion of capitalism always being in an insoluble crisis and on the verge of collapse, played over decades to license and justify all sorts of craziness in pseudo-Trotskyist organisations like the WRP (on which the SWP more and more seems to be modelling itself). They pretend that "racist" assault on the Muslim community is so all-embracing, so pervasive, so much of an immediate threat, and therefore the need to fight against it so urgent, that there is no space for socialists to assert their own identity. Socialists must commit political and moral suicide, in the interests of "anti-racism" and "defending" the Muslim communities! And not only must Marxists defend them physically, when necessary, but we must defend all their ideas and practices as well. That, I repeat: is political and moral suicide.

Ms German ends: "It would be a catastrophe for the left to bow to the witch-hunt and turn its back on the Muslim community." But so also is it a catastrophe for the "left" to colour itself Islamic green, to write, as the clever Ms German writes, reactionary political idiocies; and to commit political suicide. The choice for the left is not between one or other of these catastrophes. We can and do defend the Muslim communities against real racism, real discrimination, real injustice and real physical attacks without abjuring or compromising our own identity. Without ceasing to be hostile to the religion and much of the religion-infected culture of those we defend and, where appropriate, ally with. Without abandoning, or compromising, our own political, socialist and secularist, raison d'etre. If we can't and if we don't, then the "left" will prove to be of as little use to the young, the secularising, the women and the working class of the Muslim communities as the SWP now is to them and the broader working-class movement in Britain.

4. What is reactionary anti-imperialism?

The left is defined, grouped and regrouped, and redefined again and again, by responses to major events – for example, to the October Revolution of 1917. The left is now undergoing another redefinition, around its responses to the series of wars that began with the Kosova war of 1999 and continued through to the invasions of Afghanistan and Iraq. Those who stand for working-class socialist politics are lining up on one side, and on the other are those who are for a nameless, classless, almost depoliticised and entirely negative "anti-imperialism".

The speaker from the Iraqi trade unions was shouted down at the left-wing European Social Forum in October 2004

The shouting-down of Subhi al Mashadani, general secretary of the Iraqi Federation of Trade Unions, at the European Social Forum in London on 15 October 2004, neatly epitomised this process of differentiation. Al Mashadani had been invited not as a member or supporter of the Communist Party of Iraq – which we understand he is – but as a trade unionist, as a representative of the trade unions which Iraqi workers have been rebuilding since the fall of the Saddam Hussein regime. Free trade unions were impossible under the totalitarian regime of Saddam. On things like that, Saddam modelled himself on Josef Stalin. Those who howled down al Mashadani and would not let him speak – the meeting had to be abandoned – were, some of them anyway, people who think of themselves as Trotskyists (though the SWP, which has done most to create the political hysteria in which such things happen, has criticised those who shouted him down). In fact they are true Stalinists, and not only in their thuggish disregard for free speech. They stand squarely on the Stalinist tradition in their attitude to the Iraqi working class and to the fate of the newly reborn Iraqi working-class movement.

They say they are anti-imperialists, and their objection to al Mashadani is that the trade union movement which he represented at the ESF meeting does not call for the immediate withdrawal of US and British troops from Iraq; that it does not side with the military activities of the combination of Islamic fundamentalists and Saddamites who make up "the resistance".

There are a number of Iraqi trade union groupings, divided by political affiliations. Not one of them supports the Islamist and Ba'thist "resistance" militias. Why not? Because they know that the victory of the spiritual and political totalitarians who lead "the resistance" would create conditions in which trade unions could not exist. In which no labour movement would be possible. In which many of the militants who organise the trade union movements would immediately be killed or jailed... not as "collaborators" but as trade-unionists and "communists".

Those who howled down al Mashadani are Stalinists also because they believe that the supreme revolutionary virtue is not, as *Solidarity* maintains, commitment to the working class and to the creation, growth, and education of a labour movement, but "anti-imperialism". They do not express it like this, but they held to a rigid and fixed Stalinist-type "stageist" conception of socialist politics for Iraq. First "the resistance" must defeat "imperialism" and only then should those working-class activists who survive the tender attentions of those who set off bombs to kill Iraqi civilians and workers organise trade unions and a political working-class movement to fight for working-class power and socialism in Iraq. (The fact that some of the hooligans may think that such a policy is "permanent revolution" and that the war of "resistance" will somehow lead to socialism, does not make their program any less idiotic and any less anti-working-class or any less self-betraying.)

They are like the old Communist Parties, but worse; for they, after all, had a certain, albeit reactionary, coherence to their ideas. One-sided "anti-imperialism" for the old CPs, meant politics which helped what they identified as socialism, the USSR, which was, in fact, Russian Stalinist imperialism. What was more important for them than the working class and its development was finding ways to help the real "socialist" power in the world, the USSR. It all made a sort of horrible sense, according to their conceptions of socialism, of progress, and of contemporary history. The "anti-imperialism" of those who would not listen to a representative of the Iraqi working class at the European Social Forum makes no sense. Yet treating al Mashadani as one would treat a fascist has its own coherence and its own terrible reactionary logic. Why did they object to him? Because the trade-union movement which he represented in London – like the other trade-union groupings in Iraq – refuses to eviscerate itself on the altar of an "anti-imperialism" whose social and political banner is that of out-and-out religious, social, and political reaction. The militant and revolutionary-sounding slogans about "victory to the resistance" and the calls for US and British withdrawal now translate, in the real Iraq, into support for the unleashing of civil war and for the victory of clerical-fascist reaction (or perhaps, at best, of the Ba'thists again). Unless socialists are to shut down their minds and their commitment to the working class, and operate by mechanical, eyes-closed deductions from super-abstract notions like "imperialism" and "anti-imperialism" in the spirit of Orwell's "Two legs bad, four legs good" we must ask ourselves what such slogans mean in practice. That is the only rational, responsible, socialist and Marxist way to pose the issues.

Revolutionary socialists did not support the attempts to organise a Nazi "resistance" to the US, British and Russian occupiers of Germany, in 1945. To say that the only thing socialists can do is back the clerical fascists against Britain and the USA involves giving up on the new Iraqi labour movement. It means concluding that something like the revolutionary Islamist regime that took power in Iran in 1979 – and still, slightly softened up, holds power there today – is the least bad outcome that it is now possible to hope for in Iraq. It is to tell the Iraqi working-class and its movement that it should surrender to the clerical-fascists – and to refuse even to listen to those Iraqis who dare to disagree with the kitsch-left, toy-town anti-imperialists.

Of course, it is possible to imagine a situation in Iraq in which the "resistance" would be not what it is now, a relatively small spectrum of Islamists, Saddamite Ba'thists and others, but a movement of more or less all the peoples of Iraq, pitted against an American imperialism committed to slug it out with them in a butcherous imperialist war of conquest. In such a situation, socialists might have to decide that even the victory of outright reaction in an Iraq freed from the horrors of war would be better than the continuation of that terrible war. That is what happened in Vietnam, with other parts of Indochina, such as Cambodia, being drawn into the slaughter. Is that how things stand in Iraq? Have things reached the stage at which socialists have to recognise that all the possibilities for the development of a working-class movement that were opened up by the destruction of the Saddam regime have been crushed, and the best thing left is a war against imperialist conquest, dominated by the religious, social, and political ultra-reactionaries – clerical-fascists, to give them their generic name – who will, having defeated their enemies, including the Iraqi trade unions, then fall heir to the state power in Iraq? Are we at the stage where socialists have to recognise that the victory of political Islamists who will, in power, destroy even the quasi-secularism and root out the quasi-liberation for women that existed under Saddam's Ba'thist bloody totalitarianism, is the lesser evil now because it is preferable to continued slaughter on a Vietnamese or Cambodian scale – and there are no better possibilities in the situation that now exists?

In fact, the situation in Iraq can lead socialists to no such conclusions. The evidence from the 30 January 2005 [Iraqi] elections is that most Iraqis do not support the "resistance" – those who set off bombs with the goal of killing as many Iraqi civilians as possible. Not even the brutal stupidity of the US occupying forces has so far driven them to such a despairing conclusion. Certainly the new Iraqi labour movement has not reached such a conclusion. The Iraqi Federation of Trade Unions believes that the establishment of some sort of bourgeois-democratic system – even with the continued presence of US and British troops, which they oppose – is a better way forward for the Iraqi people. In that they are entirely correct. Socialism would be better. But if the working class is not yet able to win socialism, then the IFTU is right that the establishment and consolidation of the sort of bourgeois-democratic rights that now exist de facto, despite the bloody chaos in Iraq, and without which the trade unions cannot survive… that is the best possible option for the Iraqi working class. They are right not to rush to despair and commit the social, political and trade unionist suicide which the idiots of classless "anti-imperialism" urge on them. For socialism to become possible, the Iraqi working-class and labour movement will have to have time and space to educate and clarify themselves politically. Even the terrible situation there now is more conducive to that than the victory of clerical-fascist "anti-imperialism".

The hard truth, however, is that the "anti-imperialist" left arrive at the position of rushing to identify with Iraq's clerical fascists and Ba'thists – even against the Iraqi labour movement, as in the shouting down of Subhi al Mashadani – not by reason but by reflex, by unreflected-upon tradition, and by pixilatedly wrong-headed politics. Some of them believe that military struggle is, in itself, a politically higher order of things than the alternative road that is still, probably, possible – the evolution of Iraq, pushed along by working-class organisation and struggle, towards some sort of bourgeois democracy and the resumption of independence. They are excited and thrilled by the violent "revolutionary" struggle. The "resistance" is defined for them as "revolutionary" and progressive not by what the clerical-fascists are and aim for, but by the bare fact that they are in arms against the USA and Britain. Even clerical fascists striving for the power to repress everything progressive in Iraq – workers' rights, women's rights, free speech, any degree of secularism, freedom to organise – even they are rendered "progressive" by their all-ennobling military opposition to "imperialism". This is what might be called "apolitical" or "de-politicised" "anti-imperialism". They have learned very little from either the relatively recent experience in Iran, or the more distant experience in China in 1927 – response to which was one of the pillars of Trotsky's movement.

The policy which the kitsch left urges on the Iraqi workers is a policy of political and possibly physical suicide. These "militant idiots", despite what they intend, are with their classless and nameless "anti-imperialism", for practical purposes, simply reactionaries. They are erstwhile socialists in process of inadvertently redefining themselves as "anti-imperialist" reactionaries. The root of it is that they are people who now operate almost entirely with negative politics. They know what they are against. Apart from a vague and undefined, and increasingly "classless" socialism, they do not know what they are for. By negative repulsion against the USA and Britain, they back themselves into a de facto unity with the politics of downright anti-working-class reaction.

Those who shouted down al Mashadani on 16 October thought they represented virtuous anti-imperialism, but, no longer caring what they represent positively or with whom they ally themselves, were in fact siding with the clerical fascists against the emerging Iraqi labour movement. The brutal rulers of the USA and Britain are perfectly capable of bungling and blundering into the destruction of all the progressive possibilities that now exist – or may still exist – in Iraq, and thus into making their stated aim of a bourgeois-democratic Iraq impossible. They may already have dealt irresponsible blows to those prospects. That is one reason why the pixilated right-wing inverse of the pixilated anti-imperialists – those who let commitment to the Iraqi working class lead them into backing Britain and the USA, that is, into political suicide as socialists, are in their own way no less foolish and even more ridiculous than their mirror-images.

The toy-town anti-imperialists at least maintain a pseudo-revolutionary opposition to their own ruling class. That is something. It is not enough, but it is better than self-prostration before the British and US ruling classes. Many of the young people misled by the toy-town "anti-imperialists" can and will be helped to know better. The left that in this process is being sifted and sorted, defined and redefined, is on the "anti-imperialism first" side a purely negative populism, a politically empty receptacle willing to let itself take on the positive imprint of any "anti-imperialist" force – even, in Iraq, of clerical-fascists, as earlier (during the 2003 war) of Saddam's Ba'thists. They have let themselves be drawn into the position of opponents of the Iraqi working-class movement, so long as it refuses to become a political tool of the clerical-fascists.

The characteristics of the other side in the differentiation of the forces of the left that is now taking place are as follows. We are above all else for the development of the labour movement and the political development of the working class. We are for the freedoms without which that will not happen – without which the labour movements and the working class cannot develop politically towards socialism and the overthrow of the bourgeoisie. Everything else is subordinate to that. There is nothing – except the socialism that the working class must win – higher for us than that. "Anti-imperialism" that is indifferent or hostile to the working class and the labour movement is a contradiction in terms: it is the working class and only the working class that will finally bury capitalism and imperialism. In the early 1980s, we rejected and fought against the outlook of those who supported the Polish Stalinist state against the working-class movement, Solidarnosc, because Solidarnosc threatened state-owned nationalised property, which most of the left thought of as an all-overriding good. (The SWP was on the same side as us then.) Today we reject the view that the "anti-imperialism" of clerical fascists is superior to a labour movement that wants to see bourgeois democracy develop in Iraq. Socialists who do not support those trade unions; those who seem not to care whether the Iraqi labour movement survives and develops, or is crushed by the clerical fascists or a new Ba'thist regime; the hooligans who howled down al Mashadani; and those like the SWP who have the same politics while hypocritically distancing themselves from the hooligans – all are abandoning socialism for an "anti-imperialism" which, by analogy with what Marx and Engels in the Communist Manifesto called "reactionary socialism", is a species of "reactionary anti-imperialism".

5. The Prophet and the demoralised revolutionaries

"Religion is, indeed, the self-consciousness and self-esteem of man who has either not yet won through to himself, or has already lost himself again. But, man is no abstract being squatting outside the world. Man is the world of man – state, society. This state and this society produce religion, which is an inverted consciousness of the world, because they are an inverted world. Religion is the general theory of this world, its encyclopaedic compendium, its logic in popular form, its spiritual point d'honneur, its enthusiasm, its moral sanction, its solemn complement, and its universal basis of consolation and justification.

It is the fantastic realisation of the human essence since the human essence has not acquired any true reality. The struggle against religion is, therefore, indirectly the struggle against that world whose spiritual aroma is religion. Religious suffering is, at one and the same time, the expression of real suffering and a protest against real suffering. Religion is the sigh of the oppressed creature, the heart of a heartless world, and the soul of soulless conditions. It is the opium of the people. The abolition of religion as the illusory happiness of the people is the demand for their real happiness. To call on them to give up their illusions about their condition is to call on them to give up a condition that requires illusions. The criticism of religion is, therefore, in embryo, the criticism of that vale of tears of which religion is the halo.

Criticism has plucked the imaginary flowers on the chain not in order that man shall continue to bear the chain without fantasy or consolation, but so that he shall throw off the chain and pluck the living flower. The criticism of religion disillusions man, so that he will think, act, and fashion his reality like a man who has discarded his illusions and regained his senses, so that he will move around himself as his own true Sun. Religion is only the illusory Sun which revolves around man as long as he does not revolve around himself" – Karl Marx, *A Contribution to the Critique of Hegel's Philosophy of Right*

"The problem isn't the Muslim fundamentalists but the other funda-mentalists, the Islamophobes and racists – people like you."

The "other fundamentalists"? Anti-religious Marxists. People like me. This arresting comment came not from some Muslim or melt-ingly ecumenical Christian, or from a *Guardian* editorial writer, but from a self-proclaimed Marxist. It is typical of the self-defensive abuse SWPers throw out nowadays when confronted by Marxists who display active hostility to Islam. To be anti-Islamic is to be "racist". Since 11 September 2001, the SWP has taken on the job of so-cialist outrider for Islam in Britain.

An SWP organiser (white, English, female, her head covered Mus-lim-fashion), on a picket of the Israeli embassy, hassling secular so-cialist women to put scarves over their heads "to show respect" on a demonstration that is "mostly Muslim". SWPers accepting and ac-tively helping to enforce male-female segregation at meetings and demonstrations.

Many such stories about the SWP circulate on the secular left right now. Some of the stories one hears about SWPers made light-headed by the eruption of conflict between political Islam and the great pow-ers may be apocryphal. The story of the SWP organiser insisting that atheist women should "show respect" and solidarity by covering their heads as Muslim women are forced to do wherever Islamists make the rules is to my certain knowledge true. SWPers have ac-cepted and even half-heartedly collaborated in the segregation of women demanded by religious Muslims at anti-war meetings. Until pressed, they refused to intervene to support the right of a secular woman of Asian Muslim background to be what she was when she became a target for Muslim bigots at an anti-war meeting in Birm-ingham. At the same meeting they supported the exclusion of a stroppy ex-Muslim woman whose existence was an affront to the eyes of anti-war Muslims

These incidents indicate how far people calling themselves Marx-ist have travelled from the ABC Marxist – and even from vertebrate liberal – attitude on questions like this. The questions involved here in the dispute between the SWP and ourselves on Islam are to-be-or-not-to-be for Marxists. Is it possible for Marxists to defend Muslim people from discrimination, racism and scapegoating and at the same time proclaim our own radical hostility to religion, to Islam, and to certain social practices associated with Islam, for example, the treat-ment of women?

Does opposition to the US and British governments demand of us that we defend Islamic fundamentalist movements like the Taliban and Al Qaeda? Does solidarity with Islamic people in Britain and elsewhere against abuse, physical attack and social discrimination, demand of us that we defend Islam? That we must pretend that its specific beliefs and practices are compatible with a rational outlook on the world? In short, do we mute and suppress our own identity?

This is nothing less than the question: can people committed to war against priests as against landlords, money lords, and warlords, exist and function politically in the present situation? Can Marxism and Marxists exist?

Marxists are secularists or they are not Marxists. Why? Because we are humanists – humankind, not some imaginary God, is the centre of our concerns and endeavours. Because a viable socialist outlook can only be built on the truth about humanity's real place in the universe. Because, to one degree or another, religions direct us to live this, our only life, as preparation for an imaginary afterlife, and teach that this life is less important. Because religions tend, though there are sometimes exceptions, to breed fatalism and a sense of helplessness before social oppression, seeing it as decreed by God and not essentially by other human beings. Because Islam, like Christianity, believes that a benign God controls our lives, that he can and does intervene in human affairs, and that our prayers and solicitations can move him to such intervention. Because religion offers false consolation for things which we want to rouse up the working class and other oppressed people to fight and overcome.

We are against religion because we are for reason and science. Unlike demoralised liberals and the sub-liberal "politically correct" "Marxists", we believe that it matters whether what people believe is true or false. We continue the tradition of militant rationalism – what an Anglican priest, a socialist, whom I talked to recently, denounced as "19th century rationalism" – and secularism which the bourgeoisie have abandoned. The Islamicising "Marxists" in practice abandon it too.

Wars of religion convulsed Europe for 150 years in the 16th and 17th centuries. By the middle of the 17th century Protestants and Catholics had fought each other to a stalemate. Then a reaction set in, and an age of scepticism and comparative indifference. The Christian tide receded. Something like that has happened in the second half of the 20th century to the once-powerful secularist drive. Even though some of its leading people were anti-socialists, that current was connected to the drive to remake the world by the exercise of reason in the service of love and human solidarity. Its retreat is part of the reflux of the socialist tide, of the drive to remake the world.

If secular-minded people today are tolerant of religion and super-stition and indifferent to it, that is an aspect of the collapse of a posi-tive world outlook different from the prevailing bourgeois one, the collapse of the aspiration to transform our world and build a better one. Those who wanted to enlighten, educate and convince people that a better world was possible felt the need to challenge false ideas. They had a drive to wipe out religion and clear up its debris (such idiocies as astrology). The present tide of indifference might be called "post-Utopian". It is part of the dominant anti-Utopianism of our time, with its belief that this is as good as it will ever get. Marxists cannot go along with it without ceasing to be Marxists. We have not given up on the aspiration to build a rational world free from super-stition as well as from exploitation.

We remain hostile to all religions, irreconcilably opposed to all privileges for religious bodies, against the religious involvement in state education, and against all state subsidies for religious education, and for the strict separation of church and state. Here Marxists simply continue the tradition of the serious bourgeois radicals who over two hundred years ago wrote the separation of church and state into the constitution of the American Republic. With the liberal ideal of free-dom of religion, to which of course we subscribe, Marxists insist on coupling the demand for freedom for atheists and for atheistic pro-paganda – as the Communist International, for example, did.

Not for centuries in most of the West has the demand for freedom of atheistic propaganda had such urgency as it has now wherever Islam is strong, Muslim Britain included. The freedom not to be a Muslim; the freedom for a Muslim to abjure Islam (for Muslim fun-damentalists that is punishable with death); the freedom for people of Muslim background to make atheistic propaganda in their own communities; the freedom to brand all the basic tenets of Islam about Allah and his Messenger as lies and all-round nonsense; the right to explain that to young people of Muslim education – all that is of fun-damental importance in Islamic countries and in Islamic communities in non-Islamic countries. It is a matter of life and – sometimes literally – death for secularists, socialists and Marxists within those countries and communities.

What can you say of a political culture in which an SWP full-time organiser can think it nothing wrong to try to enforce the Islamic fun-damentalist rule of covering their heads on non-Muslim women on a political demonstration? Those who create and maintain that cul-ture have simply lost the plot, if not their minds. Now, everyone who pays attention knows that within their ritual chanting about "revolution", the operational politics of the SWP are generally pretty tame and, in fact, not socialist but reformist. "Socialism", like "revolution" and "the revolutionary party", is for them no more than a patented brand name. As someone said, the SWP is in politics often only a self-excited crowd of "*Guardian* readers with placards".

In their tolerance towards Islamic intolerance, their softness towards those who exercise a hard coercion against "their own" in Muslim countries and societies (and try to do it at demonstrations and meetings in Britain), the very revolutionary SWP simply mirror and parallel the attitudes of a large part of the post-Stalinist, post-utopian, organically demoralised, "liberal intelligentsia". They become demoralised *Guardian* readers with headscarves, so to speak.

This posture is a betrayal of the best people in the immigrant Islamic communities. It is a taking of sides with the great unenlightened mass of people of Islamic background in Britain and their priests and spiritual policemen against those of that background who have more or less broken with it or are more or less hostile to it.

"Racism" is a word that is too casually and lazy-mindedly thrown around these days. Nonetheless, it needs to be said that there is something very like racism in this business, or at least gross chauvinist stereotyping, and not on the part of those who side with the secular "Muslims" and against Islam. "Asian Muslims" are... Muslims; and, moreover, backward, bigoted, unteachable Muslims, who can only be approached on their own terms and by way of cynical would-be manipulative patronisation. That is the implication of the SWP approach. And it is not remotely true.

Large numbers of people from Islamic backgrounds have in serious part emancipated themselves from Islam, ranging from outright atheists through to "secularised" Muslims. That is one of the most encouraging things to be seen on the anti-war and pro-Palestinian demonstrations. Many ostensible Muslims take and carry placards calling for two states in Israel-Palestine. Even if they won't take the placards, you can talk about the political issues – even with seriously religious Muslims – in a way in which you cannot talk with most of the bigotedly anti-Israel and "anti-imperialist" left.

Of course, the SWP leaders have their private beliefs, which are probably the same as ours. Their motive is pure catchpenny opportunism; but its prerequisite is ideological demoralisation and political disorientation. They bring to the Islamic communities the same cross-class popular-front approach that has allowed them to have Tories on Anti Nazi League platforms.

Socialists will stand side by side with the priests and Islamic bigots to defend their neighbourhoods against racist attack. We have done that (in my direct experience, in East London). It is very different from standing side by side, so to speak, with those reactionaries against the more emancipated segments of their own communities. It is a "socialist", "Marxist" variant of the oft-repeated "treason of the intellectuals" – a betrayal of reason, an abandonment of the secular program of revolutionary socialism and of our entire tradition. It is also stupid, unless they have given up on socialism. The socialist future, not of "the Muslim community" which the SWP in Popular Front mode tries to relate to now, but of the workers and youth and the rebellious women of that community, will be wrought and secured by those secular "Muslims" who are now a despised and often persecuted minority in "the Muslim community". It is they who will act initially as the link with the broader labour movement and as the bearers of anti-religious enlightenment to the Muslim community. The fundamental job of non-Muslim socialists is to encourage and help those secular "Muslims".

The SWP's attitude to Islam is possible only because they themselves have a quasi-religious outlook which they mistakenly think is Marxist and "dialectical". They live in a hazy mental world where everything is essentially in flux; where "Revolution" is imminent, maybe, or soon will be; where things are therefore never just what they are; where everything solid dissolves into air and pseudo-political patter. Political Islam is only a transient form of something else, the unfolding "Revolution". Islamic reaction does not matter because the socialist world revolution, maybe, will clear everything up. It is not "really" reactionary because "objectively" it is part of something progressive, namely "revolutionary" opposition to "US and British imperialism". It is not a threat to anyone because it cannot last long. "After Hitler, our turn", was how the complaisant Stalinised Communist Party of Germany expressed a similar outlook in 1933 and after. "After the Islamists, our turn"?

History is a revolutionary roller-coaster. Realities dissolve into a pseudo-dialectical flurry. The SWP leaders are no longer sure of near-imminent revolution, but the pattern of thought, the old millenarian approach to "anti-imperialist" phenomena, is still in place

All sorts of accommodations are licensed, because the thing accommodated to is not fully real. Thus their "revolutionary" socialist politics dissolve into a pseudo-historical mysticism which is very much like a religious belief in a godlike spirit of History which will, eventually, "take care" of everything for us.

But in fact political Islam is real – an immensely oppressive reality for many people in Muslim societies and communities, and especially for those of them who disagree to one degree or another. Such a way of looking at contemporary history, with an uncomprehending numb indifference rooted in the belief that horrors are not real horrors but something else, if viewed through the right ideological spectacles, is to rational socialism what the religious belief that nothing matters because everything will be made right in the afterlife, is to a this-world, humanity-centred philosophy of life. It was at the heart of much 20th century socialist experience, for example of the attitude which people who should have known better took to Stalinism, and not only to Stalinism.

For Marxist socialists in Britain who have to combine defence of Muslim people from racists and scapegoaters with implacable hostility to Islam, as to other religions, the old Catholic tag offers guidance: love the sinner, hate the sin! Defend Muslim people against racism and bigotry, fight political Islam! (And fight Islam, as we fight Christianity and other religions.) Understand that political Islam is the enemy of everything that socialists stand for! Don't try to "relate" to the "Muslim community" – except in things like organising physical resistance to racists and fascists – but to the Muslim working class and to the "Muslim" secularists. Work to split the "Muslim community"; help organise the ex-Muslims, the insurgent women and the socialists within the "Muslim community" to fight the Islamic religious and cultural establishments!

Appendix: the Communist Party and Irish "anti-imperialism"

There are striking parallels between the conventional Left's attitude to Islam now and the way the Communist Party used to relate to Irish Catholic immigrants in Britain. I had some experience of that. For a while, over half a century ago, I was involved in the work of the Communist Party among Irish people of devout Catholic background in Britain, people from the nearest thing to a theocracy in Europe, where clerics ruled within glove-puppet bourgeois-democratic institutions. Hundreds of thousands of us came to Britain from small towns, backward rural areas, from communities of small commodity-producers, from places and conditions that were very different from what we encountered in big-capitalist British society. We spoke English and were ethnically indistinguishable from the natives, but we brought with us the idea of history as the struggle of the oppressed against oppression and exploitation, derived from what we had learned from parents, teachers, priests, and songs, and from reading about Ireland's centuries-long struggle against England.

Such ideas had very broad implications. It needed only a small shift – no more than a refocusing of those ideas on the society we were now in, and which at first we saw with the eyes of strangers not inclined to be approving – for us to see British – and the less developed Irish – capitalist society for the class-exploitative system it is, to learn to see our place in it, and to reach the socialist political conclusions that follow from that.

Vast numbers of Irish migrants became part of the labour movement. Quite a few of us became socialists of varying hues, a small number revolutionary socialists. The propaganda barrage against Communism, as embodied in Russia and the other Stalinist states, most of it just, worked to inhibit Irish as well as others in turning to Communism. Even so, it was primarily their Catholicism that stopped large numbers of Irish immigrants, whose mindset I have sketched above, from learning to understand, as some of us did, that Communism was not Stalinism, and developing according to the logic of our ideas about history, into communists.

The CPGB ran an Irish front organisation, the Connolly Association. Instead of advocating socialism and secularism and working to organise as communists those being shaken loose from the dogmatic certainties we had learned in a society ruled by Catholic "fundamentalists", the Connolly Association disguised themselves as simple Irish nationalists. They purveyed ideas not seriously different from those of the ruling party in Dublin, Fianna Fail, except for occasional words in favour of Russian foreign policy. The real history of 20th century Ireland, and the part played by the Catholic Church and the Catholic "Orange Order", the Ancient Order of Hibernians, in creating the conditions that led to Partition, were suppressed and forgotten. Instead, they told a tale in which only the Orange bigots and the British were villains. The concerns and outlook of narrow Catholic nationalism were taken at their own evaluation and given a pseudo-anti-imperialist twist. All that mattered was to be against Russia's enemy "British imperialism".

The CPGB thus, for its own manipulative ends, related to the broad mass of Irish Catholic immigrants – who, in the pubs of places

---

† *And if this seems just something purely personal to me, I suggest that the reader takes a look at James P Cannon's review of the novel about the mindset of the Irish American world, Moon Gaffney. It is in Cannon's Notebook of an Agitator, and also at http://www.workersliberty.org/node/29036.*

like South Manchester, in my experience, bought the Connolly Association paper, *Irish Democrat*, in large numbers – by accommodating to the Catholic nationalist bigotries we had learned from priests and teachers at home, and battening politically on them. We had, those of us who took it seriously, a cultural and religious arrogance that would have startled those who did not see us as we saw ourselves – something that, I guess, is also true of many Muslims now. The CPGB did not challenge it. † For the CPGB this approach made a gruesome sense that is entirely absent from the SWP's antics with Islam: Moscow approved of Dublin's "non-aligned" foreign policy, and its refusal to have NATO military bases in Ireland. Russian foreign policy, and the wish to exploit Irish nationalism against the UK – that was the CPGB leader's first and main concern.

In this way the Connolly Association and the CPGB cut across the line of development of secularising Irish immigrants: large numbers became lapsed Catholics, but without clearing the debris of religion from their heads. It expelled from its ranks those who wanted to make the Connolly Association socialist and secularist. Instead of helping us move on from middle-class nationalism and the Catholic-chauvinist middle-class interpretation of Irish history, it worked to lock us back into those ideas by telling us in "Marxist" terms that they were the best "anti-imperialism". What mattered, fundamentally, to the CP leaders was who we were against – Russia's antagonist, Britain.

East Berlin, June 1953. The banner calls for free elections.

6. The slogan "Troops Out" and socialist principle: the case of Iraq

Before, during, and after the 2003 invasion of Iraq, we, the AWL, said what needed to be said. AWL was against the USA's war in Iraq. We preached "no political trust or confidence" in the American, British, or any ruling class, in their states, their politicians, or their armies. We analysed the motives of the American, British and other ruling classes in their dealings with Iraq; solidarised with the new Iraqi labour movement wherever it clashed with the occupiers; indicted US/UK misdeeds unsparingly; said to those Iraqi socialists whom we can reach, and to people in Britain, that they could not and should not rely on the US and UK to bring democracy to Iraq. Long before the 2003 invasion, we pointed out that the occupation of Iraq would not curb Islamist terrorism. We said that the peoples of Iraq must have self-determination. We maintained a stance of hostility to the troops. We denounced the USA's (failed) attempt in 2008 to impose a deal on Iraq to maintain a permanent US military presence there with large authority.

That was enough.

The behaviour of the occupying forces – the senseless brutality and slaughter of Iraqi civilians, the economic looting by the US rulers, the all-shaping arrogance, the casual deployment of lethal firepower against civilians, and the sheer all-round epoch-defining ineptitude – that piled up enormous barriers against any "benign" scenario. We pointed that out.

But we refused, between 2003 and the 2008 US agreement to withdraw (completed in 2011), to raise a "demand", Troops Out Now, whose likely, calculable, practical consequences we did not want. A "precipitate" withdrawal would have maximised the chances of destruction for the Iraqi labour movement. It might well have brought on a catastrophe that would have aborted all the possibilities that the rising labour movement was opening for the working class of Iraq. (And for the region, perhaps, where, though there is a powerful working class, there is scarcely any labour movement except in Israel – at best, some elements of a labour movement among the Palestinians, in Lebanon, and in Egypt).

Democracy is a principle; but self-determination is only one of its forms; Troops Out Now in turn is only one of self-determination's possible immediate, sloganised, expressions. The only reason for not

294

deciding in 2003-8 that the best thing was that the US, Britain, etc. should immediately just get out was that that would calculably be to give up all hope for anything less bad than the scenario of civil war and destruction of the labour movement. Things may yet go that far. But it was not for us to shout, in effect: Bring it on!

Everything suggested that "immediate" withdrawal of the foreign troops would be likely to lead to the destruction of the Iraqi labour movement by the forces of Ba'thist-fascist and clerical-fascist reaction. Any distinction between sloganising for Troops Out Now and being for the victory of the reactionary Iraqi "resistance" was largely a notional one. The slogan Troops Out Now was inescapably, a siding with the reactionary resistance. Who else would gain "now" from the troops disappearing "now"? (The addled left understood that, at least, and duly backed the "resistance").

A concerned friend, one who did not share the politics of the addled left which backed the Iraqi "resistance", might ask, regarding the call for "Troops Out Now" in 2003-8: by refusing to call for the immediate and unconditional withdrawal of all occupation forces, wasn't AWL seeking a social and political gain from the crime of imperialism without actually advocating it?

Wasn't the slogan "Troops Out of Iraq Now" a matter of principle? If we let calculations about the practical, concrete – Iraqi – meaning of "Troops Out Now", inhibit us from demanding "the immediate withdrawal of imperialist forces", then weren't we:

• engaging in an impermissible "ideological compromise" with imperialism;

• engaging in "an interim appeasement program towards the status quo on this side of the imperialist battle lines";

• engaging in an objective united front with imperialism; making a "provisional and tactical military reliance on imperialism".

Ours was not to reason, calculate, or calibrate, and still less to decide on slogans and "demands" according to an analysis of the concrete situation and what they mean, or will most likely mean, in that situation.

That argument conflated socialist propaganda and socialist agitation. It resided up in the clouds somewhere, far too high above the ground. It displayed too little real, practical concern for the Iraqi labour movement. It blurred and fudged what for us was, in Iraq as in all other situations, the central question – the working class, its labour movement, and their fate. At issue was not whether socialists should give the US/ UK positive political support or political confidence, or forget for now who, socially and politically, and what they are, and who and what we are. ever do any of these things. At issue was: do we gauge the concrete meaning of a slogan like Troops Out Now, and decided on its use accordingly? Are there slogans that are above and outside of all such political calculations? Must we on principle raise a slogan whose calculable practical consequences we did not want? Do we use such slogans as tools or as a set of binding instructions which we blindly obey and serve?

If it is obligatory to call for "Troops Out Now", that implies that if the new Iraqi labour movement had benefited from the US-British destruction of the Saddam regime – and undeniably it had since 2003 – then it would be better had it never come into existence than that it should thus benefit from imperialism. The Iraqi labour activists would just have to be stoical, bear their fate bravely, and understand that though we reach the same conclusions as the "reactionary anti-imperialists" in shouting for "Troops Out Now" and thereby succouring the Sunni supremacists and clerical fascists, our motive was different – to put ourselves in the best position to resist the "gravitational pull" of imperialism and the threat that we might wind up going over to Blairism (as a few of our one-time comrades in fact did).

Brutus and Cassius both stab Caesar, but for different motives. If Brutus explains to the dying man that he was motivated by higher goals than those of the jealous Cassius and his friends, Caesar will understand and die happy…

The issue could be restated, without too much exaggeration: should we turn our backs on capitalism and start a clean new society somewhere from scratch? Should we adopt the approach of the 19th century devotees of building socialist colonies in some unpolluted wilderness? Our entire world – the world Marxists say is the basis from which the working class can make socialism – is built on the crimes of class society. The cities of Liverpool and Bristol were built on the slave trade. Early British capitalism accumulated its wealth from the slave trade, piracy against the Spanish pirates and plunderers of Mexico and Peru, and from pillage and genocidal wars in 16th and 17th century Ireland. European civilisation, on the achievements of which we propose to build socialism, rests on a gigantic mound of human skulls and bones!

We cannot in retrospect re-do the history that led us to where we are. Advanced capitalism, the dominant force in the world, amidst its horrors, and sometimes by way of its horrors, has done things on which socialists have to build and without which socialism cannot be built. World War Two and its aftermath are the clearest example. In Europe, American and British imperialism – consider said all that needs to be said about their reactionary policies, their enslavement of colonies, their atom-bombing of Hiroshima and Nagasaki, etc. – cut down the totalitarian Nazi geno-imperialism and recreated bourgeois democracy.

In 1940 the labour movement in Europe was everywhere – except in Switzerland, Sweden, Britain, and Ireland – smashed, reduced to weak underground movements, and most of them dominated by Stalinists. Modern Europe, with its tremendously powerful and potentially world-transforming labour movement, re-emerged under the wing of British and American imperialism.

Better things would have been possible had we been stronger, had Stalinism not existed? Yes, and our comrades advocated those things then. They were right to advocate them and counterpose them to what the "progressive" bourgeois-imperialists did. Better, in those times, had the European working class asserted itself as an independent "class for itself" overthrown capitalism, and driven out, or disrupted by way of agitation and propaganda among the soldiers, the occupying armies of Roosevelt-Truman, Churchill-Attlee, and Stalin. Yet it would have been metaphysics-saturated political nonsense for European socialists (and socialists in Japan) to have foresworn seeking social and political gain from the bourgeois-democratic systems and the re-risen labour movements because they were "tainted" by their origins in the victory of American and British imperialism.

The social and political system in Western Europe by, say, 1949 registered immense progress, not direct socialist progress, but immense progress nevertheless, compared to 1940 or 1944, above all for the potentialities it opened up for the working-class movement. One of the things that derailed Orthodox Trotskyism was its incapacity to understand that and adjust to it. Our attitude to such progress cannot be different from our attitude to economic progress under the capitalist system which nonetheless we want to overthrow, which we believe should and could have been overthrown long ago, and which we continue to work to overthrow.

We extend to the rulers of the USA and Britain no political credit in advance. We criticise them from our own socialist and consistently democratic point of view for what they do and don't do, and for what they license, acquiesce in, or fail to oppose. We maintain towards them the stance of mortally hostile communist opponents of bourgeois society.

Nonetheless, we recognise and utilise the imperialist-fostered bourgeois-democratic progress in Western Europe – just as we want to use the capitalist and "imperialist" improvement in economic techniques and labour productivity to build a socialist alternative to capitalism.

Could we in principle refuse to hope for advantage for the working class or the socialists out of anything advanced capitalism ("imperialism") does in the world? Surely we can not. Another way to look at this question is to pose it in terms of Stalinism. Could we properly hope for advantage or progress out of the work of Stalinism in Russia, in Eastern Europe, or elsewhere? The Orthodox Trotskyists answered that question with a clear-cut yes. A "political revolution" was necessary first, but the working class would build on the positive economic achievements of the Russian and East European Stalinist tyrannies. There was a great deal wrong with their accounts of what Stalinism was. But they were right when, in advocating working-class revolution against Stalinism ("political revolution"), they did not dream of proposing that the Stalinist-built industry be dismantled and scrapped, and that society should start again. That would have been an absurdity. A version of stop the world, I want to get off; roll back the film of history, I want to start from somewhere else. A variant of the joke about the man asked for directions who said: "If I were you, I wouldn't start from here at all".

No more can or should we propose the erasure of the achievements of monopoly capitalism in the USA or Europe. The Orthodox Trotskyists advocated the seizure of political power, and power over the economic assets – the destruction of the social and economic power of the Stalinist oligarchy – as we advocate working-class revolution and the transfer and transformation of the existing capitalist economic assets. The Workers Party and the ISL had politics much more true to the reality of the Stalinist states than the Orthodox Trotskyists had. But they had no different proposal to offer about what to do with the "achievements" of Stalinism. In the mid 1950s they argued that all-pervasive political democracy – the destruction of the autocracy, its social-political rule, and its state – would, per se, transform the economy. In terms of the economy, was that attempting to "benefit from Stalinism and Stalinist imperialism"? And, in any case, weren't they right? What other reality-grounded program could they have put forward for the Stalinist societies?

Could the AWL realistically expect to withstand the gravitational pull that such "ideological compromises" exerted over previous generations of socialist militants? Wasn't the logic, if not yet the general politics, of the AWL's refusal to raise the slogan "Troops Out Now" the same as that of groups like the Blairite, neo-connish political turncoats in Labour Friends of Iraq? And of Max Shachtman and his comrades in effectively supporting the USA in Vietnam?

The great pressure on Third Camp socialists such as Shachtman and his friends, pushing them towards allying with the bourgeoisie, was that Russian Stalinism was the second power in the world. It was the enemy of most of the achievements in history of bourgeois civilisation at its best – free speech, freedom for civic organisations to exist, etc. – all the things that allowed labour movements to exist and are prerequisites of socialism. The Third Camp socialists did not deny that on all those counts advanced capitalism was better than Stalinism and preferable to it, which they defined as the looming form of "barbarism". Socialism, in their view, was the only long-term alternative to that barbarism; yet advanced capitalism was the only large force already in existence standing athwart Stalinist domination of the world. Tremendous pressure to side with what they explicitly, and rightly, saw as the better of the two competing systems bore down on them from the end of World War Two onwards. No such logic bore down on us over Iraq. A similar logic – the pressure to opt for the lesser evil in what is already available – did account for the moral, intellectual, and political collapse of a few erstwhile revolutionary socialists. It was not their refusal to use one slogan, Troops Out Now, which led them to stop saying what needed to be said against the bourgeoisie and against capitalism.

Is advanced capitalism just "one reactionary mass", or can it sometimes and in some ways do "progressive" work? Modern history, for over 100 years, consists not only of horrors such as wars, repressions, and famines in parts of the world, but also of "progressive" things done by advanced capitalism, from the destruction of fascist totalitarianism to the overthrow, in a different way, of Stalinist totalitarianisms. Tremendous and life-expanding things have been achieved under advanced capitalism, including two general technological revolutions. The productivity of labour, on which the possibility of socialism depends, has been vastly increased. In no circumstances do we give the big capitalist powers credence, allegiance, or confidence in advance. We put forward our own working-class program, and counterpose it to theirs, in every situation. Working-class democratic socialism would have been better and achieved more. What advanced capitalism yields in the way of progress is always at risk of being annulled by its characteristic crises, including wars. But we cannot simply call it "imperialism" and say "no" to the modern world – the world shaped and reshaped, and still being shaped and reshaped, by advanced capitalism.

Here, as in our attitude to the concentration and centralisation of capital, or to bourgeois efforts towards desirable objectives (like the European Union and European unity), we have to operate within a capitalism that both blights and retards progress as compared to the socialism which is possible and necessary, but nevertheless does progressive work. It has done, in its own brutal, predator's, profit-first, way, things that take society forward and the immediate alternative to which is reactionary – for example, a return to the walled-off nation-states of pre-EU Europe. We do not and should not, in opposing advanced capitalism, as we do when we counterpose to them the possibilities of socialism, also "oppose" and contradict what we want, or give support, or implicit support, to what would take us backward.

You cannot be a Marxist and argue for a slogan on the grounds of its usefulness to you in resisting uncongenial pressures, apart from whether it makes sense in terms of reality. That way lies confusion, irresponsibility, and irrelevance. If we were to resist the "pull" of the powers that rule the world only by closing our eyes to facts, possibilities, certainties, and modern history – if we felt obliged to pretend that everything about the bourgeoisie and bourgeois society is reactionary, and that there is nothing more reactionary in the political world – then we would be paying too high a political price for anti-imperialist, or even anti-capitalist, virtue. We would also be setting ourselves up to collapse if and when awareness of a more complex reality breaks through – a very common experience with naive and even not-so-naive revolutionaries over most of the 20th century.

We felt no gravitational pull towards the bourgeoisie or its system as a result of recognising that this system, towards which we are mortally antagonistic, is not always and everywhere, and not in every single thing, only or simply reactionary; and that there are in some situations, things more reactionary things. The American big-capitalist bourgeoisie demolished Hitler's fascism and installed bourgeois democracy in post-1945 western Europe and Japan. If that was reactionary, then it was so only compared to what the working class could have achieved if better educated and better mobilised; but it was not so educated and so mobilised. In fact, of course, independent working-class politics was only a peripheral force in that situation, as it has been so far in Iraq.

Recognising such facts does not affect our fundamental hostility to capitalism and to bourgeois society. It sharpens and sustains our hostility – hostility to what they really are, as they really are, unalloyed with the patently false idea that everything in the bourgeois-dominated world is reactionary today (or has been since how far back? 1900? 1912? 1917?), or is the most reactionary thing possible.

Independent socialists are rightly chary of making positive demands on the big powers. For example, we would not try to tell them positively what to do next in Iraq. We couldn't "tell" the US what we would like them to do to ensure the best outcome, because we knew that they act for their own reasons and objectives, which are not ours. We had no illusions about that, and did not want to teach others to have illusions.

We did not, and did not want to, sloganise positive "orders" to them – "get more Iraqis killed", "get Iraqi trade unionists shot or blown up", "get the nascent labour movement extirpated". But we could, and on principle were obliged to, shout the same "orders" to them in negative form? Again – why?

Because some of our slogans are not slogans, not formulas whose use is regulated by what they might mean in a given situation, but fetishes outside of history, of politics, of society? We, AWL, refuse to take that approach. I know of no respect-worthy Marxist in the past who did. We must not obliterate the necessary distinction between self-determination as a basic programmatic principle for us and one of its possible immediate agitational translations, Troops Out Now.

In part the problem here is the dominant style of left and pseudo-left politics now – tiny propaganda groups, with no power to shape events, shouting "instructions" for immediate action to governments, and made reckless by their own powerlessness, because they know what they say will not shape, or in most cases even marginally affect, what happens. That style does not, I think, among Marxists, go back further than the Korean war and the movement against the Vietnam war. After 1945, for example, the Trotskyists demanded self-determination for Germany and that foreign troops should leave, but as far as I know they didn't do that often (if at all) in the form of demands for "Troops Out Now".

Lenin's discussion in *What Is To Be Done* (1902) of the relationship between our theory and propaganda and "calls to action" says a lot to the habits of the left and pseudo-left today.

"To single out a third sphere, or third function, of practical activity, and to include in this function 'calling the masses to certain concrete actions', is sheer nonsense, because the 'call', as a single act, either naturally or inevitably supplements the theoretical tract, propagandist pamphlet and agitational speech, or represents a purely executive function..."

Did the call "Troops Out Now" flow from an all-round analysis of Iraq? The situation was one in which the Iraqi labour movement might (we'd say, would) be destroyed, and sooner rather than later, if the occupation forces scuttled in a "precipitous" withdrawal. To make a particular "call to action" our fixed point is to turn Marxist politics upside down. We make no "call to action" on the working class, and still less on anyone else, that does not spin organically and naturally out of our theory, propaganda, program, and concrete analysis of a situation. In short: that does not make sense.

The meaning of slogans is determined variously by different sets of concrete circumstances. The meaning and implications of a particular form of words differs from circumstance to circumstance, and from time to time. Our overall picture of a situation, and of the forces and possibilities in it, determines what "calls to action" are appropriate or inappropriate. The separation or cutting loose of "calls to action" from our program and the general complex of Marxist ideas has been one of the long-term agents of destruction that has worked its way through, like syphilis, groups such as the SWP-UK. It has produced what might be called "apparatus Marxism", "focus-group Marxism", "party manager's Marxism" or, to use an older expression for such things, "wire-puller's Marxism". It reduces Marxist politics to demagogy.

If a slogan ("Troops Out Now") carries with it the extreme likelihood of disaster for the labour movement, then it contradicts our overall concerns. We do not raise it, or we do not raise it in a form which if realised implies disaster. The general principle and propagandist "position" – that is, the general explanation rather than "call to action" – is enough. We are not obliged to translate the explanation into a "call to action" which will promote forces like the Iraqi "resistance" and help them to turn the would-be summary formula against the fundamental ideas and concerns behind it.

For Marxists there is no slogan that we are obliged to treat as a fetish, something above and outside of its own concrete meaning. The very idea that there might be is ridiculous! Principles are more or less immutable. How they are translated into slogans or agitational axes is changeable. Sometimes they can't be expressed in any summary "call to action". To refuse to translate a "principle" into concrete "demands" is sometimes to make of the principle a lifeless abstraction? Yes. But you can only judge where that is being done by way of analysis of the practical meaning of the possible "concrete" slogans. Slogans are selected not according to the idea that they are self-sufficient principles, but for their immediate effect, concrete application, and practical meaning. We do not do as the "apparatus Marxists" do and, for calculations of organisational advantage or "catching a mood", raise slogans antagonistic to our program and principles (and, in this case, to the interests of the Iraqi labour movement). The idea that we are obliged to raise or hold to a slogan irrespective of its practical meaning – that, again, is absurd.

In 1920 the Bolsheviks had, as the heirs of Russian Marxism, 40 years – and Lenin, two decades – of sincerely fighting for Poland's self-determination and its right to independence. I don't know if that ever took the form of slogans for Russian "Troops Out Now" (I doubt it). But when the Red Army defeated the invading Polish army and chased it deep into Poland – with the intention, in Lenin's expression, of prodding the German revolution with the bayonet – the slogan "Russian troops out" would have meant not the "democratic affirmation" of self-determination for Poland, but radical opposition to the interests of the Russian workers' revolution, to its army, and to the international working-class revolution, that of the Polish workers too.

It makes no difference here whether Lenin was right or wrong in his calculations about the advisability of the Red Army pressing into Poland. Events seemed to prove Trotsky's contrary calculations correct. But the Russian workers' government had a right in principle to refuse to make a fetish of Polish self-determination. Something higher was involved – the interests of the working class and its revolution. Polish self-determination could easily have been restored – and, if the German workers had taken power, possibly on a higher level, with the Polish working class in power.

The point here is not to compare the US army of today with the Red Army of 1920, but to see that slogans cannot stand apart from an overall Marxist analysis of a situation and above it. To put it absurdly again: slogans cannot stand higher than their own practical meaning! To say that we are obliged to raise Troops Out Now as an affirmation of democracy and of revolutionary opposition to the USA and its British helpers, irrespective of the consequences for the Iraqi labour movement, could only make political sense if "Troops Out Now" embodied a commitment for us higher than the working class, its movement, and their immediate fate.

Of course to resist the gravitational pull of the bourgeoisie is a to-be-or-not-to-be question for socialists; but that can be achieved not by mechanically repeating set slogans, but only by having an overall picture which determines our basic posture towards the ruling power even when it does, or may be doing, something that is, or may be, itself desirable.

While honestly evaluating and recording what is happening – as we do in all things – we give the bourgeoisie no positive political support; we give them no credence or credit to go on and consistently do "what's right"; we distinguish between our reasons for wanting, or assessing as positive, something that they are doing, and their own reasons, their overall program, their "context" for it. In short we continually point out who and what they are, who and what we are, where the best interests of the working class lies, and what the working class itself must be.

Only thus can we create and sustain a rounded, realistic, revolutionary world view in those whom we reach. You cannot create or sustain a lasting proletarian class consciousness on the basis of falsely negative accounts of what in a "good" moment the bourgeoisie may do, any more than you can do it by letting the "good" moment, real or mere hope, blur your overall picture of what they are and make you forget what we are.

Suppose, for example, that the US and Britain had already carried through their "project" in Iraq and created a functioning bourgeois democracy there? Would that have changed our fundamental view of what they are and what, mainly, they and those they serve do in the world?

Would it inhibit us from encouraging and helping Iraqi workers to use the new bourgeois-democratic openings to fight against Bush and Blair? To replace theirs by a working-class socialist world? It would not. Not at all. At most it would imply an amendment to our view of them to explain why "in this period" they are doing this relatively good work – exporting and expanding bourgeois democracy. Would that blot out our overall picture of what they do in terms of expanding and increasing exploitation? No, it would not.

Would it imply that we extend them credit to do equally good work of expanding bourgeois democracy somewhere else? Not for us, it wouldn't. The same bourgeois-democratic USA and Britain that – for their own reasons, as Germany's rivals – brought down Hitler, simultaneously, and for three decades, sustained Franco, the fascist who had smashed Spanish bourgeois democracy and the Spanish labour movement with the support of Hitler and Mussolini.

What the experience of a Bush or Blair carrying through some large reform that we want, or anyway see as progressive and important – again, say, establishing bourgeois democracy in Iraq – what that would do to our thinking, of course, would be to introduce the idea that they might now behave similarly elsewhere. That would not incline us where we had the option of independent action to rely on them. It would not inhibit us from telling people in other countries to which their attention was directed neither to trust them nor to rely on them, nor to give them positive political support. As Trotsky said, "we are the party of irreconcilable opposition". As Liebknecht and Luxemburg said, "not a man, not a penny, for their system".

Any attitude that pushes the immediate fate of the Iraqi labour movement to the margin of our concerns, or leads us to fatalistically accept that the labour movement must be sacrificed to something else, something higher – "anti-imperialism", or "self-determination for Iraq" understood falsely as Troops Out Now and damn the consequences – any such attitude is radically disoriented and disorienting.

Marxists tell the truth of situations, in the first place to ourselves. We face the practical implications of our slogans candidly and squarely. We are concerned at all times with the labour movement and the working class. We would have to have very special and very good reasons indeed to even seriously consider accepting something else as higher in the scale of things and more important than the fate of the working class. "Anti-imperialism", or vicarious "national liberation", is not from our point of view, a self-sufficient world outlook. The problem with much of the "left" is that for them, it is.

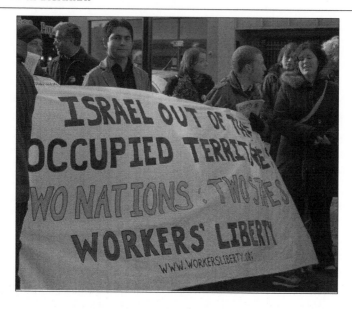

7. What is left antisemitism?

What is "left-wing antisemitism"? Where is it manifested? What is to be done about it? There are three difficulties, three confusions and obfuscations, that stand in the way of rational discussion of what we mean by "left-wing antisemitism".

The first is that left-wing antisemitism knows itself by another and more self-righteous name, "anti-Zionism". Often, your left-wing antisemite sincerely believes that he or she is only an anti-Zionist, only a just if severe critic of Israel.

The second is that talk of left-wing antisemitism to a left-wing antisemite normally evokes indignant, sincere, and just denial – of something else! "No, I'm not a racist! How dare you call me a racist?"

No, indeed, apart from an atypical crackpot here and there, left-wing antisemites are not racist. But there was antisemitism before there was late-19th and 20th century anti-Jewish racism. And there is still antisemitism of different sorts, long after disgust with Hitler-style racism, and overt racism of any sort, became part of the mental and emotional furniture of all half-way decent people, and perhaps especially of left-wing people.

Left-wingers are people who by instinct and conviction side with the oppressed, the outcasts, those deprived of human rights, with the working-class and the labour movement. We naturally side against the police, the military, and the powerful capitalist states, including our "own". We are socially tolerant; in contrast to "hang 'em, flog 'em, build more jails" people; we look to changing social conditions rather than to punishment to deal with crime – we are people who want to be Marxists and socialists, and consistent democrats. Confused some such people may be, racists they are not. We are not saying that left-wing antisemites are racists.

The third source of confusion and obfuscation is the objection: "You say I'm an antisemite because I denounce Israel. I'm not anti-Jewish when I denounce Israel, but anti-Zionist". And sometimes, at this point, you get the addition: "By the way, I am myself Jewish".

The objector continues: Israel deserves criticism. Even the harshest criticism of Israel's policies in the West Bank and Gaza, and of Israel's long-term treatment of the Palestinians, is pro-Palestinian and anti-Zionist, not antisemitic. To equate criticism of Israel with antisemitism is just crude and hysterical Zionist apologetics.

No, by "left-wing antisemitism" we emphatically do not mean political, military, or social criticism of Israel and of the policy of Israeli governments. Certainly, not all left-wing critics of Israel or Zionism are antisemites, even though these days all antisemites, including the right-wing, old-fashioned, and racist antisemites, are paid-up "anti-Zionists".

Israel frequently deserves criticism. Israel's policy in the Occupied Territories and its general treatment of the Palestinians deserve outright condemnation. The oppressed Palestinians need to be politically defended against Israeli governments and the Israeli military. The only halfway equitable solution to the Israel-Palestine conflict, a viable, independent Palestinian state in contiguous territory, side by side with Israel, needs to be argued for and upheld against Israeli power.

Solidarity condemns Israel's treatment of the Palestinians. We defend the Palestinians and champion an independent Palestinian state side by side with Israel.

The difference here between left-wing antisemites and honest critics of Israel – a category which includes a very large number of Israeli Jews as well as Israeli Arabs – is a straightforward one of politics, of policy.

The left-wing antisemites do not only criticise Israel. They condemn it outright and deny its right to exist. They use legitimate criticisms, and utilise our natural sympathy with the Palestinians, not to seek redress, not as arguments against an Israeli government, an Israeli policy, or anything specifically wrong in Israel, but as arguments against the right of Israel to exist at all. Any Israel. Any Jewish state in the area. Any Israel, with any policy, even one in which all the specific causes for justly criticising present-day Israel and for supporting the Palestinians against it have been entirely eliminated.

The root problem, say the left-wing antisemites, is that Israel exists. The root "crime of Zionism" is that it advocated and brought into existence "the Zionist state of Israel".

Bitterly, and often justly, criticising specific Israeli policies, actions, and governments, seemingly championing the Palestinians, your left-wing antisemites seek no specific redress in Israel or from Israel, demanding only that Israel should cease to exist or be put out of existence.

They often oppose measures to alleviate the condition of the Palestinians short of the destruction of Israel. Thus the petitions and chants on demonstrations: "Two states solution, no solution!" They use slogans like "Free Palestine" precisely because they can be understood in different ways, depending on your definition of "Palestine". Therefore they can accommodate those who, without having studied the complexities or the history of the Jewish-Arab conflict, instinctively side with the oppressed and outmatched Palestinians, and for whom "Free Palestine" means simply that Israel should get out of the Occupied Territories. And it can also accommodate those, like the proponents of the slogan, the political Islamists of the Muslim Association of Britain/ Muslim Brotherhood and others, who define "Palestine" as pre-Israel, pre-1948 Palestine, and by "Free Palestine" mean the destruction and abolition of Israel, and the elimination in one way or another of the Jewish population of Israel, or most of them.

The political differences spelled out here are easily understood. But why is the drive and the commitment to destroy Israel antisemitism, and not just anti-Zionism?

Because the attitude to the Jewish nation in Israel is unique, different from the left's attitude to all other nations; and because of the ramifications for attitudes to Jews outside Israel. Apart from a few religious Jews who think the establishment of Israel was a revolt against God, and some Jews who share the views of the leftists whom we are discussing here, those Jews outside Israel instinctively identify with and support Israel, however critically. For the left-wing antisemite they are therefore "Zionists", and proper and natural targets of the drive to "smash Zionism".

The attitude of the "anti-Zionist" left to Israel brings with it a comprehensive hostility to most Jews everywhere – those who identify with Israel and who defend its right to exist. These are not just people with mistaken ideas. They are "Zionists".

In colleges, for example, where the anti-Zionist left exists side by side with Jewish students, this attitude often means a special antagonism to the "Zionist" Jews. They are identified with Israel. They, especially, are pressured either to denounce Israel, to agree that it is "racist" and "imperialist" and that its existence is a crime against the Arabs – or else be held directly and personally responsible for everything Israel does, has done, or is said to have done.

In such places, where the left "interfaces" with Jews, the logic of the unique attitude to Israel takes on a nasty persecuting quality. In the past, in the mid 1980s for example, that has taken the form of attempting to ban Jewish student societies. Non-Jews who defend Israel's right to exist are not classified in the same category.

But is the attitude of the "absolute anti-Zionists" to Israel really unique? There are seeming similarities with left attitudes to one or two other states – Protestant Northern Ireland, apartheid South Africa, or pre-1980 white-ruled Rhodesia (Zimbabwe) – but the attitude to Israel is unique, because the reality of Israel cannot properly be identified with Northern Ireland, apartheid South Africa, or white Rhodesia.

In apartheid South Africa and white Rhodesia a minority lorded it over the big majority of the population, exploiting them. Israel is a predominantly Jewish state consisting of all classes. The Jewish nation does not subsist, and never has subsisted, on the exploitation of Arab labour, or depended in any essential way on such exploitation.

The general left hostility to the Northern Ireland Protestants – who are not exploiters of Catholic labour, and who are the compact majority, if not of the Six Counties, then of the north-east half of the Six Counties – is the closest to the attitude to Israel.

But it is not widely believed on the left that the Northern Ireland Protestant-Unionists simply have no right to be there. The right of the Jews to "be there" is denied in those sections of the left that we are discussing. The organisation of Jewish migration to Palestine – that was the root "crime" of Zionism, of which the "crime" of establishing Israel was only a further development. The "solution" is not only to undo and abolish Israel, but to reverse Jewish "migration" – which now includes people born there, to parents born there – and to roll the film of Middle-Eastern history backwards.

The prerequisite for left-wing antisemitism is the catastrophic decline in the culture of the left over the last decades, a decline which allows people who want to be socialists to chant "Sharon is Hitler, Israel is Nazi" and similar nonsense without checking on the words, without pausing to listen to what they are saying, or to think about it. The specific framework within which what we have been describing exists, and without which it probably couldn't exist in these "left-wing" forms, is the poisonous and systematic misrepresentation and falsification of the history of the Jewish-Arab conflict and of the Jewish people in the 20th century. We can only touch on that here.

In real history, Jews fled to Palestine, where a small Zionist colony and a small pre-Zionist Jewish community already existed, from persecution in Europe in the 1920s, 30s and 40s. In the 1930s and 40s they fled for their lives from Nazism, which killed two out of every three Jews alive in Europe in 1939, in a world in which no non-persecuting state would let them, or enough of them, in. They fled to the existing Jewish national minority in Palestine (a long-established minority which, though small, was for example the majority in Jerusalem in 1900). †

While Hitler was organising mass slaughter, Britain shut out Jews from Palestine, interning those who tried to enter. Overloaded, unseaworthy boats carrying illegal cargoes of Jews sank in the Mediterranean trying to get to Palestine (for example, the Struma, in which over 700 people died).

Israel was set up by those Jews on licence from the UN, which stipulated two states in Palestine, one Jewish and one Arab. When the state of Israel was declared in May 1948, the surrounding Arab states invaded. Jordan, Iraq, and Egypt were then British-dominated, and some of the armies were staffed by British officers.

The Israelis defended themselves and won. In the war three quarters of a million Palestinian Arabs were driven out or fled; in the same period and afterwards, about 600,000 Jews were expelled from or fled Arab countries.

In the Arab invasion of 1948, the Arab-Palestinian state was eliminated. Most of its territory went to Jordan, and fell under Israeli control in the war of 1967. That was a tremendous tragedy that will only be redressed when an independent Palestinian state takes its place alongside Israel.

This complex and tragic history is presented by the "absolute anti-Zionist" left as a conspiracy of Zionism, conceived of as a demonic force outside general history and outside Jewish history. It is not rare to find "left anti-Zionists" arguing that this Jewish-Zionist conspiracy was so all-powerful that it was able even to manipulate Adolf Hitler and the Holocaust in which six million Jews died (see the play by the

---

† J M Oesterreicher and A Sinai, *Jerusalem*, p.158.

veteran Trotskyist Jim Allen, *Perdition*, of which Ken Loach planned a performance at a London theatre in 1987). The core idea, the root of modern left-wing antisemitism, is that Israel, in one way or another, is an illegitimate state; and that therefore, in one way or another, it should be done away with. If its citizens will not be the first in history to voluntarily dismantle their nation-state and make themselves a minority in a state run by those whom they have had to fight for national existence; if they will not agree to voluntarily dismantle Israel and create a "secular democratic Arab state", in which Israeli Jews can have religious but not national rights – then they must be overwhelmed and compelled to submit or flee by the Arab states, now or when they are strong enough.

Beginning with the benign-seeming proposal to sink Israel into a broader Arab-majority entity in which "everyone could live in peace", the chain of logic rooted in the idea that Israel should not have come into existence, that it is an illegitimate state, leads directly – since Israel will not agree to abolish itself – to support for compulsion, conquest, and all that goes with it. Israel must be conquered.

Even the work of a writer like Hal Draper can feed into this poisoned stream. While Draper made valid and just criticisms of Israel, he accepted that it had a right to exist and a right to defend itself. He denounced those who wanted to destroy it. But he made his criticisms in the tone and manner of a prophet denouncing sin and iniquity. He too thought that Israel was an illegitimate state, that it should never have come into existence and should go out of existence as soon as possible.

By agreement, and only by agreement, he believed; but the subtleties get lost. There is nothing to stop someone swayed by Draper's denunciations of Israel, and accepting his idea that Israel is an illegitimate state, then impatiently insisting: if not by agreement, then by conquest.

And so an increasingly-disoriented SWP-UK could look to a Saddam Hussein to "free Palestine", that is, conquer Israel.

The point here is that states and nations are the products of history. There is no such thing as an illegitimate nation or a "bad people" which does not deserve the same rights as other peoples.

The antisemitic left today, which depicts Israel as the hyper-imperialist power – either controlling US policy, or acting as its chief instrument, the story varies – is in the grip of an "anti-imperialism of the fools". And that in practice leads to a comprehensive hostility to Jews not far from what Bebel called the socialism of fools. One of the great tragedies of contemporary politics is that many young people, whose initial instincts to oppose Bush and Blair in Iraq and to support the Palestinians are initially healthy, are being poisoned with "left-wing" antisemitism.

"Left-wing antisemitism" is, in short, first a denial of Israel's right to exist and rooted in that a comprehensive hostility to pro-Israel Jews, that is to most Jews alive, branding them as "Zionists" and seeing that description as akin to "racist" or "imperialist". It excepts only those Jews who agree that Israel is racist imperialism in its most concentrated essence, and oppose its continued existence.

The general antidote to this anti-imperialism of fools is the propagation of rational democratic and socialist politics. Such politics focus on a political solution to the Arab-Israeli conflict. They measure and criticise Israel – and the Arab states – according to their stand in relation to that just solution – the establishment of an independent Palestinian state alongside Israel.

There is an immediate "antidote" to left-wing antisemitism too, and it is a very important task for Marxist socialists like those who publish *Solidarity*: relentless exposure and criticism of their politics and antics – without fear of isolation, ridicule, or the venomous hostility of the vocal and self-righteous left-wing antisemites.

II

We need to specify what left anti-semitism consists of, in order to debate, educate, and clarify. These, I think, are its main features.

1. The belief that Israel has no right to exist. That is the core of left anti-semitism, though it comes in more than one version and from more than one root, ranging from the skewed anti-imperialism of the Orthodox Trotskyists through Arab nationalism to Islamic chauvinism. Advocacy of the destruction of Israel, which is what separates left-wing and Islamist antisemites from honest critics of Israeli policy, should not be tolerated in the labour movement and in the serious left.

2. The belief that Israeli Jewish nationalism, Zionism, is necessarily a form of racism. That this racism can only be expunged if Israel, Zionists, and Jews abandon Israeli nationalism and support of any kind for Israel. That Jewish students, for example, can only redeem themselves if they agree that the very existence of Israel or of an Israeli Jewish nation is racist.

3. The view that Israel alone is responsible for the conflict with the Arab states (and, now, with Islamic states). The idea that Israel alone is responsible for creating Arab refugees, and is uniquely evil in doing so. In real history the Arab states mostly refused the Palestinians cit-

izenship or even the right to work.

4. The claim that the Palestinian have a "right of return", that is, the right to the organised settlement in Israel of six million people (only a tiny and dying-off number of whom were born in what is now Israel) is one of the many codes for in fact demanding the self-abolition of the Jewish state and justifications for war to conquer and abolish it because it will not abolish itself. It is not the equivalent of free immigration to the UK, or even of mass migration to the UK of millions from Syria, Libya, and Africa. Its equivalent for Britain would be the settlement in the country, organised by a hostile authority, of sixty million people. Socialists should of course be in favour of agreements between Israel and the Palestinians for compensation and for letting individual Palestinians into Israel. Support for a collective right of return is only another form of the demand to conquer and destroy Israel, if it will not surrender.

5. The idea that the forced migration of 700,000 Arabs was a *unique* evil is also extravagantly wrong. In 1945, 12 to 14 million Germans were driven out of Eastern Europe. They were driven into a Germany reduced to ruins by wartime bombing, where economic life had seized up and millions were starving. Only fringe German nationalists now propose to reverse that forced population movement and to drive out the Poles, Czechs, Russians, etc. who live where Germans once lived.

6. There is a peculiar dialect of Holocaust semi-denial current on the left. I have never heard of anyone on the left who denies that six million Jews were murdered by the Nazis (though, in the nature of things, someone will now jump out from behind a bush wearing a "Hitler was Framed" badge, and call me a liar). What the anti-Zionist left habitually deny is that this unique fact of history had repercussions that we should at least recognise and try to understand, with some sympathy for the surviving Jews and their descendants. On the left the Holocaust is not denied, but it is relegated almost to the status of a "virtual fact". In truth, the Holocaust discredited all Jewish-assimilationist programs, including ours, the socialist one. It created and hardened the will for a Jewish solution to the Jewish question and for the creation of Israel. There is nothing to be surprised at or scandalised by in that. The Holocaust should be appreciated as a real fact of history, with repercussions and reverberations, and not as something outside the history we are all part of, as a sort of sideshow, as a two-dimensional hologram rather than the enormously weighty, reverberating event it was and continues to be.

7. The idea that there are good peoples entitled to all rights, and

313

bad peoples, entitled to none. That too is something I have never heard anyone voice plainly and explicitly. But it is there as an implicit subtext in the idea that we are concerned with national rights only for the presently oppressed, i.e. in this case the Palestinians.

8. There is no one-state solution. Not, as now, by Israeli domination of the whole territory and Palestinians living indefinitely in a purgatory of Israeli occupation, nor through a Palestinian state "from the river to the sea" incorporating Israel after its Jewish population have been killed or overpowered by Arab or Islamic states. The only just solution that can serve both Jews and Arabs is two states: a sovereign Palestinian state in contiguous territory, side by side with Israel. If, as may be possible, a Palestinian Arab state is made impossible by the spread of Israeli settlements, then the future will be grim indeed for both Palestinian Arabs and Israeli Jews.

Appendix: Jew or Zionist? Learn how to do it smoothly, Tammy

A small outcry greeted the assertion by the veteran Labour MP Tam Dalyell † that there are too many Jews in Tony Blair's and George Bush's entourages, and that those Jews make Britain's and the USA's policy on the Middle East. I found the responses to Dalyell encouraging, but also seriously off the point. The important and effective antisemites now are not those who talk like Hitlerites about Jewish influence and Jewish "cabals". Such people can usually expect the response Dalyell got.

Their talk is too close to what the Nazis said to justify genocide. It begs too-obvious questions and implies preposterous answers to them. Do all Jews have the same politics? How can the presence of "the Jews", or of people of Jewish faith or Jewish background, add up to "Jewish influence" or "Jewish conspiracy", when the individuals involved often have different opinions and advocate different policies? How, where the neo-conservatives of Jewish origin who are close to George Bush are out of line with the thinking of most American Jews, the big majority of whom are liberal Democrats? Where, though there may be a number of Jews who share the same opinion on certain questions, they are not alone in such opinions, and Jews can be found defending the opposite view? Where some Jews helped create the movement against the US invasion of Iraq, while others

---

† *Vanity Fair magazine, issue dated June 2003*

fervently supported the war, or, in Bush's camp, helped initiate it?

There is only one semi-coherent version of the idea that where there are Jews around, irrespective of whether they agree or fight with each other, then that is a Jewish influence. And that is the Nazi doctrine that Bolshevik Jews and Jewish international financiers, irrespective of all that divides them, are all nonetheless part of one Jewish conspiracy to dominate the world. It is the only version that allows you to note the truth that there are bourgeois Jews and Bolshevik Jews, red Jews and Rothschilds.

That stuff doesn't, I guess, have much of an open following now, though such bits of that old antisemitism as Dalyell spewed out should of course be stamped on. A number of writers in the *Guardian* did stamp on it. It was left to Paul Foot [of the SWP-UK] (*Guardian*, 14 May 2003) to defend Dalyell and put the most important present day antisemitism back in focus. Foot wrote: "Obviously [Dalyell] is wrong to complain about Jewish pressure on Blair and Bush when he means Zionist pressure. But that is a mistake that is constantly encouraged by the Zionists". Foot advises Dalyell on how he should have expressed the same idea in widely acceptable words. Call them "Zionists", not "Jews", Tammy, and no-one can accuse you of being an antisemite without also having to take on the bulk of the "revolutionary left". Learn how to do it in the modern fashion, comrade Dalyell. Of course you didn't mean "Jews", you meant "Zionists", didn't you?

Anti-Jewish feeling and ideas are usually now wrapped up in anti-Zionism. Not all "anti-Zionists" are antisemites, but these days antisemites are usually careful to present themselves as "anti-Zionists". For that reason, it is light-shedding to find a prominent pseudo-left "anti-Zionist" recognising as his political kin someone who denounces Jews – and, Foot thinks, was at fault only in lacking the finesse to say Zionist when he meant Jew.

"Anti-Zionism" is the antisemitism of today. "Anti-Zionism", that, is root-and-branch denunciation of Israel, involves comprehensively anti-Jewish attitudes – rampant or latent and implied – because it starts out from a stark refusal to recognise that the Jewish nation that had formed in Palestine by the mid 1930s had the right to exist, or the right to fight for its existence against those who would have destroyed it if they could.

In onslaughts the most important of which began in 1936, and in a series of wars, 1948, 1967, and 1973, Arab chauvinists tried to destroy the Jewish nation in Palestine. The "Zionists" had no right to defend themselves, still less to prevail! Arab pressure on the British overlords in pre-World-War-Two Palestine led to the closing of the doors to Palestine for Jews who otherwise faced death in Europe, and kept them closed all through the war and for three years after the war ended.

In his own way, Foot expresses the logic he himself sees in the "anti-Zionist" language he advises Dalyell to adopt. "There are lots of Jews in Britain who are bitterly opposed to the loathsome Israeli occupation of other people's countries and the grotesque violence it involves" (emphasis added). Countries, plural? Which countries does Israel occupy other than the West Bank and Gaza? Foot does not mean the ex-Syrian Golan Heights, Israeli-occupied since 1967. He means pre-1967 Israel.

The attitude to Israel which Foot expresses, that it does not have the right to exist at all, begins with denial of equality to the Jews of Palestine and with demonising the Jewish nation there. From that denial comes grotesque anti-Jewish bias and misrepresentation in accounts of the history of the Jewish-Arab conflict and the origin of Israel. The Jewish nation had no right to exist; Jews who fled to Palestine from the Nazis had no right to do that; they never had the right to defend themselves, and they don't have it now.

The overwhelming majority of Jews in the world, in whose post-Holocaust identity Israel is en-grafted, are guilty of racism and betrayal of Jewish internationalism when, however critical they may be of Israeli governments, they defend Israel's right to exist.

Beginning with denial of the Jewish state's right to exist, this "anti-Zionism" spreads out to also demonise most Jews in the world. The "Zionists" who are demonised by the "anti-Zionists" of Foot's kind are always Jewish Zionists, not non-Jews who defend Israel's right to exist and defend itself. (The exception is when they are those who can be denounced as renegades from pseudo-left orthodoxy on Israel and "Zionism" – like the non-Jewish supporters of *Solidarity*). "Anti-Zionism" is the most potent antisemitism in the modern world. It is especially and most venomously a property of the pseudo-left, as Dalyell's statement and Paul Foot's gloss on it shows clearly.

In fact Dalyell didn't even get his facts right. Of the three "Jews" he named in Blair's circle, two, Jack Straw and Peter Mandelson, though both have some Jewish ancestry, do not identify themselves as Jews. The daft old duffer blundered into a racist, "tell-me-who-your-ancestors-were" definition of Jewishness. By the time Foot came to defend Tam Dalyell, his mistake had been pointed out. Foot didn't notice. Just call them "Zionists" Tammy and you can't go wrong.

This "anti-Zionism" is no help at all to the Palestinians. For over half a century the Arab chauvinist demand for the destruction of Israel has been the best helper the expansionist Jewish-chauvinist Israeli right has had. If the Arab states and the Palestinians had accepted the Israeli proposal of September 1967 to withdraw from the territories it had occupied in June that year in return for Arab recognition and normalisation of relations between Israel and the Arab states, then the colonialist horrors of the last decades on the West Bank could not have happened.

People like Foot, are not socialist internationalists but vicarious Arab chauvinists. They are no friends of the oppressed Palestinians, for whom the only just and possible settlement is an independent Palestinian state side by side with Israel.

The main thing "socialists" like Foot and his mentor Tony Cliff have achieved is to infuse old left-wing anti-colonialism with virulent antisemitism, dressed up in the way Foot advises Dalyell to dress it up, as "anti-Zionism".

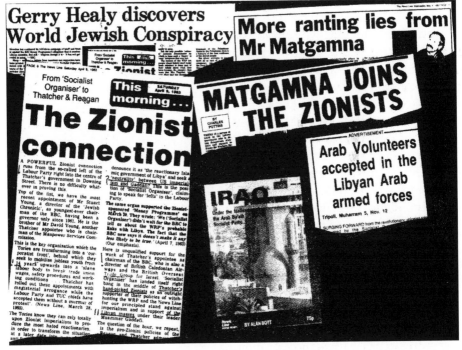

In the early 1980s Gerry Healy's WRP claimed that socialists who had indicted its financial connections with the Iraqi and Libyan regimes must be part of a world "Zionist connection" with Thatcher and Reagan. Across the page from the editorial raging about "the Zionist connection" Healy's Newsline had Ken Livingstone saying yes, talk about the WRP's dodgy financial links could only come from "Zionists". The WRP was still able to win wide left acceptance for its Labour Herald paper.

8. The Balkans, nationalism, and imperialism

If socialists operate in politics according to worked out positive principles, then they will generally be consistent. Should circumstances arise that compel them to seemingly veer from those principles, then they can explain themselves in terms of the base-line principles involved, or of some higher principle.

Socialists believe that peoples should be self-governing – that, for instance, where the compact majority wants it, Ireland has a democratic right to be free of British interference. But suppose that the British working class has taken power and a hostile Ireland is used as a base for attacking the British socialist workers' state? Defence of that state would be far more important than Ireland's national rights, and British (and Irish) socialists might choose – temporarily – to violate the democratic right to Irish self-determination in the name of a higher principle, working-class self defence.

What if you operate in revolutionary socialist politics in accordance with the belief that "tactics contradict principles" (the quotation is from Tony Cliff of the Socialist Workers Party)? You will wind up extrapolating your operational positive principles from your negativism towards capitalism. They will be imposed mechanically on you. Instead of a comprehensive picture of reality and intelligent attempts to apply your principles, you will have an utterly one-sided political picture – the part that shares your negativism. "More substance in your hate than in your love", so to speak. You will lose independence on all big questions and become a mere negative imprint of those you hate and oppose. Not guided by positive principles, you may choose to stand back, refusing to "take sides", where there is no energising anti-capitalist, anti-imperialist negativism. To an observer who does not understand your nature, you will seem to make crazy zig-zags.

For example, Serbian armies are invading Croatia, or Bosnia – in Bosnia they are "ethnic cleansing" Muslims, slaughtering and destroying. Serbia has most of the arms of the old Yugoslav state; the Bosnians do not and, moreover, they are subject to an international arms embargo. Do you defend the Bosnians' right to self-determination and side with them, denounce the arms embargo, indict the Serbs? No: you write articles saying that, for socialists, each side, each nationalism, is as bad as the other, and they are all to blame. Where

318

Lenin acutely argued that "the nationalism of the oppressed is not the same as the nationalism of the oppressor", you say in this case: "Yes, it is", adding that the massacred are as bad as those who massacre, the ethnically cleansed as bad as their murdering cleansers.

In Trotsky's appropriately disgusting image for it, you complacently "pick your nose" and remain "objectively" aloof in face of state-sponsored ethnic slaughter. You sagely comment that the victims of ethnic chauvinism today will, if they get the chance, change places with their persecutors. Your answer to the conflict? Socialism! Now! Immediately!

That was the SWP approach to events in ex-Yugoslavia in the first half of the 1990s. The democratic program of working-class politics adopted by the Balkan socialists as long ago as 1910 – for a democratic Balkan federation in which each of the participants will have the maximum national freedom consistent with the national freedom of others – was for them a spectral voice from the lost world of pre-Stalinist socialism. Yet the Balkan socialists' politics – the early Communist International took them over – were rooted in reality. They were tools elaborated by socialists concerned with positive advances, with living, suffering peoples, for whom socialism had to be the work of a working class that had found political ways of freeing itself from nationalism and chauvinism. Thus, the emergence of such formulas as that of a democratic Balkan federation – a proposal that would in the right circumstances allow the workers of the embattled people and fragments of peoples to imagine a viable national freedom within coexistence with other peoples. Thus it would enable the socialists amongst them to begin to unite across the blood-filled communal and national ditches.

But our sectist friends, positive about nothing, except for a vaguely-conceived and ever-receding socialist final goal, are uninterested – they are fixed in their obsessive negativism. They are anticapitalists of the primitive, say-no-when-they-say-yes-and-yes-when-they-say-no school; and they are "anti-imperialists" above all else. When Serbia [in 1999] starts to clear out and kill off the Albanian people of Kosova (93% of the population), and NATO, for its own reasons and in its own extravagantly brutal and incompetent way, mounts a police action to compel Milosevic to stop – then the depoliticised negativists know where they stand. They are "against imperialism". Which imperialism? Milosevic's primitive geno-imperialism? No, they are against NATO. It is not imperialism they are against, but NATO. Politics? For Marxists, war is politics by other means: what are the politics here? Politics? Who cares about politics? We are "against the war". Which war? Serbia's genocidal war in Kosova? NATO's war!

They are above all "against the bombing". They mount a – feeble, but that was not for want of trying – Stop the War campaign allied with pacifists and *Morning Star* neo-Stalinist, uncritical partisans of Milosevic. By way of negativism against advanced capitalism and NATO, they back themselves into the Milosevic camp, into positive support for the would-be geno-imperialists. They make propaganda – the pamphlet *Stop the War*, for example – which by deliberately minimising what the Serbs are doing in Kosova is effective cover-propaganda for attempted genocide. Having no positive program of their own, no standard of judgement, except a disembodied route map for future socialism, they wind up recoiling from NATO into de facto acceptance of Milosevic's program.

For the three months of the NATO-Serb war *Socialist Worker* turned itself into a vulgar, pro-Milosevic, war propaganda sheet on behalf of Serb imperialism in Kosova; they excluded mention of the Kosova Albanians except to insist that "NATO" was lying about what was going on in Kosova, and minimise it by indignant, pedantic refutations of exaggerated claims by ministers and newspapers that the Serb drive against the Albanians was the equivalent of the Holocaust. In meetings all over the country they fought against adopting slogans about Kosovar Albanians' rights, even about their right to stay alive. They achieved the difficult feat of being marginally less critical, less "objective" in their "reporting" than the *Morning Star*.

The nearest equivalent in the history of the British labour movement to *Socialist Worker* in these three months is the "anti-war" propaganda, favouring Hitler (then Stalin's ally), of the *Morning Star*, then called the *Daily Worker*, between September 1939 and the government suppression of the paper in January 1941.

Where *Socialist Worker* should have taken sides, in Bosnia, it was aloof, sectarian and politically abstentionist. Where it should have taken sides with the Kosovar Albanians, it refused to do that, and in a passion of hysterical negativism towards advanced capitalism and NATO wound up actively and positively on Milosevic's side, that is on the side of Serb imperialism as it attempted genocide against the population of Serbia's colony, Kosova.

It would be difficult to imagine a more decisive, or more horrible, demonstration that socialists need positive politics – that is independent working-class socialist politics – unless reflex negativism is to turn them into reactionaries. Without positive politics rooted in an analysis of the whole of your reality, independent working-class politics is impossible. To be merely negative, no matter how oppositional and r-r-revolutionary it sounds, is in fact to turn yourself into the imprint of whoever you are against. It is the opposite of independent politics.

The book *The Balkans, nationalism, and imperialism*, edited by Lindsey German, which came out after the end of the war, in June 1999, is a collection of pieces by various people in *Socialist Worker* over ten years. It has the general politics described above. But it has comparatively very little from *Socialist Worker*'s coverage of the events of 1999. The overall impression is a misleading one of balance – too much, sectarian, balance and "nose-picking" objectivity, in fact. From this collection, which will circulate for years, you will get no inkling of *Socialist Worker*'s crazy three months as unrestrained war propagandists for Milosevic, as he was trying to clear Kosova of ethnic Albanians. The book, so to speak, seals off that period.

It will be a pity if this rich, disruptive and spectacularly unprincipled sect is allowed to flush its three month record of Serb imperialist apologetics down the memory hole.

Kosovars flee in 1999 as Serbian troops try to massacre them or drive them out in order to secure Belgrade's rule in a territory where it had been a colonial oppressor for decades, since 1913

9. How to make your anti-imperialism sterile

The 1950s movie The Wild One is about a motorcycle "rebel" gang, led by Marlon Brando, invading a small American town and frightening the natives. Someone asks the Brando character: "And what are you rebelling against?" Famously, he replies: "What've you got?"

That film was, for decades, banned in Britain. That may have been to protect impressionable British Marxists, especially the SWP, from mistaking the Brando character's philosophy – whatever it is, I'm against it – for a serviceable political program. It is now the core and only approach of the SWP. Look at Chris Harman's review † of a book on Mao Zedong (*Mao: The Unknown Story*, by Jung Chang and Jon Halliday). The book indicts Mao as a Stalin-scale mass murderer. Oh no, says Harman. Having provided a general criticism of Mao and Maoism – but with the edge of criticism blunted by the underlying idea that Mao was historically "necessary" in backward China – he continues in a way that will be drearily familiar to all who are acquainted with the present mindset of the SWP. In full apologetic mode he says:

"The weakest point about this book is its claim that Mao was uniquely evil and responsible for 70 million peacetime deaths"– "more than either Hitler or Stalin".

What's wrong with that claim? It's unfair to Mao. "All rulers in this barbaric capitalist world are prepared to see people die if it is necessary to achieve their goals of accumulating wealth or armaments. They endorse sanctions in Iraq, which killed half a million children in ten years. They happily blast apart cities such as Belgrade or Fallujah. And they preside over a system that sees 50,000 die in the Third World each day from poverty-related causes – which means more deaths in just four years than died under Mao's brutal regime."

That puts Mao, and Stalinism in history, into perspective, doesn't it, comrade? Only the weak-spirited who do not, like Harman and his friends, "really" want to "tear the head off capitalism", will complain about millions slaughtered by someone who clashes with Washington.

The accelerated political decline of the SWP has led its press in recent times to produce many other bizarre and freakish arguments for

---

† *Socialist Worker, 18 June 2005.*

increasingly bizarre and freakish politics. Perhaps the strangest was the attempt of *Socialist Worker* of 6 October 2001 (when it was edited by Chris Harman) to "explain away" the Taliban's monstrous treatment of women. "Taliban leaders feared that their soldiers would behave as some previous Mujahedeen groups had on taking a city. The war years had seen repeated abuse and rape of women. They said that forcing women into seclusion was a means of protecting them. Of course, it meant appalling oppression."

They asked *Socialist Worker* readers to take the clerical-fascist Taliban's stated intention – "protecting women" – at their own evaluation. And why not, you might reasonably ask. The US and the British were attacking the Muslim fundamentalist Afghan regime (because it refused to give up those responsible for the 9/11 atrocity in New York). The SWP was against the British and American war (as indeed were *Solidarity* and the AWL). So, of course, was the Taliban. So, as its contribution to the "anti-imperialist struggle", the SWP did what it could to improve the "image" of its Afghan ally against Bush and Blair. Not only was its US-British enemy's enemy its friend, but the Taliban was a great deal better than Britain and the US said they were. Imperialist slanderers! The Taliban were "really" – though in an "appallingly oppressive" way – the protectors of Afghanistan's women!

The SWP did similar work in defence of the Saddam regime in the run up to the 2003 US British invasion of Iraq. They formed a long-term close partnership with George Galloway, a middle-of-the-road "soft left" Stalinist New Labour MP who, in front of BBC cameras recording the incident, had told the Iraqi fascistic dictator to his face how "courageous" and all-round wonderful he was.

And in 1999 when NATO planes attacked Serbia to force the Serbian regime to stop butchering and ethnic-cleansing the people of its colony Kosova, the SWP sided whole-heartedly and uncritically with this regional imperialist power then engaged in attempted genocide against the Kosovar Albanians. There too the SWP saw it as their political duty to defend and whitewash the regional imperialist, enemy of their imperialist enemy. Genocide? They had two responses to that: "Imperialist slander!" And: "it's already happened, and nothing can be done about it, so back Serb ethnic imperialism against NATO!" †

The SWP wasn't always like that. For many years it had policies on such questions very like the politics of *Solidarity* now. It separated half a century ago from other groups in the Trotskyist tradition be-

---

† *See Patrick Murphy's report of their performance at the National Union of Teachers conference in 1999, Workers' Liberty 55. www.workersliberty.org/node/10735*

cause the founders of the SWP, led by Tony Cliff, said that those others were insufficiently critical of Russia, China, North Korea and other Stalinist regimes. The Orthodox Trotskyists expelled Tony Cliff and his supporters for refusing to back North Korea in the Korean war of 1950-3. In turn Cliff accused the other Trotskyists of uncritically lining up with the Stalinist regimes in international politics out of an unbalanced hostility to the "market capitalist" imperialist regimes in Washington, London and Paris. As against that Cliff adopted the slogan "Neither Washington nor Moscow but International Socialism". The group, then called Socialist Review, borrowed this slogan from the American Shachtmanite organisation led by Max Shachtman, but they made it their own.

Since 1987, when the SWP suddenly came out in support of Iran because, they had realised, seven years after the Iran-Iraq war started, that the Americans favoured Iraq, they have moved further and further away from such politics. Everything has come to be determined for them not by what they are for – what they are now for no more than notionally: the interests of the working class – but by what they are against. America and British hostility to a regime – the Taliban, Saddam's, Milosevic's, whatever – is now enough to win that regime the open support of the SWP, its press and whatever arguments, excuses, "explanations" for their clients, they can muster.

When they proclaimed their antagonism to both "Washington and Moscow", in the same slogan they used to spell out what they were for – "international socialism". If they were to sum up their politics of the past few years in similar slogans they would have been something like these: "Neither London nor Washington, but Kabul!" "Neither Washington nor Berlin, but Belgrade!" "Neither Washington nor London, but Baghdad!" And now? "Neither Washington nor London but the Sunni-supremacist and Shia-sectarian 'resistance' in Iraq"!

If a time machine could take them back to the Second World War, and if they were to employ their current approach to determining where they stood in that conflict, then logically they would side with Japan and Germany against their more powerful imperialist enemies, Britain, France and the USA which between them then, in their respective colonial empires controlled large swathes of the world. It was against that dominant carve-up that the German and Japanese imperialisms made war, demanding their "fair share".

Back in 1940 the SWP current political practice would have lined them up with the Stalinist CP. During the 22 months of the Stalin-Hitler pact of peace and cooperation (up to June 1941, when Hitler invaded Russia), the CP made propaganda in Britain on behalf of

Russia's ally Germany. It denounced "the warlike imperialists", Britain and France and branded them responsible for the war and all its evil consequences. It demanded they make peace with Stalin's ally, the peace-loving Adolf Hitler.

More poignantly, perhaps, the playful time machine might deposit the leaders of the SWP back in 1950, when the SWP's lineal ancestral group was first set up after a conflict with those Trotskyists who supported Stalinist North Korea in its war with the UN, American, Britain and others. Those powers had landed in Korea to defend the puppet regime in the southern half of the peninsula from Stalinist North Korea.

With their current politics, the SWP leaders would – standing in front of a mirror perhaps – join those from whom the SWP founders broke away in denouncing Cliff and his friends as the SWP denounces *Solidarity* and the AWL today – "capitulators to imperialism", "agents of Washington", etc.

Talented and ingenious writers of science fiction weave mind-boggling plots by working out the details and implications of such transpositions and encounters as the present leaders of the SWP alighting from a time machine in 1950 to confront... themselves. With their present politics transposed to 1950, the SWP would have to support the Stalinists, including the USSR – by far the weaker of the contemporary imperialisms – against Washington-London and "NATO"!

What slogans would they counterpose to "Neither Washington nor Moscow but International Socialism"? "Neither Washington nor London but Moscow, Pyongyang, and the International Anti-Imperialist Alliance!"

In 1999, when the SWP was doing mindless and shameful propaganda work for Slobodan Milosevic's Serb regime as it started a drive to kill or "cleanse" the Albanian people of Kosova – 93% of the population – Harman and his like seized on wild statements in the capitalist press comparing Milosevic's ethnic cleansing with Hitler's massacre of the Jews and used it to deflect discussion of the living political question into a pedant's concern about whether Milosevic and Hitler really were "identical".

And if they weren't "identical"? What had that to do with one's attitude to what Milosevic's forces were actually doing in Kosova? Nothing at all!

Was Mao "uniquely evil"? Was he responsible for killing 70 million people, his subjects, in peacetime – more than Hitler or Stalin? Don't be ridiculous! 70 million? Bah! A mere detail in the sweep of history! Don't you know, comrades that "all rulers in this barbaric capitalist world" are willing "to see people die" to gain their ends! Why pick on Mao? That is to whitewash the present Great Ones of our world, who are prepared to "see" people die!

Note the word "see". It is used to obliterate the distinction between the workings of our vile capitalist system, under which millions needlessly die each year and the deliberate acts of a totalitarian state to kill its own subjects, by bullet, noose or planned starvation.

Capital does "preside over a system" under which millions needlessly die. We condemn the capitalists and their system. It is one reason why we are revolutionary socialists.

But to claim that the general workings of the system are the moral, political or logistical equivalent of what Hitler, Stalin and Mao deliberately did to tens of millions of people is to shed all the distinctions that enable us to make sense of the world. It is to be morally and politically colourblind.

It is to cease to know the difference between the casualties of the organically inhumane capitalist system which dominates our world, as humankind struggles to rise up out of our pre-history to rational control of society, on one side, and deliberate mass murder by a totalitarian state on the other.

To present the bombing of "Belgrade" – to compel the Serbian government to stop its attempted genocide in Kosova: the bombing stopped when the Serbian armies began to withdraw from Kosova – or Fallujah, as an alleged equivalent of deliberate totalitarian mass murder is no less bizarre.

In both these cases, Harman and the SWP were on one side in the war in question – with genocidal Serbian imperialism, and with the Sunni-supremacist-Islamists in Fallujah against the Iraqi secularists and the Iraqi labour movement.

Two consequences, pertinent to what we are discussing here, of the domination of Stalinism in much of the labour movement over most of the 20th century, are plainly and unmistakably identifiable in the SWP today.

The first is the separation of the two complementary and mutually-conditioning parts of the Marxist world outlook: the negative, the criticism of capitalism; and the positive, the democratic working-class alternative to capitalism.

Appropriating the Marxist critique of capitalism, the Stalinists confronted the capitalist system as forceful and just critics. But in place of capitalism they proposed to put not our working-class socialist alternative – democratic working-class power – but their own totalitarian system, of which the USSR was the pioneer.

The SWP performs exactly the same sort of operation today, divorcing criticism of advanced capitalism from the Marxist alternative to it, as well as muting Marxist, socialist, and secularist criticism of Islamic opponents of the USA and Britain.

The SWP indicts capitalism with a just and necessary ferocity. And in its place? Not "international socialism" but... the Taliban! Slobodan Milosevic! The Sunni-supremacist "resistance"! Iranian medievalist mullahs! Whatever the whirligig of history hurls up in some degree of antagonism to the capitalist great powers is, for these disoriented one-time Marxists, to be supported. To be whitewashed and prettied up. To be championed against what Britain and the USA may say against them, even when it is patently true. The much-misunderstood Taliban were, weren't they, out to "protect" women?

The second aspect of Stalinism relevant to what we are discussing is, perhaps, only a sub-division of the first: it was the long-term systematic corruption and adulteration of all the key ideas of Marxism, of socialism, of politics and even of logic itself. That too is dominant in Harman's lucubrations on Mao.

The Stalinists perfected the technique which SWP scribblers like Harman use to obliterate the distinction between mass murder and the routine working of inhumane capitalism."Freedom? But what is freedom, comrade?" the Stalinist would say, adding such typical potted wisdom as this: "The worker in the West has the freedom to starve! The workers in the USSR have freedom from such things. Therefore the worker in the USSR, really, dialectically, has more freedom", etc.

Mind-rotting conflation, purging of the real meaning of words, vandal destruction of important concepts, smart-ass apologist's attempts to obscure important distinctions – that is what Harman offers when he equates the depredation of the workings of the capitalist market system with the depredations of Mao's totalitarian state.

But shouldn't socialist critics of this capitalist system focus on and emphasise present horrors? Isn't it basic to our approach that we do not excuse the swinishness of today by harping back to the worse swinishness of yesterday; that we don't excuse the swinishness at home by emphasising the worse swinishness abroad?

Yes, the main enemy is the enemy now, not the enemy of yesterday; the evil to focus on is the evil around you, not the evil of the past or the far away. Of course! But it isn't possible to fight the evils of today by indiscriminately equating them with all kinds of horrors of the past, by blurring the distinction between the effects of market capitalism and the indifference of its criminal rulers, and totalitarian mass murder.

You can't do that without making yourself ridiculous to thinking people. Young people with only a hazy notion of history who accept what you say about capitalism now will, when they become better acquainted with the totalitarian horrors which a Harman glibly equates with the routine workings of capitalism, wind up deciding that maybe this system is not so bad after all.

And you can't do what Harman does without to one degree or another becoming an apologist for the past evil. You can't equate the evil of one side in our world (advanced capitalism) with the worst horrors of the past, in order to blur, obscure, and seem to lessen the horrors of those, like Saddam Hussein, or the Taliban, or Serbian troops attempting genocide in Kosova, who clash with the USA or Britain, without becoming an apologist for the worse horrors.

Apologists for those horrors lose the moral right to denounce the routine horrors of market capitalism.

"We are on strike": East Berlin, June 1953. Facing page: Daily Worker (USA), 6 March 1926

10. "Apparatus Marxism":
Impoverished twin of "Academic Marxism"

"Marry, sir, they have committed false report; moreover, they have spoken untruth; secondarily, they are slanders; sixth and lastly, they have belied a lady; thirdly, they have verified unjust things; and, to conclude, they are lying knaves" – Much Ado About Nothing

"Borodin… is characterised in the novel as a 'man of action', as a living incarnation of Bolshevism on the soil of China. Nothing is further from the truth! [Borodin was no old Bolshevik]… Borodin, appeared as the consummate representative of that state and party bureaucracy which recognised the revolution only after its victory… People of this type assimilate without difficulty the gestures and intonations of professional revolutionists. Many of them by their protective colouring not only deceive others but also themselves. The audacious inflexibility of the Bolshevik is most usually metamorphosed with them into the cynicism of the functionary ready for anything. Ah! To have a mandate from the Central Committee! This sacrosanct safeguard Borodin always had in his pocket…"– Trotsky, February 1931, in *Problems of the Chinese Revolution*, discussing André Malraux's novel about the 1925-7 Chinese Revolution, *The Conquerors.*

The Comintern functionary whom Trotsky discusses here, using André Malraux's fictionalised Borodin as an example, was a "revolutionary" James Bond figure – a "superman" raised above the organic processes of the labour movement and the working class, and above mundane restraints and moralities. In the service of "the cause" he could say and do anything – so long as his superiors approved. As Stalinism progressed in the Comintern, there was literally nothing such people, and the working-class organisations they controlled and poisoned, would not for an advantage say and do. There was nothing that had been unthinkable to old socialists and communists that they did not in fact do.

They could ally with fascists to break socialist strikes, suppress the proletarian revolution in Spain, become rabid chauvinists for their own countries (so long as that might serve the USSR), turn into anti-semites… Nothing was forbidden to them. Nothing was sacred, and nothing taboo. Any means to an end. "All that is holy is profaned".

Old agitational and propagandist techniques of manipulation were brought to new levels of perfection by the Stalinist rulers and their agents and allies across the world. Politics, history and, they thought, "History", were freed from the primitive slavery to facts. Politics that were virtually fact-free and virtually truth-free became possible on a mass scale. Great political campaigns could now be lied into existence. To be sure, this was not something unknown before Stalinism; but the Stalinists, beginning with their lies about what the Soviet Union was, made it an all-embracing permanent way of political life.

At different times Trotsky described this condition as "syphilis" and "leprosy". In the summaries of the proper revolutionary communist approach which he wrote in the 1930s, the demand to "be true, in little things as in big ones" is always central. The fact that such a "demand" had to be made and that it was made only by a tiny pariah minority, as incapable of imposing the necessary norms of behaviour as they were incapable of doing what they knew had to be done to defend the working class, was one measure of how far the "Marxist" movement had fallen, how deeply it had regressed, and how much had to be done to restore its health.

The "revolutionary superman" today is typically a "Trotskyist" builder of "the revolutionary party". One of the things trade union supporters of Workers' Liberty in Britain have to contend with – in the civil service union for example, where the would-be revolutionary left has had a presence for many years – is that many good trade unionists, honest, rational people, have come to hate the "revolutionary left" as liars, manipulators, people who place themselves outside the norms of reasonable political, moral and intellectual interaction. To a serious degree they do not have a common language with people who do not share their methods and habits of thought, or their special view of themselves and their "party".

II

Trotsky himself commented more than once that the small groups of Trotskyists had sometimes absorbed too much "Comintern venom" into themselves. After Trotsky's death, not at once, but over many years, and not uniformly, organisation to organisation, but more in some Orthodox Trotskyist organisations than others, a kitsch-Trotskyist political culture developed that replicated much that Trotsky had called leprosy and syphilis in the Comintern.

Its core was the degradation of the idea of a "revolutionary party" into a fetish, into something prised loose from both the social and historical context and the political content which gives it its Marxist meaning. For Marxists, the party and the class, though there is an unbreakable link between them, are not the same thing. "The Communists... have no interests separate and apart from those of the proletariat as a whole," as the Communist Manifesto puts it. The program Leon Trotsky wrote for his movement in 1938 insisted that it was a cardinal rule for Marxists to "be guided", not by the interests of "the party", but "by the logic of the class struggle". And there is at any given moment an objective truth that cannot be dismissed if it is inconvenient to "the party".

In Orthodox Trotskyism, the tendency over decades is for "the party" and what is considered to be good for "the party" to become the all-defining supreme good – to become what the USSR was to the Comintern and its Borodins. There are more limits than the Comintern functionaries had, but not too many limits. There are very few things people calling themselves Trotskyists have not done for organisational advantage. Much of the time, for many of the Orthodox Trotskyist groups, everything – perceptions of reality, "perspectives", truth, consistency, principle – is up for "construing" and reinterpretation in the light of perceived party interest. Their "Marxism" is "Apparatus Marxism": it exists to rationalise what the party apparatus thinks it best to do.

Central to this pattern, of course, was the radical falsity of many of the axial ideas of the Orthodox Trotskyist groups – on the USSR, for example, or on the "world revolution", of which the USSR's existence was both manifestation and pledge for its presently on-going "immanent" character; and on the linked idea that capitalism was perennially in a state of imminent 1930s level collapse. The survival and mutation of such ideas – the USSR is "in transition to socialism", capitalism faces immediate catastrophe – were themselves often shaped by organisational considerations.

Their "Marxist" ideas had become dogmas glaringly at odds with reality; to hold those ideas you needed a special way of construing the world; and thinking about it became a work of special pleading for the fixed dogmas, of rationalising to arrive at conclusions already set and inviolable. If "Marxism" is reduced to such a role, then there is no logical or psychological barrier against "Marxism" being used to rationalise whatever seems to "make sense" for the party on a day to day basis.

The German pre-World War One Social-Democrat, Eduard Bernstein, who proposed to shed the socialist goal of the Marxist labour movement and substitute for it a series of reforms of capitalism, notoriously summed up his viewpoint thus: "The movement is everything, the goal nothing." The Orthodox Trotskyists in their fetishistic commitment to creating an instrument, the "Revolutionary Party", that could make the socialist revolution, stumbled into a grim parody of Bernstein's notorious dictum: the party, short of the socialist revolution itself, is everything; all other things, including the actually existing working class, count for little and often for nothing.

III

This approach led to the creation of a special sort of Marxism – "Apparatus Marxism" – the neo-Trotskyist version of which is really, all qualifications granted, a dialect of the old Stalinist Comintern "Marxism". It is the predominant revolutionary "Marxism". There had been elements of "Apparatus Marxism" in the revolutionary socialist movement before the consolidation of Orthodox Trotskyism – pieces rationalising the practices of existing organisations. Now "Apparatus Marxism" overshadowed everything.

Today Marxism has retreated deeper into academia – though there is a lot less even of that than there used to be – or, in a ridiculous parody of what Marxism was to the Stalinist organisations, into the cloistered seclusion of one or other "revolutionary party", where it exists to grind out rationalisation and apologia to justify the decisions of the "party" apparatus: "Marxism" with its eyes put out, chained to the mill-wheel – "Apparatus Marxism".

Apparatus Marxism is a peculiarly rancid species of pseudo-academic "Marxism" from which everything "objective", disinterested, spontaneous and creative is banished. Creativity is incompatible with the prime function of "Apparatus Marxism": rationalising. Creativity and, so to speak, spontaneity is the prerogative of the all-shaping, suck-it-and-see empirical citizens who staff the "Party" apparatus. Everything is thereby turned on its head. The history of the Orthodox Trotskyist, or Cannonite, organisations is a story shaped by this conception of the relationship of Marxism to "the revolutionary party" – as a handmaiden of the apparatus. So, too, is the story of the British SWP. "Party building" calculations determine the "line" and "Marxism" consists in "bending the stick" to justify it.

Revolutionary theory without revolutionary practice is sterile, revolutionary practice without revolutionary theory is blind. "Apparatus Marxism" is both blind and sterile because it is not and cannot be a guide to practice. It exists to rationalise a practice that is in fact guided by something else – usually, the perceived advantage of the organisation. For Marxists, practice is guided by a theory constantly replenished by experience. In "Apparatus Marxism", the proper relationship of theory to practice and of practice to theory is inverted.

Our predominant Marxist culture is largely made up of the various "Apparatus Marxisms", protected, as behind high tariff walls, by the "party" regimes they serve. Demurrers or questionings of cloistered certainties are inimical to that culture. This segmented "Marxism" stands in the way of Marxist self-renewal. The kitsch-Trotskyist conception of the "revolutionary party" – which in fact is a conception closer to that of the Stalinists than to either Lenin's or Trotsky's conception – makes revolutionary Marxism impossible. It makes the cornerstone of revolutionary Marxism – as distinct from Academic Marxism and its gelded first cousin, "Apparatus Marxism" – the unity of theory and practice, Marxism as a guide to action, an impossibility.

Apparatus Marxism is self-righteous: it serves "the Party", which for now "is" "the Revolution", or, so to speak, its "Vicar on Earth"; it has few scruples, and recognises only those aspects of reality that serve its needs. Its progenitor is neither Marx nor Engels nor Lenin, but, ultimately, Stalin.

One reason why it thrives, even among anti-Stalinists, in our conditions, which are unfavourable to serious Marxism, is precisely its simple, uncomplicated, easily graspable logic and rationale. It is the way to "build the party", "catch the mood". You don't need background, study, work; and there aren't any very difficult or unanswerable questions – just three or four basic ideas and a willingness to listen to the Central Committee, or whomever it is that can "come up with a line" that lets "the party" have something plausible to say. This approach is much simpler and far easier than "full-strength" Marxism, for which reality cannot always be construed to fit what is best for "party-building". The contemporary kitsch-Trotskyist superhero *embodies* "Apparatus Marxism". From his collection of "Trotskyist" formulas, "lines" and rationalisation, he selects what will best advance the organisation – the "Revolutionary Party" which represents socialism – whatever it says or does. The kitsch-Trotskyist superhero has no time for Engels' comment in a letter to the German socialist Conrad Schmidt (5 August 1890):

"The materialist conception of history has a lot of dangerous friends nowadays who use it as an excuse for not studying history. Just as Marx commenting on the French 'Marxists' of the late [18]70s used to say: 'All I know is that I am not a Marxist'...

"In general, the word 'materialist' serves many of the younger writers in Germany as a mere phrase with which anything and everything is labelled without further study, that is, they stick on this label and then consider the question disposed of. But our conception of history is above all a guide to study, not a lever for construction after the Hegelian manner. All history must be studied afresh, the conditions of existence of the different formations must be examined in detail before the attempt it made to deduce from them the political, civil-law, aesthetic, philosophic, religious, etc. views corresponding to them...

"You who have really done something, must have noticed yourself how few of the young literary men who attach themselves to the Party take the trouble to study economics, the history of trade, of industry, of agriculture, of the social formations... The self-conceit of the journalist must therefore accomplish everything and the result looks like it..." – the self-conceit of the "party-building" "Apparatus Marxist".

Facing page: a high point of 1970s industrial battles. Dockers' shop steward Vic Turner rides on the shoulders of the crowd at Pentonville Jail after a great strike wave had forced the Tory government to release him, July 1972

People who shaped the left: five essays

The Great Gadsby: The paradoxes of Tony Cliff

"The miners' strike is an extreme example of what we in the Socialist Workers Party have called the 'downturn' in the movement" – Tony Cliff, *Socialist Worker*, 14 April 1984

"Sammy lugged his papers up and down Fourteenth Street yelling about a war in Europe. He used to come home with a hoarse throat and 30 or 40 cents in pennies. He would count the money and say, 'God dammit, I'm yellin' my brains out for nuttin'. Several weeks later Sammy came in with a dollar seventy-eight. Papa, Momma and Israel danced around him. 'Sammy, you sold out all the papers?' said Papa in amazement.
'Yeah,' Sammy said, 'There's a guy on the opposite corner doin' pretty good 'cause he's yellin' "U.S. may enter war". So I asks a customer if there's anything in the paper about that. So when he says no, I figure I can pull a fast one too. So I starts hollerin' "U.S. enters war" and jeez you shoulda seen the rush!'
'But that was a lie,' Papa Glick said. 'To sell papers like that is no better than stealing.' 'All the guys make up headlines,' Sammy said. 'Why don't you wise up?'" – Budd Schulberg, *What Makes Sammy Run?*

Tony Cliff (Ygael Gluckstein), who died in April 2000 a few weeks short of his 83rd birthday, was one of the most influential socialists of recent decades. He is physically dead, but, as a eulogist might put it, Cliff lives on. He taught a certain politics, and, more to the point, a certain conception of what revolutionary politics is, to generations of socialists. The biggest socialist organisation in Britain now, the Socialist Workers Party (SWP), embodies Cliff's ideas and Cliff's approach to politics. In that sense, Cliff remains very much alive. Of the generation of revolutionary socialists formed in Trotsky's Fourth International, and, most importantly for their political characteristics, in the Fourth Internationalist movement of the 1940s, Cliff was in his own terms the most successful.

When I heard that Cliff was dead, I remembered a conversation I had had with him in the middle of 1968. Tremendous prospects for working-class socialism seemed to have been opened up by the French general strike of May that year. Nine million workers had seized the factories and for a week refused even to discuss the big concessions the bosses and the government were eager to offer, if only the workers would release the grip on their throat and let them breathe again. Everything in Europe seemed to have been shaken up, including Cliff's politics.

In Britain, the Socialist Labour League (SLL), the authoritarian organisation that had dominated revolutionary politics for 20 years, was now behaving in an increasingly lunatic, and – so we fervently hoped – terminally self-destructive fashion. The possibility of a future in which we could hope to do things better than they had been done in the recent past seemed to have opened up. We agreed that we should begin to regroup the left in an open, democratic organisation. The immediate first step? To fuse the small group of Orthodox Trotskyists called Workers' Fight (WF) – which a few of us, believing the two existing Orthodox Trotskyist groups, the Socialist Labour League and Militant [now Socialist Party], to be politically bankrupt, had put together in the previous 18 months – and the more eclectic, much larger group to which Cliff was central, International Socialism (IS). It had existed for 18 years and been self-proclaimedly "Luxemburgist" for half that time. But now – if Cliff won the faction-fight – IS was turning "Leninist" and "Trotskyist". Quiet and ruminative, as if talking to himself, Cliff said: "I'm not even 52 yet. I can live to see the socialist revolution!" It was a man taking stock for a new star, having decided on his direction.

Alas, he did not live to see the socialist revolution. He lived to see tremendous defeats for the labour movement, and a tremendous reflux of socialism. He saw the fall of Stalinism in Europe and saw it replaced not by working-class power, but by chaos and capitalism. He saw the "Russian state capitalism" he had defined as the highest possible stage of capitalism – the development of capitalism in part beyond capitalism, to the degree that its economic forms overlapped with the next, socialist, stage of social development – mysteriously turn into an extremely backward capitalism (in some ways, into pre-capitalism) as if it had slipped down half a dozen notches on History's ratchet.

And he spent the third of a century left to him in building something very different from the sort of organisation we talked about in that glorious early summer of 1968. He developed an approach to the politics of "party building" that systematised traits that exist in much of post-Trotsky Trotskyism and for a very long time were exemplified in Britain by Gerry Healy and the SLL.

II

Cliff was in political flux in 1968. He had come out in support of the Vietnamese Stalinists against the war planes and troops of the USA. There were differences, but no fundamental differences, between the war in Vietnam and the Korean war, on which Cliff's refusal to take the position he now took on Vietnam had led to his separation in 1950 from the Fourth International of the Orthodox Trotskyists.

For a decade, self-proclaimedly "Luxemburgist", he had been deriding the idea that Marxists in British conditions should work to build a small "Bolshevik"-style organisation in the labour movement. That, he had insisted, was "toy-town Bolshevism". The Bolshevik Party, he would heatedly tell you, speaking as one who understood Russian and knew, was a myth. Now Cliff had rediscovered himself as a Leninist and was proclaiming the need to build a revolutionary party. But he had done it in his own peculiar fashion: by publishing a second edition of his 1960 pamphlet on Luxemburg with nothing changed in the argument and exposition, but with diametrically opposite conclusions tacked on to the old arguments. (A couple of key paragraphs were cut and surreptitiously replaced.)

He had, he would insist, been right in both his old and in his new conclusions. Or maybe he had just decided that the "myth" was a myth worth inhabiting, that it could be used as he had seen others, especially the SLL, using it. As a politician, Cliff was a capable mime-actor.

Rosa Luxemburg – Cliff's idea of Luxemburg – had, in 1960, been the best guide: "For Marxists in advanced industrial countries, Lenin's original position can much less serve as a guide than Rosa Luxemburg's." Now Lenin – Cliff's idea of Lenin – was the model.

Workers' Fight would comment: "Of course people change their minds. When Marxists do so it would be good to know why and how... A Marxist's exposition is based on an analysis of the real world, to which he brings certain conceptions: his conclusions are drawn [in this way]. Thus the train of thought is clear, the reasoning and considerations are designed to expound, to convince. In this case there is a mystery: one and the same exposition (without supplement) leads to opposite conclusions. Why? How does comrade Cliff reach his conclusions?" (WF, new series, Easter, 1969)

That is the central question in assessing the career of Cliff. The episode in which Cliff changed from a "Luxemburgist" back to a "Leninist" was emblematic of his whole career. But so, though I didn't know it then, had been the manner in which he had become a "Luxemburgist" in 1958. That too had been a sudden lurch when a big majority of Cliff's small organisation momentarily decided to join Gerry Healy's, then a sane, impressive and comparatively large "Bolshevik"-style organisation.

III

With Cliff, the space between his person and his politics, where it existed at all, was a very narrow one. In most areas, it simply did not exist, as he proudly insists in his autobiography, where he boasts of his narrowness, and though he baulks at the word philistinism, in effect he boasts about that too. He would not have noticed that what was perhaps more striking than his concentration on politics, was the extreme narrowness of his concerns within politics.

You could say that all his vices were political ones, or rooted in a conception of what revolutionary politics is. But they were all-pervasive. I spent three years after the fusion of WF and IS as Cliff's factional opponent, in a small minority most of the time. Often that was nasty, as by its nature such a thing is. But there wasn't much gratuitous nastiness on Cliff's part. You could say that he was a more than halfway decent human being. Compared with, say, his nearest equivalent, the grotesque Gerry Healy, who ran the Socialist Labour League for decades, Cliff was a decent human being. But Cliff, so to speak, was a politician, not a human being. Politics is his proper measure. What matters is what he did in politics, his way of functioning in politics. That in its turn is a matter of political judgment.

Both the practical and the political responsibility for the witch-hunt quality of much of the internal life of the post-68 IS organisation when serious political differences emerged – on Ireland, to take the most extreme but by no means the only case – was Cliff's. So was the character of the organisation that IS became in the five years after 1968. With Cliff, to try to isolate personal traits, or to decide whether, politics aside, you found him likable or not, is especially unproductive: he was his politics.

IV

The memories of Cliff that come into my mind tend to be about things that instructed, surprised or astonished me: his recklessness and complete lack of scruple when he had a point to get across – "bending the stick", he called it, adapting a phrase of Lenin's.

Late 1971, at an IS gathering at a holiday camp in Skegness. Cliff makes a very, very long speech about the history of socialism. In the audience are many who are politically very raw – youngsters and some older militants from different traditions, some of them, inevitably, influenced by Stalinism. Cliff wants to inoculate them politically against Trotsky's Transitional Program, the main document which had been adopted by the founding conference of the Fourth International in 1938. Inoculation is very urgent. The organisation's main rival, the SLL, now far gone in sectarian craziness, uses the Transitional Program, as they will eventually use such things as Leon Trotsky's death mask, as an icon for religious veneration. Cliff warns his audience: using Trotsky's Transitional Program in prosperous 1971, he tells them, is like trying to find your way around the London Underground with a map of the Paris Metro! In the course of his survey of socialist history, Cliff had greatly praised Rosa Luxemburg. Luxemburg had, in December 1918, at the founding conference of the German Communist Party, advocated such an approach, but the audience wouldn't know that. Cliff is "bending the stick". He needs to damn the whole concept of a transitional program and transitional demands: the IS opposition grouping, the Trotskyist Tendency (WF), forerunner of AWL, who are in process of being expelled, are aggressive advocates of the method of Trotsky's program.

Warming to it, whipping himself up, he screams at the audience that if they "accept" Trotsky's Transitional Program, the logic of it will lead them to Posadas, about whom he proceeds to regale them. Juan Posadas was a crazy Latin American Trotskyist who believed in flying saucers and that they came from distant socialist planets. (They implied a higher technology than anything on earth: therefore they had gone beyond capitalism: workers' states in space...)

340

V

To say that Trotsky's 1938 Program would get you believing in so-cialist flying saucers is only an especially bizarre example. One inci-dent more than any other sums up Cliff's entire approach to politics – the "tactical" surrender to British nationalism during the labour movement crisis over Britain joining the European Union – a startling political U-turn executed so that the group could have the organisa-tional benefits of joining in the very powerful campaign being run by Stalinists, left-Labour Tribunites, trade union bureaucrats, and a sizeable chunk of the Tories, against Britain entering the European Union. It was a nationalist, indeed a chauvinist, campaign, part of an upsurge of British nationalism which included the early stages of an alarming growth of the fascist National Front.

One aspect of that rising tide of nationalism was a strong current of rampant and unashamed racism even amongst industrially mili-tant workers. Already, in early 1968, London dockers, who six months earlier had fought and lost a tremendous 10-week strike against re-organisation of the ports, struck and marched in support of Tory racist Enoch Powell. Dockers would strike in the same cause and join a fascist-inspired march early in 1972, when the Tory government let in the British-passport-holding ethnic Indians being expelled from Uganda.

In 1968 Cliff had responded to the dockers' march by raising the alarm about "the urgent threat of fascism" and calling for left unity to fight it. (It was a blatantly cynical "come on" to the radical youth of the times.) By 1971, however, when the same sort of issues were coming to the boil again, things were different. The Tories had come back to power in mid-1970, and immediately launched a strong at-tempt to bring in legislation to curb the trade unions, triggering pro-longed labour movement resistance. IS was now "centralised" and "Leninist" – indeed increasingly, though not uncontestedly, run by full-time officials. It would soon ban generalised internal opposition to Cliff.

IS had grown, and had had limited but real and very promising success in implanting itself in the factories. Its anti-nationalist politics, however, so it was reasonable to believe, might cut the group off from further serious growth in the period ahead. Socialists who were stroppy about the politics of international working-class unity were not best adapted to get the most out of a situation dominated by a tide of British chauvinism.

Ruthless revolutionary choices had to be made. A proper sense of priorities had to be brought into play. And subtlety, lots of subtlety.

What, after all, was the main thing? The great abstractions and general political slogans of Marxist international socialism or building the organisation? That way of putting it is defeatist, comrade. The question is, how can the great ideas of socialist internationalism be served and the organisation built? The best way to serve the great ideas was to build the organisation.

Not bending to the nationalist wind would mean not being able to get maximum returns and "gate receipts" for the organisation that embodied and represented international socialist ideas. That would weaken international socialism. Only a blinkered pedant could fail to see that.

Thus, though it was paradoxical, international socialism could only be served in deeds if in mere words it was not stressed too much, indeed if, at the crucial point, it was abandoned. The tree that bends with the wind survives and grows; the stiff and stubborn sectarian old conifer is uprooted and left to rot. Cliff was equal to reconceptualising the issue for himself, and then selling it to his less talented comrades. First he proposed that the organisation should stick to its political guns. But, having said their piece against the left-wing nationalists, IS members should vote with them in a trade union branch, against "the right". First respond to their nationalism and advocate the alternative, European working-class unity, and then vote with them on the issue? But how could that not make your politics into a joke and convey to observers that you didn't believe in them yourself.

Arguing for this absurd solution to the problem at the IS national committee in mid-71, Cliff explained himself: "Tactics contradict principles." Unsure if I had heard right, I interrupted him. He repeated it. Principles, "theory", are in one dimension, "tactics", practice, in another... For Cliff, the "unity of theory and practice" meant not that Marxism guides practical work and is itself enriched by the experience, but that theory serves – not guides, serves – practice.

In fact, the proposal to argue one way and then vote against your own position in order to "keep in with" the nationalist left was only a trick. Once it was through the committee, the emphasis in the paper, "the arguments", became entirely anti-Common Market little Britainism: Cliff's internationalists had, so to speak, fused with the British nationalists.

You could argue that the whole issue of socialist internationalism did not hang on the attitude one took to the anti-EU campaign. Before they changed under pressure, Cliff and his friends thought it did. Internationalism that does not dare challenge rampant nationalism and chauvinism, and which dares not proclaim its own program against the nationalists in the labour movement, is a vicious hypocrisy. The approach was quintessentially Tony Cliff.

VI

Cliff picked up a phrase of Lenin's: "bending the stick", meaning that in politics you often have to push things strongly and even one-sidedly in a desired direction in order over time to achieve balance. Cliff worked the expression to death, but in fact, "bending the stick" was not quite what Cliff himself did. He did to political ideas what I used to see my father do with seven-foot long hazel rods or "scallops", which are used in thatching. A hazel sapling can be twisted until it is stringy fibre, and can then be used as a sort of rope – for example, to bind big, heavy "barths", or bundles, of other scallops together. You can even tie the, so to speak, ex-stick into loose knots. In the west of Ireland, the name for a stick thus twisted out of the normal consistency of wood but retaining considerable strength is a "gad". Cliff did not "bend" political sticks, he twisted them into gads: the Great Gadsby.

VII

Cliff spent his life – more than 60 of his 83 years – as a participant in the long march of the Trotskyists. Like other youngsters who rallied to Trotsky in the 30s, Cliff joined a movement that had inherited, and developed, the program and perspectives of the Communist International, but was far too weak to win them.

This was an epoch of convulsive capitalist crisis, in which the working class was repeatedly crushed where we might have won. In order to win, we needed a revolutionary organisation of such a size and scope that it could win the leadership of the working class.

The tragedy was that the armies of subjectively working-class revolutionaries were led by Stalin and by the agents and dupes of the Stalinist ruling class in the USSR, who had stolen the banners and symbols of communism The other "big battalions" of the working class were led by the parties of social democracy – parties that had long ago made peace with capitalism and at best sought reform.

Thus when Cliff became a Trotskyist, the entire world labour movement and all its large formations was influenced by, or tightly tied to, either the bourgeois or the Stalinist ruling classes. Politically independent revolutionary working-class parties did not exist, in a world rotten-ripe for socialist revolution and speeding towards the tremendous catastrophe of World War Two.

It was an experience that shaped most of Cliff's – and not only Cliff's – political life. Like others of his generation of anti-Stalinist Marxists, Cliff's conclusion from the tragic dichotomy between the communist program and the small forces of authentic communism fighting for it, was that a "party" had to be built on any terms, almost with any politics. He veered away from that for the decade 1958-68, then returned to it with a vengeance. For his own socialist goals, he elaborated an approach to politics not too far from mainstream politicians who take a poll before they decide what they will say. It was a refined, sophisticated variant of the approach developed by such Orthodox Trotskyist tendencies as those of Healy and Lambert.

These two, on the face of it, seem to be very different from Cliff. Not so. Gerry Healy came to dominate British Trotskyism from the late '40s, and Pierre Lambert much of French Trotskyism from about the same period, because in the 1940s and 50s the world posed big political and theoretical problems to the old-style Trotskyists, and most of the political leaders of the movement collapsed in demoralisation, confusion or perplexity. The Healys and Lamberts came to the fore because they cared about the ideas only as crude working tools that did, or did not, help build the organisation. They could propose what to do on the basis of short-term calculations, without any political or intellectual qualms.

The Trotskyists in Trotsky's time had drawn confidence, despite the gap between their tiny numbers and their very large perspectives, from the idea that "the program creates the party". What might be called the "organisation-first" schools of neo-Trotskyism turned this upside down. For them the old formula came very much to mean: arrange a program, and lesser postures, that will assist the organisation to grow. After he asserted his political independence in the early 60s, Healy's politics were blatantly cut, and frequently "recut", to fit his organisational needs and calculations. So were and are those of the Lambert groupings. (The Lambertists were, I believe, the first of these groupings to use "build the revolutionary party" as a general slogan.)

Not "the program creates the party" but "the needs of the party create, and recreate the program". Not the unity of theory and practice in the proper sense that theory, which is continually enriched by experience, guides practice, but in the sense – Tony Cliff's sense – that "theory" is at the service of practice, catering to the organisation's needs.

The very literary and "theoretical" Cliff, on one side, and the political semi-literates Healy and Lambert on the other, had a common conception of the relationship of theory, principle and politics to the revolutionary organisation. The fact that Healy couldn't easily write a hack article, and Cliff prided himself on the number of his books, is mere detail. It meant only that Cliff could do his own ideological chicane-work. What he did with theory was identical to what Healy and Lambert had their conscienceless "red professors" do (and what certain shameless academics do now for the SWP).

From 1970/71, if not from 1968, Cliff set out to adapt to his own needs the techniques and methods that had allowed the SLL to grow into a formidable organisation.

VIII

Cliff worked according to his belief that for practical politics "tactics contradict principle". His genius was for political manoeuvring and "positioning", which was also his central concern. His last three decades were spent in the elaboration of techniques for building a "revolutionary party" by way of pushing politics into the background so as to maximise the stability and possibilities of growth and self conservation of "the party" – irrespective of political events. He built up "the party" by way of a bewildering succession of political zig zags, dropping or picking up political positions according to calculations about their efficacy in "building the party". Political positions that might get in the way of the organisational needs of "the party" were ruthlessly jettisoned; those that might help embraced.

Again and again he turned himself inside-out politically. He began as an advocate of independent working-class politics and a bitter critic of the Orthodox Trotskyists who lined up behind one of the two imperialist blocs – the Stalinist one. He ended with a spectacular example of reductio ad absurdum "blockist" politics: siding with Serb imperialism in 1999 against its Albanian victims – because Serbia was against NATO.

Cliff's position came more and more to be determined not by the necessary drive to shape and win support for an independent working-class world outlook and policies, but by absolute negativism towards advanced capitalism-against no matter what. To adopt that approach is to let your politics be rigidly determined by advanced capitalism – in a negative, inverted replica of big bourgeois politics. But that doesn't matter if it helps "build the party".

In Cliff's conception of it, the "revolutionary party" rests on its own axis, is its own lodestar, its own self-sufficient point of reference. Like net revenue to a commercial enterprise, the organisation's prosperity – its rates of expansion and recruitment – is, short of the revolution, the supreme revolutionary good, the criterion against which

virtually everything else in politics is to be judged, and to which everything, including the specifics of politics and political doctrine,
must if necessary be sacrificed.

IX

The manner of Cliff's quick-change act back to being a Leninist
from 10 years as a "Luxemburgist" – simply reversing the old conclusions without changing the argument – neatly summed up the
central paradoxes of Cliff. He was a theorist, an ideologue, a revolutionary Marxist intellectual – but to an astonishing extent he dealt
with ideas just as means to an end, picking them up, using them and
discarding them as primitive man picked up, used and discarded
flints.

Shortly after Cliff's death I was talking about him with a Marxist
academic who knew him. He posed the following question, which I
would not have posed in that form for myself: "What was Cliff? He
wasn't an intellectual..." He had in mind Cliff's peculiar dealings
with ideas and the attitude thereby implied. I replied: "He was a militant."

On one level that is to say a great deal on his behalf. But a Marxist
militant, even one with none of the intellectual ambition or pretences
of Cliff or his deftness at juggling with "theory" for organisational
purposes, has to have a radically different attitude to ideas than
Cliff's dropping or picking up political positions according to calculations about their efficacy in "building the party".

Books clearly mattered to him. That was one of the things he did,
one of the things that defined his identity and gave him a gauge for
what he was: he wrote books. But books are ideas. The paradox of an
intellectual, for whom ideas, or anyway books, were important, and
who yet had the spirit of a machine politician for whom ideas, slogans, programs are all mere instruments in the service of something
else, and regards ideas as mere tokens and ciphers, loose change to
be picked up or thrown away when convenient – that was Cliff.

Cliff's near contemporary, Ernest Mandel, the representative figure of post-Trotsky Orthodox Trotskyism, lived to see all his "revolutionary perspectives" collapse with the disintegration in 1989-91 of
European Stalinism – his fancied "degenerated and deformed workers' states in transition to socialism" – and must have died (in 1995)
a bitterly disappointed, defeated man. Cliff, by contrast, to judge by
the autobiography published just after his death, approached dissolution with a sense of great achievement, of having been proved right
about Stalinism and everything else. In fact, the collapse of Stalinism

– which Cliff had considered the highest form of capitalism, overlapping in its economic forms with socialism – shattered Cliff's theories no less than Mandel's. He lived to see events refute everything specific to his theory of state capitalism, so that he could only sustain the belief that he was "right" by jettisoning all but the name and praising himself not for what was unique to his thinking, but for what he had had in common with every theory of Stalinist Russia that defined it as a class society. To Cliff, ideas, including even his own much-prized theory of Stalinism as state capitalism – though that is still in service as a "party" shibboleth to be brandished triumphantly: as someone said, sects change their doctrines more readily than their names, or the names of their fetishes – were instruments, artefacts, means to organisational ends. As with "the party", form – here a nametag without its old content – is everything.

On the record, it is difficult to say exactly what there was stable in Cliff's politics, other than a tremendous shamanistic belief in himself and in the momentary centrality he could bestow for himself on whatever ideas he found useful. There were fixed poles – building the party, and a few political generalities, positive ones about socialism and, far more importantly, negative ones about capitalism – but beyond that you are left with the record of a personality, not of political continuity. Where there appears to be continuity, it is often nothing more substantial than a continuity of words and name-tags – on state capitalism, for example.

X

First impressions are often the best. I vividly recall the first time I encountered Cliff and his entourage – and entourage is the right word – and the impression they made on me.

September 1960. The movement to demand that nuclear weapons be outlawed was reaching its peak. The Trade Union Congress had just come out for unilateral British nuclear disarmament; at the beginning of October, the Labour Party Conference would follow suit, opening up one of the most important political struggles in the history of the British labour movement. In the month between the TUC and Labour Party conferences, there took place a tremendous rolling mobilisation of the anti-bomb movement in cities and towns all over Britain, organised around a column of mainly young people – myself, an adolescent "Healyite", one of them – who were marching from Edinburgh to London.

In Manchester, where there had been an enormous turnout, I noticed Cliff, a very dark, prosperous-looking, tiny man in a crombie overcoat and frizzy hair – so my memory supplies it – surrounded by attentive, shepherding comrades. They had just published the first regular issue of a 32-page A4 journal, *International Socialism*, and were out in force at the big rallies to sell it. (They were there too when we got to Birmingham, a week later.)

I stopped to buy the new journal and wound up wrangling with an exotic, elegant creature whose exaggeratedly smooth and effete upper-class English manner and accent set my national (Irish) prejudices on edge – Cliff's comrade and brother-in-law, Michael Kidron, whose origins were in fact South African and then Israeli.

Kidron called to Cliff, "Come over here, Tony, you are better at this than at selling anyway." I remember nothing of Cliff's arguments except his strong, strange accent and jerky, hectoring manner of speaking them. I do retain a sharp memory of the impression made on me by the grouping, that of a family and a delicate, prized, cosseted child. Kidron's finessing comment about what Cliff was and was not good at suggested a fond, more worldly sibling, or an organising, fussing parent, of the sort who proudly tells you that Johnny is no good at games, but...

That impression of a favourite child and his cosseting entourage was not a false one. The capacity to create, to recreate and to sustain an admiring, sustaining, family-type structure with himself at the centre of it – "his majesty the baby", Ygael, the genius – was central in Cliff's long political life, as indeed the deep need for it must also have been. This is at the core of an understanding of Cliff's highly personalised conception of what revolutionary politics is.

XI

In an essay on the film director Roman Polanski, the late Kenneth Tynan wrote: "He has the assurance of all the great imposers. Let me clarify the concept of 'imposing'. Derived from the French verb s'imposer, it is a quality of temperament or personality. It denotes the ability not only to impose one's will on others (although that is a part of it) but to dictate the conditions – social, moral, sexual, political – within which one can operate with maximum freedom. In other words, assuming one has talent, the gift of imposing is what enables one to exercise it to the full. It does not merely stake one's claim, it asserts one's authority over a given field of work. 'Inside this field', it says, 'you will defer to me'.

"Unfortunately, many untalented people have the knack of imposing; the arts are full of them, and very nasty they are. On the other hand, many talented people are quite unable to impose, being too gentle and reticent; and these are the saddest cases of all. Success or failure, fulfilment or frustration in almost every sphere of human activity is dependent on whether or not one has the trick of imposing."

Cliff had it in spades. There is a touch of "greatness" in the sheer charlatan effrontery of the assertion at the head of this piece, designed to square the prematurely defeat-accepting concept of the "downturn" – which left the SWP utterly disoriented during the first months of the miners' strike – with the greatest eruption of the class struggle in decades. It belongs in the same category as James P. Cannon's attempt, when the shooting and bombing had finally stopped, to assert that, nonetheless, World War Two wasn't really over. Reading Cliff's remark, one has to remind oneself that this strike lasted 13 months, that at different junctures – when the dockers almost joined the miners; when the pit deputies (overseers) almost came out – the miners could have won and destroyed the Thatcher government.

XII

The dilemmas that led Cliff in 1958 to turn "Luxemburgist", mocking toy-town Leninism (and accepting Healy's toy-town antics as Leninism or rooted in Leninism) were real and they are similar to dilemmas facing us now as a result of Cliff's own work.

Bad slogans drive out good ones. Raucous, pretend, ultra-leftism – it mainly is pretend, a matter of advertising slogan politics – makes measured, that is serious, left wing politics difficult. The existence of an ostensibly revolutionary organisation that is willing to say and do virtually anything for organisational advantage and is, in Tony Cliff's style, utterly shameless about it, is a political curse. Not only is there the poisonous reality of such a sect, there are the inversions of itself it throws off repeatedly, making its effect doubly poisonous. That is Cliff's legacy.

"The revolutionary party", because it is an irreplaceable means for the socialist revolution, can seem to be a self-sufficient end in itself. That is a self-defeating delusion.

For Marxists, two ideas qualify their proper concentration on building a revolutionary organisation. One is to be found in the Communist Manifesto: the communists have no interests apart from the working class; they merely point out the necessary course of its own development to the working class and the existing labour movements, and fight to win them to that course.

The other is in the Transitional Program of Trotsky's Fourth International, listed amongst the cardinal principles that were to guide them in rebuilding revolutionary workers' parties: the communists are always and everywhere, no matter what the consequences for themselves or their "revolutionary party", guided by the logic of the class struggle.

Without these guiding notions there can be no such thing as a revolutionary socialist party, only onanistic sects. A revolutionary organisation not governed by these ideas in its quest for growth is free to counterpose itself to the labour movement, to assess events in the class struggle according to its own needs, where the proper approach is the other way around. For Marxists guided by the injunctions of the Communist Manifesto, above, to go along with the nationalist poisoning of the working class in order to build their own organisation would be deeply senseless, though it might – and did – make sense to the "organisation first" neo-Trotskyists.

The joke is that those Orthodox Trotskyists who, for good "revolutionary" reasons, make an absolute fetish of "the party", thereby stumble inadvertently into a conception of revolutionary politics that is the Second Internationalist notion of revolutionary politics – at its most degenerate. (In the case of those groups, Zinovievist and Stalinist organisational patterns are superimposed on it.)

XIII

Tony Cliff built a sect whose conception of politics puts its own structures in the central place the working class should occupy in its conception. It counterposes itself to the labour movement and puts its own perceived interests – how to recruit – above the interests of the labour movement, and even to the class struggle. It was for decades organised as a cult around Cliff, with no democratic structures in which free debate or any power of decision in the affairs of the organisation was available to the members. He leaves behind a sizeable organisation whose members have no experience of resolving political questions: that was Cliff's prerogative, and those he chose to consult. Cliff's departure will, though perhaps not immediately, throw that organisation into a crisis of self-redefinition in which his political and organisational legacy will come in for a very severe reappraisal.

Afterword, 2017

17 years after Cliff's death it is possible to see more clearly what, politically, he left behind him. In 1999, when Cliff was alive and, reportedly, still giving a political lead to the organisation, the SWP took a violent political turn. It threw its weight into organising a "Stop The

War" movement. Which war? NATO's police action against Serbia to stop its campaign in Kosova to drive out or kill its Albanian population. If Cliff was responsible for that turn – and it seems that he, at least, approved of it – it was a final gyration in an extraordinary record of zig-zags in pursuit of organisational advantage.

The SWP ran a mendacious campaign of full-throttle support for Serbia. It so happened that the Serbian-chauvinist regime was the most Stalinist of all the successor regimes in ex-Stalinist Eastern Europe. After Cliff's death the organisation continued in the same vein. In 2001 the SWP made a public virtue out of refusing to condemn the 9/11 attack on New York. It organised an "anti-war" movement in tacit support of the regional-imperialist Ba'thist regime of Saddam Hussein; and, after the occupation of Iraq, in support of the Ba'thist and Sunni-supremacist "resistance". It allied in Britain with the Muslim Brotherhood, which Cliff had once characterised as clerical-fascist (and it wasn't the Brotherhood that in the meantime had changed). When Islamists bombed London's public transport on 7 July 2005, killing 52 people, the SWP leaders rushed out a statement regretting the bombers' choice of "anti-war" London as a target but offering political rationales which the bombers had neglected to provide for themselves.

Cliff was perhaps the originator, certainly one of the originators, in the non-Stalinist left of an "absolute anti-Zionism" which advocated the destruction of Israel. Since his death that "anti-Zionism" has reached the level of mass hysteria on the Trotskisant left. Cliff must take a great part of the political and moral responsibility for that.

When Ian Birchall was interviewing people who had known Cliff for his biography, I reminded him of Cliff's statement in the dispute about Europe in 1971, mentioned above, that "tactics contradict principles". Birchall, who had once been on the IS Executive, the small committee that ran the organisation from day to day, told me that the idea was one Cliff frequently expressed on the Executive, provoking resistance and even mockery from some members of the committee.

It was a true statement of Cliff's political guiding principle. His guiding principle was that there was no guiding principle. Principles were one thing, agitation another. They did not "talk" to each other. There was virtually nothing that was forbidden to the organisation in pursuit of an organisational advantage. That is how it has always been with the organisation he primed and shaped.

Cliff had been a member in Palestine of the rightist international current known as "the London Bureau", which included the American Lovestoneites, so called after their leader Jay Lovestone, who were known to the Trotskyists as spectacularly unprincipled people. Cliff's family name Gluckstein translates into English as Luckstone. In his methods Luckstone was the political descendant and heir of Lovestone. The result since Cliff's death in 2000 has been a spectacular series of bizarre zig-zags. The organisation even took money from right-wing Arabs (it gave it back when it was exposed, and those directly responsible went on to form Counterfire). The Socialist Review and IS groups had prided themselves, under the rubric "Neither Washington, nor Moscow, but international socialism", on resisting the Orthodox Trotskyists' magnetisation by Stalinism. The SWP has let itself be magnetised by Islamic clerical fascism, and taken up something like the quasi-apologetics the worst Orthodox Trotskyists sometimes took up in relation to Stalinism.

The perverse dictum that "tactics contradict principles" is Cliff's legacy to his followers and his most fitting epitaph.

The young Tony Cliff with his partner Chanie Rosenberg

Ernest Mandel and the historic process

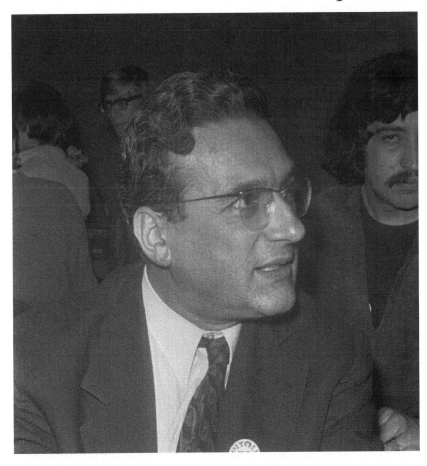

"The leadership oriented itself without any synthesised understanding of our epoch and its inner tendencies, only by groping (Stalin) and by supplementing the fragmentary conclusions thus obtained with scholastic schemas renovated for each occasion (Bukharin). The political line as a whole, therefore, represents a chain of zigzags. The ideological line is a kaleidoscope of schemas tending to push to absurdity every segment of the Stalinist zigzags. Blind empiricism multiplied by scholasticism – such is the course" – Leon Trotsky, The Third International After Lenin, 1928.

"To the Executive Committee of the Fourth International: You have reached a point where... it is impossible for me to remain any longer in your ranks.... Obsessed by old and outlived formulas, you continue to regard the Stalinist state as a workers' state. I cannot and will not follow you in this.... There is hardly a country in the world where the authentic ideas and bearers of so-

353

cialism are so barbarously hounded. It should be clear to everyone that the revolution has been completely destroyed by Stalinism. [The Stalinists] are the worst and the most dangerous enemies of socialism and the working class.... [in Eastern Europe] it was not the masses that won power and it was not a workers' state that was established... It was the Stalinist counter-revolution that won power, reducing these lands to vassals of the Kremlin by strangling the working masses... In 1932 and 1933, the Stalinists, in order to justify their shameless capitulation to Hitler, declared that it would matter little if the Fascists came to power because socialism would come after and through the rule of Fascism. Only dehumanised brutes without a shred of socialist thought or spirit could have argued this way. Now, notwithstanding the revolutionary aims which animate you, you maintain that the despotic Stalinist reaction which has triumphed in Eastern Europe is one of the roads through which socialism will eventually come. This view marks an irredeemable break with the profoundest convictions always held by our movement and which I continue to share" – Natalia Sedova Trotsky, May 9, 1951

Ernest Mandel was the pre-eminent post-Trotsky "Official Trotsky-ist". A central leader of the reorganised Orthodox Trotskyist move-ment from the middle 1940s, for 50 years, until he died in his native Belgium in July 1995, Mandel produced magisterial, super-objective commentaries on everything, from the Jewish question to Stalinism. In history he, not James P Cannon, Michel Raptis-Pablo, or anyone else, is the representative leader of Orthodox Trotskyism, the prolific thesis-writer and polemicist of the organisational mainstream of the Fourth International. Often Mandel's magisterial expositions would propound and defend ideas he had at first opposed, on Stalinism in Eastern Europe, for example.

A second-generation Trotskyist, he joined the movement at the age of 16 in 1939. Showing a fortitude and a courage difficult for us to imagine, in 1940 Mandel and other young Trotskyists set about reor-ganising the Trotskyist movement under the guns of the Nazi occu-pation forces. Arrested, Mandel persuaded his guard to help him escape. A man of Jewish background, he survived a period in a con-centration camp. As well as being a central leader of the reorganised Trotskyist movement, Mandel was also a talented writer who tried to reach out to wider circles interested in Marxism, producing several studies in economic theory. I deal here only with Mandel as a leader of Orthodox Trotskyism.

When, at the end of World War 2, a great wave of working-class revolt swept Europe, it was controlled or repressed by the Stalinist apparatus. In Eastern Europe systems like that of the USSR were created; in China and other countries, Stalinists made revolutions which were against the big capitalist powers, and against the bourgeoisie, but also against the working class. In France and Italy, the Stalinist movements, on Russia's orders, helped the bourgeoisies to rebuild their states.

Capitalism, which had seemed almost on its last legs in 1940, entered a post-war boom. The mass labour movements of the advanced countries settled in to live with capitalism. From about 1950, Mandel and his associates described the Stalinist states as "degenerated and deformed workers' states", socially in advance of, and superior to, capitalism.

The USSR, Eastern Europe and China were, they believed, "post-capitalist" societies in transition between capitalism and socialism. Thus, despite the crushing of the working class in the Stalinist states, and its quietness in the big capitalist countries, the "world revolution" was continuing to "develop" – albeit, said Mandel, in a deformed way. Mandel and others reinterpreted the ideas of Trotskyism so as to present the expansion of Stalinism and the creation of totalitarian states in large parts of the world as the first stage of the socialist revolution. He accepted on their own terms such systems as Mao's China and Tito's Yugoslavia, and for decades adopted the role of loyal critic. It was twenty years after Mao's victory before he came out for a working-class "political" revolution in China.

Keeping Trotsky's label for the USSR – "degenerated workers' state" – and adapting it to the whole cluster of Stalinist formations, the Orthodox Trotskyists, assembled behind the "workers' state" label ideas and assessments starkly at variance with those that Trotsky expressed in the same terms. Trotsky's label was retained; all his analyses, perspectives and definitions – all the ideas for him encapsulated in that term – were radically changed. The Marxist politics of honestly settling theoretical accounts with the past gave way to the ancient arts of palimpsestry, and to the survival techniques of the chameleon. This would be the cause of much obfuscation and confusion.

For Trotsky, the USSR was an unstable, transitional regime; the Stalinist bureaucracy was a "cancerous growth" on the society created by October, not a necessary social organism capable of defending the USSR, or of creating the USSR's post-World War Two empire of 90 million people. Trotsky admitted for the first time in *The USSR in War* (September 1939) the theoretical possibility that the USSR as it was, property remaining collectivised, might be assessed as a new form of class society. He believed that the USSR must in months, or in a year or two, give way either to capitalist restoration or to working-class "political" revolution. His belief in Stalinism's short life expectancy was one of his central arguments for not yet (that is, 1939-40) accepting that it was a new form of class society.

In stark contrast to the views Trotsky expressed in the term "workers' state", Stalinism was now seen as stable; as an agency for accumulating and defending the gains of a continuing world revolution, which, tangibly, was identical with Stalinism itself. Changes could come only by way of reform (Yugoslavia, China) or political revolution (the USSR), not by regression. These were societies "in transition to socialism", not, as the USSR was for Trotsky, an aberrant, hybrid formation that could not possibly last. The Stalinist formations were progressive, post-capitalist, on the broad highway of history – unconditionally progressive, not, as Trotsky at the end said of Stalin's nationalised property, potentially progressive, on condition that the workers overthrew Stalinism. Trotsky had in 1939-40 already recognised "elements of imperialism" in Stalin's foreign policy, and said: "We were and remain against the seizure of new territories by the Kremlin." Though the USSR had a vast empire, for Mandel and his friends it was not "imperialist".

Stalinism destroyed labour movements and imposed totalitarian regimes on the working class of the Baltic states, Poland, Czechoslovakia, Hungary, Romania, and Bulgaria, regimes like that of the USSR which Trotsky in 1938, in the founding document of the Fourth International, proclaimed that same year had rightly described as differing from Hitler's regime "only in its more unbridled savagery". But this was still the – deformed – workers' revolution.

According to every criterion by which the labour movement throughout its history had measured its progress – civil liberties, political democracy, the free existence of labour movements, free press, speech, sexuality – the USSR, China, etc., were at least as much of a regression as Nazism had been. But, because of the – totalitarian – state monopolised property, these systems, vis a vis capitalism were, for Mandel, unconditionally progressive.

Stalinist bureaucratic formations independent of the USSR – Yugoslavia, China, Vietnam – had made their own revolutions, but for the Orthodox Trotskyists these were no new ruling classes. Does the bureaucracy play a necessary role in production? You could not, on the facts, continue to give Trotsky's negative answer, not even for the USSR. If these were workers' states, it was not according to Trotsky.

356

Mandel became the word-spinning high priest of the vast, unstable and inchoate ideological edifice which grew up around the Stalinist bloc in the 40 years before the USSR collapsed. Ernest Mandel and his friends accepted on their rulers' terms, "critically", of course, such systems as Mao's China and Tito's Yugoslavia, and for decades took the role of loyal critic, adopting for these Stalinist states the "reform" politics which the Brandlerites, Lovestonites, ILPers, etc., had in the later 1930s counterposed to Trotsky's call for a new "political" revolution to overthrow the bureaucratic caste in the USSR. It was 20 years after Mao's victory before he came out for a working-class "political" revolution in China.

For the post-Trotsky official Trotskyists, the workers' state label expressed new ideas, not what it had expressed in Trotsky. Whose ideas did the term now express? Bruno Rizzi's! Trotsky had polemicised with Bruno Rizzi's acceptance of Stalinism as a stable system of post-capitalist rule by a collectivist new class. In fact, Rizzi, mimicking Fabians such as Bernard Shaw, believed that Stalinism and Fascism were essentially the same, and that – though Trotsky's polemic ignored this aspect of his thought – both were progressive, both transitional between capitalism and socialism, evolving towards socialism; he saw their horrible features, such as Nazi antisemitism, as mere kinks in an immature but sufficient anti-capitalist consciousness.

By the end of the 1940s Orthodox Trotskyism was expressing not Trotsky's but, essentially, Rizzi's – and Shaw's – ideas about Stalinism in the terminology Trotsky had used to express his radically different ideas. Mandel proclaimed that the survival and expansion of Stalinism meant defeat for Stalin's "Socialism In One Country", and posthumous triumph for Trotsky and his Permanent Revolution. Mao and Ho were Trotsky's legatees, not Stalin's. In fact, this assessment of the Stalinist states and the Stalinist-led world revolution implied acceptance of the essentials of Socialism In One Country.

The point for Trotsky and his comrades, as for all earlier Marxists, was that socialism had to come after advanced capitalism, and could not come otherwise. Though the workers might take power in a backward country, socialism could not be built in backwardness. If the revolution did not spread to countries ripe for socialism, it would be doomed. The idea of stable, evolving socialist growth from peripheral backwardness to socialism, in competition with advanced capitalism, was a revival on a gigantic scale of the pre-Marx colony-building utopian socialism of people like Etienne Cabet, who built small socialist colonies, parallel worlds, in the American wilderness in the

1840s. Mandel in World Congress documents (*The Rise and Decline of Stalinism* (1954), and *The Decline and Fall of Stalinism* (1957)) vainly chopped logic to hide this. One country? No longer one country! socialism in isolation? Not isolated now! Etc., etc.

It was the work of a religious zealot, reasoning around daft, unquestionable, fixed ideas, not Marxism. The need for it arose because all the "revolutionary" perspectives and hopes of Mandel's Orthodox Trotskyism were spun from the survival, expansion and likely continuing success of "Socialism In One Country", that is, of the USSR, a world power "in transition to socialism".

Worse than that. In Lenin and Trotsky, as in Marx and Engels, the historical protagonist of the anti-capitalist revolution is the proletariat. The Trotskyism of Trotsky was the revolutionary working-class politics and perspectives of the early Communist International minus, deprived of, the working-class armies assembled by the Communist International to make the revolution. Stalinism had "captured" and perverted them. Thus the terrible combination in 1930s Trotskyism of acute awareness, accuracy in understanding and prediction – in pre-Hitler Germany, and in Spain for example – combined with an incapacity to affect events of tiny, tiny groups whose natural identity, like their "constituency", had been stolen.

All Trotsky's "optimistic" hopes and perspectives were premised on the shifts and regroupments in the proletariat and its parties which he worked to bring about. There would be working-class self-clarification, self-regeneration and political regroupment in the heat of class struggle. Wrong, certainly. Fantastic, possibly. But Trotsky's was a perspective in which the ends of democratic workers' power and the means – working-class risings, the creation of soviets – were appropriate to each other.

By contrast, in Orthodox Trotskyism – "Mandelism" – the identification of Stalinism and Stalinist expansion as the "actually existing" unfolding, albeit deformed, workers' revolution led ineluctably to the destruction of all rational notion of ends and means. The "official Trotskyist" fetish of nationalised property – which for Marxists is a means, not an end, and by no means a self-sufficient means – took the central question out of rational assessment: Stalinist statification and its alleged working-class character was a "given", something to reason from, not about.

When the Orthodox Trotskyists transformed themselves into an epiphenomenon – critical, of course – of Stalinism, they thereby became millenarians. Christian, primitive millenarian sects, often Communistic in their desires, have looked to supernatural events like the second coming of Christ to transform the world into an ideal place. They had no notion of ends and means such as the labour movement would develop – action by named human forces for specific goals. In practice, they would look to some bandit, warlord or lunatic to begin the designated change. Central for our purposes here was their lack of a rational notion of ends and means.

In Orthodox Trotskyism, circa 1950, both the ends and means of the proletarian revolution in the original Trotskyism, as in traditional Marxism, disappear – or are pushed to the far horizon of history. The "world revolutionary perspectives", which Mandel wrote and refurbished for successive world congresses were, though dressed up in the husks of ideas taken from Trotsky and Lenin, now spun around the USSR, not around the proletariat or its methods or its old socialist goals. The protagonist in the workers' revolution is, for now, the Stalinist bloc, not, as in Trotsky, the working class, self clarified and politically regrouped. Mandel's mentor Raptis-Pablo once speculated that Stalinism would last for centuries. The protagonist is the Stalinist state, the "Red" Army, the Chinese peasant army. Though "perspectives" and hopes for bureaucratic reform and for working-class democracy are plentiful in Mandel, they are just tagged on.

The proletariat may be crushed under regimes akin to Fascism, despite such "details" this is the proletarian revolution. "Nationalised economy" conditions and defines all. How could a Chinese peasant army, led by declassed intellectuals, be seen as a workers' party? By circular logic: only a workers' party could do what the Maoists did, replicating Stalin's USSR. Ergo, this is a workers' party. Rationalising the Stalinist phenomenon, Mandel's Marxism became arid, eyeless scholasticism. Trotsky's ideas of 1940 were turned into their opposite.

The point at which millenarianism triumphed can be dated: the Korean War and the belief that the seemingly inevitable Third World War would be a war-revolution, an international civil war. The nuclear Armageddon – albeit with early nuclear weapons – would also be the revolution. The "Red" Army and its Communist Party allies in Western Europe would bring working-class victory in the looming war-revolution. You could not go much further from the idea of the socialist revolution – protagonist, ends, means – in Trotsky, and in all previous Marxism. When, a decade later, the Posadas wing of Mandel's organisation took to advocating that "the Russian workers' state" start the Third World War, because this would accelerate the world revolution, it only brought out the crazy other-worldly millenarian logic with which Mandel's group had replaced the Trotskyism of Trotsky at the time of the so-called Third World Congress of the Fourth International.

The tight millenarianist scenario of 1951-53 centred on Stalinism and war as the agency. Eventually that gave place to a looser millenarianism, promiscuous in its ever-changing choice of saviours. Various nationalist forces, plausibly and implausibly assessed, were anointed – though Stalinism always would be central to Mandel's perspective of world revolution. Trotsky's tradition and Trotsky's political terminology were thus reduced to mere building blocks in scholastic constructions. Ernest Mandel was from his youth the pre-eminent master in this work.

Of course Mandel's adaptation to Stalinism was never uncritical adaptation – those who ceased to be critical ceased to be even nominally Trotskyist – never inner acceptance of it, never a surrender of the idea that the Stalinist states had to be democratised and transformed. But Mandel used his erudition and his intellectual talents to weave, from the ideas of Lenin and Trotsky, ideological clothing which could be draped on Stalinism to identify it as part of the world revolution of the proletariat. Directly and indirectly, Mandel and his organisation over the years tied large numbers of anti-Stalinist militants into accepting, tolerating or justifying, "critically", Stalinist regimes and aspects of Russian Stalinist imperialism.

He played a role similar to that of Karl Kautsky two generations earlier, who rationalised, from the point of view of a hollow "orthodox Marxism", what the leaders of the German Social Democracy and trade unions did. Here Mandel was worse than Kautsky. Kautsky devised ideological schemes to depict the time-serving activities of a bureaucratised labour movement as an effective drive for working-class liberation; Mandel produced similar rationalisations for totalitarian Stalinist machines, convinced that they embodied the spirit of history, and that it was his job to interpret and rationalise it. Mandel was the Kautsky of "the historic process" itself.

And then, 50 years after Trotsky's death, Stalinism collapsed in Europe. It was revealed as nearer to being pre-capitalist than post-capitalist. Far from "defending and extending, in its own distorted way, the gains of the 1917 workers' revolution", Stalinism must be judged historically to have had no relationship to socialism and working-class emancipation but that of a destroyer of labour movements and an enslaver of working classes.

Had he died four years earlier, Ernest Mandel would possibly have died happier, for that would have been before the collapse of the USSR – the event which showed conclusively that his version of

Trotskyism was radically wrong, and that it had been wrong for 50 years.

In the later '40s, as a young man, Mandel saw the old Trotskyism – Trotsky's Trotskyism – go into a profound crisis and waste away. That Trotskyism had been based on the idea that – for the working class – Stalinism was irredeemably counter-revolutionary, and in its political regime akin to or (as Trotsky put it in the Transitional Program) worse than fascism.

Mandel saw that movement come to the point of collapse when faced with the defeat and disappointment of its hopes of workers' revolution, and with the unexpected survival and expansion of Stalinism. Not long before his death, he saw the "new Trotskyist" perspective he had built collapse along with the Stalinism he had reluctantly redefined as the "deformed" but continuing world revolution.

Mandel died while the cadres of his version of Trotskyism were still trying to come to terms with the collapse of what most of them, following Mandel himself, saw as the USSR workers' state. He leaves them politically orphaned, trying to come to terms with the collapse of the alien systems around which they had woven fantasies for five or six decades.

If they do not now face up to the facts, and critically reassess everything "Trotskyist" after Trotsky's time, then either they will drop out of revolutionary politics, or, utterly defeated in the ideological struggle with the bourgeoisie, they will take refuge in fantasies and delusions of the sort made familiar to us by the Lambertists, the Healyites, the Posadists, the American SWP and the other sectarian – and often scarcely sane – splinters from Mandel's mainstream Orthodox Trotskyism.

Has "Trotskyism" a future? For ourselves, we continue to believe that the future of working-class politics lies with a cleansed and regenerated Trotskyism. Trotskyism, which took over and fought for the ideas of the early Communist International, was no arbitrary or personal creation. That International itself inherited the progressive work and root ideas of the previously existing socialist movement. The root ideas of Trotskyism are the continuation and summation of the whole history of the socialist working-class movement. They embody the best conscious expression of the working-class side in an irrepressible class struggle. Not even the terrible errors committed by the Orthodox Trotskyist movement which Mandel led can destroy Trotsky's great tradition, or discredit the socialist program, on which history has stamped the name of "Trotsky". In a post-Stalinist capitalist world wracked by economic dislocation, famines and wars, those Marxist ideas – and new ideas developed out of them – are not only relevant, they are irreplaceable for the working class.

Mandel's personal tragedy here epitomises the tragedy of unknown millions throughout the world who to one degree or another saw Stalinism as a stage – a grotesquely distorted one, maybe, but still a stage – on the road to the emancipation of humanity from class society.

Ernest Mandel leaves all of us one thing to learn from: the courage and tenacity which made him as a lad of 16 defy all ordinary prudence and all narrow self-interestedness to join the Trotskyist movement. It kept him actively loyal to his best notion of revolutionary socialism all the rest of his life, through terrible disappointments and set-backs. Those of us who are committed to Trotsky's politics will, as we go forward, have to criticise and reject most of what Ernest Mandel, for 50 years, misrepresented as Trotskyism.

The young Ernest Mandel (left), with Abram Leon, another young leader of the Belgian Trotskyists. Leon died in Auschwitz, but left the manuscript of a book on the Jewish Question which Mandel published in 1946.

Tony Benn and the left

Tony Benn with Arthur Scargill during the 1984-5 miners' strike

The first thing that should be said and remembered about Tony Benn, who died on Friday 14 March 2014, is that for over four decades he backed, defended, and championed workers in conflict with their bosses or with the "boss of bosses", the government. That put him decidedly in our camp. The political ideas which he too often linked with those bedrock working-class battles detract from the great merit of Tony Benn, but do not cancel it out or render it irrelevant.

Politically, Benn's story was a strange one. An editorial in *The Times* neatly summed up the shape of Benn's long career. His was "A Life Lived Backwards". For the first half of his long life he belonged to the Establishment, socially and in his politics. To the dissenting old radical-Liberal and right-wing Labour part of the Establishment, but the Establishment nevertheless. Both his parents had MPs for fathers. Four generations of Benns have been MPs. Benn's son, Hilary, has been the third generation of cabinet-minister Benns. His father was Ramsey MacDonald's Secretary of State for India in the 1929 government.

Benn went to one of the leading "public" schools and then to Oxford University, where he climbed up onto that milestone in the careers of so many Establishment politicians, the presidency of the Oxford Union debating society. He became a pilot in the hierarchical Royal Air Force, in which pilots came from the upper classes, and in 1950, at 25, a Labour MP in a safe seat. His wife, Caroline, was rich, as was Benn himself. This sincere champion of the working class was a millionaire. Benn became a minister in Harold Wilson's Labour government in 1964-70, and was a minister again in the Wilson-Callaghan government of 1974-9.

Out of office after 1970, he turned left, at the age of 45. Publicly, he shifted during the great occupation and work-in at the giant Upper Clyde Shipyards, in 1971. The decision by Edward Heath's Tory government to end subsidies to ailing industries meant shut down for UCS. In office Benn had subsidised UCS, so there was logic and continuity in this. He marched alongside the Stalinist UCS leaders, Jimmy Airlie and Jimmy Reid, at giant working-class demonstrations in Glasgow.

Interviewed in the *Observer* at that time, he said of himself that in office one was a pragmatist, and in opposition one's idealism held sway. That might have been a summing up of the Parliamentary Labour Party side of what socialist critics called the old "fake left" culture of the labour movement: left talk combined with right-wing and conventional bourgeois actions at all the crucial turning points.

Benn's "pragmatism" had kept him in the government that brought in the first statutory wage controls (1966) and tried in 1969 to bring in laws to shackle the unions – an attempt to pioneer what the Heath Tories would ineffectively make law in 1971, and which Thatcher would succeed in shackling on to the labour movement in the early 1980s. He had supported the Wilson government's unsuccessful attempt to join the European Union (then called the Common Market).

After UCS the second Tony Benn started to emerge. He opposed the Heath version of the union-restricting laws he had supported in their pioneering Wilson government form in 1969. He sided routinely with striking workers. He came out against the Common Market (EU), opposition to which had by then become an article of faith with the conventional left (Communist Party, *Tribune*, some trade union officials, and most of the revolutionary left). He came out against nuclear weapons. He championed nationalisation of industries in difficulty.

None of that went far enough to stop him serving as a minister all through the 1974-9 Wilson-Callaghan government, which demobilised the militant working class which had brought it to power. It would be only after Labour's general election defeat of 1979 that Benn shifted fully and decisively. But after UCS he often spoke for the conventional left at meetings and conferences. He came to reflect the conventional left in his attitude to the Stalinist states. The modification in his preferred name summed up the shift. "The Right Honourable Anthony Wedgwood Benn" said he now wanted to be known as plain "Tony Benn", and he was.

In 1960 he had refused to inherit his father's title, Lord Stansgate, because that would have made him ineligible for the House of Commons. He fought and won two by-elections in his seat, Bristol South East, in a campaign to be allowed to renounce his title and sit in the Commons. That episode had produced the first "left" and "anti-Establishment" Benn. In its politics, it was a piece of old 19th century radicalism revisited. It even had precedents. The atheist Charles Bradlaugh had stood in a series of by-elections in Northampton to win the right to take his seat without first swearing a Christian oath; and in the late 18th century, John Wilkes had fought a similar series of by-elections in the Middlesex seat.

Benn moved left, seeing himself more and more as the modern embodiment of the old radicalism. He took to making frequent historical references in his speeches, and commemorated calendar-occasions – the Levellers of the 1640s, the Peasants' Revolt of 1381, the suffragettes, the Chartists (whose call for annual parliaments, however, he rejected).

Ostentatiously, he played his chosen part, visibly relishing it. To say that is not necessarily to question his sincerity, and sincerity does not rule out calculated self-positioning. His enemies said of him that in 1979 Benn calculated that Labour would lose the election, and started to position himself as the instrument of a break with the Labour government's record, in the expectation that he would become party leader. In any case, he played the role he assumed in 1979 for the remainder of his life.

In 1918 the Bolshevik Anatoly Lunacharsky wrote about Leon Trotsky that he "treasures his historical role and would probably be ready to make any personal sacrifice, not excluding the greatest sacrifice of all – that of his life – in order to go down in human memory surrounded by the aureole of a genuine revolutionary leader".

Benn also treasured his role, but the differences between Trotsky and Benn, and their respective traditions, are defining ones. Trotsky, from the age of 18, was a Marxist, immersed in the doctrines, the politics, the history that made up the Marxist tradition. He could be and was consistent in aims, goals, and in the tradition he sought to personify and continue. Trotsky was both politically and personally an integrated, organic whole. The doctrine he upheld was coherent.

Benn? He shifted radically halfway through his life – back to the Radical seam in British political history, but by about 1980 it was a very thin seam. Its old unwon causes – abolishing the House of Lords and the monarchy, for instance – were now of only marginal importance. Even the right-wing Blair government could essay to abolish the House of Lords. Benn's posture translated in the real political world of the 1980s into a comprehensive accommodation with the extant conventional left; and, except for points of historical continuity, that left had very little in common with the old democratic Radicalism he wanted to conjure back into life. (Moreover, that old Radicalism itself had bred antagonistic political currents – Joseph Chamberlain, the Radical imperialist, as well as Liberal anti-imperialism).

The labour movement left of the early 1980s was a chaos trying to make sense of itself. Shaped by Stalinism in varying dilution, its dominant model of "socialism" was cross-bred from Britain's wartime state-regulated economy on one side and on the other from the USSR and its East European satellites. Most of the left believed in the goodwill of Russia's rulers and their peaceful intentions and priorities, even while Russian Stalinism was expanding its areas of control and semi-control, as it did all through the 70s and early 80s. In 1982 Benn's constituency Labour Party, Chesterfield, with Benn's evident agreement, wrote an open letter to the Russian dictator Brezhnev, accepting the good intentions and desire for peace of the government that had invaded Afghanistan in 1979 and triggered the Second Cold War.

Playing the demagogue to the existing left and its causes and assumptions, Benn won tremendous popularity among people eager for a prominent and capable tribune who, moreover, knew how to play the media's game. Benn walked from his position of upper-class privilege into leadership of a wide coalition of leftists like a man casually walking into a different part of his own house. Visibly glorying in the applause and approbation which it brought to him, he became the central leader of a loosely defined left. And in Benn's role there was much of the old "Dancing Elephant Act". The elephant trainer moves his hands and the elephant dances to the gestures. But in fact the reality is the opposite of what it appears to be. The trainer's skill is to move in time with the elephant.

Benn appeared to "conduct" the left orchestra, but in fact he accommodated to what he found already there. He did that as a calculated role. For instance, he talked much of the radical Christian tradition and of the affinity of the Christian tradition with the socialist attitudes to which Benn appealed. He presented himself as in that Christian tradition. He was widely accepted as a Christian. In fact he was an atheist! The late John Mortimer, in a published interview, had to ask Benn, repeatedly, insistently, again and again, if he believed in God. Finally, after dodging the question many times, Benn admitted that he didn't.

A political event, a picture, an image that summarises his political trajectory, stands at each end of Benn's career as a radical.

The first is Benn marching with the leading stewards from UCS through Glasgow. The second is the aged Benn, no longer an MP, on the eve of the invasion of Iraq conducting a fawning interview with Saddam Hussein – producing in effect a "party political television broadcast" from Saddam to the people of Britain. There was no "speaking truth to power" there! Benn would have seen what he did then as part of the "fight for peace".

Accepting all the problematic causes of a confused and disintegrating left, Benn joined in the pro-Milosevic, pro-Serbia "Stop The War Coalition" in 1999, making an outcry to "stop the war" against Serbia which in the event succeeded in stopping the genocidal Serbian war against the Albanian population of Serbia's colony, Kosova. (It was not necessary to back NATO, or to give the Western powers any political credence or support, to understand what was going on).

Yet, in this bitter political chronicle, it is necessary to return to where we began: Benn stood with the workers in all the clashes after 1979. With a critical edge to his old-style radicalism, he might have usefully interacted with the existing left in the ideologically battered condition it was in by the time he joined it. But that would not have been popular with the conventional left. Benn chose to seek popularity, to be the chief demagogue, to ingratiate himself with what existed. From the (politically speaking) rotten timbers, decaying carcases, bits of broken stone, and crumbling dusty cinders that he found to hand, nothing worthwhile could be made.

Benn's relationship with the left and labour movement after 1979 – that of speaker, orator, articulator, political chameleon to the coloration of his audience – is most reminiscent of the role which freelancing radical leaders of 200 years ago played with the nascent labour movement and the broader plebeian anti-Establishment stirrings they found to hand – manipulation, demagogy. Such people as, for example, "Orator Hunt", one of the speakers at the meeting in St Peter's Square, Manchester, that became the site of the Peterloo Massacre in 1819.

At that time, the labour movement was only coming into being and taking shape, as the Industrial Revolution transformed Britain. Benn's career was part of the decline and decay of the old left, the old trade unions, and the old working class.

In old age Benn found himself widely popular even with people who disagreed with his political ideas or knew little or nothing about them. He appeared to be a man of principle who stuck to his guns against the Establishment. There was some justice in that, too. And symbolism. Benn did play, personify, and project himself as a rebel and anti-establishment nay-sayer – irrespective of the politics involved – and, for us, despite his politics.

At the beginning, this article recalled the great fact that for four decades Tony Benn stood with workers and the labour movement against their ruling-class enemies, and in his own way tried to defend our interests. For that he should be remembered with respect and affection.

Tony Benn with UCS shop stewards, 1971

Gerry Healy:
The revolutionary as gangster

Gerry Healy, around 1980   *... and in 1942*

"Our comrades in America and everywhere should not think that 'gangster-ism' is confined to the American [Stalinist] movement. Stalinism has intro-duced police tactics and bureaucratic centralism into the whole international radical movement. Even the fights between the Bolsheviks and the anarchists and Narodniks were on an entirely different plane from this. Even in the vacuum of emigre politics – in the Bolshevik past – there has never been such corruption as Stalinism has brought to the workers' struggles. It is natural that our comrades should react sharply to any evidence that this is creeping into our own movement, and it is better at the present time to exaggerate 'democracy' than to tolerate tendencies to Stalinist methods" – Leon Trot-sky, Conversation with Earle Birney (1935), *Writings Supplement 1934-40*, p.622

During the two decades of the great labour militancy, roughly from the mid 50s to the mid 70s, the most important revolutionary socialist organisation in Britain was the Healy group, from 1959 called the Socialist Labour League. The fundamental responsibility for the failure of the left then has to be laid on the SLL and on its leader Gerry Healy.

It is a matter of simple justice to remember the Healy of the late 1940s and early 50s as the man who had the courage and conviction to pull together what was left of the British Trotskyist movement during and after a general political and organisational collapse. From the end of the 40s to the mid 70s, the Healy group dominated the world of revolutionary politics, overshadowing even sizeable organisations like the RSL / Militant (now the Socialist Party, and Socialist Appeal) and the SWP (then called IS) and blocking the road of development for the tiny Workers' Fight group, a forerunner of the Alliance for Workers' Liberty.

This was a time when it was probably possible for Marxists to make a real breakthrough in re-moulding the mass labour movement, or, failing that, to create a large revolutionary organisation linked organically to the mass labour movement.

No such breakthrough was made. Fuelled by the mass youth radicalisation of the late 60s, there was a wide diffusion amongst middle class youth of generally revolutionary ideas, but too often ideas of a populist, quasi-anarchist or diluted Maoist nature, hostile or contemptuous towards the real, the only existing, working class and its movement. One variant of this politics of middle-class ambivalence and half-contempt for the real working class took the form of patronising lionisation of the "working-class heroes" when they engaged in militant trade-union action, and giving up on them when they didn't. Another, the SWP's, combined lionisation with an all-defining focus on "building the party" as a substitute for the working class. Sects were built but no serious revolutionary organisation rooted in the working class was built. The most important sect during the decisive period was the SLL. It became the "Workers' Revolutionary Party" in 1973, and would finally break up in 1985.

II

To understand Healy, we have to trace some of the development of Orthodox Trotskyism, and of the "Orthodox Trotskyism Mark II" which informed Healy. There have been two "Orthodox Trotskyisms", both invented by James P Cannon. The first emerged after the death of Trotsky. Cannon enunciated Orthodox Trotskyism Mark I in his speech at the New York memorial meeting for Trotsky. † Trotsky was dead, but Trotsky's ideas were down on paper, his teachings

---

† *The Two Trotskyisms Confront Stalinism, pp.527ff*

were there as a guide, and Cannon knew exactly which were, at any given time, the important and relevant ideas in that legacy.

The Trotskyist movement had split four months before Trotsky's death over their attitudes to Russia's invasion of Poland and war with Finland. James P Cannon led one side in the split, Max Shachtman the other. The Shachtmanite Workers Party concluded less than a year after the split that Russia was not a degenerated workers' state. The organisation adopted the position that the USSR was a new, hitherto unknown, form of exploitative class society. † It was an imperialist or sub-imperialist state, allied with Hitler's Germany (and then, after Germany invaded the USSR, with the UK-US bloc).

Trotsky's evolving politics had moved step-by-step towards rejection of the idea that Russia was any sort of workers' state. Initially, up to 1933, the Trotskyists had what is called a perspective of reform in the USSR. "Reform" here is misleading. They thought that the Stalinists, during forced collectivisation and breakneck industrialisation, would lead the system to a breakdown, perhaps involving a mass peasant revolt. In that breakdown, the elements of the old Bolshevik movement would recreate the party which Stalin had destroyed as a party, and take back control from the Stalinists. By 1933 the Stalinist social system and totalitarian regime had weathered their initial storms and, relatively speaking, stabilised. Trotsky came to think that a new revolution – from 1936 he would call it "political revolution" – was necessary to overthrow the Stalinist autocracy. He sharpened that position.

In 1937 Trotsky separated "defence of the USSR" from the notion that it was a workers' state: he argued that, though he still thought Russia to be an increasingly degenerating workers' state, it was in any case progressive, workers' state or not. Its nationalised economy was free of the defects of capitalism in the slump-ridden 1930s. In September 1939 Trotsky shifted his position further. He wrote that the USSR, exactly as it was, without further degeneration, might have to be reconceptualised as a new form of exploitative class society. It was too early for that, he argued. Russia was facing the test of war, and he thought that Stalinist bureaucracy was sure to be overthrown in that war, either by the working class or by the capitalist class inside

---

† *A minority, C L R James and some others, characterised Russia as state capitalist. The initial view of the Workers Party on bureaucratic collectivism was that it was a freak of history which could not last long – just like Trotsky's perspective on what he called the degenerated workers' state. That view would be amended in 1946-7. The WP would then come to see Russia's as a viable semi-slave social system that was capable of replacing capitalism everywhere.*

or outside Russia. On the eve of his death, in an Open Letter to the Russian workers, he wrote that "the conquests of the October Revolution" – the nationalised property – "will serve the people only if they prove themselves capable of dealing with the Stalinist bureaucracy, as in their day they dealt with the Tsarist bureaucracy and the bourgeoisie…" That was a tremendous qualification to the idea that the nationalised property was progressive in and of itself, regardless of the political control under which it operated.

The Orthodox Trotskyists Mark I stuck to the letter of Trotsky's conclusions – "degenerated workers' state" – and shed all the framework of ideas within which Trotsky saw Russia as, pro tem, a degenerated workers' state. † For them, the existence of nationalised property came to be the sole and sufficient criterion for a state to be some species of workers' state.

After 1944, Russia conquered a large part of Europe, oversaw the nationalisation of economies there, and emerged as the greatest power in Europe and the second power in the world. The Orthodox Trotskyists at first – at their Second World Congress, for example, in April-May 1948 – said that the East European satellite states were state-capitalist police dictatorships, while Russia, with and because of a more-or-less identical economic structure, was a degenerated workers' state. They used one criterion for judging Eastern Europe – the working class did not rule there – and another for Russia. The workers did not rule in Russia, either, but for Russia they identified nationalised economy, per se, as defining some form of working-class rule. After much agonising around this contradiction, they finally chose nationalised property, and nationalised property alone, as the decisive criterion for the character of a state.

By the early 1950s, Stalinist victory in China, the war raging in Korea, and the seeming imminence of World War Three, combined to make the Orthodox Trotskyists a mere tail of Russia in international affairs – a critical and cavilling tail, but a tail nonetheless.

The Fourth International leadership was a small coterie of journalists in Europe, at the centre of which was Michel Pablo (Raptis), an Alexandria-born Greek, the secretary of the International. It included Ernest Mandel. The group round Pablo, though its Fourth International comprised only very small and rather scattered organisations, tried to act as a central leadership, instructing its sec-

† *Trotsky's framework for seeing Russia's nationalised economy as the empirical evidence that Russia was still a workers' state comprised its origin in the workers' revolution, its uniqueness in the world, and the unstable and transitory character of the Russian system as Trotsky saw it.*

tions in detail on what to do. It evolved the tactic of immersion in so-cial-democratic mass parties – in Britain, the Labour Party, within which the Healy group worked. However, like many others at the time, they thought World War Three was certain. In that war, the Stal-inist parties, the biggest working-class-based parties in France and Italy, would rally to the Russian army, which was certain to invade, and rise in its support. Together the Communist Parties and the Rus-sian army would make of Western Europe what Russia had made of Eastern Europe. The Orthodox Trotskyists wanted to be part of that "process". Pablo extended the idea of entry into mass parties to the mass Communist Parties.

But these were tight totalitarian parties, everywhere, even before they had state power. Trotskyists publishing or even whispering their views would certainly be expelled or killed. Trotskyists had been killed on a large scale in Greece and Vietnam by Stalinist organisa-tions not in power (or, in Vietnam, not yet).

They would have to work completely underground in the Com-munist Parties. People known as Trotskyists would have to pretend to renounce Trotskyism; they would have to heap abuse on Trotsky and publicly repeat the stock Stalinist lies about Trotsky and Trotsky-ism and any new ones Moscow issued. The French Trotskyists re-belled against this decree and in summer 1952 the majority of them were expelled from the Fourth International.

The reverberations spread, and in November 1953 James P Can-non and the SWP-USA issued a "Letter to Trotskyists Throughout the World", calling for the repudiation of "Pabloism". They set up an "In-ternational Committee of the Fourth International", supported also by the French and British organisations. Their opponents said that they were in revolt against the idea that an organisation such as the Fourth International was then should be tightly centralised. That was true: they objected to having a centre composed of a few "young men" in Paris (as Cannon put it) issuing orders to relatively substan-tial organisations, in the first place the SWP-USA. The International Committee would be a loose international grouping around the SWP-USA. They were hotly anti-Stalinist, accusing the Fourth Interna-tional's leaders of failing to side effectively with the East German workers in 1953.

What the International Committee was doing and saying put in question the innovative political course which the Fourth Interna-tional had embarked on since 1948, when the Tito-Stalin break led them to adopt radically new attitudes to Stalinism, and codified at the Third World Congress in 1951. It implicitly raised questions about the whole history of the Orthodox Trotskyists since 1940. Recoil from "Pabloism" on the question of the "deformed and degenerated workers' states" pushed them in the direction of "Shachtmanism". But the leaders of the new IC were not having any of that. They stood by "the decisions of the Third Congress". Their difference with Pablo, Mandel, etc. were in interpreting the political line that flowed from those decisions. Thus Cannon launched what might be called "Orthodox Trotskyism Mark II", fiercely but incoherently anti-Stalinist.

Healy backed Cannon. This surprised those who had known him as a member of the Pablo group, with the rank, so to speak, of a prominent lieutenant.

The Healy group was politically very incoherent. For instance, in 1956, Healy wrote an article in the British Labour paper *Tribune* arguing that Stalinism in Russia could not last long because the modernisation and technological advance of the economy called for a liberalisation of society. †

The International Committee was a healthy recoil from the drift which had caused Natalia Sedova Trotsky to break publicly with the Fourth International in May 1951. But it was a self-stifled and bureaucratic recoil. As a movement to regenerate the Fourth International politically, it was still-born.

The organisations of the International Committee had in common that they were, all of them to different degrees, tightly controlled groups with leaderships and party apparatuses which were very strong against the members and politically all-defining. The upshot of the 1953 split was that Healy had a tightly-controlled organisation with a leadership (Healy) that could dictate its politics more or less arbitrarily. (A small group of ostensible supporters of the Pablo-Mandel International Secretariat, led by John Lawrence, split off, and soon went over to the Communist Party). After the SWP-USA went for reunification with Mandel in 1963, and the International Committee split, Healy's domination in Britain became even more complete and arbitrary. Widely disparate but underdeveloped and incoherent political currents within the organisation were held in balance by Healy.

---

† *Tribune, 9 March 1956. "The historical causes which produced Stalin have now dramatically changed. The Soviet Union has been joined by China and Eastern Europe; the Colonial Revolution has set millions moving along the road to freedom. Moreover, thanks to the economic foundations of the Soviet Union, established by the October Revolution, the productive forces of the country have enormously increased despite the bureaucracy. This in turn has raised the cultural level of the people... Khrushchev has assumed the mantle of power under enormously different conditions from Stalin; he, therefore, pursues a different course". (www.workersliberty.org/node/21390).*

The Banda brothers, for example, were always half-Maoist. A small strand of the later Healy organisation explicitly supported the suppression of the Hungarian revolution in 1956.

Even when, in the 1950s, it did serious and constructive work in the labour movement, the Healy group was organisationally authoritarian and, as a consequence, intellectually stultified. Healy dominated the organisation in an unchallengeable rule sustained by both ideological and (petty) physical violence against anybody who dared disagree with him – or with whatever political strand in the organisation's leading layer he was, for the moment, backing. For example, the SLL "went Maoist" to support the Chinese "Cultural Revolution" in 1967.

In the 1960s the SLL progressively cut loose from the Labour Party – that is, from what was then the working-class movement in politics – and, though it remained in the trade unions, its activity there became more like Third Period Stalinism than serious work. It recruited and exploited – exploited is the word! – mainly raw youth.

Healy was a highly volatile fellow who tended to believe what he wanted to believe, and ever more so as he got old at the heart of an organisation where his every whim was law. At the centre of a machine where no-one could make him take account of anything he wanted to ignore, Healy slowly went mad – or, if you like, retreated into such a childish me-centred solipsistic view of the world and of "his" organisation that it came to the same thing. Not the least of the arguments against the "Zinovievist" form of organisation of the typical Orthodox Trotskyist groups is what that does to those who rise to personal dictatorship within them.

For example, by 1968 the SLL was going on a 100,000-strong anti-Vietnam-war demonstration with leaflets explaining that it was "not marching" because the march was a conspiracy by the press to boost the march organisers at the expense of great Marxists like Healy. Yet the SLL machine survived, as an increasingly sealed-off youth-fuelled sect, and expanded. Not accidentally, its main "industrial" base by the early 1970s was among actors and other theatre people.

The SLL published a daily paper from 1969. But, more and more it inhabited an onanistic world where its own rigidly exclusive marches and theatrical pageants were more important to the organisation than anything else. One incident summed that up neatly. The annual summer camp was the greatest event in the Healyite year. Healy would preside, living in a big tent at the campsite: no-one was allowed to have a bigger one. There would be lectures, and selected people, pitifully loyal to Healy, would be publicly bullied and denounced. The 1972 camp was under canvass when the political crisis erupted over the jailing on 21 July of five dockworker pickets arrested under new anti-labour laws. For five days, thousands laid siege to Pentonville Jail, where the five men were locked up. A quarter of a million workers struck, and the TUC called a one-day general strike for the following Monday, 31 July. The Tory government buckled and released the five. And the SLL? Healy refused to let events in the class struggle impinge on his routine. He decided that the camp would continue. And it did, during the crisis that engulfed Britain and the labour movement.

One consequence of the SLL's undisguisable sectism was that by the late 1960s and the early 1970s, the then saner IS/SWP had space to grow substantially. A disconcerting feature of the SWP today is that it has grown more and more like the SLL of the 60s.

Healy was always, even in his best days, given to paranoid self-importance and paranoid fear of the State, and now his derangement got completely out of control. A terrible panic seized him during the 1973-4 miners' strike that led to the defeat of the Tory Government in the election of 28 February. At one stage members of the organisation were instructed to hide their "documents" because a military coup was only days away.

Then Healy discovered that other Trotskyists who opposed him, such as Trotsky's one-time secretary, the American, Joseph Hansen, were really secret "agents" of the US or Russian governments, or of both. A great barrage of lies and bizarre fantasies was poured out "exposing" them.

A vast world-wide campaign – the Healyites had small "children groups" in many countries – was launched to "explain" much of the tortured history of Trotskyism after Trotsky as a convoluted spy story. All of the world, and much of recent history, was reinterpreted as an affair of "agents" and double-agents. This stuff bore a horrible family-likeness to the paranoid world of Russia and the Stalin-controlled East European regimes in Stalin's last years, as during the Moscow Trials in the 1930s.

Perhaps as part of his increasingly dominant paranoia, Healy now transmuted into a "philosopher." † Living the life of a multi-millionaire, while members often went short to give money to the organisation, and full-time organisers were sometimes going half-hungry because their wages were not paid, Healy concentrated more and more on expounding a pseudo-Marxist, pseudo-Hegelian gooblede-gook reminiscent, despite its verbiage about "dialectics" and so on, of nothing so much as L Ron Hubbard's dianetics, around which the

Church of Scientology has been constructed. It eventually came out that Healy was cribbing the stuff from Russian "Marxist" textbooks. The "philosophy" mixed oddly with his continuing "political" concerns and the lines were often crossed: it was not unknown for the WRP press to denounce someone as both a police agent and a "philosophical idealist."

By the mid-70s the organisation was in serious decline, financially over-extended, and threatened with collapse. At that point, Healy sold the organisation to Libya, Iraq and some of the Arab sheikhdoms as a propaganda outlet and as a jobbing agency for spying on Arab dissidents and prominent Jews ("Zionists") in Britain. Arab gold flowed into the shrunken and isolated organisation. Printing presses were bought, more modern than those on which the bourgeois papers were then printed. To get away from the London print unions, they were installed in Runcorn, Cheshire, anticipating by a decade Rupert Murdoch's move from union-controlled Fleet Street to Wapping.

They churned out crude Arab-chauvinist propaganda lauding Saddam Hussein and Libya's ruler Colonel Gaddafi and denouncing Israel and "Zionism." Numerically still in serious and progressive decline, the organisation, nevertheless, built up a property empire of bookshops and "training centres" around Britain. To earn their wages, they, still calling themselves Trotskyists, publicly justified Saddam Hussein's 1980 killing of Iraqi Communist Party members, and provided reports on London-based Arabs and on Jewish capitalists. This organisation could not any longer be considered part of the labour movement. ††

The final act came in October 1985. Healy, who had run the organisation by bullying, bluster, and the personal terror he inspired, was now 72, weakened by age and by a bad heart. Those who rule by personal forcefulness and emotional violation of others should not grow old. With Healy dithering on the margin between retirement and ex-

---

† *The predominance of this philosophical aberration was new, but, with Healy, the substance of it was not. The late Vladimir Derer, a Czech émigré socialist in London in the war years, a member of the German émigré Trotskyist Internationale Kommunisten Deutschlands, once described to me a meeting then at which Healy had expounded "Marxist philosophy" and "dialectics" – and the embarrassment of those in the meeting who knew anything about the subject at the fact that Healy did not know what he was "teaching" the meeting.*

†† *As we insisted at the time – paying for our insistence with a costly libel case brought in the name of the actress Vanessa Redgrave. In fact the WRP was still widely accepted as part of the labour movement, but that's another story. See "The Last Time We Were Heresy Hunted", by this writer: http://www.workersliberty.org/wrp.*

ercising his old control and prerogatives, the WRP imploded. Faced with continued decline and, despite the flow of Arab gold, a new financial crisis, the WRP apparatus divided. Healy himself was probably getting ready for a purge. He was suddenly denounced as a rapist of 20-something female comrades and expelled from the organisation. The WRP fell apart in a great outburst of long bottled-up hysteria. The subgroups which Healy had kept in line fell on each other, and on Healy, who had exploited and then disappointed their political hopes.

People whom he had oppressed for many years, using them as demoralised tools, butts, and whipping boys, allied with the quasi-Maoist Banda brothers, his lieutenants of 35 years, and drove Healy out. It was a satisfying but not a pleasant thing to see. With Vanessa Redgrave – a splendid actress politically short of more than a few of the pages necessary for a full shooting script – playing Cordelia to his Lear, Healy fled from the wrath of his political children. He died in December 1989 an enthusiastic Gorbachevite. Asserting to the end his right to believe what he wanted to believe, he imagined that he saw Gorbachev carrying out Trotsky's program in the USSR. Thus the "Gerry Healy story" would have a happy ending! At the end, and for a long time before the end, the "Gerry Healy story" was a series of episodes from the theatre of the grotesque, which is where Healy himself really belonged politically and personally.

He claimed Irish peasant origins, from Galway. That was 30-odd miles north of where I came from, and, the first time I talked to him, he told me that his father had been shot by the British occupation force there, the Black and Tans, in 1920. He spun out that story as from a repertoire, in a way that made me doubt it. Altogether too pat, it inadvertently suggested someone with only a broad big-events acquaintance with Ireland and Irish history, and Healy was a notorious liar. The story is repeated by Paul Feldman in his biography of Healy, co-written with Corinna Lotz.

Healy's leadership, first in the 40s of the Revolutionary Communist Party faction which favoured entry into the Labour Party, and then of the main British Trotskyist group, in the late 40s and through the 50s, was that of a mere political "branch manager", local representative of the Orthodox Trotskyist leaders, Michel Pablo (Raptis) and Ernest Mandel, and then Cannon in the USA. Healy took most of his broader politics ready-made. He came to play the role he played in British Trotskyism from the mid-40s onwards not despite but because of his indifference to political ideas except as organisation-building tools. A similar political type, Pierre Lambert, came to dominate much of French Trotskyism in the same period. Healy, like Lambert, came to the fore because he was a lightweight politically, not caring very much about the political ideas.

In the 1940s and 50s, the world posed big problems to old-style Trotskyists, and most of the political leaders of the movement collapsed in demoralisation, confusion, and perplexity. The Healys and the Lamberts became central, partly because they had the courage and will to continue, but also because they cared about the ideas only for their immediate organisational consequences, and could propose what to do on the basis of short-term calculations without any political or intellectual qualms.

If James Cannon, Healy's early mentor, was fond of saying, after Trotsky, "the program creates the party", Healy reinterpreted this guiding principle to mean: arrange to have a "program" that will maximise party growth and change it where you need to; "the organisational needs of the party create the program". Here Healy's most important disciple would be Tony Cliff...

In appearance, Healy was extraordinary. Small – perhaps 5 feet 2-3 inches – and pudgy in middle age, he had an enormous, disproportionately large (or so it seemed), high-coloured head, with only thin strands of hair on it, looking like they had been painted on with an eyebrow pencil. His face was large and fleshy, with small features. What he called to my mind was Karl Marx's description, in *The Civil War in France*, of the politician Thiers, one of those who suppressed the Paris Commune: "a monstrous gnome."

He dominated his organisation by uninhibitedly brutal force of character, impervious alike to reason and to decency. The "cadre" of the group, including all or almost all the other leaders, was the product of "selection" – survival – through a never ending series of savage sado-masochistic rituals, involving at one time or another the pillorying, hounding, denouncing and self-prostrating of most of the hard core. † In this way Healy built a machine that was essentially depoliticised, ready at his whim for any "turn." Here, it was a farcical caricature of Stalinism despite its thin veneer of Trotskyism. That the SLL mutated like that was a great tragedy for working-class politics in

---

† At one such "criticism"(ritual bullying) session, at an SLL summer camp, Healy was denouncing Bob Shaw, a veteran cadre of the group. Shaw sat meekly on a stool as Healy denounced and character-assassinated him, jabbing his finger at him. He jabbed him in the chest, or pushed him, so fiercely that Shaw and his seat overbalanced backwards, tipping Shaw onto the much-trampled muddy ground. Shaw got up, put the stool back where it had been, and took his seat again so that they could resume their sado-masochistic ritual.

Britain. Much of the history of that organisation is properly explained by the personality of Healy; the fact that the most important ostensibly revolutionary organisation in Britain took this form needs a broader and deeper explanation. But that is a major subject in itself.

After Healy's death in 1989, Paul Feldman and Corinna Lotz published a biography (1994). They are badly informed politically: for example, they think Lenin was "secretary" of the Bolshevik Party. They naively believe in Healy: dollops of his "philosophical" gibberish, notes from his lectures, lace the text. But Lotz gives a touching account of Healy in his last years as a charlatan-guru for rich and silly theatricals – Maharishi Guru Gerry, so to speak, and L Ron Healy, rolled into one – globe-trotting to interesting places with Vanessa Redgrave's name on his calling card.

Lotz paints a fanciful picture of a gallant old man struggling for his truth against strong enemies, including the unbeatable ones, old age and ill-health. She made me forget for a while, though I have indelible adolescent experiences to remind me, that this man spent 25 years bullying – politically, financially, emotionally, sexually – and exploiting young people who thought he represented the legacy of Leon Trotsky – towards which his real relationship was that of Cain to Abel.

When Lotz describes Healy moaning to himself shortly before he lost consciousness and died, I felt what both humanity and convention say you should feel about such things, though Gerry Healy would have been the first to scorn that sort of "weakness": "He kept sighing, and saying, 'Oh my God'..."

Then my real feelings about the old reptile came to the surface in involuntary speculation about the meaning of the great philosopher's "last words". Was this last-minute appeal to "Oh my God" a prayer? Did the old purveyor of "dialectical" pidgin-religion get real, God-bothering, religion at the end? Or is the correct political interpretation that it was something akin to Christ's despairing cry on the cross: "My God! My God! Why have you forsaken me?" Had he thought he had a special relationship with the Supreme Leadership in the sky?

If you exclude these possibilities, you are left with the sense of Edward G Robinson's dying words at the end of "Little Caesar" when, playing Rico the small-time gangster, he staggers around, shot through the chest, gasping out his astonishment that he is, after all, mortal: "Can this", he cries, "be the end of Rico?" And a miserable end Healy's was too – thirty years too late.

Ted Grant and the workers

Ted Grant (1913-2006) was the leader of the "Militant Tendency" of the 1970s and 80s, and of its 1950s-60s forerunners; before that, he was the chief writer of the Revolutionary Communist Party of the 1940s. The Socialist Party of today, although it expelled the aged Grant in 1992, still relies for theories, in so far as it has any, on Grant's work. To understand its politics, we must first pose the question: what should Marxists do, what must Marxists do, in the working class and its movements?

Theory without practice is sterile; practice without theory is blind. The central goal of Marxist socialists in politics is to reach the working class and educate it – the actually existing working class, as it is at any given time, in any circumstances, no mat-

Top pic: Ted Grant appeals against expulsion at the Labour Party's 1983 conference. Lower pic: Ted Grant in 1942

ter what. James Connolly put it about as well as it can be put: "To increase the intelligence of the slave, to sow broadcast the seeds of that intelligence that they may take root and ripen into revolt; to be the interpreters of that revolt, and finally to help in guiding it to victory

381

is the mission we set before ourselves." We go through its experiences with the working class. For instance, when there is conscription, we do not become conscientious objectors as a matter of principle, no matter how much we may disapprove of what the army is being used for. We act always to help the working class to understand capitalist society, to see it in history as one of a number of exploitative class societies; to see its own place in capitalist society, to learn that it can be replaced with a better, socialist, society. In practice, except at the height of a revolutionary working-class drive against capitalism, that almost always involves relating to a minority. The point here is that, although of course we use our heads in deciding what we select, stress, focus on at a given moment, we do not, on pain of political self-annihilation, dilute what we say in order to reach the maximum number of workers; we do not adulterate what we say in order to have more effective agitation. Our agitation must be consonant with our basic ideas, our program. To do otherwise would be to work against our own fundamental, longer term, objectives.

To take something nobody on the left would think of doing, we do not use racist agitation or xenophobia in order to reach the mass of the white working class. That would contradict and defeat the whole purpose of our work. We should not – to take something that almost everybody on the left does, and has done for decades – counterpose the increasingly defunct nation-states of Europe to the bourgeois attempt to unite Europe in the European Union. That is reactionary.

In my opinion, one of the great sources of political and intellectual corruption on the left is the dominance in its work of free-wheeling, opportunist, catch-penny agitation. Everything is agitation-led. "The party" must be built – and we don't need to be too fastidious in our agitation or ask how it squares with our general outlook on the world, what it says or implies about our picture of the world, to our "propaganda". The late Tony Cliff used to put it with inimitable crassness: "Tactics contradict principles".

We work by way of general education. We use agitation against aspects of day-to-day life and conditions under capitalism to help workers see the system as a whole. We help the working class to organise. We act to organise the working class in trade unions, political organisations, ephemeral specific-issue organisations, all the way to organising armed insurrection, when that becomes necessary. In all these phases, our central, all-governing concern, is to educate and prepare the working class, or a sizable minority of the working class that can then reach the rest of the workers. That central concern tells us what we can and cannot do. It is the fundamental reason why Trotsky, living in a political, world-flooding deluge of Stalinist lies, again and again insisted that lying to the working class, misinforming the workers, misleading then, manipulating them is impermissible.

For ourselves, the tendency that is now called Alliance for Workers' Liberty has tried to live by those rules all through its existence. We regard the working class as central to all our concerns, as any Marxist must. That is why we have focused to a serious extent on the existing organisations of the working class, including the Labour Party. Even the best Marxists are condemned to sterility if, ultimately, they cannot reach and transform the working class.

But to go from that general rule, the basic guiding rule, to the conclusion that the social composition of small propaganda groups – and all the Trotskyist groups are small propaganda groups – is the all-important thing, or that having working-class members goes a long way towards compensating for political deficiencies – is to turn things on their head.

Marxist politics and the working class

The other side of the dictum is also true, and fundamental: a working-class organisation will, to one degree or another, be blind unless it is armed with Marxism. And a supposedly Marxist organisation with rotten politics is not only blind: it is an active, malignant force working, sometimes against its own best intentions, to prevent the working class from seeing capitalism as it is.

The Stalinist Communist Parties of Italy and France were, each in its own country, the mass parties of the working class. For decades they brought disaster after disaster, political betrayal after political betrayal, down on the working class they misled. They would have brought even worse disaster if they had taken power (as we Orthodox Trotskyists used to urge them to do, and condemn them for not doing).

Before the Second World War, the majority of the working class in Czechoslovakia backed the Communist Party. After 1945 that party, with help from the Russian army, led the workers into a terrible half-century of totalitarian subjugation.

Sections of the Romanian working-class, some miners for example, were prepared in 1989 to fight for Ceausescu. Militant in Britain backed those Stalinist workers at the time, just as their predecessors in the Revolutionary Communist Party in 1948 publicly backed the Stalinist coup that put the airtight totalitarian lid on Czechoslovakia.

I have known people who had few political illusions about the Communist Party of Great Britain who yet remained in that party, or joined it, because of its vaunted "working-class base". And it certainly did have a solid working-class base for most of its existence.

Politics and sociology

The Socialist Party prides itself on the number of union national executive posts it holds. The SP, and before it, Militant, have prided themselves on having a majority of people of working-class background in their ranks. But the Healy organisation, in its various stages, also had a majority from working-class backgrounds, and a lot of black workers and black young people. Many of the people who still, occasionally, sell the paper of its *Newsline* remnant are both working-class and black.

Am I saying that it doesn't matter whether or not socialists influence workers and recruit workers to their organisation? Of course I'm not! I am saying that just looking at the class composition of small Marxist organisations doesn't even begin to answer the decisive questions about those organisations and their contribution to the working class. The sad truth is that since the political collapse of the Communist International, revolutionary working-class politics, as they had been understood all the way back to Karl Marx, have mainly been in the custody of small organisations that, more often than not, have been sociologically not working-class.

Winston Churchill, of all people, put it very well in an article I happened upon recently, written just before World War Two. Writing on the Stalinist-Trotskyist division he said: "Stalin has inherited Lenin's authority, but Trotsky has inherited his message". Of course it was a different sort of "authority" in organisations that were very different from Lenin's organisation. But Stalin did "inherit" the internationalist would-be communist working class and its movement.

The tragedy of the working class in the mid-20th century – and of course of Trotskyism, which cannot thrive when the working class is defeated – was that though Trotsky and his very small movement could see and foresee the political realities with tremendous clarity (in pre-Hitler Germany for example, and in mid-30s Spain) they were unable to affect what the mass working-class movement did. In the diary he kept for a while, in 1935, when he was living in France, Trotsky compared himself to a wise old surgeon compelled to watch quacks and charlatans kill someone he loves. And they did kill the old revolutionary socialist working-class movement.

Militant a force for backwardness and confusion in the workers' movement

Militant has been a source of backwardness and mis-education in the labour movement. It has never been anything else. In the decade and a half during which they ran the Labour Party Young Socialists, from the early 70s to the late 80s, that movement was on many key questions to the right of typical young people in Britain, socially backward compared to large sections of working-class youth at that time. On such things as gay rights and the legalisation of soft drugs like cannabis, for instance. But not only on things like that.

Take racism, for a particularly scandalous example. In a notorious case in the 70s Militant refused to back Asian workers striking against racial discrimination at Imperial Typewriters. Why? Because in part they were striking against white workers they accused of racism and of benefiting from discrimination.

Plainly, where the workers are divided like that you should tread very carefully. You should advocate working-class unity, as Militant no doubt did. But not unity on the basis of keeping quiet about discrimination and the special ill-treatment of some of the workers in question! Not on the basis of implicitly or explicitly telling the most oppressed workers, in this case the doubly oppressed workers, not to split the working class. That is, not to fight back until they had first won over the white workers.

Has the Socialist Party learned from this? I'll be astonished if they have. To learn from your own history you have to know and understand it. The Socialist Party's way with awkward facts in its history is to bluster and deny them. Their nonsensical bluster and lying to cover what they did in Liverpool during the miners' strike is the worst example of that.

The work of another organisation, the Communist Party of Northern Ireland, is an instructive example of the same method of dealing with a divided working class. From 1941 until they reunited in 1970, there were two Communist parties in Ireland, one on each side of the border. The Northern Ireland Communist Party built up a strong working class following during the war, on de facto Unionist and pro-war policies, having thus put themselves in line with the outlook of the Orange workers.

It retained considerable influence in the unions for decades after the war. They had leading positions in the engineering union; Betty Sinclair, a woman of Protestant background and a one-time student at the Stalinist "Lenin University" in Moscow, was secretary of the very important Belfast Trades Council. How did they handle the fact that Catholics were discriminated against? They helped build up a tacit acceptance in the unions, where Catholics and Protestants were united on trade-union issues, that the discrimination against Catholics in jobs, in housing, in voting rights, etc., would not be raised.

That helped build the Communist Party of Northern Ireland. It kept a deceptive facade of working-class unity, but its influence in the working-class movement was malign. There might have been a principled political campaign in the relatively quiet years before 1969 – when the Protestant-Unionists did not feel actively threatened with incorporation against their will into an all-Ireland Catholic state – against such discrimination, in conditions where they could appeal to the class consciousness of the workers, and perhaps have educated that class consciousness.

Then there was the explosion that began to engulf Northern Ireland in 1967, 1968 and 1969, with the rise of the Catholic civil rights movement. Of course the Communist Party backed that civil rights movement, and indeed, helped get it started. They said the "right" things. But there the CPNIers were being liberals, having failed to be any sort of working-class communist politicians where it mattered – in the labour movement. They called for a Trade Union Defence Force in 1969. That slogan was raised first by the Healyite Socialist Labour League, echoed by the CP, then picked up by the Maoist British and Irish Communist Organisation for a while, and finally by Militant, which for decades used it as an "abracadabra" magic, a-historical slogan.

When Militant dominated Liverpool's Labour council, in the mid 80s, and came into conflict with the local black community, which had been subject to institutional racism for many decades, how did they explain the issues to their own people, and the Labour Party Young Socialists, which they led, and which had raw young people in and around it? They spread the story that the black people agitating against them in Liverpool were "spivs and gangsters". They resorted to the worst sort of racist prejudice-mongering and stereotyping of black people.

Militant's idea of socialism

What was their general role amongst those workers they reached? They preached "socialism". What was socialism? It was the "nationalisation" of "the monopolies" – by the bourgeois state. What else was it? What existed in the Stalinist states. These of course were not fully socialist. They were degenerated and deformed workers' states that needed "political revolutions" to make them properly socialist. But, they were the first stage of the world socialist revolution unfolding in a perverted form in response to the needs of "the development of the productive forces".

And by god, they were altogether better than anything else that existed on this sinful and imperfect earth! They were to be defended in all circumstances, even while being criticised. Those who were trying to create similar states had to be supported. The Russian army had to be supported in its terrible colonial war in Afghanistan – and was, for the duration of the ten-year war. Those "defending the nationalised property", even Ceausescu, were to be supported, as the 1948 Stalinist coup in Czechoslovakia had been supported by the British Trotskyist group of the time, one of whose key leaders had been Ted Grant.

One of the oddest things was that Militant did not even sloganise about nationalisation under workers' control. In the 60s, you could find vehement arguments in the Labour Party's Young Socialists about whether socialism was workers' control (IS, today's SWP), or it was only and fundamentally nationalisation (Militant). That was even odder when you knew that in the late 1940s, the RCP, whose leadership included Ted Grant, later of Militant, had used the demand for workers' control to differentiate their politics from the nationalising Labour government.

Or take international affairs. Sometimes Militant's policies beggared belief. During the British-Argentina war over the Falklands Islands, what did they have to say? They were very wary of seeming to oppose the war, though they did "make the record" in the small print somewhere that they were against it. What did they think of the issues over which the war was being fought, the Argentine invasion of the Falklands Islands? What did they try to get workers who listened to them to accept? They said that Britain, Argentina and the Falklands should immediately unite in a socialist federation! It was the art of political evasion taken to the level of quasi-lunatic genius! The reader doesn't believe it? I don't blame you, but it's true. †

The working class and the unfolding Stalinist revolutions

Militant even in its heyday was a strange sectarian formation, incor-

---

† *http://www.socialistparty.org.uk/militant/mil2frame.htm?ch20.htm*

387

porating no more than strands of Marxism and Trotskyism, making a quasi-religious fetish of some of its vocabulary. Certainly, its definition of socialism, either in relation to Britain or to the Stalinist world, had little in common with Marxist, working-class, socialism.

It parted company with Marxism and its view of the working class's role in the socialist revolution and in its attitude to the working class and its movements. Its view of the world was a hybrid species of "bureaucratic collectivism". It saw as positive what a Max Shachtman saw as utterly negative. Ted Grant, Peter Taaffe and Alan Woods were "bureaucratic collectivists" because what they described as going on in the world, as distinct from what they labelled it, was the rise of a distinct new exploitative ruling class, with an essential role in the economies created, in the revolutions which created them, and in the societies which they shaped, on the model of Stalin's Russia. Grant called this class the "proletarian Bonapartist bureaucracy".

Trotsky's "degenerated workers' state" assessment of Stalin's Russia depended on the idea that the ruling bureaucracy, though, as he once put it, it had all the worst features of all the exploitative ruling classes in history, had no necessary role in the economy created by the 1917 workers' revolution. It was a usurper, a historical "excrescence". For Grant, the rulers of what he chose to call "Bonapartist workers' states" had a positive economic and social role to play in the underdeveloped world for an entire historical period, a role comparable to that attributed to the bourgeoisie by the Mensheviks in the Russian revolution. This "proletarian Bonapartist bureaucracy" was the blind creation of the needs of "the development of the forces of production" and in turn created its own sort of collectivist property.

And the working class? It would have the role it had had in the Stalinist revolutions in China, Vietnam, etc. – no role beyond supporting the revolution-makers. Eventually, at the end of a whole historical epoch, after the "proletarian Bonapartists" had industrialised the country, doing what the West European bourgeoisie had in its time done, the working class – then the workers could make their own "political revolution".

This had nothing in common with the Trotskyism of Trotsky's time. And what had it to do with Marxism? Or with working-class socialism? It was a vision of a two-stage world revolution, in which the Stalinists (but not exclusively the Stalinists: other, non-Stalinist, forces had also turned Burma and Syria and Ethiopia, etc., into "deformed workers' states") were the protagonists in creating an immensely progressive form of totalitarianism which replaced the working class "in the period ahead".

And it wasn't just a matter of trying to define reality as Ted Grant saw it. The idea of progressive "proletarian Bonapartist" totalitarianism was incorporated into their own program by way of their support for Stalinist revolutionary movements – as the inevitable "next step". The Stalinists, the bearers of a new form of production, had a progressive role to play even in a country like Portugal, or so said Grant in their magazine, as late as 1978.

The "socialist consciousness" of the British workers' movement, or: what "the workers" would and would not "understand"

Grant, Taaffe, Woods and their comrades also had a full quiver of rationalisations for accommodating to the bureaucratic leadership of the existing labour movement. Take their idea of the "existing socialist consciousness of the labour movement". This was an issue in dispute between them and those of us who founded what is now the AWL in 1966.

There was, undoubtedly, a mass "socialist" consciousness in the broad labour movement – a belief in statism, a preference for nationalised and municipalised industry over profit-driven-private enterprises. And, certainly, the then very widespread workplace struggles over working conditions, over seemingly small things like tea breaks, were a form of struggle for control by workers of their industries, and their working lives. There was a very high degree of de facto workers' control in a number of industries. On the docks, for instance, a powerful element of workers' control had emerged within the peculiar employment structures set up under the National Docks Labour Board. (Dockers were employed permanently, at a very low guaranteed minimum wage, by local Docks Labour Boards, and hired out as they were needed to the employers working the ships.)

But all this was tremendously inadequate, measured against what was necessary if the working class were to overthrow capitalism and replace the bourgeoisie as the ruling power in society. Workers had to understand about the nature of the capitalist state and what they needed to do about it; about the difference between nationalisation and democratic working-class socialisation of the means of production and exchange; about the need for international working-class unity. In reality the best of the labour movement in the 50s, 60s and 70s came to be in the grip of a sort of headless syndicalism.

In the largely syndicalist "Great Unrest" before World War One, and its continuation during and after that war, its thinkers and writers, such as James Connolly, saw the movement they were building as a means to overthrow the bourgeoisie. They saw the industrial unions they advocated and built as the infrastructure within capitalism of the future Workers' Republic. The de facto syndicalism in mid-20th-century Britain was an often tremendous movement of rank-and-file workers that relied on direct action. It was very often, also directed against the union bureaucracy. But it remained politically tied to Labourism, and many of its militants and rank-and-file leaders to the Communist Party. They had very little notion of their movement as a mobilisation and an education in action that would eventually overthrow capitalism. They looked to Parliamentary action to achieve political ends, even when they themselves acted to achieve political ends, as when hundreds of thousands struck work to force the release of five dock workers jailed for illegal picketing in 1972. When the labour movement brought down the Tories in February 1974, all we had to replace them in government was Harold Wilson's Labour Party!

In that situation the revolutionaries, the Marxists, were those who told the labour movement the truth about its own situation and about its own weaknesses, and what needed to be done about it. The idea that the socialist consciousness of the labour movement, such as it was, was adequate, or anything remotely like adequate, was simply preposterous. The idea that all that was necessary for socialism, for working-class rule, was to generalise the widespread labour movement support for nationalisations into the demand that all "the monopolies" should be nationalised, was both foolish and pernicious. Militant's activities were the preoccupations of a self-cultivating sect for which the class struggle was at best, less important than their own organisation.

What Militant did in all its activities was batten on the existing movement, accepting and reinforcing but also mystifying the ideas that existed – and sometimes even the most backward ideas – in the movement, at every point and in every way. Today the Socialist Party explicitly opposes freedom of movement for workers in Europe; in doing so it builds on a long record of refusing to agitate against immigration controls.

Militant's propaganda for "socialism" was a species of miseducation of the workers it reached. In its unrealism, its attitudes, its sectish schema-mongering, Militant peddled a kind of utopian socialism. It had an essentially manipulative attitude to the working class. Their formula to excuse saying whatever would help the organisation to survive and grow and avoid clashing with widespread working-class public opinion was "The workers wouldn't understand that, comrade!" It generated such scarcely-believable idiocies as the British-Argentina-Falklands Federation and was a manipulative license for virtually anything, for ignoring the Marxist idea that you function to educate the workers, that you stand against the tide of opinion when necessary. Trotsky's advice was "To face reality squarely; not to seek the line of least resistance; to call things by their right names; to speak the truth to the masses, no matter how bitter it may be; not to fear obstacles; to be true in little things as in big ones; to base one's program on the logic of the class struggle; to be bold when the hour for action arrives." Those were his "rules" for the Fourth International. It had "shown it can swim against the stream". With Militant, the rule was to preach "socialism" in general and beyond that adapt to what the workers would or wouldn't "understand".

And who knew what the workers would or wouldn't understand? The wise men at the centre, licensed thereby to cut and trim, evade and obfuscate. The truth is that they had contempt for the workers. The leaders of such groups always do. One of their youth organisers at a Labour Party Young Socialists summer camp, where there were quite a lot of "raw" young workers, rowdy and factionally primed-up against the minority there (which was essentially the forerunner of the AWL), said to one of our organisers, speaking "man-to-man", wised-up Marxist to wised-up Marxist: "If we let them off the leash, they'd tear you to pieces!" (Kevin Ramage speaking to Mick O'Sullivan). With that spirit, and I cite it because I think it sums up their real spirit, the fundamental attitude of the organisation's leaders was not to try to develop and raise up and broaden the outlook and the real understanding of the youngsters they organised, courtesy of the Labour Party. They didn't teach them to think. Instead they taught them political parrot work.

Marxism is not something given, a finished program

The Socialist Party operates with the idea that "Marxism" is a given, that it is fixed. In reality it has to be sifted, applied, and redefined again and again in the light of experience. The Marxists have to learn and go on learning before they can be adequate interpreters and teachers for the working class. The Socialist Party is still making propaganda for the wonders worked by the defunct "planned economy" in Stalinist Russia!

People like Peter Taaffe are evidently incapable of learning. The bureaucratic sect-structures of the Socialist Party and the foul religious spirit cultivated in and around it by its leaders, prevent others from discussing and maybe learning from their own and other people's experiences.

The key idea of Marxist socialism, that the liberation of the working class must be self-liberation, is put like this in "The Internationale": "No saviours from on high deliver/ No faith have we in Prince or peer/ Our own right hand the chain must shiver/ Chains of hatred, of greed and fear".

Least of all will a socialist sect like the Socialist Party, teaching political and intellectual docility to those it influences, liberate the working class.

In the early-1980s revolt against Thatcher, sexist or even misogynist themes ("ditch the bitch") were common in anti-Tory agitation. Militant coined some of the chants. This Militant image of Thatcher as an over-sized, flabby "Plunderwoman" in a bikini indicted her for supposedly disgusting femininity.

How not to fight the kitsch left: the Euston Manifesto:

That'll teach me to make silly jokes! A few weeks back, in a fit of self-indulgent whimsy, I mocked some ex-comrades of ours who had abandoned socialist politics to enlist in George W Bush's neo-conservative crusade to bring bourgeois democracy and American-style capitalism to Iraq. In a little skit, I had one of them confuse the Communist Manifesto with "the Bourgeois-Democratic Manifesto". Now [2006] they and others have in all seriousness produced what I conjured up as an absurdist joke – a "Bourgeois-Democratic Manifesto". Politics today, as many have already noticed, has become satire-proof!

Mysteriously but appropriately, perhaps, for people evidently travelling fast to the right, they have named their manifesto after a railway station – the Euston Manifesto.

They say – and as if they have just discovered the political equivalent of penicillin – things that *Solidarity* and Workers' Liberty have said, defended, and fought for over the last three decades. In 1990, for example, we wrote:

'We live in a labour movement grown spiritually cross-eyed from the long pursuit of realpolitik and the operation of double standards, a movement ideologically sick and poisoned. In terms of moral ecology, the left and the labour movement is something of a disaster area because of the long-term use of methods and arguments which have corrupted the consciousness of the working class. The most poisonous root of that corruption was the Stalinist movement". (*Socialist Organiser* 447, 10 May 1990).

But where we have said those things in an effort to build a better left, they say them as part of breaking from the left.

The "Euston Manifesto" consists of a preamble; a "statement of principles", fifteen of them; an "elaboration" of them; and the conclusion.

"Many of us", they say, "belong to the left" – but not all. They reach beyond the left to "egalitarian liberals". They "pay attention to liberal and conservative voices and ideas if they contribute to strengthening democratic norms and practices and to the battle for human progress". Boldly they "reject the notion that there are no opponents on the left" and "that there can be no opening to ideas and individuals to our right".

Curiously, in the form of a general manifesto we are offered a very narrow polemic against the kitsch-left. The Travelling People of the Euston Manifesto define themselves by negativism towards the kitsch-left, and mainly to the SWP part of it.

Yet, though their impulse is to oppose the kitsch-left, with their "democratic" and "progressive" popular front the Euston Travellers parallel the SWP's "popular front with clerical fascists". They disagree with their choice of allies, not with their approach.

Doppelganger: At least Euston's popular front with "egalitarian liberals" is better than a popular front with clerical fascists.

Is it? It might be, I suppose. All right, it is. But in both cases, the ally to the right limits what the accommodating "Popular Front" "left" can do. For practical purposes the grouping can go no further than its most right-wing element agrees to. That is as true for the Travellers' ideological popular front with liberals and conservatives as it is for the SWP's electoral and political popular front with Islamic clerical-fascists.

Doppelganger: They don't claim to be socialists.

Some of them do, but evidently it doesn't matter much to them. They say that their project "involves making common cause with genuine democrats, whether socialist or not".

Doppelganger: What about their principles?

They want "democratic norms, procedures, and structures... freedom of opinion and assembly, free elections", and "the separation of state and religion". They "value the traditions and institutions, the legacy of good governance, of those countries in which liberal, pluralist democracies have taken hold". They want "the separation of executive, legislative, and judicial power".

Their second principle is: "no apology for tyranny". They "draw a firm line" between themselves and those "left-liberals" who "'explain', indulgently 'understand', or apologise for tyrannical regimes, and movements that aspire to create such regimes".

Number three is "human rights for all. We hold the fundamental human rights codified in the Universal Declaration" of the UN in 1948, to bind "all states and political movements, indeed... everyone".

Doppelganger: Aha. The categorical imperative in politics – do unto others as you would have them do to you. About time someone thought of that!

They proclaim themselves "egalitarians". But nothing rough or precipitate, mind you! They "look towards progress in relations between the sexes (until full gender equality is achieved)... [and] between those of various religious affiliations... [or] diverse sexual orientations".

Doppelganger: They are firmly in the ranks of progressive, liberal humankind? And that's all?

No, they're better than that. They "look towards progress... towards broader social and economic equality all round". More even than that. "We support the interests of working people everywhere" – and even "their right to organise in defence of those interests". "Democratic trade unions are the bedrock organisations for the defence of workers' interests and are one of the most important forces for human rights, democracy-promotion and egalitarian internationalism".

Doppelganger: I bet I know what comes next. "Workers of the world, unite!" Am I right?

No: they want "the universal adoption of the International Labour Organisation Conventions – now routinely ignored by governments across the globe". That, they say, "is a priority for us".

Doppelganger: Remind me what the ILO is.

It was set up by the Treaty of Versailles, as part of the League of

Nations, in 1919.

Euston gets even better. "We are committed to the defence of the rights of children, and to protecting people from sexual slavery and all forms of institutionalised abuse".

Doppelganger: Ah, sure the poor craeters! *They mean well, anyway. Don't be so* meaen *and snide about them! How are they going to achieve these things?*

They think trade unions are a good thing.

Doppelganger: And how will they move "towards broader social and economic equality all round"?

There's the rub! They "leave open... the question of the best economic forms of this broader equality". "There are differences of viewpoint amongst us" on that.

But the Travelling People are "progressives". They are against "structural economic oppression".

Doppelganger: They are against wage-slavery then – against the exploitation of workers? Nothing is more "structural" than the means of production being in the hands of the capitalist class, and the workers having to sell their labour power and thereby themselves into exploitation.

You may think that. The Euston people feel that they could not possibly comment. They differ on the economic "solution".

They also want "the benefits of large-scale development... to be distributed as widely as possible in order to serve the social and economic interests of workers, farmers and consumers in all countries".

Doppelganger: How?

Evidently, they don't know, but "we support radical reform of the major institutions of global economic governance (WTO, IMF, World Bank) to achieve these goals, and we support fair trade, more aid, debt cancellation and the campaign to Make Poverty History". They explain: "Development can bring growth in life-expectancy and in the enjoyment of life, easing burdensome labour and shortening the working day".

Doppelganger: They are against privilege?

Not so fast! They are against "unjustified" privilege and "unjustified" power. What "privilege" do they consider justified? They don't say.

Doppelganger: These are youngsters – right? Cutting their political teeth? Students? Sixth-formers?

No, no. These are grown-ups, some deep in their tired and disabused middle age, or even elderly. The main author of the manifesto, Norman Geras, is a retired professor at Manchester University. The other is the *Observer* journalist Nick Cohen.

Doppelganger: Jaysus! *But they're new to politics, surely?*

Geras was a member or supporter of the Mandelite Fourth International for decades. He has written a book on Rosa Luxemburg.

Doppelganger: They'll have some stuff to say outside the common run, then?

Well, they are against racism. They "oppose... the anti-immigrant racism of the far Right".

Doppelganger: And the racism-fomenting agitation of the New Labour government?

Don't know. They don't mention that.

Doppelganger: But at least they nail their colours firmly to the mast. They are against racism.

The truth, though, is that it would be very hard to find other than fascist morons in Britain who are not "against racism" in general. The problems begin after you have proclaimed "anti-racism" as a principle. Then, what?

When the Travellers repeat a very tame and delimited version of what almost everybody proclaims, they are reinventing the wheel...

Doppelganger: They do a lot of that?

Lots and lots of it. Sometimes, as in their notions on democracy, it is the square wheel they reinvent! Perhaps that's why they take the name of a railway station.

Doppelganger: Give up! There's nothing funny left to say about the politics of Euston station.

Don't be a faint-heart! Maybe it's because they know that their grouping is a badly-buckled fifth wheel on the left-hand side of the neo-con float in the post 9/11 carnival of reaction?

The Travellers are for a two-states settlement between Israel and the Palestinians. They are vehemently against anti-semitism, which they think is growing alarmingly. But they even manage to be just a little peculiar and seriously off-target on anti-semitism. They write that things have "now developed to a point where supposed organisations of the Left are willing to entertain openly antisemitic speakers and to form alliances with antisemitic groups".

Well, yes! But where have they been for the last twenty or thirty years? The SWP stepped up the level of its "anti-Zionism" as least as far back as 1987-8. It was part of a turn to kitsch anti-imperialism then. They suddenly decided to back Iran in the Iran-Iraq war on the grounds that the USA was on the side of Iraq – as it had been for the whole near-decade of the war!

The significant antisemitism of the kitsch left is not in occasional association with open antisemites, but in their own "anti-Zionism" –

the wish to destroy Israel, and to back those who go beyond merely wishing it to try to do it. The formula in the manifesto is perhaps deference to signatories who have only lately cottoned on to left-wing antisemitism.

The Travellers are "united against terror" –"in all its forms". "The deliberate targeting of civilians" is, they note sternly, "a crime under international law". That it is done in a just cause cannot make it right.

Doppelganger: That's fine, surely? No cause can justify the deliberate slaughter of civilians. No militants in a truly good cause would want to.

You don't think a would-be democratic manifesto should at least refer to terror by US governments, for example, or by Israeli governments?

Doppelganger: That's the kitsch-left line: "Bush is the world's no.1 terrorist".

In terms of civilians killed – with indifference or criminal recklessness, if not with deliberate intent – surely there is truth in calling the "great statesmen" terrorists. Equating Bush with bin Laden is a reductio ad absurdum of something that is nonetheless true.

And "terrorism"? Terrorism today is the deliberate slaughter of civilians. What about terrorism that targets rulers and tyrants?

Doppelganger: Marxists have always opposed that!

Yes, but we sided morally with the terrorists – lauded, for instance, those who killed the Russian Tsar in 1881. Marx himself praised those of them tried and hanged for their heroism.

Doppelganger: Quibbling! You agree with the Travellers on "modern" terrorism!

With the branding, by an Unholy Alliance of Establishments, of all struggles which use "unofficial" violence as evil, wrong, unjust? Leftists who had not lost their political bearings, who had not suffered a complete moral collapse, would insist on the distinctions and brand the "war on terror" for the hypocrisy and sham and succour for tyrant regimes that most of it is.

Doppelganger: Ah, but surely they oppose Bush's wars?

Read their tenth principle: "a new internationalism". For practical politics, this is the most important thing in the manifesto.

"Humanitarian intervention, when necessary, is not a matter of disregarding sovereignty, but of lodging this properly within the 'common life' of all peoples. If in some minimal sense a state protects the common life of its people (if it does not torture, murder and slaughter its own civilians, and meets their most basic needs of life), then its sovereignty is to be respected. But if the state itself violates this common life in appalling ways, its claim to sovereignty is forfeited and there is a duty upon the international community of intervention and rescue. Once a threshold of inhumanity has been crossed, there is a 'responsibility to protect'." They "stand for an internationalist politics and the reform of international law – in the interests of global democratisation and global development".

In practice, this means open-ended support for "intervention" by the USA – "a great country and nation… the home of a strong democracy with a noble tradition" – wherever its interests can be presented as pursuit of democracy, or desirable "regime change".

Now, it is true that there is more to imperialism than the true idea – which came to some of us with our mother's milk – that it is a foul, dirty thing.

Marx thought that the British rule in India was immensely progressive – ending the thousands of years of a stagnant Asiatic mode of production, opening up new possibilities. Engels applauded the seizure of Texas and California from stagnant Mexico by the dynamic and progressive USA.

And British rule did bring the progress Marx expected in India, though more slowly than he expected. Bourgeois democracy in India is the child of the British Empire. World War Two was an imperialist war on both sides. Nonetheless it brought the liberation of Europe from Nazi rule, and created the possibility of reconstructing bourgeois democracy in western Europe.

Doppelganger: So you are saying imperialism may be progressive?

It is a matter of historical fact that imperialism, throughout the 20th century, as well as bringing the immense destruction of two World Wars and countless lesser wars, also triggered progressive developments, and opened immense possibilities not there before. So, after all, has capitalism!

Without the epoch of capitalism creating its preconditions and, so to speak, putting it on History's agenda, socialism would be impossible.

It is not even entirely ruled out – though it looks increasingly unlikely – that imperialism will bring some approximation to bourgeois democracy, or at any rate something better than the rule of the quasi-fascist Ba'th party, to Iraq.

Doppelganger: So we should support the imperialism of the USA, the UK, and other advanced countries! You say Marx supported the British in India?

Honest analysis and recognition of what is happening in the world is a duty we owe to reason. It is not "support" for capitalism, or abandonment of socialism, to say that the dominant world capitalist system continues to do "progressive" things.

But if we recognise progress, or potential or probable progress, we do it from our point of view. We do it as socialists, mortal enemies of capitalism.

We do not need to tell lies – least of all to ourselves – about capitalism and imperialism. They are bad enough without that!

Marx on India is a good model here. He saw great historical progress in the British rule in India, and yet when the "Indian Mutiny" broke out in 1857 – a backward-looking, reactionary (or mainly reactionary) movement – he indicted the British rulers for the savagery with which they put it down. "We have here given but a brief and mildly-coloured chapter from the real history of British rule in India. In view of such facts, dispassionate and thoughtful men may perhaps be led to ask whether a people are not justified in attempting to expel the foreign conquerors who have so abused their subjects".

Marx recognised progress; but he stood apart from the British bearers of progress to India. He took no responsibility for them or their deeds – from which, remember, he expected, in the long term, immense advantage. He maintained his own viewpoint and his political independence.

He did not banish from the record the venality, profiteering, and robbery by the colonial power, or the terrible consequences of the neglect by the British of the hydraulic requisites for Indian agriculture, which the old Asiatic despotism had maintained.

Doppelganger: He was irresponsible, then!

No, he was responsible to the task of maintaining an independent, revolutionary, communist, working-class outlook on the world. Politically he was not a "developmentalist", but a class-struggle revolutionary.

The Travellers are "developmentalists", people for whom progressive development triggered from above is all-important.

There is a curious continuity here. For many decades, "socialist" – Stalinist – politics was defined by the pursuit of industrial development, as measured by crude economic statistics, regardless of human cost. That was supposedly development towards socialism. Would-be Trotskyists, too, bought into that view. For them, the USSR was "in transition to socialism". Stalinism defined the core purpose and value of "socialism" as the cultivation of economies from backwardness to industrialisation.

With the Travellers we have something similar, but they are talking about capitalist development and imperialist-sponsored "progress".

The Travelling people declare themselves for "a critical openness". Self-preening, they say: "political honesty and straightforwardness are a primary obligation for us".

But in fact the Travellers themselves now stand with forces in contemporary society that can't tell the full truth.

Thus, they say nothing about the casual barbarity with which their "good guys" of contemporary history – because they are bourgeois, because they are imperialistic – lace, poison and subvert even potentially good works, like smashing the Saddam regime.

They justly denounce the kitsch-left for dishonesty and for double standards. Yet they themselves use double standards. In a revealing sleight of mind, for example, they misquote the slogans of the Great French Revolution of the 18th century (in the last point of their statement of principles, no.15).

"We reaffirm the ideas that inspired... the democratic revolutions of the eighteenth century: liberty, equality and solidarity".

"*Solidarity*"? The French revolution said: "fraternity". Fraternity did not explicitly exclude the competition of capitalism, the "war of all against all"; indeed, historically, it cleared the way for it. Solidarity explicitly does.

Here the crusaders for truth themselves employ the same sleight of mind and lamentable standards as the kitsch left.

Fighting the dragon of kitsch-leftism, they adapt to the shape of what they fight.

Doppelganger: Try not to be so f...ing pretentious!

All right then, forget Nietzsche! Take what Lenin said about what he saw as the warping of Rosa Luxemburg's ideas by her over-preoccupation with the fight against Pilsudski's Polish Socialist Party.

"To a mouse there is no stronger beast than the cat, it is said. To Rosa Luxemburg there is evidently no stronger beast than the... 'Polish Socialist Party'... If [they say] 'yes', Rosa Luxemburg considers it her sacred duty to say an immediate 'no'." (*CW* 20 (393-454)). Loathsome though the politics of the SWP and much of the "revolutionary left" are – the allies of Islamist clerical fascists, Ba'th quasi-fascists, and reactionary "anti-imperialists" – there are more powerful, and not less loathsome, forces in society!

The Travellers are an anti-SWP group, an inversion of the SWP. The SWP's mechanical inversion of official bourgeois politics makes them not an independent force but only a foolish negative imprint. The Travelling people's inversion of the SWP turns them into a positive offprint of bourgeois politics. No. 13 of their principles is commitment to "the traditional liberal freedom of ideas". But don't run away with the idea that they'll cut up rough in defence even of that. They hasten to add that it must be "within the usual constraints against defamation, libel and incitement to violence". Britain has immensely restrictive libel laws (laws which, like so much else in liberal bourgeois-democratic society, greatly favour the rich). Who decides what is "defamation"? Especially under Blair's "anti-terror" laws, who decides what is "incitement to violence" (or "glorifying terrorism", as the law puts it)? The liberal democratic courts, of course!

The Travellers say boldly, however: "Respect for others does not entail remaining silent about their beliefs where these are judged to be wanting". The philistinism and cliche-clotting of the language is itself an important part of their new politics!

Doppelganger: But look here: they support "human rights; the pursuit of happiness... the brotherhood and sisterhood of all men and women. None should be left out, none left behind". Here at last they raise a rallying cry; they nail their theses to the door of the cathedral. Here they stand; they can do no other! The Martin Luther touch. Something they will dig in and fight for. It's good!

Not quite. They hasten to add – and it is characteristic of their whole enterprise: "We are partisans of these values. But we are not zealots. For we embrace also the values of free enquiry, open dialogue and creative doubt, of care in judgement and a sense of the intractabilities of the world".

Doppelganger: These are our truths, but, er...they may be wrong! Here we stand – but we may be persuaded to move!

They desire to have more backbone than the invertebrate liberals they criticise, but – moderate in all things, and with a proper sense of the intractabilities of the world – not too much!

I prefer Trotsky. "Revolutionary ardour in the struggle for socialism is inseparable from intellectual ardour in the struggle for truth".

Only the most feeble, liberal notion of class (as a duty of care to the poor), and no notion at all of class struggle, is in this manifesto. In a revealing passage, they complain that "even educated and affluent people" have bad attitudes, as if "affluent" people are those who can normally be expected to favour enlightenment, and it is scarcely surprising if the proles are yahoos.

Do not think, however, that they merely defend the status quo. Within their bourgeois-democratic "defencism", they understand that "these democracies have their own deficits and shortcomings".

Doppelganger: Because they are bourgeois class democracies, pluto-democracies? They bear the stamp of the bourgeoisie and embody – in access, control of assets, etc., if not in formal rights – the rule of the capitalist class over the working class.

No, none of that Marxist old guff! They say it is now a "battle for the development of more democratic institutions and procedures, for further empowering those without influence, without a voice or with few political resources". This, they affirm "is a permanent part of the agenda of the Left".

Doppelganger: Permanent? So a society where no-one would be left without influence, voice, resources is a myth-mirage, a will-o-the-wisp that can never be attained?

They state that "the proper concern of genuine liberals and members of the Left should have been the battle to put in place in Iraq a democratic political order and to rebuild the country's infrastructure".

Doppelganger: Surely you agree with that?

Yes, but also no! Read what they mean by it. They bundle Third Camp socialists into the same ash-can as the sharia-socialists and reactionary "anti-imperialists". They are opposed not only to those, "but also to others who manage to find a way of situating themselves between such forces [the sectarian militias in Iraq] and those trying to bring a new democratic life to the country" [Bush, Blair, etc.]

Those who are not entirely with them, and with Bush and Blair and their allies in Iraq, are against them. The parallel with the attitude of Stalinism when it was vigorous and expanding is striking here. These are the "Pabloites" of post-Stalinist bourgeois arrogance and expansion!

Doppelganger: Remind me who the Pabloites were?

"Pabloites" were people of Trotskyist background who looked to Stalinism to carry through the socialist revolution and saw their own role as friendly critics and propagandists for democratic improvements in the Stalinist states.

Doppelganger: But they do not agree with the invasion?

No, not all of them. But they all defer to those who did and do support the invasion. They agree to denounce those "many left opponents of regime change in Iraq" who perversely refuse to understand why "others on the Left" supported it. By "dishing out anathema" they "betray the democratic values they profess".

Doppelganger: What are they themselves doing if not anathematising those who reject their – in fact, Bush's and Blair's – politics?

But that's all right! Double standards against the double-standards-blighted left are perfectly all right. Not only do they reject the idea that there are no enemies on the left; they reject the idea that there are friends on the left who disagree with their conversion to

Bush and Blair. They are fed up with left and liberal "progressive opinion" operating with "double standards" which make it see "lesser (though all too real) violations of human rights" at home, or in countries it dislikes, as "more deplorable than other violations that are flagrantly worse".

Doppelganger: What's wrong with that? The kitsch left operates with stark double standards.

Indeed. But, as we'll see, they slip into the stance that "the main democratic friend is at home".

They "roundly" condemn "the violation[s]... at Abu Ghraib, at Guantanamo, and by the practice of 'rendition'... [These] must be roundly condemned [as] a departure from universal principles, for the establishment of which the democratic countries themselves, and in particular the United States of America, bear the greater part of the historical credit". Then they direct their fire at the "double standards" by which "too many on the left... treat as the worst violations of human rights those perpetrated by the democracies, while being either silent or more muted about infractions that outstrip these by far".

As a general statement about the left, it is true. But the idea that the main enemy is at home and our proper first concern is with the crimes of "our own" is also true. True now as when Karl Liebknecht first proclaimed it in World War One – knowing that Russian Tsarism was also an enemy, and a worse one than the German government. The core idea can be separated from its kitsch left corruptions – those that arise if all notion is lost of scale and proportion; if the idea that there are, or may be, worse in the world than "our own" bourgeoisie and its allies, is lost; or if the guiding idea becomes "my enemy's enemy is my friend".

The Travellers' motto is, by contrast: the main enemy is *not* at home. Certainly not in the USA! That is where the hope of the democratic future lies. You must keep that in mind! Don't forget that you must defend the workers' state – sorry... bourgeois state – because it is "progressive".

Don't be unfair to our rulers; even where they fall, it is from the standards for the establishment of which they "bear the greatest historical credit". None of the enemies of that "great nation", the USA, with its "noble tradition" is fit even to clean its moral galoshes, so to speak. (The Euston Travellers will do that!)

Amnesty International compared Guantanamo with the Stalinist gulag (in a comment by its secretary-general, Irene Khan, in her preface to AI's 2005 annual report). She presumably meant it was similar in type, not the same in scale. The Travellers are outraged at this "grotesque" comparison!

Doppelganger: But surely Guantanamo is the same sort of thing as the gulag – even if it would be nonsensical to compare the US regime in general and as a whole with Stalin's Russia.

The point is that, like the Stalinists and "Pabloites" of old, the Travelling people feel that the righteousness of the perpetrating powers' cause mitigates, if it doesn't excuse, what they do.

Nowhere is the parallel with the attitudes of the old Stalinists and present kitsch-left so blatant. For example, in the late 1940s and early 1950s, when a great outcry arose in the West in response to hard knowledge becoming widely available about Stalin's slave labour camps, Ernest Mandel and others of the Orthodox Trotskyists denounced the left-wing organisers of the outcry, and worked to blunt public awareness of the camps. The outcry was preparation for war, don't you see, and you must never forget that the USSR is progressive compared to its opponents!

On things like Guantanamo, it is indispensable for any socialist or serious democrat to be hard and merciless in criticising "their own" government. The travellers claim to "roundly condemn" Guantanamo – but immediately hasten to defend its perpetrators from too-rough criticism. The kitsch left could not ask for better help in its foul attitudes than that its critics adopt such a posture.

The Travellers' conclusion sums up what they are: "We must define ourselves against those for whom the entire progressive-democratic agenda has been subordinated to a blanket and simplistic 'anti-imperialism' and/or hostility to the current US administration". Just as the Islamic fundamentalists who want to go back to the 7th century cannot do that, and in fact would construct a present-day caricature of it, so too the would-be time-travellers of an idealised capitalist democracy end up backing the all-too-real and none-too-democratic capitalism of Bush and Blair.

They are the anti-anti-Bushites! But, to repeat and finish, if you define yourself as the inverse of people who are themselves shaped by a simple-mindedly rigid and mechanical inversion of the dominant capitalist and imperialist policies and governments, then you turn into... a positive image and epitome of the Establishment. And you name your duff manifesto after an innocent and blameless railway station.

Index

Some texts included here are expanded or edited versions of articles previously published.

"The warmongering anti-war demonstrations": Solidarity 144, 15 January 2009

"Real and invented differences on political Islam": Solidarity 3/55, 15 July 2004

"What is reactionary anti-imperialism?": Solidarity 3/60, 23 October 2004

"The Prophet and the demoralised revolutionaries": Solidarity 3/9, 25 June 2002

"Is the slogan Troops Out a principle?": Solidarity 3/84, 17 November 2005 (where it was a reply to an article by Barry Finger in Solidarity 3/81, available at www.workersliberty.org/node/29354)

"What is left antisemitism?": Solidarity 3/82, 20 October 2005; the text here also includes sections from "How to wipe out left-antisemitism": Solidarity 404, 11 May 2016

"Learn how to do it smoothly, Tammy!": Solidarity 3/31, 29 May 2003

"The Balkans, nationalism, and imperialism": Workers' Liberty 57, September 1999

"Making anti-imperialism sterile" (under the headline "Neither Washington nor London, but... er... anywhere!"): Solidarity 3/75, 23 June 2005

"'Apparatus Marxism', Impoverished Twin of 'Academic Marxism'": Workers' Liberty 2/1, September 2001

"The Great Gadsby": Workers' Liberty 64/5, September 2000

"Ernest Mandel, 1923-1995": Workers' Liberty 24, September 1995

"Tony Benn, 1925-2014": Solidarity 317, 19 March 2014

"Ted Grant and the workers" (under the headline "Every sect is religious"), Solidarity 214, 24 August 2011

"The Euston Manifesto": Solidarity 3/95, 22 June 2006